Physical Activity and Health

This timely and comprehensive textbook deals exclusively and in depth with the benefits of physical activity in the prevention and treatment of various health conditions which are of growing concern worldwide. In each chapter the authors describe the cause of the condition and then discuss the role of physical activity in its prevention or improvement, drawing on research literature and helping students to evaluate the quality and extent of this. Hazards of exercise are discussed as well as benefits, with critical appraisal of current recommendations for physical activity. The emphasis throughout is on topics relating to conditions that are major health issues in western societies – cardiovascular disease, obesity, type 2 diabetes, the insulin resistance syndrome, osteoporosis – but also includes new and developing research areas. Especially designed to be user-friendly, *Physical Activity and Health* includes:

- chapter overviews and summaries plus information boxes
- study activities and tasks for self-evaluation
- suggested further reading including landmark papers
- glossary of key terms, bibliography and extensive index
- over 100 supporting tables, figures, examples and plates.

Physical Activity and Health will appeal to degree-level students of sport and exercise science as well as to students in related areas such as medicine, public health, physiotherapy, nursing and nutrition, worldwide.

Adrianne E. Hardman has an international reputation as one of the most respected teachers and researchers in the field. She is Emeritus Professor of Human Exercise Metabolism at Loughborough, the UK's leading university for sport and exercise science. She has over 25 years of university teaching experience, has published widely and given invited lectures in many countries.

David J. Stensel is a Lecturer in Exercise Physiology at the School of Sport and Exercise Sciences at Loughborough University. He is an experienced researcher and an outstanding teacher.

Physical Activity and Health
The evidence explained

Adrianne E. Hardman and
David J. Stensel

With a foreword
by Professor Jeremy N. Morris, CBE

Routledge
Taylor & Francis Group

LONDON AND NEW YORK

First published 2003
by Routledge
2 Park Square, Milton Park, Abingdon, Oxon, OX14 4RN

Simultaneously published in the USA and Canada
by Routledge

270 Madison Ave, New York, NY 10016

Reprinted 2004 (twice). 2005, 2006 (twice)

Routledge is an imprint of the Taylor & Francis Group

© 2003 Adrianne E. Hardman and David J. Stensel

Typeset in Garamond by
Newgen Imaging Systems (P) Ltd, Chennai, India
Printed and bound in Great Britain by
The Cromwell Press, Trowbridge, Wiltshire

British Library Cataloguing in Publication Data
A catalogue record for this book is available from the British Library

Library of Congress Cataloging in Publication Data
A catalog record for this book has been requested

ISBN 0–415–27070–7 hb
ISBN 0–415–27071–5 pb

Contents

Figures

Tables

Boxes

Foreword

It is a privilege and pleasure to welcome this fine work by a leading investigator and her colleague, both of them experienced teachers in the famous school at Loughborough. The text meets the needs of countless students of physical activity and health now to be found in university sports sciences, clinical medicine, epidemiology, and in the social domain, from transport planning to the fitness industry. Many of these students, like myself, have not had systematic teaching in the physiology of exercise. Yet, we are constantly meeting its concepts and observations that are plainly fundamental to understanding and to application. Until now, there hasn't been a book to meet our needs. Two features, moreover, characterize their contribution: throughout, the nature and quality of the evidence are clearly described, and the collective – the population – aspects as well as the individual and personal are emphasized.

Our field today presents some remarkable features. In the half-century since the Second World War, there has been an explosion of research and thinking on the needs for, and benefits of, physical activity/exercise across the lifespan and bodily systems. This knowledge is widely not being applied in practice. In consequence there is an epochal waste of human potential for health, functional capacities, well-being. This the authors document and illuminate.

Three of today's major associated issues may be cited. First, the pandemic of obesity in the developed and, increasingly, the developing world. The scientific consensus now is that physical inactivity bears much and possibly most of the responsibility. The authors devote two chapters to the issue, giving us a lucid straightforward description plus a highly instructive account of the metabolic, insulin resistance, syndrome, a seminal concept that Public Health has not yet begun to take on board. The characteristic 'modern epidemic' of coronary heart disease is dealt with again in two chapters. These are typically helpful in elucidating the roles of physical activity and physical fitness and in distinguishing disease and risk factors for disease. A third instance is the welfare of old people. When history comes to be written, society's failure to apply modern knowledge of normal ageing processes, in particular the loss of muscle, and the remedial possibilities, is likely to shame us. Scientific evidence in randomized controlled trials is impeccable. And yet, one of the great gifts of physiology to public health is massively ignored. There cannot be any excuse for any in health care with such a convincing demonstration now so readily available in this book.

We are, the generality of us, the first generation in history to require little, often scarcely any, physical activity in our everyday lives. We have therefore deliberately to introduce this ourselves, and commonly in an unhelpful environment. Many readers will be seeking one way and another to serve in this field. They will find much support in this splendid book. It is surely a tract for the times. Bon voyage!

Jerry N. Morris
Public and Environmental Health Research Unit
London School of Hygiene and Tropical Medicine

Authors' preface

The aim of this book is to introduce students, particularly those studying exercise science, to the research evidence that links physical activity to a range of health outcomes that are major public concerns. In doing this, we also seek to develop in students an understanding of the process of evaluation of scientific evidence. This is important, not least because new observations in our field are often rapidly disseminated through the media, with little critical comment. In writing the book, we have drawn selectively on the vast and rapidly increasing research literature on physical activity and health, rather than attempting at comprehensive reviews of each topic.

We begin by describing the prevalence of physical inactivity and low fitness in different populations and identifying current trends that underline the burden of ill health associated with sedentary living. Our experience in teaching is that students may not be familiar with all the different types of research evidence we later refer to and so these are discussed in a chapter entitled 'The nature of the evidence'. Thereafter, we have adopted a consistent approach to each topic. Information on the prevalence and aetiology of a condition precedes discussion of the extent and quality of the evidence that links a particular condition with physical inactivity and/or low fitness. The issue of the relationship between the 'dose' of activity and its effects is addressed where there is evidence. Where possible, we have also attempted to answer the question 'Are the associations found in epidemiological studies biologically plausible?' and to indicate new and developing research areas. While most of the text is concerned with the putative role of physical activity and prevention, a chapter is also included on its important therapeutic role. Evidence related to the hazards of exercise is dealt with, as a prelude to the final chapter on public health. Here we describe and comment critically on current recommendations for physical activity and propose some priorities.

Our book is written primarily for students of exercise science but we hope that it will also attract readers from the fields of public health, health promotion and professions allied to medicine. Whatever your personal perspective, we hope that you will find it interesting.

Personal acknowledgements

Both authors thank their close colleagues, collaborators in research and research students for lively discussions over many years. In particular, they thank Professor Clyde Williams for his interest and encouragement throughout their professional lives. Professor Jeremy Morris, who also kindly provided a foreword, has been a source of inspiration and contributed endless thought-provoking questions. Adrianne thanks Peter, not only for his unremitting support during the writing of this book, but also for giving her the confidence to begin. David thanks Para for keeping him sane, Chandini and Rohini for their rapturous welcome each time he arrived home after a day of writing and his mother and father for their continued support and encouragement.

We are indebted to Drs Lettie Bishop, Michael Morgan, Greg Atkinson, Katherine Brooke-Wavell and Jason Gill and to Leslie Boobis FRCS, FRCS (Edinburgh) who read and constructively criticized drafts of individual chapters. Professor Peter Jones and Para Stensel each read several chapters, providing specific and general comments that we valued. Particular thanks are due to Professor Steve Bird who read and commented on the entire manuscript. We also thank Len Almond for photographs used in the plates. Finally, we wish to thank Moira Taylor and the staff of Routledge for their belief in our project, their forbearance when writing was slow and for their help in the realization of the final product.

Illustrations acknowledgements

The authors and publishers would like to thank the institutions below for permission to use tables and figures in the book which originated from other original works. Every effort has been made to trace copyright holders but in a few cases this has not been possible. Any omission brought to our attention will be remedied in future editions.

Figure 2.1, copyright Harvard University Press (adapted from Keys, A. (1980) 'Seven countries: a multivariate analysis of death and coronary heart disease', figure 8.2).

Figure 3.3, copyright Massachusetts Medical Society (Myers, J., Prakash, M., Froelicher, V., Do, D., Partington, S. and Atwood, J.E. (2002) 'Exercise capacity and mortality among men referred for exercise testing', *New England Journal of Medicine* 346(11): 793–801, figure 2, p. 798).

Figure 3.4, copyright Massachusetts Medical Society (Myers, J., Prakash, M., Froelicher, V., Do, D., Partington, S. and Atwood, J.E. (2002) 'Exercise capacity and mortality among men referred for exercise testing', *New England Journal of Medicine* 346(11): 793–801, figure 1, p. 797).

Figure 3.6, *Journal of the American Medical Association* (Blair, S.N., Kohl, H.W., Barlow, C.E., Paffenbarger, R.S., Gibbons, L.W. and Macera, C.A. (1995) 'Changes in physical fitness and all-cause mortality: a prospective study of healthy and unhealthy men', *Journal of the American Medical Association* 273: 1093–98, figure 2, p. 1096).

Table 3.1, *Journal of the American Medical Association* (Blair, S.N., Kohl, H.W., Paffenbarger, R.S., Clark, D.G., Cooper, K.H. and Gibbons, L.W. (1989) 'Physical fitness and all-cause mortality: a prospective study of healthy men and women', *Journal of the American Medical Association* 262: 2395–401, table 2, p. 2397).

Figure 4.1, British Heart Foundation, London ('Death rates from CHD in 1996 in men and women').

Figure 4.2, *American Scientist* ('Atherosclerosis. An understanding of the cellular and molecular basis of the disease promises new approaches for its treatment in the near future' (1995) Vol. 83, figure 2, p. 462).

Figure 4.3, reprinted with permission from Elsevier (*Basic Histopathology: A Colour Atlas*, 1985, figure 7.4).

Figure 4.4, Academic Press ('Natural history of human atherosclerotic lesions' in *Atherosclerosis and its origins* (1963) Sandler, M. and Bourne, G.H. (eds) figure 1, p. 42).

Figure 4.5, copyright Massachusetts Medical Society ('Work activity and coronary heart disease' (1975) in *New England Journal of Medicine*, 292, figure 1, p. 546).

Table 5.2, *Circulation*, Lippincott Williams & Wilkins (Pescatello, L.S., Fargo, A.E., Leach, C.N. and Scherzer, H.H. (1991) 'Short-term effect of dynamic exercise on arterial blood pressure', *Circulation* 83: 1557–61, table 2, p. 1559).

Figure 5.1, Katch, F.I. and McArdle, W.D. (1993) *Introduction to Nutrition, Exercise and Health*, 4th edn. Lea and Febiger, Philadelphia/London, figure 4.3, p. 67.

Figure 5.6, Massachusetts Medical Society (Currens, J.H. and White, P.D. (1961) 'Half a century of running. Clinical, physiologic and autopsy findings in the case of Clarence DeMar ("Mr. Marathon")', *New England Journal of Medicine* 265: 988–93, figures 7 and 8, pp. 992 and 993).

Figure 5.9, McGraw-Hill, Boston (Vander, A., Sherman, J. and Luciano, D. (2001) *Human Physiology. The Mechanisms of Body Function*, 8th edn, figure 14.72, p. 455).

Figure 6.1, Reprinted with permission from Elsevier (Alberti, K.G.M.M., Boucher, B.J., Hitman,G.A. and Taylor, R. (1990) *Diabetes mellitus. In The Metabolic and Molecular Basis of Acquired Disease*, vol. 1 (Cohen, R.D., Lewis, B., Alberti, K.G.M.M. and Denman, A.M., eds), pp. 765–840, Baillière Tindall, London, figure 36.21, p. 805. I have used a modified version of this figure which appears in the following book: Frayn, K.N. (1996) *Metabolic regulation – a human perspective*. Portland Press, London, figure 9.2, p. 223.

Figure 6.11, Massachusetts Medical Society (Tuomilehto, M., Lindström, J., Eriksson, J.G., Valle, T.T., Hämäläinen, H., Ilanne-Parikka, P., Keinänen-Kiukaanniemi, S., Laakso, M., Louheranta, A., Rastas, M., Salminen, V. and Uusitupa, M. (2001) 'Prevention of type 2 diabetes mellitus by changes in lifestyle among subjects with impaired glucose tolerance', *The New England Journal of Medicine* 344: 1343–50, figure 2, p. 1348).

Figures 6.13 and 6.14, The American Physiological Society (Rogers, M.A., King, D.S., Hagberg, J.M., Ehsani, A.A. and Holloszy, J.O. (1990) 'Effect of 10 days of physical inactivity on glucose tolerance in master athletes', *Journal of Applied Physiology* 68: 1833–37, figure 2, p. 1835).

Figure 6.15, Massachusetts Medical Society (Diabetes Prevention Program Research Group (2002) 'Reduction in the incidence of type 2 diabetes with lifestyle intervention or Metformin', *The New England Journal of Medicine* 346: 393–403, figure 4, p. 400).

Figure 7.1, Danny Hickey photo, reprinted by courtesy of Paul Harris Photography and the family of Danny Hickey with donation to the Children's Hospice South West, Barnstaple.

Figure 7.2, National Audit Office (2001) Tackling Obesity in England. Report by the Comptroller and Auditor General. HC 220 Session 2000–2001: 15 February 2001. Available at: accessed 8 May 2002, figure 29, appendix 4, p. 52.

Figure 7.6, Massachusetts Medical Society (Stunkard, A.J., Sorensen, T.I.A., Hanis, C., Teasdale, T.W., Chakraborty, R., Schull, W.J. and Schulsinger, F. (1986) 'An adoption study of human obesity', *New England Journal of Medicine* 314: 193–8. figure 1, p. 195).

Figure 7.8 (Poehlman, E.T. (1989) 'A review: exercise and its influence on resting energy metabolism in man', *Medicine and Science in Sports and Exercise* 21: 515–25, figure 1, p. 516).

Figure 7.9, British Medical Journal (Prentice, A.M. and Jebb, S.A. (1995) 'Obesity in Britain: gluttony or sloth?', *British Medical Journal* 311: 437–9 figure 5, p. 439).

Figure 8.4, Archives of Internal Medicine (William, P.T. (1997) 'Relationship of distance run per week to coronary heart disease risk factors in 8283 runners', *Archives of Internal Medicine* 157: figure 1, p. 195).

Figure 8.5, reprinted with permission from Elsevier ('Role of body fat loss in the exercise-induced improvement of the plasma lipid profile in non-insulin-dependent diabetes mellitus' (1996) Metabolism 45, figure 1, p. 1385).

Figure 8.6, reprinted with permission from Lippincott Williams & Wilkins (Arteriosclerosis, Thrombosis, 1989, vol. 9, figure 1 from pp. 217–23).

Figure 10.1, reprinted with permission from Elsevier (*Functional Histology: A Text and Colour Atlas*, 2nd edn (1987) figure 1, p. 145).

Figure 10.2, reprinted with permission from Human Kinetics (Khan, K.M. *et al.* *Physical Activity and Bone Health*, figure 1.6, p. 7).

Figure 10.5, American College of Physicians-American Society of Internal Medicine (Kannus, P. *et al.* 'Effect of starting age of physical activity on bone mass in the dominant arm of tennis and squash players (1995) vol. 123, figure 1, p. 31).

Figure 10.6, reprinted with permission from Elsevier (*Bone* (1995) vol.17, figure 1 from pp. 197–203).

Figure 10.7, reprinted with permission from Elsevier (*The Lancet* (1996) vol. 348, p. 1344).

Figure 11.5, *Circulation* 104: figure 4, p. 1362, Lippincott Williams & Wilkins (adapted from McGuire, D.K. *et al.* (2001) 'A 30-year follow-up of the Dallas bed rest and training study. II. Effect of age on cardiovascular adaptation to exercise training'.).

Figure 12.1, *Circulation* 96: 2534–41, Lippincott Williams & Wilkins (Neibauer, J. *et al.* (1997) 'Attenuated progression of coronary artery disease after 6 years of multifactorial risk intervention: role of physical exercise').

Figure 12.2, Blackwell Scientific ('Effects of exercise on glucose tolerance and insulin resistance. Brief review and some preliminary results', figure in *Acta Medica Scandinavica* 711: 55–65).

Figure 12.4, North American Association for the Study of Obesity (Bouchard, C., Tremblay, A., Despres, J.P., Nadeau, A., Lupien, P.J., Theriault, G., Dussault, J., Moorjania, S., Pineault, S. and Fournier, G. (1990) 'The response to long-term overfeeding in identical twins', *New England Journal of Medicine* 322: 1477–82, figure 1, p. 1479 and figure 2, p. 1481.

Figure 12.5 (Ross, R. (1997) 'Effects of diet and exercise induced weight loss on visceral adipose tissue in men and women', *Sports Medicine*, 24 (1): 55–64, figure 4, p. 62).

Figure 13.2, copyright Massachusetts Medical Society ('Triggering of acute myocardial infarction by heavy physical exertion', Mittleman, M.A., Maclure, Tofler, G.H. *et al.* (1993) *New England Journal of Medicine* 329: figure 2, p. 1680).

Figure 13.5, Journal of the American Medical Association ('Menstrual history as a determinant of current bone density in young athletes', *Journal of the American Medical Association*, 263: figure on p. 546).

Figure 14.1, The British Heart Foundation, London (Coronary heart disease statistics. British Heart Foundation database 2000. Also available at http/www.dphpc.ox.ac.uk/bhfhprg/stats/k accessed 27.11.00).

Figure 14.2, The American Physiological Society (Hardman, A. *et al.* 'Postprandial lipemia in endurance-trained people during a short interruption to training', *Journal of Applied Physiology* (1998) vol. 84, figure 1 between pp. 1895 and 1901).

Figure 14.4, copyright Massachusetts Medical Society ('Walking compared with vigorous exercise for the prevention of cardiovascular events in women', Manson, J.E., Greenland, P., LaCroix, A.Z. *et al.* (2002) *New England Journal of Medicine*, vol. 347, figure 4, p. 722).

Plate on p. 207, SportEx health.

Plate on p. 227, SportEx health.

Conversion factors for commonly used units

Length: 1 kilometer = 0.62137 mile
1 cm = 0.3937 inch
Mass: 1 kilogram = 2.2046 pounds
Energy: 1 kJ = 0.23889 kcal
Concentration cholesterol: 1 mmol l^{-1} = 38.67 mg dl^{-1}
Concentration triglycerides: 1 mmol l^{-1} = 88.6 mg dl^{-1}
Concentration glucose: 1 mmol l^{-1} = 18 mg dl^{-1}
Concentration insulin: 1 pmol l^{-1} = 0.1389 μU ml^{-1}

Part I
Assessing the Evidence

Knowledge assumed
Principle of energy balance
Procedures for testing aerobic
fitness, including prediction of
maximal oxygen uptake

1 Introduction

EARLY OBSERVATIONS

Physical activity and physical fitness have been linked with health and longevity since ancient times. The earliest records of organized exercise used for health promotion are found in China around 2500 BC. However, it was the Greek physicians of the fifth and early fourth centuries BC who established a tradition of maintaining positive health through 'regimen' – the combination of correct eating and exercise. Hippocrates (*c.*460–370 BC), often called the Father of Modern Medicine, wrote

….all parts of the body which have a function, if used in moderation and exercised in labours in which each is accustomed, become thereby healthy, well-developed and age more slowly, but if unused and left idle they become liable to disease, defective in growth and age quickly.

(Jones 1967)

Modern day exercise research began after the Second World War in the context of post-war aspirations to build a better world. Public health was changing to focus on chronic, non-communicable diseases and the modification of individual behaviour. Whilst Doll and Hill worked on the links between smoking and lung cancer, Professor Jeremy Morris and his colleagues set out to test the hypothesis that deaths from coronary heart disease (CHD) were less common among men engaged in physically active work than among those in sedentary jobs. In seminal papers published in 1953, they reported that conductors working on London's double-decker buses who climbed around 600 stairs per working day experienced less than half the incidence of heart attacks as the sedentary drivers who sat for 90% of their shift.

Subsequent studies by Morris and others, in particular Morris's close friend Ralph Paffenbarger in the US, have confirmed that the postponement of cardiovascular disease through exercise represents a cause and effect relationship. For their contribution, Morris and Paffenbarger were in 1996 jointly awarded the first International Olympic Medal and Prize for research in exercise sciences.

In the 50 years since Morris's early papers, research into the influence of physical activity on health has burgeoned. This book is not a comprehensive account of this literature; rather it is an attempt to illustrate its extent, strengths and weaknesses and to help students to understand the process of evaluation of evidence. Our emphasis will be on topics related to major public health issues. But first, it is necessary to 'paint a picture' of some relevant features of today's societies.

MODERN TRENDS

Three modern trends will increase the prevalence of chronic diseases in the twenty-first century. These are the epidemic of obesity, inactivity in children and the increasing age of the population.

Epidemic of obesity

Obesity is on the increase in most countries. Its prevalence in England has almost tripled during the last two decades, a more rapid increase than seen in other parts of Europe; by 1998, 21% of women and 17% of men in England were obese. In the US, 22% of adults are obese and more than 50% are above the desirable range of weight for height. Worse still, the rate of increase in the prevalence of obesity appears to be accelerating. The increase in obesity is not restricted to westernized countries; all the signs are that this is increasing rapidly also in developing countries. For example, in South Africa, more than 44% of black women have been reported to be obese. It is well established that obesity and overweight are hazardous to health and so these figures give rise to concern. The health hazards of obesity and the ways in which physical activity influences weight regulation are discussed fully in Chapter 7 but some general points will be made here.

First, for many people today, everyday life demands only low levels of physical activity and hence energy expenditure. The modern phase of the obesity epidemic (from 1980 onwards) is therefore probably mediated more by inactivity than by overeating (Prentice and Jebb 1995). The average decline in daily energy expenditure in the UK from the end of Second World War to 1995 has been estimated as 3360 kJ (800 kcal) (James 1995), the equivalent of walking about 16 km (10 miles) less. This calculation fits well with empirical data from a small informal Australian study in which actors from an historic theme park in Sydney lived the life of early soldiers, convicts and settlers for a week (Egger *et al.* 2001). During this time their movement levels were monitored using an accelerometer. The actors expended between 1.6 and 2.3 times more energy per day as the typical modern man, equivalent to walking between 8 and 16 km (5–10 miles) more.

Inactivity in children

Obesity takes decades to develop, as small excesses of energy intake over expenditure accrue. Suggestions that children are becoming less active may therefore presage even greater problems with obesity and obesity-related illnesses in years to come. Obesity is already increasing in children and adolescents. In the US, for example, the prevalence in girls and adolescents has more than doubled since the early 1960s (Baur 2002).

Physical inactivity has been linked to the increase in obesity through both a high prevalence of sedentary behaviours and a decrease in physical activity. Adolescents in western societies typically spend more than five and a half hours a day in media use (watching television or videos, computer use) and there has been a dramatic decline in physically active transport to school and a general decline in children's walking and cycling. Estimates of total physical activity in children show a decline after around age 8–10, with a particularly steep fall in girls. For example, by the age of 15, fewer than 1 in 5 English girls reach the recommended 60 minutes on five or more days a week (Figure 1.1). Data from the US suggest that the decline during early adolescence is even steeper in black girls than in white girls. A large cohort was followed from the ages of 9 or 10 to the ages of 18 or 19 years (Kimm *et al.* 2002). The median physical activity score declined by 64% in white girls and by 100% (to 0) in black girls (Figure 1.2). Thus the summary by the World Health Organization (WHO) that 'In many developed and developing countries, less than one-third of young people are sufficiently active to benefit their present and future health' (WHO 1999b) may well understate the problem.

Ageing population

The world is experiencing a demographic transition characterized by an improvement in life expectancy for both men and women, leading to an increase in the total number of older people worldwide. To illustrate this using New Zealand as an example, Figure 1.3 shows population 'pyramids' for 2001 and 2050. Data for 2050 are projections. The 2050 pyramid has a narrower base and a broader top, indicating a smaller number of children and a larger number of old people. The median age of New Zealanders is expected to rise by more than 10 years by 2050. Moreover, by comparison with some developed countries, this population is actually rather young.

Figure 1.1 Percentage of children in England participating in at least 60 minutes of physical activity on five or more days a week, by sex and age in 1997.

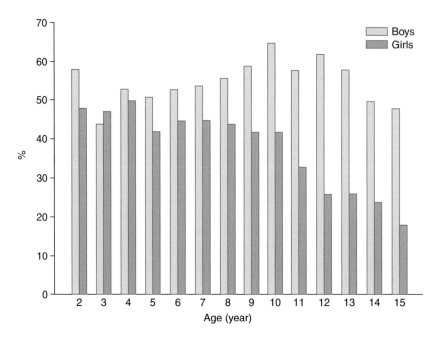

Source: Joint Health Surveys Unit (1998).

A number of countries can expect a median age of over 50 by 2050, including Germany (51), Greece (52), Japan (53), Italy (54) and Spain (55).

The impact, worldwide of the ageing of populations is shown in Table 1.1 that presents projected increases in median age and the percentage of individuals over 65. It is clear that the ageing of populations is not restricted to developed countries. The same trends are expected in those that are less well developed, although the median ages of these populations are lower.

The ageing of a population has enormous social and economic implications, including an increase in age-related diseases and an increased number of frail elderly people who have difficulty living independently. Physical activity has a lot to offer the elderly in terms of personal and public health: it helps to prevent some important age-related diseases (e.g. type 2 diabetes, osteoporosis[2] and cardiovascular disease); and it enhances functional capacities, leading to a better quality of life and increased capability for independent living (see Chapter 11). Public health policies to attenuate the marked age-related decline in physical activity levels (see later in this chapter) are therefore sorely needed.

PHYSICAL ACTIVITY LEVELS IN POPULATIONS

Governments and other agencies monitor health behaviours, including physical activity, to inform public health policy and to review the progress of interventions that aim to

Figure 1.2 Median values for physical activity scores in 1,166 white girls and 1,213 black girls in the US. Participants were studied over a period of 10 years.

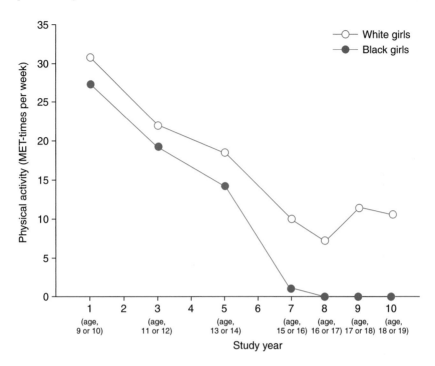

Source: Kimm *et al.* (2002).
Notes: Scores exclude activities performed in physical education classes at school. The units used here (MET-times per week) are unusual and take no account of the duration of each session of activity. Girls reported the number of occasions on which they participated in specific sports/activities over the previous year. Researchers computed the score by multiplying an estimate of the metabolic equivalent (MET)[1] by the reported weekly frequency and the fraction of the year during which it was performed. Typical values are: bicycling one or two times per week for 52 weeks of the year, 8.0 MET-times per week; and swimming three or more times per week for 13 weeks of the year, 4.5 MET-times per week.

change behaviours. Many countries survey only leisure-time physical activity because this type of activity is assumed to be most amenable to interventions and because occupational work is now uncommon in westernized countries, which are the source of most national data. The assessment methods used to monitor physical activity are, however, very varied. A brief review of the surveys conducted during the 1990s illustrates just how difficult it is to make valid comparisons between countries.

Seven countries have included questions on physical activity as part of surveys based on some sort of representative national sample during this decade, namely Australia, Canada, England, Finland, Ireland, New Zealand and the US. The size of the samples studied broadly reflected population size, ranging from 1798 in Ireland to 69,524 in Canada. The most common mode of enquiry was a household interview but some were telephone or postal surveys. Five surveys had no upper age bound but Australia, Finland and Ireland restricted participants to those under 75, 64 and 69 years, respectively. The

Figure 1.3 Age structure of the population of New Zealand in 2001 and 2050.

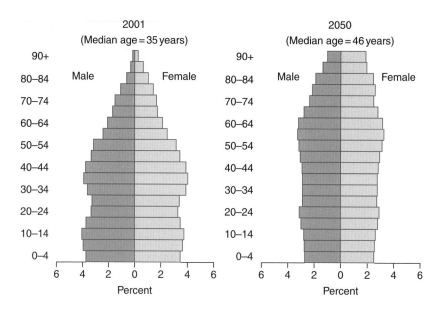

Source: Statistics New Zealand (2002).
Note: Data for 2050 are projections, based on assumptions about future levels of births, deaths and migration.

Table 1.1 Population projections for world regions during the first half of the twenty-first century

YEAR	MEDIAN AGE (YEARS)			PROPORTION ≥ 65 YEARS (%)		
	2000	2030	2050	2000	2030	2050
More developed regions	37.4	43.8	43.9	14.2	21.8	24.7
Less developed regions	24.3	31.5	35.6	5.0	9.4	13.8
Least developed regions	18.3	23.6	31.1	3.0	4.4	7.7

Source: Adapted from Australian Bureau of Statistics (1999).
Note: More developed – Northern America, Japan, Europe, Australia and New Zealand. Less developed – all regions of Africa, Asia (excluding Japan), Latin America and the Caribbean and Oceania (excluding Australia and New Zealand).
Least developed – the 48 least developed countries in the world (of which 33 are in Africa, 9 in Asia, 5 in Oceania and 1 in Latin America and the Caribbean).

recall period varied from a usual working day to the prior year (both Finland), with several surveying the last 2–4 weeks. All countries recorded leisure-time activity. Four also recorded occupational activity and two countries (Finland and New Zealand) also assessed transport to and from work. The questionnaires used to elicit this information and the methods of presenting summary scores varied considerably.

Table 1.2 shows the proportions of individuals in the lowest, middle and highest categories of activity designated in each of these surveys, based on these summary scores.

Table 1.2 Prevalence (%) for leisure-time physical activity among people in national surveys

COUNTRY	LOWEST ACTIVITY	MODERATE ACTIVITY	HIGHEST ACTIVITY
Australia	14.6	40.2	45.2
Canada	56.7	22.7	20.6
England	38.0	31.0	31.0
Finland	10.7	26.6	62.8
Ireland	39.0	48.3	12.7
New Zealand	31.0	41.0	28.0
United States	24.3	52.2	23.5

Source: Adapted from International Agency for Research on Cancer (2002).

For the lowest levels, prevalence ranged from 10.7% to 56.7%. However, those countries recording very low prevalence adopted restrictive definitions of low activity that were hard to meet; for example, the Australian criterion 'performing absolutely no physical activity during the previous week' describes only truly sedentary persons and will be one reason why the low prevalence of 14.6% was recorded. Methodology is also clearly a confounding factor in comparing the highest levels of activity between countries. For example, the proportion of people in this category was least for countries using criteria that were difficult to meet, for example, only 12.7% of the Irish sample met the stringent

Figure 1.4 Prevalence of people aged 15 and over reporting no physical activity in a typical week for 15 member countries of the EU.

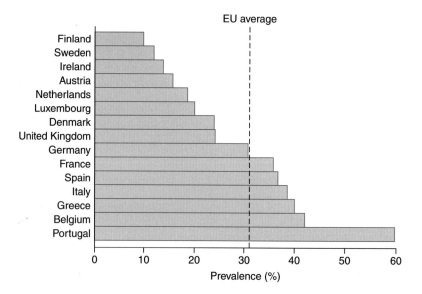

Source: Adapted from Institute of European Food Studies (1999).
Note: EU average weighted according to population size.

definition of running (or comparable activity) for ≥3 hours per week. The need for greater consistency of methodologies across countries is clear and is being addressed.

A Pan-European Union survey permits more meaningful comparisons between countries because methodology was standardized. Figure 1.4 shows the percentage of each randomly selected sample who reported no recreational physical activity. The lowest prevalence (8.1%) was in Finland and the highest (59.8%) was in Portugal, a difference of nearly 3-fold. The average for all European Union (EU) countries was 30.9%, with Mediterranean countries tending to have higher than average prevalence. Figure 1.4 understates the potential health burden of inactivity, however, because people who are deemed to be active but at a level insufficient to benefit their health are excluded. For example, in the UK only 24% of people are classed as sedentary but 63% of men and 75% of women do not meet the guideline for health benefits, that is, at least 30 minutes of activity at a moderate level or above on five days per week (British Heart Foundation 2002a).

Two features of data on physical activity are common to most developed countries: the rapid decline with increasing age; and higher levels of activity in men than in women. As an example, data from the UK are shown in Figure 1.5 (Joint Health Surveys Unit 1999). Whereas 58% of men and 33% of women aged 16–24 fulfil the guideline for health benefits, this declines to 17% of men and 12% of women in the age group 65–74 years. Ethnicity also appears to be an important influence on activity, in the UK at least. Compared with the general population, South Asian and Chinese

Figure 1.5 Prevalence of physical activity level by age, in men and women over 16 in England, 1998.

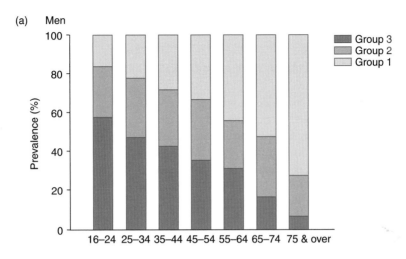

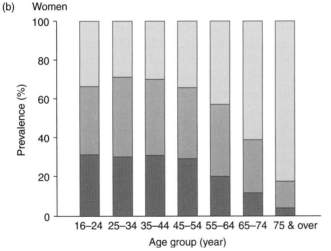

Source: Joint Health Surveys Unit (1999).
Notes: Group 3, 30 minutes or more on at least 5 days per week; Group 2, 30 minutes or more on 1–4 days per week; Group 1, lower level of activity.

men and women in the UK are less likely to participate in physical activity, with the lowest levels found in the Bangladeshi community.

In developing countries, a decline in physical activity appears to follow in the wake of economic growth. For instance, in the South Pacific Islands decreases in physical activity have been associated with urban residence and modernization (Popkin 1994). Among civil servants in Nigeria, men with higher socio-economic status have been reported to have a lower level of physical activity than those of lower status (Forrest *et al.*

2001). These observations suggest that the prevalence of inactivity worldwide may be expected to rise as the economies of countries like these develop further.

TEMPORAL CHANGES IN PHYSICAL ACTIVITY

Physical activity levels are monitored to reveal trends and to review the progress of interventions but few countries have collected comprehensive data in a standardized manner over time. Exceptions are Canada and Finland.

Canada has a long history of commitment to the study of physical activity levels. National surveys of leisure-time physical activity were carried out in 1981 (fitness as well as activity), 1988, 1995, 1998, 1999, 2000 and 2001. From 1995 onwards the same instrument, the Physical Activity Monitor, has been used. Comparison over time revealed that substantial inroads were made in reducing sedentary living during the eighties and early nineties (Canadian Fitness and Lifestyle Research Institute 2002). In 1981, over three-quarters of adults aged 18 and older were considered insufficiently active for health benefits but levels of inactivity decreased to 71% in 1988 and to 63% by the mid-1990s. Subsequent progress has been slow, with 64% classified as insufficiently active for health benefits in 1999, 61% in 2000 and 57% in 2001. Thus, a majority of adult Canadians are still not sufficiently active, despite considerable efforts to promote physical activity by government agencies.

Health behaviours have been monitored in Eastern Finland at 5-year intervals since 1972 when a community-wide project (The North Karelia Project) was initiated with the aim of reducing their high rates of cardiovascular diseases (CVD). Twenty-five year changes in leisure-time, occupational and commuting physical activity have now been described (Barengo *et al.* 2002). The proportion of both men and women engaging in high levels of leisure-time physical activity has increased, as has the proportion of women participating at a moderate level (Figure 1.6). On the other hand, the proportion of people reporting low levels of all types of activity (leisure, occupational and commuting) has remained the same (6–8% in men, 7–9% in women). Thus, despite an intensive community-based effort lasting over 25 years, 75% of men and 82% of women in Finland are still classified as either sedentary or having only moderate physical activity during their leisure time.

In the UK, it appears that the prevalence of sedentary living has actually increased during the 1990s. Since 1994, although the proportion of people meeting current recommendations has remained stable at 37% of men and increased slightly from 22% to 25% of women, the proportion classed as sedentary (<1 occasion of physical activity of 30 min duration per week) increased between 1994 and 1998 from 30% to 35% in men and from 35% to 41% in women (British Heart Foundation 2002).

In summary, despite the lack of uniformity in measures of physical activity/inactivity, it is clear that the prevalence of physical inactivity remains high in many countries. The WHO Active Living initiative summarizes the available data thus: 'More than 60% of the world population is inactive or insufficiently active to gain health benefits' (World Health Organization 1999).

Figure 1.6 Changes in leisure-time physical activity among 30- to 59-year-old men and women in eastern Finland during 1972–97.

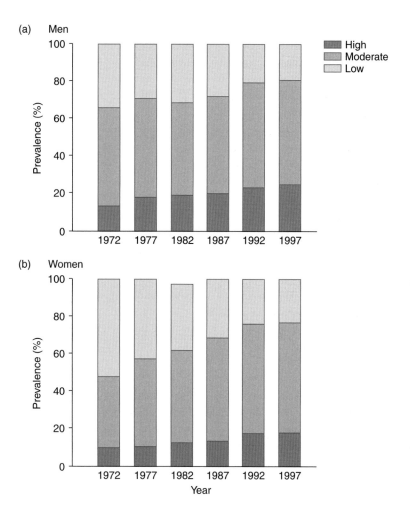

Source: Barengo *et al.* (2002).
Notes: Criteria for categories of leisure-time physical activity were: High: participation in recreational sports or in intense training or sports competitions for at least 3 h per week; Moderate: walking, cycling or practising some other form of light exercise at least 4 h per week; Low: reading, watching television or working in the household without much physical activity.

NATIONAL SURVEYS OF FITNESS

Only two countries have published representative national surveys of fitness, Canada (1981 and 1988) and England (1992) and their approaches were quite different. In the Canadian Survey, more than 20,000 participants completed a battery of tests. Cardiorespiratory fitness was assessed on the basis of the heart rate response to a standard step test and participants were allocated to one of three fitness levels: 'an undesirable personal fitness level'; 'the minimum personal fitness level' or 'a satisfactory personal fitness level'. This approach reflected the original purpose of the step test (to give individuals a means to monitor changes in their own fitness) but it made it difficult to relate the data to epidemiological findings. Average values for maximal oxygen uptake ($\dot{V}O_2$max) were predicted, without direct measurement of respiratory gases, and found to correspond quite closely with 'world averages' (Shephard 1986). The latter were not drawn from representative samples, however, and the prediction of $\dot{V}O_2$max from the step test data was fraught with problems. Repeat measurements were made in 1988 on most of a 20% subset of the original sample but results have not been widely disseminated.

The English National Fitness Survey used a graded treadmill test to estimate $\dot{V}O_2$max from measurements of oxygen uptake and heart rate in a much smaller, but still representative, sample (858 men, 883 women). These values were reported by age and sex but researchers used functional criteria as the main outcome measures. (Did people have sufficient aerobic capacity or muscle strength to carry out everyday tasks without fatigue?) For example, it was determined that nearly one-third of men and two-thirds of women would find it difficult to sustain a walking pace of about 4.8 km h^{-1} (3 mile h^{-1}) up a 1 in 20 (5%) slope for more than a few minutes (National Fitness Survey 1992). The proportion of men who could not do this rose sharply with age, that is, from 4% of 16–24 year olds to 81% of 65–74 year olds. Equivalent figures for women rose from 34% to 92%. These findings strongly suggest that the prevalence of low fitness is widespread in England.

DEFINITIONS OF KEY TERMS

Disease is relatively easy to define, either according to aetiology (e.g. tuberculosis is caused by a bacterium, *Mycobacterium tuberculosis*) or in terms of symptoms (e.g. the term asthma describes a disease characterized by fits of laboured breathing). Defining health is more problematic. Is health merely the 'other side of the coin', that is, the absence of disease? Somehow this fails to convey the essence of our everyday use of the term health as encapsulated in phrases such as 'picture of health' and 'rude health'. Something wider is needed. The most ambitious definition is probably that proposed by the WHO (1946): 'health is a state of complete physical, mental and social well-being and not merely the absence of disease or infirmity'. This definition, although crit-icized because of the difficulty of defining and measuring well being, remains an ideal. It is helpful in the context of this book because physical activity contributes more to health than just helping to prevent disease.

Finally, a note on our use of the terms 'physical activity' and 'exercise'. We have adopted the definitions that have acquired currency over recent years (Howley 2001). Thus physical activity is 'any bodily movement produced by contraction of skeletal muscle that substantially increases energy expenditure'. Hence the title of this book is broad – *Physical activity* and health. Exercise (or exercise training) is defined as 'a sub-category of leisure-time physical activity in which planned, structured and repetitive bodily movements are performed to improve or maintain one or more components of physical fitness'. Thus, for example, we have written about therapeutic *exercise* as this is invariably planned and structured. However, the distinction between physical activity and exercise is sometimes neither helpful nor necessary so there are occasions in the text where these terms are used more loosely.

SUMMARY

- The contribution of physical activity to health has been recognized since the fifth century BC but the modern history of exercise science began after the Second World War when epidemiologists began the scientific study of the role of exercise in protection against heart disease.
- An epidemic of obesity in adults and children will lead to more obesity-related disease. The average decline in daily energy expenditure in westernized countries since the early part of the twentieth century may be the equivalent of walking as much as 16 km (10 miles) less.
- In many developed and developing countries, less than one-third of young people are sufficiently active to benefit their present and future health.
- The world is experiencing a demographic transition characterized by an improvement in life expectancy for both men and women, leading to an increase in the total number of older people worldwide. This will mean an increase in age-related diseases and an increased number of frail elderly people. Increasing levels of physical activity among older persons should be a public health priority.
- Differences in methodology make it difficult to compare the findings of national surveys of physical activity levels but two features of these are common to most countries: there is a rapid decline with increasing age; and levels of activity are higher in men than in women.
- In developing countries, a decline in physical activity appears to follow in the wake of economic growth so that the prevalence of inactivity worldwide may be expected to rise as the economies of such countries develop.
- The National Fitness Survey for England determined that nearly one-third of men and two-thirds of women would find it difficult to sustain a walking pace of about 4.8 km h^{-1} (3 mile h^{-1}) up a 1 in 20 (5%) slope for more than a few minutes.

STUDY TASKS

1 Typical daily energy expenditure in western countries is estimated to have fallen by around 3360 kJ (800 kcal) in the last 50 years. Is this a lot or a little? Explain your answer as fully as possible. Explain why the figures shown in Table 1.2 should not be taken at face value.

2 Using Figure 1.3, estimate the expected change in the proportion of over 65s in the New Zealand population in the first-half of the twenty-first century.

3 Based on Figure 1.5, describe how age influences the level of physical activity among English women.

4 Which two countries have the best data on temporal changes in physical activity? With reference to Figure 1.6, compare the main trends in physical activity levels over the last 25 years between Finnish men and Finnish women.

NOTES

1   MET, multiple of resting metabolic rate, used as a measure of exercise intensity. See Chapter 2 for further explanation.
2   There are more women than men in the older age groups and this proportion is expected to rise still further as the population ages. Thus the prevalence of osteoporosis will increase.

FURTHER READING

Booth, F.W., Gordon, S.E., Carlson, C.J. and Hamilton, M.T. (2000) 'Waging war on modern chronic diseases: primary prevention through exercise biology,' *Journal of Applied Physiology* 88: 774–87.

Paffenbarger, R.S., Blair, S.N. and Lee, I.-M. (2001) 'A history of physical activity, cardiovascular health and longevity: the scientific contributions of Jeremy N Morris, DSc, DPH, FRCP,' *International Journal of Epidemiology* 30: 1184–92.

Prentice, A.M. and Jebb, S.A. (1995) Obesity in Britain: gluttony or sloth? *British Medical Journal* 311: 437–9.

Sallis, J.F. and Owen, N. (1999) *'Physical Activity and Behavioural Medicine'*, Thousand Oaks, CA: Sage.

2 Nature of the evidence

Knowledge assumed
Principles of measurement and categories of measurement scales
Basic statistics (including inference, estimation and statistical power)

INTRODUCTION

Evidence concerning physical activity and health takes a variety of forms. Like evidence on other topics, it is constrained by the nature of investigations and the methods employed. The reader needs to understand these constraints and to be able to identify good research. Good research requires that data are collected and interpreted with adequate allowance for potential sources of error. It also has to be concerned with the complexity caused by the inter-relation of physical activity levels with social and environmental factors.

Research in physical activity and health can be divided into epidemiological and laboratory-based studies. Within each category, studies may be either observational or experimental. However, in this field, most epidemiological studies are observational and most laboratory-based studies are experimental. In observational studies researchers allow nature to take its course and merely collect information about one or more groups of subjects. The simplest observational studies are purely descriptive, but most go further by analysing relationships between health status and other variables. In experimental studies the researchers intervene to affect what happens to some or all of the individuals.

WHAT IS EPIDEMIOLOGY?

Epidemiology has been defined by the World Health Organization as 'the study of the distribution and determinants of health-related states or events in specified populations,[1] and the application of this study to control of health problems' (Last 1995). The use of the phrase 'health-related states or events' (rather than the older term 'disease frequency') reflects the fact that our concept of health now includes aspects of positive health, for example a good quality of life, and not only the absence of disease. For simplicity, the term health-related outcome will be used in this text to include both disease and other health-related states or events. Health-related outcomes may be defined simply, for example, as 'disease present' or 'disease absent', or graded, for example 'normal weight', 'overweight' or 'obese'.

Types of study

The main types of epidemiological study are summarized in Table 2.1.

Case reports or case series describe the experience of a single patient or group of patients with a similar diagnosis. Such studies usually report an unusual feature and may lead to the formulation of a new hypothesis. Few studies on physical activity or fitness are of this form but one example is the autopsy study of Clarence DeMar, a runner who had participated in over 1,000 distance races, including 100 marathons; the diameter of his coronary arteries was estimated to be 2 or 3 times the normal diameter, leading to conjecture that years of running training might lead the arteries to adapt to the larger demand for blood flow (Currens and White 1961).

Table 2.1 Types of epidemiological study

CATEGORY	TYPE OF STUDY	UNIT OF STUDY
Observational		
Descriptive studies	Case reports or case series	Individuals
Analytical studies	Correlational	Populations
	Cross-sectional surveys	Individuals
	Case-control studies	Individuals
	Cohort studies	Individuals
Experimental	Randomized, controlled trials	Individuals

Source: Adapted from Beaglehole *et al.* (1993).

In correlational studies (sometimes called ecological studies), the characteristics of the entire populations are used to describe the frequency of a health-related outcome in relation to some factors relevant to the research question or hypothesis. An example would be the Seven Countries Study where patterns of mortality from coronary heart disease (CHD) were highly correlated with the median plasma cholesterol concentration in the different populations (Figure 2.1). One interpretation of this finding is that CHD mortality in a community depends strongly on the typical plasma cholesterol concentration of its people.

Cross-sectional surveys describe the prevalence of a health-related outcome in representative samples and relate this to personal or demographic characteristics. For example, the 1981 Canada Fitness Survey found distinct differences between active and sedentary Canadians in measures of their health. If such surveys are repeated, they offer a means to evaluate population-based interventions.

In a case-control study (also called a retrospective study), the occurrence of a possible cause is compared between people known to have a disease (the cases) and a reference group who do not have the disease (the controls). The investigators look back from disease to a possible cause, seeking associations with exposure to the factors of interest. The most difficult aspect of this design is the selection of controls because this can introduce bias (systematic error). However, case-control studies offer a way to identify adequate numbers of patients even when the outcome under study is relatively rare. Many studies of physical activity and the risk of cancer are therefore of this type.

Figure 2.1 Relationship between the median serum cholesterol concentration and 10-year mortality from CHD in 16 cohorts of men in the Seven Countries Study.

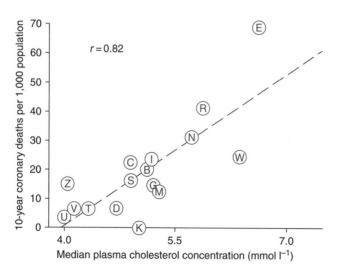

Source: Keys (1980).
Notes: B = Belgrade (Yugoslavia, formerly Serbia); D = Dalmatia (Yugoslavia, formerly Croatia); E = East Finland; G = Corfu; I = Italian railroad; K = Crete; N = Zutphen (the Netherlands); T = Tanushimaru (Japan); R = American railroad; U = Ushibuka (Japan); V = Velike Krsna (Yugoslavia, formerly Serbia); W = West Finland; Z = Zrenjanin (Yugoslavia). Add C = Crevalcore (Italy); M = Montegiorgio (Italy); S = Slavonia (Yugoslavia, formerly Croatia).

Cohort studies, sometimes called follow-up studies, are conceptually simple. They begin with a group of people who are free of disease (or other health-related outcome) and determine their exposure to a suspected risk factor. Subgroups are defined on the basis of exposure to the risk factor. For a study of physical (in)activity, subgroups might comprise: sedentary individuals; those engaging in moderate activity; and those engaging in vigorous activity. Participants are then followed for a period of time, usually some years, so that the occurrence of the specified outcome can be compared between subgroups. In contrast to case-control studies, a range of outcomes can be studied. For example the Harvard Alumni (graduates) Health Study, a cohort study which began in 1962, has investigated physical inactivity as a risk factor for cardiovascular diseases, longevity, diabetes, several site-specific cancers, gallbladder disease and even depression and suicide. Such studies are expensive but offer the best potential for establishing causality.

Experimental studies are sometimes called intervention studies because the researchers attempt to 'intervene', that is, change a variable in one or more groups of people and measure the effect on the outcome of interest. In a randomized controlled trial, considered to be the strongest design, subjects are assigned to one or more intervention groups and a control group in a random manner. This ensures that any differences between groups are due to chance rather than to bias introduced by the investigators. One framework for summarizing research on health-related issues assigns the highest level of evidence (Category A) only when a 'rich body of data' from randomized controlled trials is available (National Institutes of Health 1998). However, obvious ethical and practical constraints mean that this type of epidemiological study will probably never be conducted with a physical activity intervention because researchers cannot ask people to remain physically inactive for 20 years to see if this increases their risk of developing, say, CHD.

Measures of health-related outcomes

Measures of the occurrence of health-related outcomes are basic tools of epidemiology. They permit comparison of the frequency of the outcome(s) of interest between populations as well as among individuals with and without exposure to a particular risk factor. A number of measures are in common usage, giving different types of information. All require correct estimates of the population at risk. For instance, sports injuries only occur among people who play sport so the population at risk are sports people.

Prevalence and incidence are the measures most commonly used. Prevalence quantifies the proportion of individuals in a population that exhibits the outcome of interest at a specified time. For example, in the Health Survey for England 1995–97, the prevalence of smoking among women aged 18 was 30%. Prevalence is helpful in assessing the need for health care or preventive strategies. The formula for calculating prevalence (P) is:

$$P = \frac{\text{number of people with the health-related outcome at a specified time}}{\text{number of people in the population at risk at the specified time}}$$

Incidence quantifies the number of new occurrences of an outcome that develop during a specified time interval (the numerator) in an at-risk population (the denominator). The most accurate is the person-time incidence rate because the denominator is the best

Figure 2.2 Calculation of person-time incidence rate.

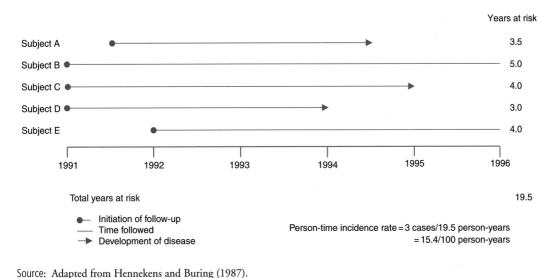

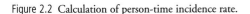

Source: Adapted from Hennekens and Buring (1987).

available measure of the total time for which individuals are free of the outcome in question. Each person in the study population contributes one person-year for each year of observation before the outcome develops or that person is lost to follow-up. Figure 2.2 illustrates this schematically, based on a study of five subjects over a 5-year observation period. The formula for calculating the person-time incidence rate (I) is:

$$I = \frac{\text{number of people who develop the health-related outcome in a specified period}}{\text{sum of the periods of time for which each person in the population is at risk}}$$

The commonest outcome measures are rates of morbidity (illness) and mortality (death). Because the age structure of a population affects both rates, these are often reported as age-specific or age-adjusted rates. This is essential when older people are more likely to become ill, as is the case, for instance, for CHD or stroke. Measures of health status may also encompass some measure of the quality of life, for example life expectancy free from disability, quality-adjusted life years or disability-adjusted life years lost.

Comparisons of disease occurrence between exposed and unexposed groups, for example, smokers versus non-smokers or sedentary people versus physically active people, are essential tools in epidemiology. These include risk difference, relative risk and population-attributable risk. Box 2.1 gives examples of each, taken from studies of physical activity. The risk difference (also called the excess risk) is the absolute difference in rates of occurrence between groups of individuals who have and have not been exposed to the factor of interest. The relative risk (also called the risk ratio) is the ratio of the risk of occurrence among exposed people to that among the unexposed; it measures the strength of an association. For example, let us assume that the incidence of stroke is 17.7 per 100,000 person-years among non-smokers and

BOX 2.1 COMPARISONS OF DISEASE OCCURRENCE

In Table 2.2, the absolute difference in risk of CHD between men reporting no vigorous sports and those reporting between 8 and ≥ 12 episodes is (5.8 − 2.1), that is, 3.7 cases per 1,000 man-years. This gives no indication of the *strength* of the association, however, which is estimated by calculating the relative risk. Relative risk is expressed in two ways.

1. Taking men reporting no vigorous sport as the reference group, the relative risk in men reporting between 8 and ≥ 12 episodes is (2.1/5.8) = 0.36. Thus, the men who were most active in vigorous sport had a risk of developing CHD that was around one-third of that experienced by the men least active in such sports.
2. Taking men with the highest level of participation in vigorous sports as the reference group, the relative risk of not engaging in these is (5.8/2.1) = 2.76. Thus, men who did not engage in vigorous sport were more than two-and-a-half times as likely to develop CHD than those with the highest level of participation in such sport.

Although the relative risk of death among alumni (Table 2.3) was nearly 9-fold greater for cigarette smoking than for a sedentary lifestyle, the estimates of population-attributable risk for these two exposures were similar. This is because the prevalence of a sedentary lifestyle was much higher than the prevalence of smoking.

49.6 per 100,000 person-years among smokers. The relative risk of stroke in smokers compared with non-smokers is therefore 2.8 (49.6/17.7). Put another way, smokers are 2.8 times more likely to have a stroke than non-smokers. When dealing with exposures that are associated with a *de*creased risk of disease – as is often the case for physical activity – researchers sometimes take the *un*exposed group (the *in*active group) as the reference category. The relative risk in the group exposed to physical activity is thus less than one. Box 2.1 illustrates both approaches. The odds ratio is used to measure the association between an exposure and a disease (or other outcome) in case-control studies; it is very similar to the relative risk, particularly if the outcome is a rare disease.

For public health policy, it is interesting to estimate the incidence of a disease (or other health outcome) in a population that can be attributed to exposure to a particular risk factor. This measure is the population-attributable risk. It reflects not only the strength of the risk associated with an exposure (information vital for assessment of the risk to an individual) but also on its prevalence. It can therefore help to determine which exposures have the most relevance to the health of a community. For example, the relative risk of developing lung cancer in smokers is high (14 in a classic study of British doctors). Nevertheless, if only 1% of the population smoke, the population-attributable risk is low; on the other hand, if 30% of people smoke, then the population-attributable risk is high and this behaviour represents a considerable public health burden that justifies investment in strategies to reduce its prevalence.

Table 2.2 Vigorous sports and attack rate of CHD in male civil servants

EPISODES OF VIGOROUS SPORT IN PREVIOUS 4 WEEKS, REPORTED IN 1976	CHD CASES	MAN-YEARS	AGE STANDARDIZED RATE* (CASES PER 1000 MAN-YEARS)
None (reference group)	413	72,282	5.8
1–3	37	7,786	4.5
8 to ≥12	7	3,349	2.1

Source: Adapted from Morris *et al.* (1990).
* rates are slightly different from values obtained from calculations based on data in columns 2 and 3 because of adjustment for age.

Table 2.3 Relative and population-attributable risks of death from all causes among 16,936 male Harvard Alumni, 1962–78

CHARACTERISTIC	PREVALENCE (% OF MAN-YEARS)	RELATIVE RISK	POPULATION-ATTRIBUTABLE RISK (%)
Sedentary lifestyle	62.0	1.31	16.1
Hypertension	9.4	1.73	6.4
Cigarette smoking	38.2	11.76	22.5

Source: Adapted from Paffenbarger *et al.* (1986).

ASSESSMENT OF PHYSICAL ACTIVITY AND FITNESS IN EPIDEMIOLOGY

Health-related outcomes are often compared between groups differing in their levels of physical activity and/or fitness. However, most researchers have opted to study physical activity because of the practical and economic difficulties of assessing physical fitness in large numbers of people.

Physical activity

A number of methods have been used to characterize exposure to leisure-time physical activity. These include: completion of a questionnaire or diary (in 'real-time' or retrospectively); monitoring of activity using a mechanical or electronic sensor; and classification of occupation. An example of the latter is the classic study by Morris and co-workers that compared the incidence of CHD in London postmen who delivered mail on foot or by bicycle (a physically active group) with that in colleagues who sorted the mail (designated as less active) (Morris *et al.* 1953). More rarely, occupational tasks have been classified according to 'on-the-job' measurements of oxygen uptake (reflecting energy expenditure). This was done in Paffenbarger's study of San Francisco longshoremen (dockworkers) and CHD risk in the 1970s (Paffenbarger and Hale 1975). For some purposes, population indices of sedentary living such as number of cars per family or hours spent watching television provide useful information on the *lack* of physical activity.

In practice however, the instrument of choice for measuring physical activity has usually been the questionnaire. The simplest classifies people as active or inactive, based on two or three questions. However, physical activity is a complex behaviour, with components of type, intensity, frequency and duration and, if a more comprehensive measure is desired, researchers have to ask those questions that elicit information relevant to their study hypothesis. If the hypothesis is that improvements in fitness arising from physical activity determine the health outcome, then the questionnaire needs to obtain information on the intensity of activity (because fitness improvements are positively related to exercise intensity). A direct approach is to ask about participation in specific activities known to demand a high rate of energy expenditure. Alternatively the questionnaire may ask how often the individual participates in exercise that he or she would describe as 'vigorous' or which elicits physiological responses associated with vigorous exercise. An example of the latter approach is 'How many times per week do you engage in exercise which makes you sweat?' These indirect questions are probably a good way to tease out the level of 'physiological stress' on the individual that is determined by the relative, rather than the absolute, intensity[2] of physical activity. Yet another way to characterize the intensity of activity is to use metabolic equivalents (METs). This unit measures intensity in multiples of the resting metabolic rate (assumed to be 3.5 ml kg^{-1} min^{-1}). For example, light house work demands about 2.5 METs, very brisk walking at 6.4 km h^{-1} (4 mile h^{-1}) 4 METs and doubles tennis 6 METs (Ainsworth *et al.* 2000).

If the research hypothesis is that the total energy expended in physical activity, rather than its intensity *per se*, determines its effects on the outcome under study, data must be collected to describe the absolute intensity, the duration and the frequency of physical activity, collectively describing its 'volume' (Howley 2001). This information can be converted into energy units by referring to data on typical rates of energy expenditure during a whole range of physical activities (McArdle *et al.* 2001). Energy expenditure in activity is then reported as kJ (or kcal) over a specified time, often per week. An alternative is to report activity in MET-h or MET-min per week. For example, if a woman did 2 h of high impact aerobic dance (intensity 7 METs) each week, as well as 3 h of brisk walking (say, 6.4 km h^{-1} or 4 mile h^{-1}, intensity 4 METs), her total physical activity could be described as $[(2 \times 7) + (3 \times 4)] = 26$ MET-h week^{-1}. The woman's energy expenditure in these two activities can then be estimated, provided that body mass is known, because the resting metabolic rate is fairly constant at 4.2 kJ kg body mass^{-1} h^{-1} (1 kcal kg body mass^{-1} h^{-1}). For a 65 kg woman, 26 MET-h week^{-1} is equivalent to an energy expenditure of approximately $(4.2 \times 26 \times 65)$ kJ, that is 7,098 kJ or 7.1 MJ.

In order to assess exposure, researchers ask participants about 'usual' or 'habitual' physical activity. Alternatively, participants may be asked to recall their physical activity levels in earlier years. This may be necessary if the hypothesis is that physical activity exerts its influence on the outcome mainly at particular stages of life. For example, in one case-control study of breast cancer, women aged between 36 and 40 years were asked to estimate their participation in various sports and leisure activities when they were 10, 16 and 25 years old (see Figure 2.3). This approach requires recall over long periods, with obvious potential for error. An alternative is to ask questions about activity during a specified period, for example, the last four weeks. This improves recall but the validity of the data is limited by the extent to which the period sampled reflects each individual's usual behaviour. Researchers have to prioritize the need for data on long term and/or current exposure, according to the outcome under study. If, as for CHD, there is reason to suppose that physical activity may influence both the long-term development of the disease and the acute events that precipitate a heart attack, both sorts of information are relevant.

The precision (repeatability) of questionnaires, assessed by test–retest correlation coefficients, is high (at an interval of 1 month this mostly exceeds 0.75) (Jacobs *et al.* 1993). It is, however, best for high intensity leisure-time activities and much poorer for those of moderate and light intensity. It also tends to be poorer in women than in men, mainly because women report very little vigorous exercise and because questionnaires do not record household activities comprehensively. Questionnaires have been validated using a variety of approaches, including; detailed interview by a trained interviewer; use of a motion detector, usually an accelerometer; assessment of cardiorespiratory fitness; and assessment of body fatness. The relationships between questionnaire scores of

Figure 2.3 Recall of lifetime participation in physical activity.

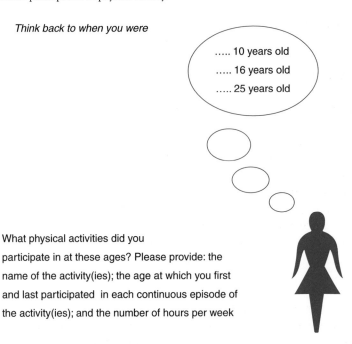

physical activity and fitness tend to be modest (typical correlation coefficients 0.3–0.5); this may reflect the genetic influence on fitness and/or the imprecision involved in measuring physical activity. Questionnaire measures do not correlate well with accelerometer recordings, perhaps because these measure different dimensions of physical activity. Thus, there is no widely accepted 'gold-standard' against which to validate questionnaires.

Fitness

Some epidemiological studies classify individuals according to a measure of fitness. Direct measurements of $\dot{V}O_2$max have been made during cycle ergometry or, less commonly, treadmill walking/running. Usually, however, because of practical and ethical constraints, a sub-maximal test has been employed. Maximal oxygen uptake may be predicted from sub-maximal heart rates (and sometimes oxygen uptake) measured during cycling. Alternatively, the heart rate at a given work rate may be adopted as a marker. In one large cohort of men and women, time to 'volitional fatigue' during an incremental treadmill test has been used as a surrogate measure of $\dot{V}O_2$max (Blair *et al.* 1989). The validity of this method derives from the strong, essentially linear, relationship between $\dot{V}O_2$max and treadmill test performance. As with measures of physical activity, each approach has its strengths and limitations. Indirect measures are less

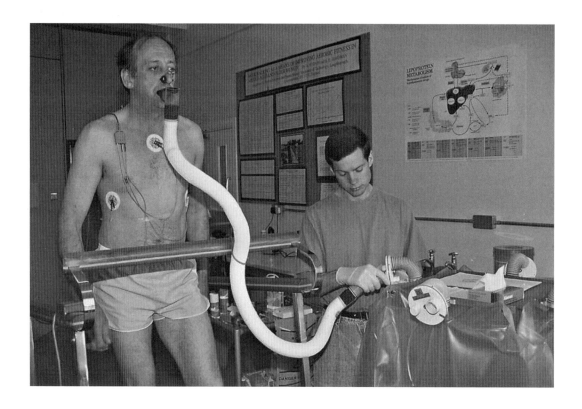

accurate but can permit larger numbers to be studied. Maximal testing improves accuracy but has to be restricted to apparently healthy people. Treadmill walking/running may reflect performance in weight-bearing activities better than cycle ergometry but will be more time-consuming if subjects require lengthy familiarization.

LABORATORY-BASED RESEARCH

Laboratory-based studies of physical activity/fitness and health complement epidemiology and help to establish causality, often by examining potential mechanisms. They may be either observational (descriptive or analytical) or experimental. Observational studies have limited potential to identify causal factors but often lead to the generation of a hypothesis that is subsequently tested experimentally. For example, early descriptive studies reported that people with exercise-induced asthma could undertake repeated short bouts of exercise without undue distress. This led to experimental studies that tested the hypothesis that intermittent exercise was better tolerated by asthmatics than continuous exercise. Cross-sectional comparisons of athletes with inactive controls have often indicated potentially fruitful lines of enquiry. For example, studies in the 1960s found that endurance athletes have low plasma insulin responses to a glucose tolerance test, something later found to derive from their enhanced sensitivity to this hormone. Such cross-sectional studies are always dogged by the problem of self-selection, however. Some genetic factor common in athletic individuals may influence the health outcome under study.

Experimental studies, by manipulating single factors independently, can remove this problem and provide good control of extraneous influences. A range of designs can be used. Randomly controlled studies generate the highest degree of confidence and have strong internal validity. In other words, the findings are unlikely to be influenced by chance, bias or confounding. (These sources of error are discussed later.) Such studies are commonly employed to test hypotheses related to the effects on health outcomes of increasing (or decreasing) levels of physical activity or fitness over weeks, months or sometimes years. The steps in setting up a randomly controlled study are shown in Figure 2.4.

Without control groups, studies risk being confounded by systematic effects unrelated to the intervention. For example, participants in an uncontrolled exercise intervention study may respond to advice to the population at large to decrease their consumption of saturated fat. Investigators might conclude that exercise decreases plasma total cholesterol when this was, in reality, due to the change in diet. (Decreasing the intake of saturated fat lowers plasma total cholesterol.) Figure 2.5 shows another example. Heart rates were measured during an incremental treadmill-running test in an intervention group and a control group, before and after the intervention group did 13 weeks of running training. The decrease in heart rate in the control group may be explained by lower levels of anxiety on the second test occasion and/or by improved running economy through getting used to running on a treadmill. The true effect of training in reducing heart rate is the difference between the decrease in the intervention group and that in controls.

Moreover, without randomization, even a controlled laboratory study can be biased. For example, given the choice, 'couch potatoes' will typically choose to be controls

Figure 2.4 Steps in setting up a randomized, controlled, laboratory-based intervention study.

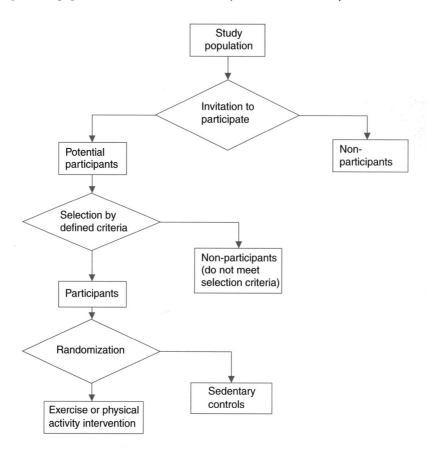

while those who are already active and fit will happily volunteer to be exercisers. This will lead to differences in variables of interest between the two groups.

Laboratory studies of exercise often use a repeated measures design where subjects act as their own control. Where the research question permits, a counterbalanced design will be used, with subjects allocated randomly to different orders of presentation. For example, if researchers wish to investigate the effects of a single session of exercise on markers of bone metabolism, each subject will be studied in two conditions, that is, with and without prior exercise. If all subjects were to do the exercise trial, first findings could be confounded by order-of-testing effects. These effects might derive from, for example, the environment (hot weather during the first trials, followed by a cold snap) but more often relate to changes in the subjects themselves. Subjects' anxiety levels decrease with repeated trials, resulting in changes to physiological and metabolic responses.

Laboratory studies of human volunteers can encounter problems with both statistical power and generalizability (external validity). A hypothesis is never proven to be true or false, it is accepted or rejected on the basis of statistical tests. Two types of

Figure 2.5 Heart rate during treadmill running in runners (upper panel) and in controls (lower panel) before and after runners completed a 13-week programme of running training.

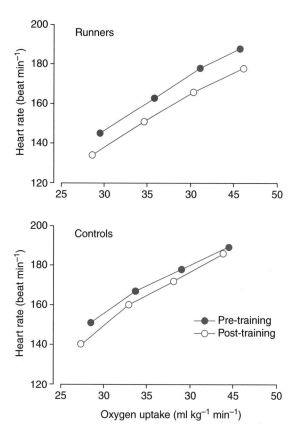

Source: Unpublished data.

error are associated with this decision: to reject the null hypothesis when it is true (type I or alpha error), and to accept the null hypothesis when it is false (type II or beta error). The probability of making a type I error is the level of significance of a statistical test. The probability of rejecting the null hypothesis when it is in fact false and should be rejected is known as its power. This reflects the potential of a study to detect an important effect. ('Important' has to be defined by the investigators, often on the basis of what is judged to be clinically important. A statistic called the effect size[3] is sometimes also used.)

Power depends on the size of the sample, the level of significance (alpha) chosen and the error variance. Particularly when complicated, time-consuming and/or invasive measurements are proposed, it may be difficult to recruit volunteers and the sample size may be inadequate. There is then a risk in the study of not finding an effect when one is really there, that is, a type II error. With adequate sample size, good control and accurate, complete and reliable measurements, a study will be valid. The issue of generalizability must be considered subsequently because one cannot generalize from an invalid study. The extent to which findings will apply to different populations has to be judged, based on the known or postulated mechanisms that might explain the findings. For example, numerous studies have shown that brisk walking improves fitness in middle-aged and older Caucasian women from developed countries. This activity has also been shown to elicit a sufficiently high proportion of $\dot{V}O_2$max to elicit a training effect. On the basis of these findings, it is reasonable to assume that brisk walking will have similar effects in women of this age group from other ethnic groups or from less developed countries.

ERROR: NATURE, SOURCES AND IMPLICATIONS

Evaluation of the validity of the findings of a study depends on the extent to which these could also be explained by chance, bias or confounding. A critical appreciation of the literature on exercise and health requires an understanding of all three source of error. First, however, it is essential to make the distinction between precision and accuracy, both essential features of measurement. Figure 2.6 depicts these important concepts. Briefly, data are accurate if they are close to the true values and precise if the same measurement, when repeated, consistently yields similar values. Good data has to be both accurate and precise (top left corner of Figure 2.6); neither is sufficient, alone (Box 2.2).

Random error is due to chance and leads to imprecision in measurement. It derives from several sources including: individual biological variation; sampling error (studies almost always study a sample of people, not a population); and measurement error. These errors cannot be eliminated but they can be reduced by making individual measurements as precise as possible and by increasing the size of the study. In the laboratory, precision is achieved by calibration of instruments, by making careful measurements and by increasing the number of measurements. Precise measurements are often impossible in epidemiology because it is difficult to measure physical activity or fitness and, often, health outcomes. This imprecision may be compensated by studying a large sample.

Researchers evaluate the degree to which chance variation may account for the results by calculating either the significance value (P value) or a confidence interval. Their hypothesis is accepted or rejected on the basis of these statistical tests. The P value describes the probability that the result may be due to chance alone. In medical research, investigators conventionally adopt a critical P value (α) of 0.05. This means that the probability of obtaining the observed association (or difference) is less than 5% or 1 in 20, if the null hypothesis was in fact true. In other words, the researcher is reasonably certain that the observed data are 'unusual' enough to rule out the null hypothesis. The confidence interval is more informative and its use has increased in recent years. It gives the range within which the true magnitude of the effect lies, with a certain level of assurance. For example among Norwegian women, physical activity equivalent to walking or bicycling for at least 4 h per week has been associated with a relative risk of developing colon cancer of 0.62. The 95% confidence interval for this relative risk was 0.40–0.97 so we can be assured that, if the study were repeated 20 times on different samples, on 19 occasions the relative risk would lie between 0.40 and 0.97.

BOX 2.2 ACCURACY AND PRECISION

- If an individual's $\dot{V}O_2$max is measured on four occasions during 1 week and recorded as 25 ml kg^{-1} min^{-1}, 35 ml kg^{-1} min^{-1}, 15 ml kg^{-1} min^{-1} and 42 ml kg^{-1} min^{-1}, the measurements have low precision; they are so different that no meaningful interpretation can be placed on them – even if the average of these values is close to the true value (lower left corner of Figure 2.6).
- On the other hand, repeated measurements of 34 ml kg^{-1} min^{-1}, 32 ml kg^{-1} min^{-1}, 33 ml kg^{-1} min^{-1} and 33 ml kg^{-1} min^{-1} indicate high precision but are inaccurate if the subject's *true* $\dot{V}O_2$max is 19 ml kg^{-1} min^{-1} (top right corner). This is important because the average value recorded (33 ml kg^{-1} min^{-1}) suggests that brisk walking at 4.5 METs would be very light exercise for this person (<50% of $\dot{V}O_2$max), whereas it would actually be very vigorous (>80% $\dot{V}O_2$max)!
- Only if repeated values are close to each other (high precision) and cluster around the true value (high accuracy), can we have confidence in the data.

Figure 2.6 Schematic representation of accuracy and precision in measurement.

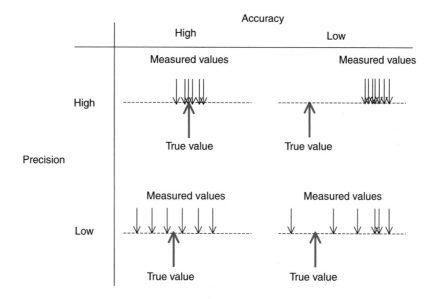

Source: Adapted from Beaglehole *et al.* (1993).

Bias is error in research design or collection of data that produces results which differ in a systematic manner from the true values. It can take many forms but the most important are selection bias and measurement bias. Selection bias arises when the characteristics of people selected to participate in a study differ systematically from those of people who are not. In a laboratory study, selection bias may influence the subsequent generalizability of findings but not its validity. In epidemiology, where associations between a putative risk factor and a health outcome are sought, selection bias threatens the validity of a study. For example, if people are asked to participate in a study of physical activity, responders are likely to differ in their exercise habits from non-responders. An investigator can also introduce bias (knowingly or unknowingly) by including people who appear more (or less) receptive to the notion that physical activity improves health rather than other potential participants. Another source of selection bias is the 'healthy worker effect'; people in employment have to be healthy enough to do their job whereas those who are ill or disabled may often be excluded.

Systematic error in measurements is an issue in both laboratory and epidemiological studies. For example, one chemical pathology laboratory may consistently measure plasma cholesterol concentrations lower than another. This bias can be evaluated if each laboratory participating in a study analyses a portion of a 'pooled' serum sample and a correction factor is applied. Other sources of bias are more difficult to deal with. One of the most important relates to measurements that rely on human memory (e.g. consumption of coffee or of foods high in fat or, of course, participation in physical activities) and these are common in epidemiology. For example, underweight individuals tend to over-report food intake on questionnaires, while obese subjects under-report it. This error is called recall bias and is particularly important in case-control studies when individuals recently diagnosed with a disease tend to recall their past exposures with greater accuracy than controls, especially if it is widely known that the risk factor under study may be associated with that disease.

Bias is not confined to individual studies but may be evident in the literature as a whole. For example, there is a tendency for editors of journals to accept research papers reporting 'positive' findings (where the research hypothesis is supported) more readily than those who report 'negative' findings. This tendency is compounded by the fact that researchers are less likely to submit studies with negative findings for publication.

As explained early in this chapter, an epidemiological study seeks to identify an association between exposure to a designated causal (or risk) factor and a health-related outcome. Often, however, a third factor is associated both with the exposure being studied and the outcome being studied. If this third factor is unequally distributed between the exposure subgroups, it may confuse the findings. This problem is called confounding. It can even create the appearance of a cause and effect relationship that does not exist. For example, researchers investigating the associations between physical activity or fitness and CHD have to address the concern that people may be physically active because of some constitutional factor(s) which, in reality, is what protects them from heart disease. Another example would be studies of physical activity and colon cancer. Dietary factors can confound findings because physically active people may be more likely than sedentary people to eat a low-fat, high-fibre diet. Randomization is the best way to control the problem of confounding factors. In case-control and cohort studies, the problem is most commonly addressed at the analysis stage by statistical modelling to estimate the strength of associations while controlling simultaneously for confounding variables. However, this approach cannot alter the fundamental quality of the data and confounding will inevitably introduce biases that cannot be controlled statistically.

ESTABLISHING CAUSALITY

Epidemiological studies, laboratory-based studies and clinical studies all contribute evidence on physical activity and health. Assessment of the strength of this evidence involves consideration of each type of research. As pointed out in the previous section, large randomly controlled trials of physical activity with disease endpoints will probably never be undertaken. Epidemiological research in this area is therefore essentially observational and, because of bias and confounding, a rather blunt tool. Indeed these two sources of error have been described as 'a plague upon the house of epidemiology' (Taubes 1995). How then does the research community assess whether physical inactivity is a causal factor for a particular health outcome? (In considering the diseases which are big public health problems in the twenty-first century, for example, heart disease, diabetes, osteoporosis, it is appropriate to talk about 'causal factors', rather than a cause because this invariably has several components.)

Several criteria for causal significance in epidemiological studies have been proposed and these are summarized in Box 2.3. One of the most important criteria is the strength of the association between the causal factor and the outcome. Some authorities take the view that no single epidemiological study is persuasive by itself unless the relative risk of exposure is three or more. If this were the only criterion, very few studies would indicate that physical inactivity and low fitness are causal factors for important health-related outcomes. However, judgements on causality need also to take other aspects of the evidence into account. These include whether or not associations reported in epidemiological studies are concordant with biologically plausible mechanisms. In this way, evidence from laboratory-based studies complements and extends that from epidemiology. The former demonstrate mechanisms but cannot show links with disease endpoints: the latter can establish links with morbidity and mortality but cannot by themselves establish causality. Reaching a conclusion on whether or not physical

---

BOX 2.3 CRITERIA USED TO ASSESS WHETHER EPIDEMIOLOGICAL EVIDENCE IS SUFFICIENT TO CONCLUDE THAT A RISK FACTOR IS CAUSAL

- Appropriately sequenced – does the measure of level of physical activity (or fitness) precede the onset of disease?
- Plausibility – is the association consistent with other knowledge? (Mechanisms of action; animal studies.)
- Consistency – are findings consistent in different populations?
- Strength – what is the strength of the association between the causal factor and the effect, that is what is the relative risk?
- Dose–response – are increased levels of physical activity or fitness associated with a greater effect?
- Reversibility – is becoming less active or fit associated with a reduction of disease risk?
- Strong study design – are findings based on strong study designs? (The randomly controlled trial is the 'gold-standard'.)

inactivity or low fitness may be causal factors in specific health outcomes therefore involves making judgements based on the totality of the evidence.

Conventions for describing the strength of research evidence are now widely used, particularly among medical researchers. That adopted in the US was mentioned earlier (National Institutes of Health 1998). The accepted convention in the UK is the SIGN (Scottish Intercollegiate Guidelines Network) system (Petrie *et al.* 1995). Both conventions place the greatest confidence in randomly controlled trials. In the SIGN system, the highest level of evidence (Grade A, level 1a) requires meta-analysis of such trials, while Grade B evidence requires 'well-conducted clinical studies but no randomized controlled trial'; the weakest grade of evidence, Grade C, is based on 'expert committee reports or opinion ... (and) indicates absence of directly applicable studies of good quality'.

Systematic reviews in a particular area attempt to consider all aspects of all the evidence. However, this process is not straightforward. For example, searches of electronic databases (MEDLINE, PubMed) typically identify only 70–80% of relevant literature. The Cochrane Collaboration – a collaboration of international groups initiated in 1992 to review clinical areas – limit the material they review to randomized controlled trials. This approach excludes potentially valuable evidence and does not recognize that such trials do not necessarily present good data because measurements may lack accuracy and/or precision. Nevertheless, Cochrane reviews are highly regarded and will be referred to in this book, particularly in Chapter 12 on therapeutic exercise.

SUMMARY

- Epidemiology is the study of the distribution and determinants of health-related states or events in specified populations, and the application of this study to control of health problems. It can identify risk factors but not causality.
- Outcome measures include mortality and morbidity but also indices of quality of life. The most accurate measure of disease frequency is the person-time incidence rate, for example, heart attacks per 1,000 person-years. These are compared between groups, yielding a relative risk that estimates the strength of an association with the risk factor under study.
- In epidemiological studies, physical activity levels are usually measured by questionnaire. This introduces bias and imprecision (misclassification) which will decrease the strength of observed associations with health outcomes.
- It is argued that measuring physical fitness may be a more objective measure than physical activity. Fitness – as commonly measured – is, however, strongly influenced by genetic factors and difficult to measure in epidemiological studies.
- Laboratory-based studies can achieve excellent control and precision and indicate potential mechanisms. However, their outcome measures are removed from the clinical endpoints of morbidity and mortality.
- Establishing causality requires evidence from epidemiology for strong and consistent associations as well as evidence for plausible mechanisms from laboratory-based studies. These types of evidence are complementary and neither is sufficient alone. The totality of the data is what matters.

STUDY TASKS

1 In epidemiology, what is considered the strongest study design and why? Discuss the reasons why this design will probably not be implemented in the study of physical activity and the risk of heart disease.

2 What is meant by confounding? Identify several factors that might be confounding factors in a case-control study of the association between the risk of colon cancer and physical activity.

3 In the Aerobics Center Longitudinal Study (a cohort study), time to exhaustion during an incremental treadmill test has been adopted as a surrogate measure of physical fitness. In this context, what are the strengths and weaknesses of this test?

4 Table 2.3 presents data, for three risk factors, on the relative risk of dying over the observation period and on the population-attributable risk. Comment on the relevance of these findings for (a) the individual and (b) public health policy.

NOTES

1 Usually it is not possible to study the entire population in which one is interested. It is therefore necessary to draw a sample and to relate its characteristics to the defined population.

2 Relative intensity may be calculated as the oxygen uptake demanded by an activity, expressed as a percentage of the individual's $\dot{V}O_2max$. For individuals with low values of $\dot{V}O_2max$, the percentage of oxygen uptake reserve ($\dot{V}O_2max$ – resting oxygen uptake) demanded by a given exercise is a better measure of its relative intensity.

3 This statistic describes the size of the difference between two means, relative to the standard deviation. An effect size of 0.8 or more is usually deemed to be large, around 0.5 moderate and 0.2 or less, small (Thomas and Nelson 2001).

FURTHER READING

Ainsworth, B.E. and Macera, C.A. (1998) 'Physical inactivity', in R.C. Brownson, P.L. Remington and J.R. Davis (eds) *Chronic Disease Epidemiology and Control*, 2nd edn. Washington: American Public Health Association, pp. 191–213.

Barker, D.J.P., Cooper, C. and Rose, G. (1998) *Epidemiology in Medical Practice*, 5th edn. New York: Churchill Livingstone.

Paffenbarger, R.S., Blair, S.N., Lee, I.-M. and Hyde, R.T. (1993) 'Measurement of physical activity to assess health effects in free-living populations', *Medicine and Science in Sports and Exercise* 25: 60–70.

Schriger, D.L. (2001) 'Analyzing the relationship of exercise and health: methods, assumptions, and limitations', *Medicine and Science in Sports and Exercise* 33 (Suppl.): S359–63.

Taubes, G. (1995) 'Epidemiology faces its limits', editorial, *Science* 269: 14 July, 164–9.

Thomas, J.R. and Nelson, J.K. (2001) *Research Methods in Physical Activity* 4th edn. Champaign, IL: Human Kinetics.

3 Physical activity and total mortality

Knowledge assumed
Basic statistics, relative risk,
population-attributable risk,
basic exercise physiology

INTRODUCTION

The Norwegian epidemiologist Gunnar Erikssen asserts that '… modern day humans are dying because of a lack of physical exercise' (Erikssen 2001). In this chapter, we will examine the evidence that physical activity and physical fitness reduce the risk of dying prematurely. The studies included in this chapter are those which have addressed all-cause mortality, that is, death from any cause. Studies that have examined the link between activity/fitness and specific causes of death such as cardiovascular disease (CVD) and cancer are covered elsewhere in the book (Chapters 4 and 9, respectively, for CVD and cancer). Moreover, the studies discussed in this chapter are all epidemiological cohort studies. Therefore, they do not begin to answer the question 'why do active/fit people live longer than inactive/unfit people?' Answers to this question are provided in later chapters.

PHYSICAL ACTIVITY AND ALL-CAUSE MORTALITY

Although there was some limited information linking physically active occupations to longevity in the eighteenth and nineteenth centuries, systematic study of the relationship between physical activity and longevity only began in the twentieth century. Initially research focussed on occupational activity and longevity. One such study was that of US railroad industry employees. This study examined mortality rates over a 2-year period (1955–56) and found lower rates among section men (classified as the most active group) compared to clerks (classified as the least active group) and switchmen (Taylor *et al.* 1962). However, there were limitations to these early studies. It was possible, for example, that the relationship between occupation and mortality risk was simply due to self-selection, that is, men who were in the process of developing chronic diseases (and therefore likely to die prematurely) might have chosen physically less demanding jobs. Also, other characteristics predictive of mortality, such as smoking, obesity and diet, were not accounted for. Moreover, leisure-time physical activity was not measured and thus there was no clear assessment of total physical activity. Nevertheless, such studies were the catalyst for future investigations with improved study designs.

In the latter half of the twentieth century, attention switched to leisure-time physical activity and the findings of several cohort studies were published in the 1980s and 1990s. The most notable of these investigations was the Harvard Alumni Health Study. This was a cohort study of men enrolled in Harvard College between 1916 and 1950. Questionnaires were used to estimate the amount of energy expended in walking, stair climbing, sports and recreational activities. One publication from this study concerned the relationship between physical activity and all-cause mortality in 16,936 men aged 35–74 years at baseline (Paffenbarger *et al.* 1986). Baseline data was collected either in 1962 or 1966. Follow-up was conducted 12–16 years later in 1978, by which time 1,413 alumni had died. The findings revealed an inverse dose–response relationship between physical activity and the risk of all-cause mortality (Figure 3.1). Death rates were 25–33% lower among alumni expending 2,000 kcal week^{-1} (8,400 kJ week^{-1}) or more in weekly physical activity compared with those expending less than this amount. These findings remained significant following control for smoking, hypertension, body mass change and early parental death. Moreover, the inverse association between activity and mortality risk held when findings were examined within different age bands (35–49, 50–59, 60–69 and 70–84).

There was evidence in the Harvard Alumni Health Study of a slight increase in the relative risk of death in the most active group (i.e. those expending >3,499 kcal week^{-1} (14,700 kJ week^{-1})) compared to the groups expending >2,000 kcal week^{-1} but <3,499 kcal week^{-1} (Figure 3.1). This suggests that very high levels of activity may increase mortality risk slightly compared to moderate levels. This issue remains contentious but it is important to note that the relative risk was still lower in the most active group compared with the groups expending <2,000 kcal week^{-1}.

Figure 3.1 Findings from the Harvard Alumni Health Study indicate that there is an inverse association between the amount of physical activity performed per week and the risk of all-cause mortality.

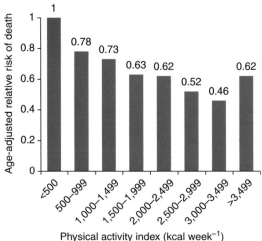

Source: Paffenbarger *et al.* (1986).

The findings of the Harvard Alumni Health Study are broadly consistent with the findings from other investigations of the association between physical activity and all-cause mortality (see Lee and Paffenbarger 1996 for a comprehensive review of these studies). These investigations suggest that physically active individuals have a lower risk of dying prematurely compared with their sedentary counterparts. Thus, there is a reassuring consistency in the data. However, the studies are observational in nature and therefore do not provide proof of cause and effect for reasons outlined in the previous chapter. Nevertheless, there is other evidence supporting an association between physical activity and all-cause mortality risk including an association between physical fitness (which is partly determined by physical activity) and all-cause mortality risk.

PHYSICAL FITNESS AND ALL-CAUSE MORTALITY

The major advantage of studying physical fitness and mortality risk rather than physical activity and mortality risk is that physical fitness can be measured more objectively than self-report of physical activity. Most studies examining the association between fitness and mortality risk have used treadmill tests to give an indication of physical fitness. Often treadmill time on a maximal exercise test has been used as a surrogate marker for $\dot{V}O_2$max because these two variables are closely related. However, some studies have used recovery heart rate as a measure of fitness while others have estimated exercise capacity in METs. Virtually all studies in this area have defined fitness in aerobic terms (using surrogate markers for $\dot{V}O_2$max) although other forms of fitness such as musculoskeletal fitness have been examined (Katzmarzyk and Craig 2002).

One of the first studies to demonstrate an association between physical fitness and all-cause mortality risk was the Aerobics Centre Longitudinal Study (Blair *et al.* 1989). In this study, a maximal treadmill exercise test was conducted in 10,224 men and 3,120 women and time to exhaustion on this test was used to indicate fitness. The average period of follow-up was just over 8 years during which there were 240 deaths in men and 43 deaths in women. Participants were classified into quintiles: quintile one contained those with the shortest treadmill times (lowest fitness); and quintile five contained those with the longest treadmill times (highest fitness). Those with the lowest fitness levels had the highest risk of death during follow-up. The lowest risk of death was seen in those with the highest fitness in men and in those in quintile four in women (Table 3.1). These trends remained after statistical adjustment for age, smoking habit, cholesterol level, systolic blood pressure, fasting blood glucose level, parental history of coronary heart disease (CHD) and follow-up interval. Blair and colleagues concluded that high levels of physical fitness appear to delay all-cause mortality primarily due to lowered rates of CVD and cancer.

In a follow-up study with a larger number of subjects, Blair and colleagues (1996) compared the strength of the association between low-fitness and all-cause mortality with that of other established disease risk factors including smoking, hypertension, high cholesterol level and overweight. In this study, low fitness was defined as the least fit 20% of the study sample. This was based on the finding from the previous study that the greatest difference in mortality risk was between fitness quintiles one and two in both men and women (Table 3.1). After adjustment for age, examination year and all other risk factors, low fitness was associated with an equal or greater increase in mortality risk than other established risk factors in both men and women (Figure 3.2).

Table 3.1 Physical fitness (time to exhaustion on a treadmill test) was associated with a reduction in the risk of all-cause mortality in both men and women in the Aerobics Centre Longitudinal Study

FITNESS GROUP	PERSON-YEARS OF FOLLOW-UP	NO. OF DEATHS	AGE-ADJUSTED RATES PER 10,000 PERSON-YEARS	RELATIVE RISK
Men				
1 (low)	14,515	75	64.0	3.44
2	16,898	40	25.5	1.37
3	17,287	47	27.1	1.46
4	18,792	43	21.7	1.17
5 (high)	17,557	35	18.6	1.00
Women				
1 (low)	4,916	18	39.5	4.65
2	5,329	11	20.5	2.42
3	5,053	6	12.2	1.43
4	5,522	4	6.5	0.76
5 (high)	4,613	4	8.5	1.00

Source: Blair *et al.* (1989).

Figure 3.2 Low physical fitness was associated with an equal or greater risk of all-cause mortality as other established risk factors in the Aerobics Centre Longitudinal Study.

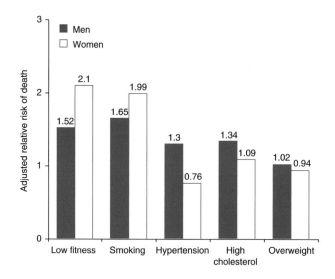

Source: Blair *et al.* (1996).

Notes: Low fitness: the least fit 20% of participants, smoking: current or recent smoker, hypertension: systolic blood pressure $\geq$140 mm Hg, high cholesterol: total cholesterol $\geq$6.2 mmol l^{-1}, overweight: body mass index $\geq$27 kg m^2. The relative risk of death was adjusted for age and for each of the other variables in the figure.

These findings suggest that low fitness should be considered as seriously as other established risk factors for disease.

Many other studies have confirmed the association between low levels of physical fitness and all-cause mortality risk. One recent example is a Californian study involving 3,679 men with CVD and 2,534 men without CVD (Myers *et al.* 2002). Exercise capacity (METs) was estimated in these men, based on the treadmill speed and incline achieved during a maximal exercise test. The average duration of follow-up was 6.2 years during which there were 1,256 deaths. As with the Aerobics Centre Longitudinal Study, the participants were divided into quintiles based on exercise capacity. The relative risk of all-cause mortality for those in the lowest quintile of fitness was 4 times higher than for those in the highest quintile of fitness. This finding applied both for those with CVD and for those without CVD (Figure 3.3). When these two groups were combined, every 1 MET increase in exercise capacity was associated with a 12% improvement in survival. Moreover, in both groups of subjects exercise capacity was a stronger predictor of all-cause mortality than established CVD risk factors including hypertension, smoking and diabetes.

Myers and colleagues (2002) also examined the influence of fitness on mortality risk in subgroups of participants who were at increased risk of death due to the presence of other risk factors including a history of hypertension, chronic obstructive pulmonary disease (COPD), diabetes, smoking, obesity and hypercholesterolaemia. In all subgroups, the risk of death from any cause was approximately twice as high in subjects whose exercise capacity was below 5 METs compared with those whose exercise

Figure 3.3 Exercise capacity (METs) was inversely related to the risk of death in Californian men with and without CVD.

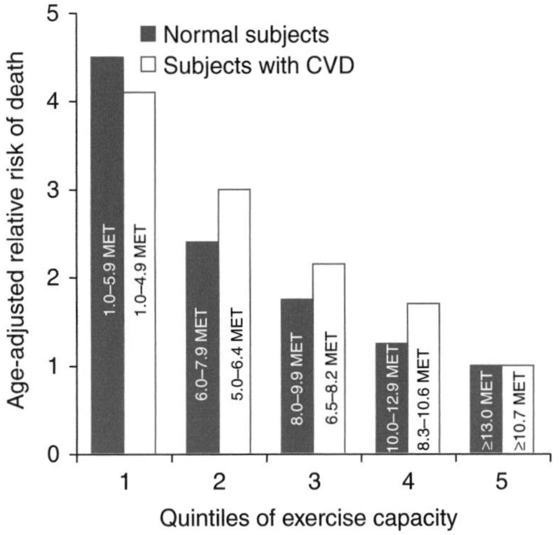

Source: Myers *et al.* (2002).

capacity was above 8 METs (Figure 3.4). In an editorial accompanying this study, Balady (2002) summarized its importance as follows: '… Myers *et al.* place valuable and readily applicable conclusions on the desk of the clinician. Absolute fitness levels … represent a continuum of risk – i.e., greater fitness results in longer survival. Fitness levels are important predictors of survival in persons with and without cardiovascular disease, as well as in those with specific cardiovascular risk factors'.

As with studies of physical activity, the studies of physical fitness are consistent in suggesting a protective effect of exercise. Moreover, there is also evidence of a dose–response relationship between fitness and mortality risk. However, studies of fitness are constrained by some of the limitations that apply to studies of activity, the main one being that the studies are observational. A further source of controversy is the extent to which fitness levels are determined by activity as opposed to genes. Both play a role but which factor has the major influence within large populations remains unclear. Nevertheless, genes have an influence on other established disease risk factors so this alone cannot detract from the importance of the fitness–mortality risk association. Moreover, changes in physical activity can have a profound effect on physical fitness, suggesting that individuals can modify their mortality risk by altering their activity levels and thus their fitness. Evidence to support this assertion is available in the form of studies that have examined changes in either activity or fitness to determine whether or not there is an associated change in the risk of all-cause mortality.

CHANGES IN PHYSICAL ACTIVITY AND ALL-CAUSE MORTALITY

The first major epidemiological study to examine changes in physical activity and risk of all-cause mortality was the Harvard Alumni Health Study (Paffenbarger *et al.* 1993).

Figure 3.4 High exercise capacity was associated with a reduced risk of all-cause mortality even in the presence of established risk factors in a study of Californian men.

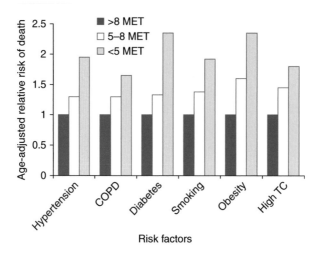

Source: Myers *et al.* (2002).
Notes: The figure shows the age-adjusted relative risk of death from any cause in subjects with various risk factors classified according to exercise capacity in METs. COPD: chronic obstructive pulmonary disease. Obesity was defined as a body mass index ≥ 30 kg m^2. High TC: high total cholesterol, that is, ≥ 5.7 mmol l^{-1}.

In this study, exercise habits were assessed via a questionnaire at baseline (either 1962 or 1966) and again in 1977 in 10,269 men aged 45–84 years in 1977. These men reported being free from life-threatening disease at both observation points. Follow-up was continued until 1985 during which time 476 men died. At each observation point individuals were grouped according to: (1) their weekly physical activity levels ($<$2,000 kcal week^{-1} (8.4 MJ week^{-1}) versus $\geq$2,000 kcal week^{-1}) and (2) their participation or lack of participation in 'moderately vigorous' sports activities (defined as those requiring an intensity $\geq$4.5 METs) such as swimming, tennis, squash, racquetball, handball, jogging and running.

The findings revealed that changes in exercise habits between observation points were associated with differences in mortality risk during follow-up. Specifically, there was a lower mortality rate in those who became more active and/or increased the intensity of their physical activity between observation points than in those who did not (Figure 3.5). These findings have been confirmed by the findings of the British Regional Heart Study (Wannemethee *et al.* 1998). Such studies provide firmer evidence to support the hypothesis that inactive people can lower their risk of dying prematurely by becoming more active. They also support the notion that 'moderately vigorous' activities such as those defined above are more effective in reducing mortality risk than 'light' activities such as 'golf, walking for pleasure, gardening and housework'. Finally, the findings of the Harvard Alumni Health Study suggest that past activity alone is not protective and that benefits may be lost following the cessation of regular exercise. This conclusion arises from the observation that mortality risk appears to increase in those reporting a reduction in the amount and/or intensity of physical activity between observation points (Figure 3.5).

Figure 3.5 Increases in the amount and/or intensity of physical activity over time are associated with a lower risk of all-cause mortality in comparison to the risk in those who remain sedentary.

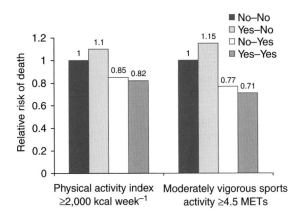

Source: Harvard Alumni Health Study (Paffenbarger *et al.* 1993).
Notes: This study involved 10,269 men assessed in 1962 or 1966 and again in 1977 and followed-up until 1985. The figure legend indicates group classifications, for example, those in the 'no-no' group expended less than 2,000 kcal week^{-1} (8.4 MJ week^{-1}) at both observation points.

CHANGES IN PHYSICAL FITNESS AND ALL-CAUSE MORTALITY

At least two studies have examined all-cause mortality in relation to changes in physical fitness. The first of these was the Aerobics Centre Longitudinal Study (Blair *et al.* 1995). This study involved 9,777 men aged 20–82 years at baseline who completed two maximal treadmill tests between 1970 and 1989. The mean interval between treadmill tests was 4.9 years and the mean follow-up duration after the second test was 5.1 years during which time there were 223 deaths. For each of the treadmill tests, participants were grouped into quintiles based on treadmill time and those in quintile one (shortest treadmill time) were classified as unfit while those in quintiles 2–5 were classified as fit. The age-adjusted relative risk of death was 1.0 for those who were unfit on both occasions, 0.56 for those who were unfit on the first occasion but fit on the second occasion, 0.52 for those who were fit on the first occasion but unfit on the second occasion and 0.33 for those who were fit on both occasions. This pattern – highest risk of all-cause mortality in those who were unfit on both occasions, lowest risk in those who were fit on both occasions, intermediate risk in those who were unfit on the first occasion but fit on the second occasion – held throughout all age groups (Figure 3.6). Furthermore, crude analysis within a subgroup of 1,512 men indicated that changes in fitness were related to changes in activity, providing evidence for a cause and effect relationship.

More recently, a study of Norwegian men has confirmed the association between changes in physical fitness and changes in mortality (Erikssen *et al.* 1998). In this study, 1,428 healthy middle-aged men completed a bicycle exercise test between 1972 and

Figure 3.6 Findings from the Aerobics Centre Longitudinal Study demonstrate that improvements in physical fitness are associated with reductions in the risk of all-cause mortality regardless of age.

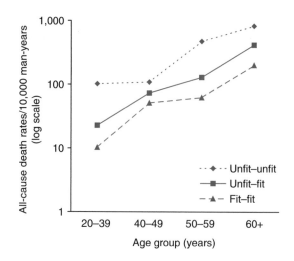

Source: Blair *et al.* (1995).
Note: Values are plotted on a log scale. Unfit: men in quintile one of their age-specific fitness distribution. Fit: men in quintiles 2–5 of their age-specific fitness distribution.

1975 and again between 1980 and 1982. Follow-up continued until 1994 during which time there were 238 deaths. Physical fitness was defined as the sum of all work done during the bicycle test (kJ) divided by body weight (kg). Change in physical fitness was calculated by dividing the physical fitness score on test two with that obtained on test one. A graded inverse relationship was observed between change in physical fitness and mortality irrespective of physical fitness status at survey one (Figure 3.7).

Collectively, these studies provide convincing evidence that changes in activity habits have an influence on mortality risk, particularly if such changes result in an improvement in physical fitness. Thus, these studies suggest that human beings have an element of control over their own mortality. It is important to re-emphasise, however, that these studies are observational and are not proof of a cause and effect relationship. Furthermore, the studies highlighted here all pertain to men. Findings regarding change in activity/fitness and all-cause mortality have not yet been reported in women. However, there is no reason to believe that such findings would be inconsistent with those in men.

PHYSICAL FITNESS, BODY COMPOSITION AND ALL-CAUSE MORTALITY

Most of the studies discussed so far relate to 'healthy' men, although some studies have included 'healthy' and 'unhealthy' groups based on the presence or absence of disease at baseline. An issue that has been debated more recently is the extent to which exercise influences mortality risk in obese individuals irrespective of any influence on body

Figure 3.7 Improvements in physical fitness were associated with a significantly lower risk of all-cause mortality irrespective of initial fitness levels in a study of Norwegian men.

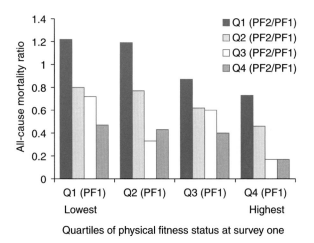

Source: Erikssen *et al.* (1998).
Notes: Q: quartile. PF1: the level of physical fitness attained on the first survey. PF2: the level of physical fitness attained on the second survey.

fatness. This issue has been addressed with reference to data collected in the Aerobics Centre Longitudinal Study.

Lee and colleagues (1999) studied the relationship between fitness, fatness and all-cause mortality risk in 21,925 men aged 30–83 years. Body composition was measured using hydrostatic weighing, skinfold thickness or both. Physical fitness was assessed using time to exhaustion on a maximal treadmill exercise test. As in previous studies men in the least-fit 20% of each age group were classified as unfit, and all others as fit. Men were also assigned to categories with respect to body fatness – lean, normal or obese – corresponding to <25th, 25th to <75th and ≥75th percentile scores. This resulted in the following body fatness categories: lean <16.7% body fat, normal 16.7 to <25.0% body fat, obese ≥25.0% body fat. Baseline tests were completed between 1971 and 1989 and the average period of follow-up was 8 years during which there were 428 deaths.

After adjustment for age, examination year, smoking, alcohol intake and parental history of heart disease, unfit, lean men were found to have double the risk of all-cause mortality compared to fit, obese men (Figure 3.8). Similar findings emerged in a sub-group of 14,043 men stratified according to waist circumference. Unfit men with a low waist circumference (<87 cm) had a much greater risk of all-cause mortality than fit men with a high waist circumference (≥99 cm) (Figure 3.9). These findings suggest that obese men are not homogeneous with respect to physical fitness and that obese men who are fit do not have an elevated risk of all-cause mortality. They also suggest that the benefits of leanness are restricted to those who are fit. It is important to note, however, that only 6% of the men in the lean group were classified as unfit whereas 40% of those in the obese group were classified as unfit. Similarly, only 4% of men in the low waist

Figure 3.8 Findings from the Aerobics Centre Longitudinal Study indicate that men who are obese and fit have a similar risk of all-cause mortality compared with those who are lean and fit.

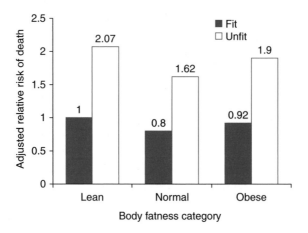

Source: Lee *et al.* (1999).
Notes: Percentage body fat values are: lean <16.7, normal 16.7 to <25.0, obese ≥25.0. Unfit: men in the least-fit 20% of their respective age group. Fit: all other men. Mortality risks were adjusted for age, examination year, smoking, alcohol intake and parental history of heart disease.

Figure 3.9 Findings from the Aerobics Centre Longitudinal Study indicate that fit men with a high waist circumference have a similar risk of all-cause mortality compared with fit men who have a low waist circumference.

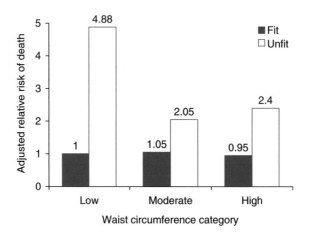

Source: Lee *et al.* (1999).
Notes: Waist circumference categories are: low <87 cm, moderate 87 to <99 cm, high ≥99 cm. Unfit: men in the least-fit 20% of their respective age group. Fit: all other men. Mortality risks were adjusted for age.

circumference category were classified as unfit as opposed to 30% of men in the high waist circumference category.

Another obesity-related issue addressed by the Aerobics Centre Longitudinal Study is the strength of the association between low fitness and mortality in comparison to that of other established risk factors for mortality including CVD, diabetes, hypercholesterolaemia, hypertension and smoking (Wei *et al.* 1999). To examine this 25,714 men (mean age: 44 years) completed a maximal treadmill exercise test and were given a medical examination and then followed for an average of 10 years, during which time there were 1,025 deaths. Thirteen percent (3,293 men) of the men in this sample were obese (body mass index $\geq$30 kg m^2). Within this group, obese men with low fitness had more than double the risk of all-cause mortality compared to obese men not classified as such. This was comparable to, or higher than, the risk associated with other established predictors of mortality (Figure 3.10). Moreover, when the population-attributable risk was calculated for each of these risk factors, the findings indicated that low fitness was associated with far more deaths amongst obese men than any other risk factor (Figure 3.11). The results of the Aerobic Centre Longitudinal Study concerning obese men require confirmation in women. These results would also be strengthened if they were shown to hold true for physical activity in addition to physical fitness.

Figure 3.10 Among obese men, the association between low fitness and mortality was comparable to that of other mortality predictors in the Aerobics Centre Longitudinal Study.

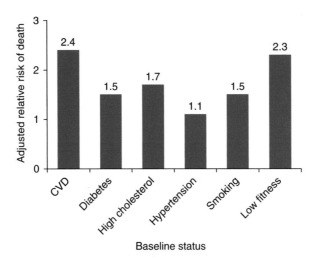

Source: Wei *et al.* (1999).
Notes: Obesity was defined as a body mass index $\geq$30 kg m^2. High cholesterol: TC >6.2 mmol l^{-1}, hypertension: blood pressure > 140/90 mm Hg, low fitness: least fit 20% in each age group. Relative risks were adjusted for age and for each of the other risk factors in the figure. For each risk factor the referent group is obese men without that risk factor.

Figure 3.11 Among obese men, the population-attributable risk associated with low fitness was higher than that associated with any other mortality predictor in the Aerobics Centre Longitudinal Study.

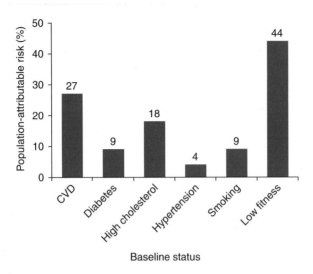

Source: Wei *et al.* (1999).
Notes: Obesity was defined as a body mass index ≥ 30 kg m^2. High cholesterol: TC > 6.2 mmol l^{-1}, hypertension: blood pressure > 140/90 mm Hg, low fitness: least fit 20% in each age group. Relative risks were adjusted for age and for each of the other risk factors in the figure. For each risk factor the referent group is obese men without that risk factor.

Nevertheless, the findings do suggest a complex relationship between fitness and fatness. Specifically, the findings suggest that the hazards of fatness may be limited if a certain level of fitness is maintained. Moreover, the findings indicate that overweight and obese individuals may gain benefit from exercise even in the absence of weight loss.

EXERCISE FOR LONGEVITY

What is the optimum amount of exercise for longevity? This is a difficult question to answer with confidence due to the difficulty in measuring physical activity accurately and to differences in the methods used to classify individuals in various studies. In some studies physical activity energy expenditure has been estimated whereas other studies have placed individuals into discrete groups such as 'active' and 'sedentary' without reference to energy expenditure.

In a recent review, Lee and Skerrett (2001) concluded that an energy expenditure of 4,200 kJ week^{-1} is associated with a 20–30% reduction in the risk of all-cause mortality. This expenditure would be obtained by minimal adherence to current US guidelines ('30 minutes or more of moderate-intensity physical activity on most, preferably all, days of the week'). Moreover, Lee and Skerrett (2001) found 'clear evidence' of an inverse dose–response relationship between the volume of physical activity (or level of physical fitness) and all-cause mortality rates. This suggests that the risk of dying over

a given period continues to decline with increasing levels of physical activity (beyond 4,200 kJ week^{-1}) rather than displaying a threshold effect. It was also noted that this relationship has been shown in men and in women and in younger and older ($\geq$60 years) subjects.

Is there an optimal intensity, duration and frequency of exercise for longevity? An analysis of data from the Harvard Alumni Health Study found that energy expended in vigorous ($\geq$6 METs) but not non-vigorous (<6 METs) activities was associated with longevity suggesting that exercise must be 'vigorous' to be beneficial (Lee *et al.* 1995). However, caution is required regarding the interpretation of the word 'vigorous'. In the Harvard Alumni Health Study, vigorous activities included 'walking briskly, running or jogging, swimming laps, playing tennis, and shovelling snow'. Exercise intensity may vary greatly between these activities all of which were classified as vigorous and further research is needed to clarify the relationship between exercise intensity and longevity. Moreover, few if any studies have compared all-cause mortality rates in individuals matched for total energy expenditure but exercising at different durations or frequencies. Therefore, further research is also required here.

Is activity or fitness more important in determining longevity? This is another question that is difficult to answer at present. For both activity and fitness, evidence supports a dose–response relationship with all-cause mortality. This relationship appears to be stronger for fitness than for activity. In several of the studies examining fitness, mortality rates were 3–4 times lower in groups with the highest fitness compared to those with the lowest fitness. In studies of activity, the difference between groups is smaller. It is unclear, however, whether this is a genuine difference or is simply due to differences in the accuracy of measuring activity and fitness. The epidemiologist heading the Aerobics Centre Longitudinal Study, Dr Steven Blair, believes that the latter is true. He argues that the use of self-report questionnaires to determine physical activity levels has inevitably led to some misclassification thus weakening associations with mortality risk. Since physical fitness is measured more objectively there is less potential for error. In other words, Blair believes that fitness is simply a better marker for activity levels than questionnaires. Conversely, it is possible that fitness is the more important determinant of mortality risk because it reflects the combined influence of activity and genes in prolonging life. At present, there is insufficient evidence to answer this question with certainty.

How much longer can active/fit people expect to live – by avoiding premature mortality – compared with inactive/unfit people? This is another question for which there is no definitive answer. Estimates from the Harvard Alumni Health Study suggest that the amount of additional life attributable to adequate exercise, as compared with sedentariness, is two or more years (Paffenbarger *et al.* 1986). This may not sound impressive but it is important to remember that health is about much more than avoiding premature mortality. Health is also about living without illness and with the functional capacities to do things (what might be termed 'positive health') and about feeling good (well-being). This is where physical activity has most to offer. In the chapters that follow, we will examine a wide variety of evidence to explain: (1) the aetiology of the major diseases/conditions that might be influenced by physical activity; (2) the associations between these diseases/conditions and physical activity/fitness and (3) the mechanisms by which physical activity can enhance health.

SUMMARY

- Observational studies have consistently shown that physical activity and physical fitness are inversely related to all-cause mortality risk.
- The findings of these studies remain statistically significant following control for possible confounding factors including the existence of disease and/or disease risk factors at baseline.
- Evidence is strongly supportive of a dose–response relationship and indicates that mortality rates are between 20% and 80% lower in active/fit individuals compared to inactive/unfit individuals over a defined period.
- The strength of the association between physical fitness and all-cause mortality risk suggests that it is of equal or greater importance as a mortality predictor than other established disease risk factors.
- The association between physical activity/fitness and all-cause mortality holds true for adult men and women of all ages. Most studies have been conducted in Caucasian populations from the US and Europe and there are limited data on other ethnic groups. There is no compelling reason, however, why this relationship should not hold true for all ethnic groups.
- Recent studies indicate that obese individuals who are physically fit have a similar risk of all-cause mortality as lean individuals who are physically fit. This suggests

that physical activity may provide important health benefits for obese individuals, regardless of any influence on body fatness.

- Evidence suggests that expending 4200 kJ week^{-1} (1000 kcal week^{-1}) in physical activity is sufficient to lower all-cause mortality risk. Greater amounts of activity are likely to produce greater benefits. Vigorous exercise is probably more effective than non-vigorous exercise.
- Although physical activity and physical fitness are associated with the prevention of premature mortality, they do not appear to extend the natural lifespan.
- There are many plausible biological mechanisms to explain the association between physical activity/fitness and all-cause mortality. These will be discussed in the chapters that follow and provide strong evidence for a cause and effect relationship.

STUDY TASKS

1. Make a list, in order of importance, of all the possible confounding factors that may preclude a cause and effect relationship between physical activity/fitness and all-cause mortality.
2. List the aspects of the evidence linking physical activity/fitness with all-cause mortality that are supportive of a cause and effect relationship.
3. Discuss the strengths and limitations of studies examining changes in physical activity/fitness and all-cause mortality risk.
4. What are the strengths and limitations of the evidence indicating that obese individuals who are fit have a similar risk of all-cause mortality as lean individuals who are fit?
5. How much exercise is required to avert premature mortality? Justify your answer with reference to the research literature.

FURTHER READING

Blair, S.N., Cheng, Y. and Holder, J.S. (2001) 'Is physical activity or physical fitness more important in defining health benefits?', *Medicine and Science in Sports and Exercise* 33(6)(Supplement): S379–99.

Erikssen, G. (2001) 'Physical fitness and changes in mortality: the survival of the fittest', *Sports Medicine* 31: 571–6.

Lee, I-Min and Paffenbarger, R.S. (1996) 'Do physical activity and physical fitness avert premature mortality?', *Exercise and Sport Sciences Reviews* 24: 135–71.

Lee, I-Min and Skerrett, P.J. (2001) 'Physical activity and all-cause mortality: what is the dose-response relation?', *Medicine and Science in Sports and Exercise* 33: S459–71.

Oguma, Y., Sesso, H.D., Paffenbarger, R.S. and Lee, I.-M. (2002) 'Physical activity and all-cause mortality in women', *British Journal of Sports Medicine* 36: 162–72.

Part II
Effects of Physical Activity on the Risk of Disease

4 Cardiovascular disease

Knowledge assumed
Basic histology
Anatomy and physiology of the cardiovascular system
Basic methods in epidemiology

INTRODUCTION

Cohort studies that started in the late 1960s discovered that, as an epidemic condition in Western countries, coronary heart disease (CHD) (the cardiovascular disease, CVD with the highest prevalence) is mostly due to environmental influences. These can be modified, so this finding opened the way for prevention.[1] These studies developed the concept of risk factors. Three were consistently found to be predictors of CHD in different populations, that is, high concentrations of serum cholesterol, high blood pressure and cigarette smoking. More than 30 years on, numerous other risk factors have been identified, for example, diabetes mellitus, a low serum concentration of high density lipoprotein cholesterol, a high circulating level of homocysteine and central adiposity – to name but a few. Risk factors interact synergistically. For instance, the excess risk of CHD death attributable to high cholesterol and high blood pressure is much greater for cigarette smokers than for non-smokers.

In the last chapter we looked at evidence that showed that people who are physically active or fit are less likely to die over a defined period than those who are inactive and/or unfit. This chapter shows that one important reason for this is that individuals who are active and fit experience a lower incidence of CVD. More than 50 years after Professor Jeremy Morris's pioneering studies, the evidence that physical inactivity and low fitness are risk factors for CVD is compelling. We will now evaluate this evidence in accordance with the principles set out in Chapter 2. First, however, it is important to clarify the term CVD.

WHAT IS CARDIOVASCULAR DISEASE?

Cardiovascular disease is the name given to a group of disorders of the heart and blood vessels (listed in Box 4.1). The disease endpoints that have been studied in relation to physical activity or fitness are CHD, stroke and hypertension. In CHD the blood flow

BOX 4.1 CATEGORIES OF CVD

- Hypertension (high blood pressure).
- Coronary heart disease (ischaemic heart disease). This category includes angina and myocardial infarction (heart attack).
- Cerebrovascular disease (stroke). This can be due to the formation of a thrombus (blood clot), that is, a thromboembolytic or ischaemic stroke, or to bleed into the brain, that is, a haemorrhagic stroke.
- Peripheral vascular disease. Narrowing of peripheral arteries compromises blood flow. Most often affects the femoral artery, causing pain on walking.
- Heart failure. The heart is unable to pump blood forward at a rate sufficient to meet the metabolic demands of the body, usually because of impaired left ventricular function.
- Rheumatic heart disease. The valves of the heart are damaged, impairing its capability to control the direction of blood flow.
- Cardiomyopathies. Disorders that occur due to major structural abnormalities of the myocardium.

to the myocardium is compromised because of progressive narrowing or sudden blocking of a coronary artery or arteries. A heart attack happens when blood flow to the myocardium is impaired, either because a thrombus forms or because the artery goes into spasm. The extent of the damage depends on the site of the obstruction; if flow is interrupted to a large area of the myocardium the attack is life-threatening because the heart can no longer function as an effective pump. A stroke causes neurological damage, either because a blood vessel in the brain becomes blocked or because of a bleed into the tissues of the brain. Hypertension is the term given to abnormally high arterial blood pressure. It increases the work of the heart, damages the arterial wall and increases the possibility that a small blood vessel in the brain will rupture, causing a stroke.

Other types of CVD have been little studied in relation to exercise but they are included in Box 4.1 for the sake of completeness. The components of the classification in Box 4.1 are not mutually exclusive. For example, heart failure is the principal manifestation of coronary atherosclerosis, heart attack, damaged valves or hypertension.

Cardiovascular disease accounts for almost a third of global deaths. More than one in three people in the UK die from CVD, mainly CHD and stroke. Whilst the highest death rates are evident in affluent Western countries, the incidence is rising rapidly in developing countries; in 1999, 78% of CVD deaths were in low and middle-income countries. Whilst death rates worldwide are much lower among women than among men (Figure 4.1), CHD is not a trivial problem in women; for instance, twice as many women die from heart and circulatory disease as they do from cancer. Stroke and hypertension also have high prevalence. Stroke accounts for about 10% of all deaths worldwide; and a substantial minority of Western populations have hypertension. In the UK, for example, more than 40% of men and more than 30% of women have hypertension.

Worldwide, death rates from CHD differ 14- to 17-fold (Figure 4.1) and trends over recent years vary greatly. For example whilst the death rate in Australia for men aged

Figure 4.1 Death rates from CHD in 1996 in men and women aged 35–74 in selected countries.

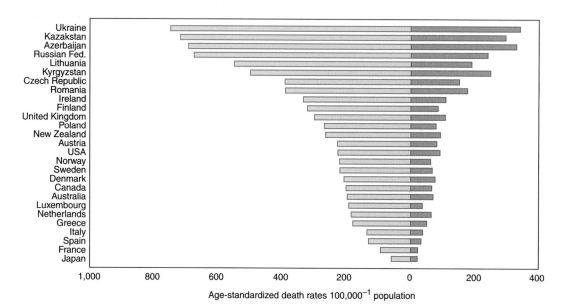

Age-standardized death rates 100,000^{-1} population

Source: British Heart Foundation (2002a).
Note: Men, light bars; women, dark bars.

35–74 fell by 44% between 1984 and 1994, it has risen rapidly in recent years in countries of eastern and central Europe. In Singapore, heart disease accounted for 4% of deaths in 1948 but 23% by 1991. These strong temporal changes, within populations with (presumably) a rather stable gene pool, illustrate the important contribution from environmental factors, including physical inactivity, to the aetiology of CHD.

This chapter discusses the epidemiological relations of physical activity and fitness with CHD, stroke and hypertension. By far the most important cause of these diseases is atherosclerosis and its complications.

ATHEROSCLEROSIS

Atherosclerosis begins in childhood and progresses over many decades. In a landmark study published in 1953, pathologists who conducted autopsies on US soldiers killed in the Korean War found that only 23% of these young men (average age 22) were free of obviously visible atherosclerotic lesions in their coronary arteries (Enos *et al.* 1953).

The pathological hallmarks of atherosclerosis are the fatty streak (the earliest visible lesions) and the fibrous plaque. (Plaques are more advanced lesions that are the source of clinical symptoms.) The mechanisms responsible for atherosclerosis are incompletely understood but current models are based on the 'response to injury' hypothesis. This was proposed in the early 1970s and states that the disease begins with an injury to the lining of an artery, that is, the endothelium. The wall of normal muscular arteries consists of three orderly layers: the intima (the most 'intimate' with the blood), the media (the middle layer) and the outer adventitia. The intima – the battleground of the atherosclerotic process – comprises a single layer of endothelial cells that rests on a bed of connective tissue.

Normal endothelial cells serve critically important functions: they comprise a barrier restricting the passage of large molecules and cells; they resist thrombosis through releasing anti-clotting molecules and platelet inhibitors; they help regulate blood flow to metabolic needs by secreting vasodilator substances; and they inhibit the proliferation and migration of smooth muscle cells. Endothelial injury or dysfunction thus leads to the accumulation of molecules, especially lipids, and a proliferation of cells in the intimal layer of an artery. The intima enlarges and appears yellow and streaky to the naked eye – hence the term 'fatty' streak. Progression of atherosclerosis involves adhesion of white blood cells called monocytes to the endothelium. Once they cross the endothelium these cells become macrophages and ingest oxidized lipids, taking on a 'foamy' appearance. Macrophages and smooth muscle cells proliferate in the intima, the latter producing collagen and other molecules that increase the bulk of the lesion. This process is depicted in Figure 4.2. Molecular factors such as cytokines, growth factors and nitric oxide all play a role in the proliferation and migration of smooth muscle cells. The size of the fatty streak increases and a cap of connective tissue may cover the core of fat and cellular debris, forming a fibrous plaque. The site of the lesion can also become calcified, reducing the artery's elasticity.

Figure 4.3 shows the narrowing of an artery by an atherosclerotic plaque. Plaques grow gradually and only when a lesion restricts blood flow by around 45% do symptoms develop as the tissues supplied by that artery become ischaemic. This threshold is described as a 'clinical horizon' or 'clinical threshold' because the disease process then begins to limit normal functioning. Complications of atherosclerosis also derive from sudden events. For example, rupture of a vulnerable plaque is often associated with thrombus formation, leading to a heart attack or stroke. An artery wall weakened by atherosclerosis can rupture, leading to internal bleeding. Common sites of this complication include the aorta (an aneurysm) or an artery in the brain (haemorrhagic stroke). The progression of the atherosclerotic process to the clinical horizon is shown schematically in Figure 4.4.

EPIDEMIOLOGY OF PHYSICAL ACTIVITY AND CHD

The observation that physical activity can protect against heart attack was first made in cross-sectional studies comparing incidence rates in men in a variety of occupations. Jeremy Morris and colleagues studied the drivers and conductors of London's double-decker buses. The conductors (who walk up and down stairs 11 days a fortnight, 50 weeks a year, often for decades) experienced roughly half the number of heart attacks and 'sudden death' due to heart attack as the drivers. Similar differences in CHD attack and death rates were found between physically active postmen (who spent 70% of their shift time walking, cycling and climbing stairs) and their sedentary colleagues who sorted the mail (Morris et al. 1953). The self-selection bias in such studies is obvious,

Figure 4.2 Schematic representation of the early events in atherosclerosis within the innermost layer of an artery, the intima.

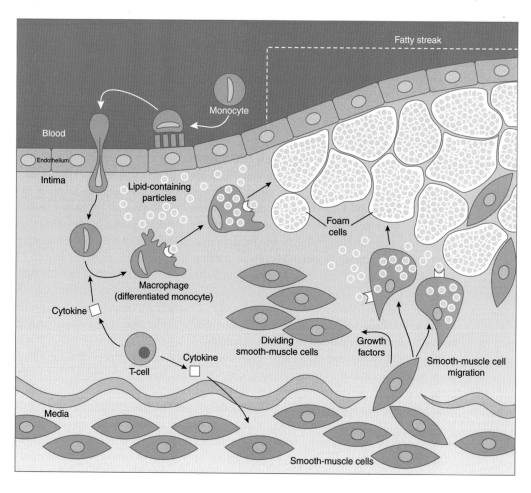

Source: Hajjar and Nicholson (1995).
Note: The media (middle layer of the artery wall) can be seen at the bottom of the diagram. Foam cells are the primary constituents of the fatty streak.

however: did leaner, generally healthier men seek the more physically active jobs? Morris and colleagues subsequently published data on the waist size of the uniform trousers issued to the men – a crude measure of what is now termed central obesity. Lean, average and portly conductors all experienced CHD rates about half those of the sedentary drivers. It appeared therefore that the protective effect of physical activity was independent of body fatness (at least as crudely assessed).[2]

Occupational studies in other countries, notably those in San Francisco dockworkers (called 'longshoremen'), confirmed the protective effect of occupational work. The longshoremen ($n = 6,351$), whose exercise intensity at work was categorized as light, moderate or heavy according to measurements of oxygen uptake, were followed for 22 years (Paffenbarger and Hale 1975). (The steps by which oxygen uptake

Figure 4.3 Narrowing of a coronary artery branch by a large plaque of atheroma. The consequent reduction in blood flow leads to ischaemia of an area of the myocardium.

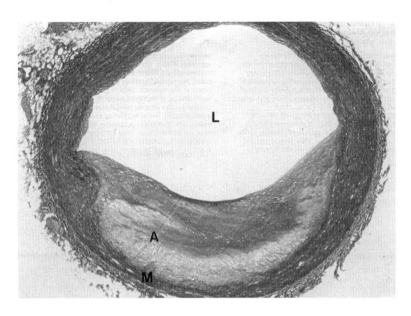

Source: Wheater *et al.* (1985).
Notes: Artery is seen in cross-section. A, atheroma; L, lumen (space inside artery); M, media.

measurements were converted to rates of energy expenditure are shown in Box 4.2.) Death rates of the dockworkers from CHD are shown in Figure 4.5, within 10-year age-bands. Overall, men engaged in light or moderate work were twice as likely to die from CHD as those whose work was classified as heavy. The protective effect of heavy occupational work was evident at all ages but greatest in the oldest men. Selection bias was not a major problem because men enrolling in the industry were not allowed to choose their job assignment.

By the 1960s it was clear that differences in physical activity level within populations would derive mainly from leisure-time activity – heavy occupational work was decreasing. Two large studies were thus begun, on opposite sides of the Atlantic. Morris and colleagues studied English civil servants, adopting a 5-minute by 5-minute record of how they had spent the previous Friday and Saturday as the index of leisure-time physical activity. Eight-and-a-half years later the men who reported engaging in 30 or more minutes of vigorous exercise (estimated as entailing peak rates of energy expenditure of 31.5 kJ min^{-1} (7.5 kcal min^{-1}) or more) had an incidence of CHD less than half that of their colleagues who recorded no vigorous exercise (Morris *et al.* 1980).

One of the most comprehensive data sets derives from the Harvard Alumni Study referred to in Chapter 3. The reader will recall that Paffenbarger and colleagues studied the physical activity habits of men who had graduated from Harvard University between 1916 and 1950, collating replies to questionnaires sent out in 1962 or 1966. Information was obtained not only about current physical activity but also about

Figure 4.4 Schematic representation of the progression of atherosclerosis from the fatty streak (depicted as a reversible process) to a clinical horizon where the ensuing ischaemia leads to organ damage and symptoms develop.

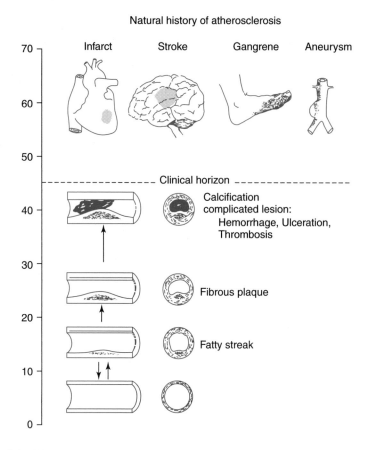

Natural history of atherosclerosis

Source: McGill *et al.* (1963).

participation in student sport whilst at University. Researchers found that the risk of heart attack was inversely related to total energy expenditure in physical activity over the range < 2.1 to 8.4 MJ week^{-1} (< 500 to 2,000 kcal week^{-1}) (Paffenbarger *et al.* 1978). As in the study of English civil servants, active men had lower risk both in the presence and in the absence of smoking, hypertension and a high body mass index, confirming that effect of exercise is not acting through these other factors.

One finding from the Alumni Study gives a clue as to possible mechanisms. Men who participated in University sport – who might be expected to have a robust cardio-vascular system – did not have a lower CHD risk unless they maintained a high level of physical activity (Figure 4.6). The finding that recent – but not past – exercise offers protection against CHD was confirmed among English civil servants. Playing vigorous sport some years earlier conferred no protection among men who did not continue to practise such exercise. Moreover, a report from The Netherlands, found that light activities like walking, gardening or cycling were associated with a lower risk of acute

BOX 4.2 ENERGY EXPENDITURE DURING EXERCISE – RELATIONSHIPS WITH OXYGEN UPTAKE

During sub-maximal exercise the majority of energy comes from the oxidation of fat and carbohydrate. The rate of oxygen uptake therefore reflects the rate of energy expenditure (metabolic rate). The exact energy expenditure per litre of oxygen depends on the proportion of fat and carbohydrate being oxidized but if it is assumed that both contribute equally to energy metabolism, each litre of oxygen taken up is equivalent to an energy expenditure of 20.5 kJ ($\approx$5 kcal).

Examples from the epidemiology:

- Morris's studies of male English civil servants defined exercise as vigorous if the rate of energy expenditure reached peaks of $\geq$ 31.4 kJ min^{-1} (7.5 kcal min^{-1}). This is equivalent to an oxygen uptake of (31.4/20.5) or 1.53 l min^{-1}.

  Question – What does this mean in terms of exercise for these men?
  Answer – Metabolic rate depends on body mass. For purposes of estimating and describing exercise intensity, metabolic rate has been defined as 3.5 ml oxygen per kg of body mass per minute, that is, 3.5 ml kg^{-1} min^{-1} or 1 MET. If we assume that the civil servants typically weighed 78 kg, then an oxygen uptake of 1.53 l min^{-1} represents about 20 ml kg^{-1} min^{-1} or 5.7 METs. Activities such as easy cycling or doubles tennis typically demand this rate of oxygen uptake.

- In the Harvard Alumni Study, a threshold value for gross weekly energy expenditure in physical activity of 8.37 MJ (2000 kcal) has often been used.

  Question – What does this equate to in terms that are readily understood?
  Answer – Let us look at this from the point of view of, say, brisk walking. Walking briskly at 6.4 km h^{-1} (4 mile h^{-1}) demands about 4 METs, an oxygen uptake of (3.5 × 4) or 14 ml kg^{-1} min^{-1}. Assuming a body mass of 78 kg, this means 1.09 l min^{-1} and expends energy at a rate of (1.09 × 20.5) or 22.3 kJ min^{-1}. Thus, a total gross energy expenditure of 8.37 MJ per week is equivalent to (8370/22.3) minutes of brisk walking, about 40 km (25 miles).

- In the US Nurses Health Study walking is expressed in (MET-h) week^{-1}.

  Question – The median value for nurses in the top quintile for walking was 20 MET-h week^{-1} (Manson et al. 1999). For how many hours did they walk?
  Answer – Walking at a 'normal' speed of 4.8 km h^{-1} (3 mile h^{-1}) demands 3.5 METs. So, walking for 1 h at this speed gives 3.5 MET-h and 20 (MET-h) week^{-1} means walking for 5.7 h during a week, covering some 27.4 km (17 miles).

Thus, adjectives such as 'vigorous', 'heavy' or 'moderate' do not have precise meaning in the literature. For example, much of the work activity classified as 'heavy' in Paffenbarger's studies of dockworkers (Paffenbarger and Hale 1975) would have been well below the threshold for 'vigorous' exercise adopted in the studies of English civil servants (Morris et al. 1980, 1990).

Figure 4.5 Death rates from CHD in San Francisco dockworkers between 1951 and 1972, according to intensity of physical activity at work and age at death.

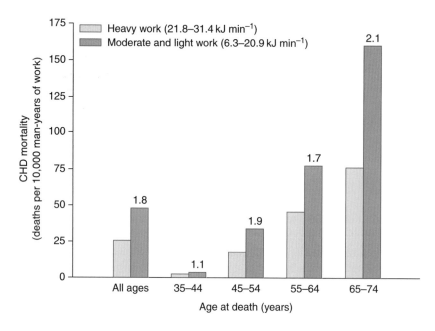

Source: Adapted from Paffenbarger and Hale (1975).
Notes: Light bars, moderate/light work at 6.3–20.9 kJ min^{-1} (1.5–5.0 kcal min^{-1}); dark bars, heavy work at 21.8–31.4 kJ min^{-1} (5.2–7.5 kcal min^{-1}). Figures over bars show relative risk, with reference group as moderate/light work. Difference between heavy and moderate/light work significant for all ages ($P < 0.001$) and for men in all 10-year bands ($P < 0.01$) except 35–44.

coronary events only among men who pursued them all-year-round. There was no effect if these activities were seasonal. All these findings suggest that the protection afforded by physical activity is mediated, at least in part, by some effect on the acute phases of CHD (thrombosis, vascular spasm, loss of normal heart rhythm).

In their second study of civil servants, Morris and colleagues gathered comprehensive information on possible interactions of exercise with other risk factors (Morris *et al.* 1990). They found that the protective effect of vigorous exercise was independent of stature, reported attitude to healthy behaviours, weight change, 'health-conscious diet' and a personal history of CVD – in addition to the factors examined in earlier studies. Figure 4.7 displays death rates from CHD among men with and without these potentially confounding factors and shows that the effect of vigorous activity is consistent across subgroups. Thus confounding by known risk factors could not account for the effects of physical activity.

During the 1970s and 1980s many other epidemiological studies of work and leisure-time physical activity were published. Almost all were of men (mainly because the disease incidence is so much lower in women) and the majority were from the US. Other countries contributing to the studies were the UK, The Netherlands, Italy, Yugoslavia, Greece, Finland, Sweden, Israel and Puerto Rico. This evidence was

Figure 4.6 Age-adjusted rates of first heart attack in alumni reporting high (> 8.37 MJ week^{-1}) and low (< 8.37 MJ week^{-1}) levels of estimated gross energy expenditure in physical activity as adults, according to past participation in University sport.

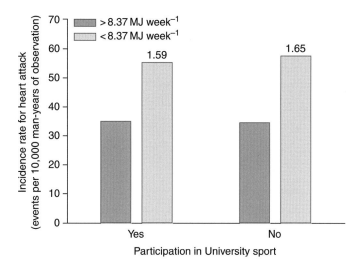

Source: Paffenbarger *et al.* (1978).
Note: Figures over bars show relative risk with reference group as moderate/light work.

subjected to critical review (Powell *et al.* 1987) and meta-analysis (Berlin and Colditz 1990) to provide an overall picture. (Meta-analysis is the statistical analysis of a collection of analytic results for the purpose of integrating the findings.) About two-thirds of studies found a significant effect of exercise and, tellingly, no study found a *higher* risk among active people. The conclusions reached by structured review and meta-analysis were reassuringly similar: first, better studies (assessed on quality of information about both physical activity levels and cause of death) were more likely than poorer studies to report an inverse relationship between physical activity level and incidence of CHD; and, second, the relative risk of physical inactivity (median 1.9) was similar to that associated with high total cholesterol, hypertension or smoking cigarettes – all strong risk factors.

Since 1990 many more studies have been published on physical activity and CHD. What have they added that is new? First, they have provided strong evidence that the benefit is also seen in women, in older men and in more racially diverse groups. Second, they have examined the relationship between 'dose' of exercise and the 'response' in terms of reduced risk of CHD. Evidence on this topic, crucial for the development of promoting exercise as part of a public health strategy, is discussed here, after consideration of studies of fitness.

EPIDEMIOLOGY OF FITNESS AND CHD

The difficulties of measuring physical activity were discussed in Chapter 2. Some investigators have sought to avoid these by measuring the characteristics exhibited by

Figure 4.7 Relative frequencies of potentially confounding factors according to frequency of vigorous exercise in English male civil servants.

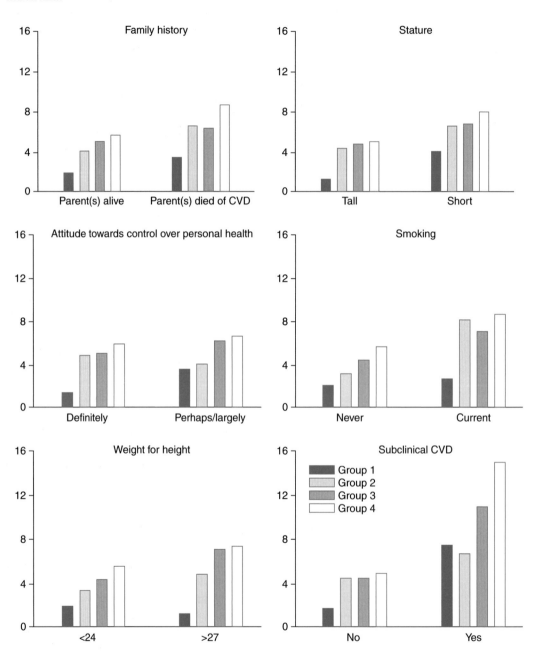

Source: Adapted from Morris *et al.* (1990).
Notes: Groups 1–4 indicate level of 'vigorous aerobic exercise': Group 1, frequent intense; Group 2, next lesser degree; Group 3, residual, little; Group 4, none. Middle panel on left: participants' view of the degree of control they have over their future health was assessed by their answer to the question 'Can you do anything to prevent ill-health in the future?'.

people who are physically active, that is, fitness, rather than the behaviour (physical activity/exercise) that leads to fitness. They argue that this reduces the chance of individuals being misclassified and, by increasing the precision of measurement, increases the likelihood that true findings will not be missed. The extent to which traditional measurements of fitness are independent of genetic factors is a matter of debate. However, some studies have found close relationships between physical activity and measures of fitness, suggesting that the environmental influence is dominant. What is certain is that information relating CHD incidence to fitness complements and extends that based on relationships with self-reported activity.

The view that fitness improves the objectivity of investigations is supported by reports that low fitness appears to be a stronger risk factor for CVD than physical inactivity. Findings from the Aerobics Center Longitudinal Study (Dallas, Texas) constitute a major part of this literature. Fitness was measured as time on a maximal treadmill test (a surrogate for $\dot{V}O_2max$) in more than 25,000 men. Steven Blair and colleagues found that the relative risk of low fitness (bottom quintile of study population) versus all other men was 1.70 (Blair *et al.* 1996), a higher relative risk than often reported for physical inactivity. Based on comparisons within the same study population, the relative risk of low fitness was also higher than that observed for smoking (relative risk 1.57), systolic BP $\geq$140 mm Hg (1.34), high cholesterol $\geq$6.2 mmol l^{-1} (1.65) or parental death from CHD (1.18). These estimates, which are depicted in Figure 4.8, represent the independent risk associated with each factor as they are corrected for each other, as well as for body mass.

Studies of fitness can make comparisons of CHD incidence among multiple ordinal fitness categories, and thus provide new information on the level of fitness below which there seems to be an important increase in risk. A few investigators have attempted to identify such thresholds, which might be important for public health policy. For middle-aged men, this is probably of the order of 8–9 METs (28–32 ml kg^{-1} min^{-1}). There is little information for women but, based solely on the Aerobics Center Study, the comparable level is probably of the order of 6–7 METs (21–25 ml kg^{-1} min^{-1}). The potential of popular activities like walking to elicit values at these levels will be discussed in Chapter 14.

CHANGES IN PHYSICAL ACTIVITY OR FITNESS AND CHD

All the studies referred to above used a single baseline measure of physical activity/fitness as the exposure variable. This assumes, probably wrongly in many cases, that participants' levels of physical activity or fitness are rather stable over years and leads to misclassification. Studying *changes* in activity or fitness between two observations several years apart increases the precision with which exposure to inactivity or low fitness is measured. It also allows the hypothesis that changing exposure is associated with a change in risk to be tested.

Several cohort studies have been able to obtain repeated measurements. The first of these was the Harvard Alumni Study that reported deaths from CHD in men who returned questionnaires about their activity levels in 1962 or 1966 and again in 1977. Previously sedentary men who, over this period, increased their total physical activity

Figure 4.8 Relative risk associated with six different risk factors among men in the Aerobics Center Longitudinal Study.

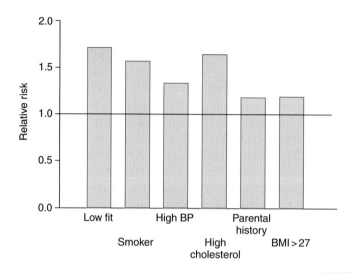

Source: Blair *et al.* (1996).
Note: In each category risk is relative to men who did not exhibit the risk factor. Relative risks are independent, that is, data were adjusted for each of the other factors shown.

index to ≥ 8.4 MJ week^{-1} had a 17% lower risk of death from CHD than those who remained sedentary (Paffenbarger *et al.* 1993b). Even greater benefit was seen in the sub-group of men who took up moderately vigorous exercise at ≥ 4.5 METs; they had a 41% lower risk of death from CHD than those who continued to be sedentary. This difference in risk was similar to that seen among men who gave up cigarette smoking (44% lower risk than continuing smokers) or who avoided becoming overweight for height (41% lower risk than those whose BMI increased to ≥ 26). Similar findings were reported among men from the British Regional Heart Study studied for changes in activity level at an interval of 12–14 years. In this study, the benefit of increasing physical activity was evident among men already diagnosed with CVD as well as among healthy men.

We might expect therefore that improvements in fitness would also reduce the risk of CHD. Findings from the Aerobics Center Longitudinal Study support this argument. Men who were unfit, that is, in the bottom quintile for performance on a maximal treadmill test, on one assessment but who improved their fitness when assessed 5 years later, had a 52% lower age-adjusted risk of CVD mortality (CHD deaths were not reported separately) than men who remained unfit (Blair *et al.* 1995). Furthermore, men designated as fit when first assessed (quintiles 2 or 3) but who improved their fitness so that they were in a higher quintile when reassessed, also had a 28% lower risk of CVD mortality than those who remained in quintiles 2 or 3. These findings were independent of confounding by other risk factors at baseline or by changes in risk factors during follow-up.

Collectively, these findings strongly suggest that the relationships between fitness or physical activity and cardiovascular mortality are not due solely to hereditary factors. They also go some way to addressing concerns that low fitness and inactivity may be a consequence in some individuals of undetected, pre-existing disease. These data, from cohort studies, do not prove a causal link with reduced CVD mortality, but they strengthen the argument that, if activity or fitness improves, risk can be modified.

DOSE–RESPONSE: WHAT LEVEL OF ACTIVITY OR FITNESS CONFERS PROTECTION AGAINST CHD?

This question is important for two reasons: first, if the relationship between physical activity or fitness and the risk of CHD is causal, then there should be a graded effect – more activity/higher fitness should be associated with greater benefit; and second, public health initiatives demand an understanding of what constitutes a sufficient level of activity or fitness to confer a worthwhile decrease in risk.

Only studies where several gradations of physical activity or fitness are reported can help address dose–response issues. More than 30 publications relate dose[3] or level[4] of physical activity to risk of CHD. Of these, about two-thirds provide evidence for a dose–response relation, 3 are equivocal and 8 do not support such a relationship. In a few studies there is evidence for an *increase* in risk at the very highest levels of activity. Fewer studies are available with fitness as the exposure variable and these are mostly from the Aerobics Center Longitudinal Study. However, these are compelling in their consistency and in the steepness of the gradient across fitness groups.

Evidence on dose–response from major cohort studies of either physical activity or fitness is summarized in Figure 4.9. The inverse gradient is clear, although the shape of the relationship clearly differs between studies. Morris's study of English civil servants stands out because men had a significantly lower risk only if they engaged in 'vigorous' activity. By contrast, the biggest difference in risk for men in the Aerobics Center Study was between the lowest quintile and the next lowest, suggesting that modest improvements in fitness (acquired through moderate intensity activity) would confer a cardioprotective effect in previously sedentary men.

Based on the available evidence on dose–response, the conclusion may be drawn that, while moderate levels of physical activity or fitness confer a measurable decrease in the risk of CHD, more vigorous activity or higher levels of fitness confer a greater benefit. The exact shape of the relationships with risk is not known so future epidemiological studies will attempt to describe this in more detail.

Information on the independent effects of different components of physical activity is beginning to appear. Two papers from the Harvard Alumni Health Study are important. One examined the influence of the duration of exercise episodes, through the range <15 min in 15-min increments to >60 min (Lee *et al.* 2000). Longer sessions of exercise did not have a different effect on the risk of CHD than shorter sessions, as long as the total energy expended was similar. The second paper examined the influence of the relative intensity of exercise (assessed using participants' ratings on the Borg scale of perceived exertion) and found a strong relationship with the risk of CHD that was independent of total energy expenditure (Lee *et al.* 2003). This ties in well with evidence from laboratory studies that the physiological 'stress' of exercise depends on the proportion of individual VO_2max it demands, rather than on its intensity measured in absolute terms.

It is difficult to investigate the links between specific physical activities (e.g. racquet sports, swimming, cycling) and CHD risk because even large studies lack the statistical

Figure 4.9 Reduction in coronary mortality or events, according to level of physical activity or fitness.

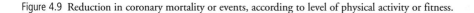

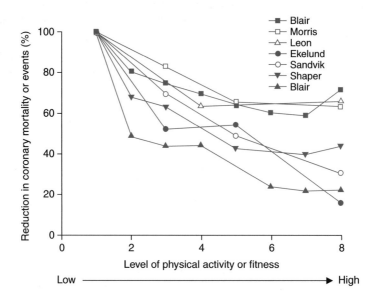

Source: Adapted from Haskell (1994).
Note: Original data from Paffenbarger *et al.* (1986), Morris *et al.* (1990), Leon *et al.* (1987), Shaper and Wannamethee (1991) (all of whom measured physical activity) and Blair *et al.* (1989), Ekelund *et al.* (1988) and Sandvik *et al.* (1993) (all of whom measured fitness).

power to do this. The data available are mainly for walking because exposure to this activity is high. For example, Morris and colleagues reported data on walking habits in English civil servants and CHD risk. There was a clear inverse gradient of risk according to reported walking speed, with a particularly low rate of disease in men claiming to be fast walkers ($\geq$4 mile h^{-1} or 6.4 km h^{-1}) (Morris *et al.* 1990). In the Honolulu Heart Program, elderly men who walked <0.25 mile day^{-1} had twice the risk of CHD than those who walked >1.5 mile day^{-1} (Hakim *et al.* 1999). Walking has also been associated with a lower risk of CHD in women. For example, in the US Nurses Health Study (a large cohort study), there was a strong inverse gradient between the amount of walking reported and the risk of coronary events (Manson *et al.* 1999). This relationship persisted even after correction for a whole range of potentially confounding factors, including vigorous activity (women who are 'sporty types' might tend to walk more). Excluding the few women who reported that they were 'unable to walk', did not alter the results. This analysis nicely demonstrates how hard epidemiologists work to address the difficult issue of confounding.

ARE PHYSICAL INACTIVITY AND LOW FITNESS CAUSAL FACTORS FOR CHD?

Collectively the evidence discussed here is strongly supportive of the proposition that physical inactivity and low fitness are causative factors in CHD. However, because of the enduring problem of self-selection and because people in whom disease is developing but undetected may be more likely than others to be sedentary, epidemiological studies cannot by themselves establish causality. Moreover, as pointed out in Chapter 2, a randomized, controlled trial with disease endpoints as the outcome measure is not feasible. Complementary evidence that examines potential biological mechanisms is therefore vital (Chapter 5). The features of epidemiological evidence that can contribute towards establishing causality were explained in Chapter 2. The evidence discussed in this chapter appears to fulfil these criteria (Box 4.3).

STROKE

There are good reasons why the hypothesis that physical activity reduces the risk of stroke is attractive. Clear evidence links physical inactivity to CHD, and thromboembolytic stroke (ischaemic stroke, the commonest type) and CHD share similar pathophysiology and risk factors (raised blood pressure, obesity, glucose intolerance, smoking).

The number of epidemiological studies examining the relationships of physical activity with stroke incidence is small relative to the numbers of studies of CHD. However, over the last decade a number of comprehensive reports have been published, the majority from cohort studies. Some report a lower incidence of stroke (fatal and/or non-fatal) but the evidence lacks the consistency observed for CHD. Studies that have found an effect tend to be those with more cases and comprehensive information on physical activity, but available data are insufficient to draw a conclusion.

BOX 4.3 FEATURES OF EVIDENCE FOR THE PROPOSITION THAT PHYSICAL ACTIVITY AND FITNESS PROTECTS AGAINST CHD

- Findings are remarkably consistent in diverse populations.
- Better studies are more likely than poorer studies to observe an inverse relationship.
- The majority of evidence is in middle-aged men but there is some also in older men and in women.
- The relationships between CHD risk and physical activity or fitness are inverse and graded. Whether intensity and/or frequency of sessions of physical activity have separate effects over and above that of the total energy expenditure is not yet clear, although these are issues of much research interest.
- The relative risk of inactivity or low fitness is at least two.
- The majority of studies have demonstrated that they measured activity/fitness before the onset of CHD. This decreases the likelihood that participants were not inactive because they had pre-clinical disease.
- The findings are not confounded by other major risk factors (hypertension – repeatedly confirmed, cigarette smoking – repeatedly confirmed, total cholesterol – much less data).
- Becoming more active or fit is associated with a lower risk than remaining inactive or of low fitness.

Figure 4.10 Relative risk of stroke according to reported walking among women in the US Nurses Health Study.

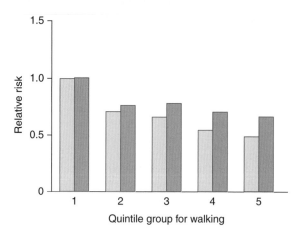

Source: Hu *et al.* (2000).
Notes: Lighter bars, adjusted for age; darker bars, adjusted for multiple potentially confounding variables, that is, vigorous exercise, smoking, BMI, menopausal status, use of hormone-replacement therapy, myocardial infarction before age 60 years, alcohol consumption, aspirin use and history of hypertension or hypercholesterolaemia.

As an example, data from the US Nurses Health Study are shown in Figure 4.10. This figure shows physical activity level, measured as MET-h per week, in relation to stroke incidence (Hu *et al.* 2000). Data are the average of reports gathered on three occasions 8, 6 and 2 years prior to assessment of outcome and adjusted for age. Two points may be made: first, the relationship is inverse, graded and statistically significant; and second, although further adjustment for potentially confounding factors somewhat attenuated the risk, this remained significant. The relationship was primarily observed for thromboembolytic stroke. The multivariate analysis adjusted for participation in vigorous exercise, so these findings can be regarded as describing the association of the risk of stroke with walking *per se*. By contrast with the CHD data from the same cohort referred to earlier, data were adjusted for alcohol consumption. This is because high consumption of alcohol is one of the most important risk factors for stroke but is not a risk factor for CHD.

Few studies have allowed estimation of the separate effects (if any) of exercise intensity or frequency. One – a case-control study in Manhattan – found a significant effect of both intensity (light–moderate versus heavy) and duration (<2 h week^{-1} versus >2 <5 h week^{-1} versus ≥ 5 h week^{-1}) of exercise. However, several studies show a U-shaped relationship between physical activity and the risk of stroke. This implies an increase in risk with very high levels or intensities of physical activity and is a cause for concern.

One study of fitness and stroke incidence is available. The US Aerobics Center Longitudinal Study analysed stroke incidence among 16,878 men during a 10-year follow-up (Lee and Blair 2002). Compared with the least fit 20% of men, the relative risk of stroke was 0.37 in those with moderate fitness (next 40%) and 0.32 in those designated as high fit (top 20%). The numbers of cases are inevitably much lower than for CHD, illustrating the difficulty of examining different types of strokes separately. (It is possible that activity is not related in the same way to both thromboembolytic and haemorrhagic stroke.) Only 32 strokes were documented in the Aerobics Center study, 14 in the low-fit group, 11 in the moderate-fit group and seven in the high-fit group. Thus, although there is mounting evidence for a beneficial effect of physical activity on the risk of stroke, it is premature to draw a conclusion.

HYPERTENSION

When people say 'The doctor says I've got blood pressure', they mean of course that they have *high* blood pressure, specifically high arterial blood pressure. What constitutes abnormally high blood pressure? Table 4.1 shows widely accepted values for increasing severity of hypertension. Remember that blood pressure varies during each cardiac cycle, being highest in systole and lowest in diastole. Blood pressure is therefore usually written as two figures, for example 120/80 mm Hg. When talking informally, the convention is to say '120 over 80'.

In about 95% of patients the cause of the blood pressure elevation is unknown. This condition is termed 'essential hypertension'. Where a definite cause can be identified, the condition is termed 'secondary hypertension'. Causes of secondary hypertension include: malfunction of the kidneys (not surprising, given the crucial role of the kidney in control of blood pressure); and hormonal disturbances that interfere with fluid balance (and therefore blood volume).

Hypertension increases the risk of CHD, stroke (particularly thromboembolytic stroke), peripheral vascular disease, congestive heart failure and kidney failure. Its links with insulin resistance and obesity will be discussed in Chapter 8. Because of its complications and high prevalence, hypertension is a major public health problem. Moreover, because many hypertensive people do not have symptoms, its prevalence is probably underestimated.

A few cohort studies have addressed the question 'Are people who are physically active and fit less likely to develop hypertension than their inactive, unfit peers?' Among

Table 4.1 Severity of hypertension according to measurements of systolic and/or diastolic blood pressure

CATEGORY	SYSTOLIC (mm Hg)	DIASTOLIC (mm Hg)
Normal	<130	<85
High-normal	130–139	85–89
Hypertension		
Stage 1 (mild)	140–159	90–99
Stage 2 (moderate)	160–179	100–109
Stage 3 (severe)	180–209	110–119
Stage 4 (very severe)	≥210	≥120

the Harvard alumni studied by Paffenbarger and colleagues, men who did not report engaging in vigorous sports were 35% more likely to develop hypertension during the 6–10 year follow-up than other men (Paffenbarger *et al.* 1983). Among men and women in the Aerobics Center Longitudinal Study, individuals with low fitness (least fit quintile) were 52% more likely than those with high fitness (most fit quintile) to develop hypertension (Blair *et al.* 1984).

SUMMARY

- Cardiovascular diseases are a major cause of mortality and morbidity in developed countries and their prevalence is increasing in developing countries.
- Atherosclerosis is the major cause of many CVD. It has a long clinical history and may be well progressed before symptoms occur.
- Evidence that inactivity and low fitness are strong risk factors for CHD is compelling. Both confer an increase in risk similar to that associated with smoking, hypertension or high blood cholesterol.
- Only recent exercise is protective against CHD, suggesting an effect on some aspect(s) of the acute phase of the disease.
- Evidence that being physically active or fit reduces the risk of becoming hypertensive or having a stroke is suggestive but not as compelling as that for CHD. However, as some aetiological factors are common to these different types of CVD, benefits from activity and/or fitness are biologically plausible.

STUDY TASKS

1 Using the data in the Table 4.2, calculate the relative risk of death from CHD associated with low fitness. Express this first with the low-fit group as the reference category and then with the high-fit group. As well as working out the figures, put each relative risk into words as if you were explaining the findings to someone else. In addition, explain (a) why it is necessary to use person-years as the units for the death rate, (b) why the death rates were adjusted for age and (c) why the person-years of follow-up are not simply 10 times the numbers of subjects in each fitness group.

Table 4.2 Deaths from CHD over an average follow-up period of 10 years

	NUMBER OF SUBJECTS	PERSON-YEARS OF FOLLOW-UP	NUMBER OF DEATHS	DEATH RATE PER 10,000 PERSON-YEARS*
Low fitness	5,130	46,098	112	20.70
High fitness	5,075	45,650	44	8.25

* Adjusted for age.

2   In the example given in Box 4.2 the women in the top quintile for walking in the US Nurses Health Study completed an average of 20 MET-h of walking. It was estimated that this meant about 5.7 h of walking at a 'normal' pace (assumed to be 4.8 km h^{-1} or 3 mile h^{-1}). Estimate the gross weekly energy expenditure of these nurses in walking, assuming an average body mass of 60 kg.

3   What further information could epidemiology provide to strengthen the argument that physical inactivity and low fitness are causal factors in CHD? Discuss the problems that would have to be faced in seeking this information.

NOTES

1   This is not to deny the importance of genetic predisposition in modifying susceptibility – an area of active research. However, the disease is caused as much or more by 'nurture' as it is by 'nature'.
2   Body fatness is a confounding factor because of its associations with diabetes, dyslipidaemias and hypertension, all of which increase the risk of heart attack.
3   Measured as total energy expenditure in physical activity.
4   Group within a study, allocated according to energy expenditure or some surrogate for this.

FURTHER READING

Berlin, J.A. and Colditz, G.H. (1990) 'A meta-analysis of physical activity in the prevention of coronary heart disease', *American Journal of Epidemiology* 132: 612–28.

Blair, S.N. (1994) 'Physical activity, fitness and coronary heart disease', in C. Bouchard, R.J. Shephard, T. Stephens (eds) *Physical Activity, Fitness and Coronary Heart Disease*, Champaign, IL: Human Kinetics, pp 579–90.

Fagard, R.H. (2001) 'Exercise characteristics and the blood pressure response to dynamic physical training', *Medicine and Science in Sports and Exercise* 33(Supplement 6): S484–92.

Kohl, H.W. (2001) 'Physical activity and cardiovascular disease: evidence for a dose response', *Medicine and Science in Sports and Exercise* 33(Supplement 6): S472–83.

Morris, J.N. (1996) 'Exercise versus heart attack: questioning the consensus', *Research Quarterly for Exercise and Sport* 67: 216–20.

Wannamethee, G.S. and Shaper, A.G. (2001) 'Physical activity in the prevention of cardiovascular disease: an epidemiological perspective', *Sports Medicine* 31: 101–14.

5 Risk factors for cardiovascular disease

Knowledge assumed
Basic knowledge of lipid metabolism, cardiovascular physiology and exercise physiology

INTRODUCTION

The previous chapter reviewed the epidemiological evidence suggesting that high levels of physical activity or fitness confer protection from cardiovascular disease (CVD). Although this evidence is convincing, at least for coronary heart disease (CHD), it is limited by the fact that it is observational – demonstrating association rather than cause and effect. Intervention studies, particularly randomized intervention studies, provide much more convincing evidence for causality. Such trials have been conducted to assess the role of physical activity and fitness in modifying CVD risk factors. These studies demonstrate that activity/fitness can influence many of the risk factors for CVD.

In doing so they provide evidence for biologically plausible mechanisms linking high levels of activity/fitness with protection from CVD. This evidence will now be examined, starting with an identification of the risk factors for CVD.

CVD RISK FACTORS

The major risk factors for CVD are listed in Table 5.1. These are categorized into modifiable and non-modifiable risk factors. These include family history, age, gender and ethnicity. CVD risk is elevated in those whose first-degree relatives (mother, father, sister, brother) have died prematurely from CVD. The risk of CVD also increases with age and is higher in males than in females. However, this does not mean that women are immune to CVD, merely that they develop it later. In fact, in the 75 years and above age group more women than men die each year from heart disease in the UK (British Heart Foundation 2003). CVD risk is also elevated in some ethnic groups, particularly South Asians (Indians, Bangladeshis, Pakistanis and Sri Lankans) for whom the risk of premature death due to CVD is approximately 50% higher than average in the UK (British Heart Foundation 2003). Although ethnicity is listed as a non-modifiable risk factor in Table 5.1 it is possible that differences in diet and physical activity habits partly explain the differences in CVD prevalence between ethnic groups.

Modifiable CVD risk factors are those that can be altered to some degree by diet, physical activity, drugs, stress control or a combination of these. Table 5.1 lists the major modifiable CVD risk factors. The three most well-accepted modifiable risk factors for heart disease are hypertension, high blood cholesterol and smoking. Risk ratios were calculated for these in the Pooling Project (Pooling Project Research Group 1978). The age-standardized relative risk of myocardial infarction for men was estimated to be 2.1 for hypertension (systolic pressure >150 mm Hg versus ≤120 mm Hg), 2.4 for high cholesterol (total cholesterol >6.9 mmol l^{-1} versus ≤5.6 mmol l^{-1}) and 2.5 for smoking (≥1 pack per day versus non-smokers). As noted in Chapter 4, the relative risk for physical inactivity is similar in magnitude to that of these three well-accepted risk factors (Powell *et al.* 1987).

Table 5.1 The major risk factors for cardiovascular disease

MODIFIABLE RISK FACTORS	NON-MODIFIABLE RISK FACTORS
Dyslipidaemia	Family history
Hypertension	Age
Cigarette smoking	Gender
Diabetes mellitus	Ethnic background
Obesity (particularly abdominal obesity)	
Physical inactivity	
Pro-coagulant state	
High plasma homocysteine	

Physical activity may modify CVD risk via multiple direct and indirect mechanisms. Direct mechanisms are those that are independent of other risk factors. Indirect effects include the role of physical activity in modifying other CVD risk factors. Apart from cigarette smoking and elevated plasma homocysteine (which will not be mentioned further), all of the factors listed in Table 5.1 may be influenced by physical activity to some degree. In the remaining sections of this chapter we will examine the direct and indirect effects of physical activity on CVD risk.

LIPOPROTEIN METABOLISM

Before discussing the role of exercise in preventing or ameliorating dyslipidaemias we need to have a basic understanding of lipoprotein metabolism. For a more comprehensive review of this area the reader is referred to Frayn (1996). Lipoproteins are required to transport triglyceride and cholesterol in the blood. Triglyceride (sometimes termed triacylglycerol) is a form of fat, which provides the major source of energy to the human body. Cholesterol is a steroid necessary for the synthesis of steroid hormones and bile salts and is integral component of cell membranes. Both triglyceride and cholesterol are water insoluble and therefore cannot circulate in the blood without the aid of lipoproteins. Lipoproteins contain a hydrophilic (water-loving) shell and a hydrophobic (water-hating or water-fearing) core. The shell is composed of phospholipids (a major component also of cell membranes) and free cholesterol and the core is composed of triglyceride and cholesterol esters (a cholesterol ester contains cholesterol and a long-chain fatty acid and is highly hydrophobic). Lipoproteins also contain proteins, often referred to as apoproteins or apolipoproteins. These proteins have a variety of important functions. For example, they act as recognition sites for receptors, they act as cofactors for enzymes of lipoprotein metabolism and they contribute to the structural stability of lipoproteins.

There are four major classes of lipoproteins, each with distinct functions (Figure 5.1). Chylomicrons are composed almost entirely of triglyceride and their main function is the transport of dietary fat that has been absorbed from the intestine to adipose tissue and muscle. Consequently chylomicron concentration is high after a meal but low during periods of fasting once the triglyceride has been removed and stored either in adipose tissue or muscle. Very-low-density lipoprotein (VLDL) particles are also rich in triglyceride and their main purpose is to transport endogenous (produced within the body) triglyceride from the liver to adipose tissue and muscle. Low-density lipoprotein (LDL) particles arise as metabolic products of VLDL and carry the bulk of cholesterol in the blood. Their function is to deliver cholesterol to cells. High-density lipoprotein (HDL) particles are also involved in cholesterol transport but their role is to return excess cholesterol from the cells back to the liver in a process termed reverse cholesterol transport.

Cholesterol and triglyceride are essential for human life, as are the lipoproteins that transport them. If the concentrations of cholesterol and/or triglyceride become too high, however, then the risk of CVD may be increased. The general term dyslipidaemia is often used when referring to abnormal concentrations of lipids and/or lipoproteins in the blood. The main forms of dyslipidaemia are a high cholesterol concentration

Figure 5.1 Composition of the four major lipoproteins.

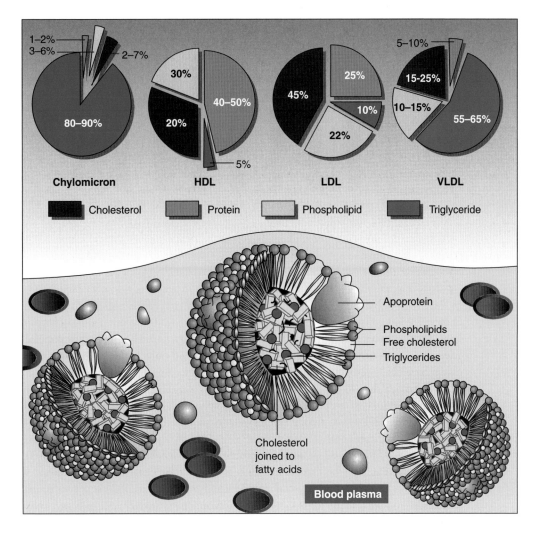

Source: Katch and McArdle (1993).

(hypercholesterolaemia) and high triglyceride concentration (hypertriglyceridaemia). Dyslipidaemia may also refer to abnormally low concentrations of HDL-cholesterol. This is because HDL-cholesterol concentration is inversely related to CVD risk, that is, high HDL-cholesterol concentrations are associated with a lower risk of CVD, possibly due to their role in reverse cholesterol transport. The role of HDL-cholesterol in CVD risk should not be underestimated since calculations suggest that for every 0.26 mmol l^{-1} (10 mg dl^{-1}) increment in HDL, there is a 50% change in heart disease risk (Kannel 1983).

In England, the mean blood cholesterol concentration for men aged 16 and above is 5.5 mmol l^{-1}. For women the mean is 5.6 mmol l^{-1} (Figure 5.2). These values are high

Figure 5.2 Total cholesterol concentrations by sex and age in England in 1998.

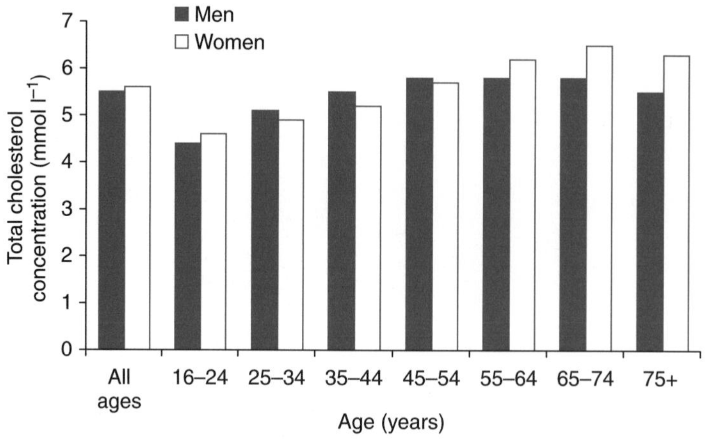

Source: British Heart Foundation (2003).

by international standards. The commonly adopted risk factor cut-off point for total cholesterol is a concentration in excess of 5.2 mmol l^{-1} (200 mg dl^{-1}) although optimal levels are somewhat lower. In England, approximately two-thirds of the adult population have cholesterol concentrations above 5.0 mmol l^{-1} and only 20% of those aged 55 and above have cholesterol concentrations below this value. As a result of such figures it has been estimated that 45% of deaths from CHD in men and 47% of deaths from CHD in women, in the UK, are due to raised blood cholesterol. The prevalence of high triglyceride and low HDL-cholesterol is not so well documented as that of high cholesterol but recent data indicate that 17% of men and 5% of women in England have low (<1.0 mmol l^{-1}) HDL-cholesterol concentrations (British Heart Foundation 2003).

Dyslipidaemia may be caused by genetic or environmental factors. In most cases environmental factors (diet, physical inactivity and other aspects of lifestyle) are probably responsible. So what evidence is there that physical activity influences lipids and lipoproteins? Many cross-sectional studies have demonstrated an association between physical activity and favourable lipid/lipoprotein profiles. One unique study examined HDL-cholesterol in several groups of men with widely differing levels of physical activity ranging from almost complete inactivity in those with recent spinal cord injuries to 80 miles week^{-1} of running in a group training for the Boston marathon. The findings revealed a clear gradient in HDL-cholesterol, ranging from a mean of 0.7 mmol l^{-1} (27 mg dl^{-1}) for new spinal cord injured patients to 1.6 mmol l^{-1} (61 mg dl^{-1}) for the marathon runners (Figure 5.3). Moreover, HDL-cholesterol concentration was below the 5th percentile of the normal population in all of the new spinal cord injured patients.

The findings from cross-sectional studies of lipids/lipoproteins have been confirmed in intervention studies. A notable example is the Stanford Heart Disease Prevention Program (Wood *et al.* 1985). In this study, which did not involve dietary intervention, 14 previously sedentary middle-aged men participated in a running programme for 2 years, averaging 12 miles week^{-1} throughout the second year. By the end of the

Figure 5.3 High-density lipoprotein (HDL) cholesterol concentrations in seven groups of individuals characterized by widely differing habitual physical activity levels.

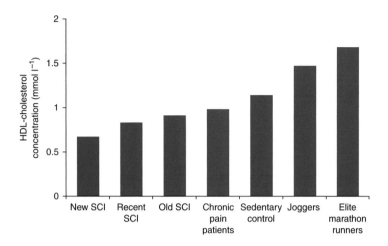

Source: Adapted from LaPorte *et al.* (1983).
Note: SCI: spinal cord injury.

programme body fatness was reduced in these men from 22% to 18% and $\dot{V}O_2$max increased from 35.6 ml kg^{-1} min^{-1} to 46.6 ml kg^{-1} min^{-1} (a 30% increase). There were significant reductions in total and LDL-cholesterol and a significant increase in HDL-cholesterol (Figure 5.4). These changes occurred despite a 15% (1260 kJ day^{-1}) increase in daily energy intake by the end of the study. A follow-up randomized controlled trial by the same group of researchers demonstrated that changes in plasma lipid and lipoprotein concentrations did not differ significantly when fat loss was accomplished via exercise alone or diet alone in overweight men (Wood *et al.* 1988).

The beneficial influence of exercise on lipids and lipoproteins has been confirmed in many studies which collectively demonstrate that physical activity has the potential to elevate HDL-cholesterol and to lower total cholesterol, LDL-cholesterol and triglyceride. The most consistent findings are for HDL-cholesterol (Leon and Sanchez 2001). Moreover, the effects of exercise are greatest when weight (fat) loss occurs although a recent study has demonstrated that beneficial changes in lipids and lipoproteins can occur with only minimal reductions in weight (Kraus *et al.* 2002). There are some indications of a dose–response relationship between physical activity levels and lipid/lipoprotein concentrations (e.g. LaPorte *et al.* 1983) and there is also some evidence to suggest that the amount rather than intensity of exercise may be the key to modifying lipid metabolism (Kraus *et al.* 2002). Changes are more likely to occur in individuals who are initially inactive and/or overweight. It has also been suggested that exercise is more likely to be beneficial in individuals with dyslipidaemia than in those with normal lipid/lipoprotein concentrations but this is not always supported by the literature (Zmuda *et al.* 1998).

Exercise modifies lipids/lipoproteins via an influence on several key enzymes involved in lipoprotein metabolism including lipoprotein lipase, hepatic lipase and

Figure 5.4 Changes in total cholesterol (TC), low-density lipoprotein cholesterol (LDL-C) and high-density lipoprotein cholesterol (HDL-C) following a 2-year running programme.

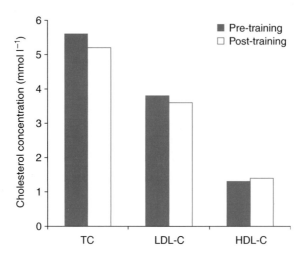

Source: Adapted from Wood *et al.* (1985).
Note: This study involved 14 previously sedentary middle-aged men who averaged 12 miles per week of running during their second year of training.

cholesterol ester transfer protein. More is said regarding the influence of exercise on lipoprotein lipase in Chapter 8 when discussing the insulin resistance syndrome. Chapter 8 also includes more information regarding the role of exercise in modifying triglyceride and HDL-cholesterol concentrations with specific reference to metabolism in the period following meals.

Do exercise-induced changes in lipoprotein metabolism result in a reduction in coronary atherosclerosis? This question is difficult to answer with certainty because few studies have addressed this issue. A study in monkeys, however, suggests that changes in lipids as a result of exercise training can reduce atherosclerosis. This study examined two groups of monkeys consuming atherogenic (atherosclerosis inducing) diets over a 2-year period. One group was maintained in a sedentary state throughout the study while the other group was trained to 'run' on a motorless treadmill wheel for 1 h, 3 times per week. By the end of the study, total cholesterol was substantially elevated in both groups of monkeys and did not differ significantly between groups (mean values were approximately 15.5 mmol l^{-1} in both groups as compared to normal values of around 2 mmol l^{-1}). However, HDL-cholesterol was significantly higher and triglyceride significantly lower in the trained compared to the sedentary monkeys. Moreover, assessments of the degree of coronary artery narrowing (using angiography) revealed that this was much greater in the sedentary monkeys than in those who exercised (Figure 5.5). The authors concluded that '...the benefits derived from such moderate exercise for one hour three times per week in the presence of hypercholesterolaemia were less atherosclerosis in wider coronary arteries supplying a larger heart that functioned at a slower rate' (Kramsch *et al.* 1981, p. 1488).

Whether such findings apply to humans is not known with certainty. However, observational evidence suggesting that exercise ameliorates coronary atherosclerosis is

Figure 5.5 The percentage narrowing (reduction in cross-sectional area) in the coronary arteries of two groups of monkeys who consumed atherogenic diets over a 2-year period. One group of monkeys remained sedentary throughout this time, the other group exercised for 1 hour, 3 times per week.

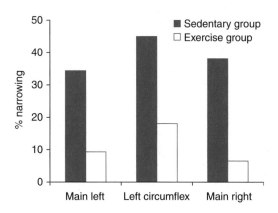

Source: Kramsch *et al.* (1981).
Note: Percentage narrowing was determined by angiography.

Figure 5.6 Cross-sections of the left and right coronary arteries of Clarence De Mar 'Mr Marathon'. De Mar was a prolific marathon runner and following his death an autopsy of his heart revealed that his coronary arteries were two to three times the normal diameter. Note the large lumens and minimal atherosclerosis.

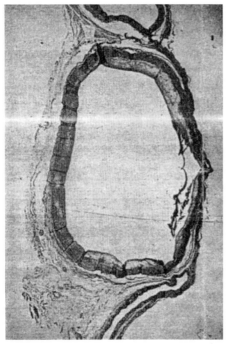 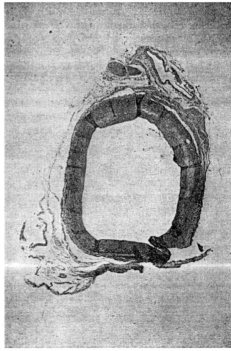

Left coronary artery   Right coronary artery

Source: Currens and White (1961).

available in the form of autopsy studies. An example is the case study of Clarence DeMar ('Mr Marathon') mentioned briefly in Chapter 2. DeMar was a prolific marathon runner who competed throughout his adult life. He died of cancer at the age of 70. Autopsy of his coronary arteries revealed that they were two or three times the normal diameter (Figure 5.6). Although there was some evidence of atherosclerosis in DeMar's arteries, no impairment of blood supply was apparent because of their large size. The question this study cannot answer is whether these large coronary arteries were the result of genetic inheritance, regular vigorous exercise or a combination of the two.

Another source of indirect evidence suggesting that physical activity may be able to offset the effects of an atherogenic diet is provided from the study of the Fulani ethnic group of northern Nigeria. They are semi-nomadic people whose main occupation is cattle rearing. Their diet is very high in fat (close to 50% of total energy intake) and saturated fat (25% of total energy intake). However, their blood lipid profile is indicative of a low risk of CVD and it has been speculated that this is due to a combination of their high physical activity level and their low total energy intake (Glew *et al.* 2001).

We will now examine the influence of exercise on blood pressure, high levels of which are also a risk factor for CVD. We will say more regarding the effects of exercise on coronary arteries when we examine the influence of exercise on endothelial function later in the chapter.

BLOOD PRESSURE

Elevated blood pressure (either systolic or diastolic) is a major risk factor for CVD. As noted in Chapter 4, the underlying cause of this increase is usually unknown. Hypertension is diagnosed if systolic blood pressure is 140 mm Hg or higher and/or if diastolic blood pressure is 90 mm Hg or higher. Currently the prevalence of hypertension in England is 40% in men and 39% in women. Blood pressure tends to increase with age, as does the prevalence of hypertension. The current (as of 2000) prevalence of hypertension in those aged 65–74 in England is 70% in men and 72% in women (British Heart Foundation 2003). In Scotland, the prevalence is even higher in this age group at 74% and 76% for men and women, respectively, in 1998 (Figure 5.7).

The fact that the prevalence of hypertension increases so dramatically with age suggests that high blood pressure is an inevitable consequence of ageing. This is not the case, however, and there are reports from several groups around the world demonstrating that blood pressure does not always increase with age. One such group are the Kung Bushmen of northern Botswana. This is an isolated group who live as hunter–gatherers all year round. In contrast to the situation in developed countries, systolic and diastolic blood pressure remain low throughout life in male and female Kung Bushmen (Figure 5.8). Several factors may explain the low blood pressure values of the Kung Bushmen including a low salt intake, freedom from the stresses of civilization and high levels of physical activity which are characteristic of a hunter–gatherer lifestyle.

The rationale for the proposition that physical activity (or fitness) will help prevent hypertension is based on the cardiovascular responses to exercise and the adaptations of

Figure 5.7 The prevalence of hypertension in men and women in Scotland in 1998.

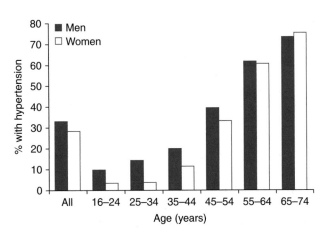

Source: The Scottish Executive Department of Health (2000).
Note: Hypertension was defined as systolic blood pressure ≥140 mm Hg or diastolic blood pressure ≥90 mm Hg.

Figure 5.8 High physical activity levels may partly explain the low systolic and diastolic blood pressure values observed across all age groups in the Kung bush-men/women of northern Botswana.

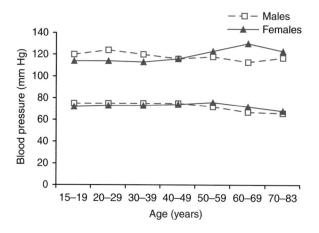

Source: Truswell *et al.* (1972).

this system to training. To understand these, it is important to remember two things: first, the most fundamental equation in vascular physiology:

Mean arterial blood pressure = cardiac output × total peripheral resistance;

and, second, that regulation of arterial blood pressure is the most important homeostatic mechanism in man.

During endurance exercise with the body's large muscles the cardiac output increases several-fold. Vasodilation of the arterioles in the exercising muscle causes a decrease in total peripheral resistance which, in turn, attenuates the rise in blood pressure which would otherwise follow from the increased cardiac output. During recovery from exercise, cardiac output quickly falls back to the resting level but the vasodilation, and thus the decrease in total peripheral resistance, persists for some hours. According to the equation above, blood pressure will be lower after exercise. Table 5.2 shows average values over a period of 12.7 h after 30 min of exercise in men with borderline to moderate hypertension. Bearing in mind the length of the post-exercise effect, someone who regularly and frequently engages in endurance exercise may well spend most of their lives in a state of 'post-exercise hypotension'. (It is important to note that these responses are typical of endurance exercise. During resistance exercise blood pressure increases sharply, mainly because the high tension generated in muscle temporarily occludes the blood vessels in muscle, increasing resistance and thus blood pressure. This is the main reason why sedentary people should increase their activity through endurance exercise before attempting sports or exercises which involve resistance work.)

Another mechanism which may lead to a decrease in blood pressure with increased physical activity is a decrease in sympathetic activity. Whole-body resting sympathetic

Table 5.2 Average blood pressure values in mildly hypertensive men before exercise and over 12.7 h after 30 min of low or moderate intensity exercise

	BEFORE EXERCISE	AFTER EXERCISE
Systolic BP (mm Hg)	136	130
Diastolic BP (mm Hg)	91	82
Mean arterial BP (mm Hg)	106	98
Heart rate (beat min^{-1})	83	80

Source: Pescatello *et al.* (1991)

'tone' is reduced with training, with a decrease in the plasma catecholamine response to standardized exercise. It is also possible that training may modify the baroreceptor reflex.

Many intervention studies have been undertaken to examine the proposition that regular exercise lowers blood pressure. The design of the early studies was often inadequate, primarily because of a lack of control groups. Blood pressure is difficult to measure accurately because of a phenomenon known as 'white coat syndrome'. When people are anxious, for example at the sight of a doctor, nurse or scientist, the ensuing rise in sympathetic activity increases their blood pressure. When the subjects/patients return for subsequent measurements the situation is less novel, they are less anxious and their blood pressure is lower than on first measurement. Thus intervention studies without a control group are more likely to find a significant effect of exercise or to overestimate its magnitude. This is an example of a type I error, sometimes called a 'false positive'. The problem is overcome by studying a control group to determine the effect of the process of measurement *per se* in lowering blood pressure. This effect is then subtracted from the gross effect of the intervention in the exercisers.

Recent appraisals of this literature have therefore focussed on randomized controlled trials. For example, meta-analysis of 68 trials published before August 1998 found that the net change, that is, change in exercisers minus the change in controls, as a result of training averaged −3.4 mm Hg for systolic blood pressure and −2.4 mm Hg for diastolic pressure (Fagard 2001). As might be expected, baseline blood pressure was an important determinant of the response to exercise: for 52 groups of subjects with normal blood pressure at baseline the effect of training averaged −2.6/−1.8 mm Hg; for 15 groups of subjects with high blood pressure (defined as systolic pressure ≥140 mm Hg or diastolic pressure ≥90 mm Hg), the effect of training was −7.4/−5.8 mm Hg. There is no strong evidence that the blood pressure response to dynamic endurance training differs according to intensity of training. Indeed a recent review by Hagberg and colleagues (2000) concluded that low to moderate intensity exercise (<70% of $\dot{V}O_2$max) is more effective in lowering blood pressure than high intensity exercise (>70% of $\dot{V}O_2$max). The response also appears to be similar for frequencies between 3 and 5 times per week and for session times between 30 and 60 min.

Thus, exercise is an effective non-pharmacological means of lowering blood pressure and is advocated by the World Hypertension League. The effect is modest compared with those of hypertensive drugs and will not normalize blood pressure in hypertensive people. It is, however, sufficient to decrease the risk of diseases attributable to hypertension.

ENDOTHELIAL FUNCTION

Earlier in this chapter it was speculated that frequent physical activity results in large coronary arteries which would enhance blood flow to the myocardial tissue. One mechanism responsible for such an effect may be the prevention of dyslipidaemia thus limiting the development of atherosclerosis. Aside from the size of the coronary arteries there is also some evidence to support the hypothesis that frequent exercise has a direct effect on myocardial perfusion by facilitating the recruitment of coronary collaterals that is, accessory vessels to the main coronary vasculature that provide an increased flow of blood to the myocardial tissue. More recently evidence has emerged suggesting that exercise training enhances myocardial perfusion via an effect on endothelial function.

Endothelial function refers to the ability of the endothelium (the thin layer of cells lining blood vessels) to interact with vascular smooth muscle to influence blood flow. Endothelial cells exert their effects by secreting various agents that diffuse to the adjacent vascular smooth muscle and induce either vasodilation or vasoconstriction. One important vasodilator released by endothelial cells is nitric oxide. This is released continuously in the basal state but its secretion can be rapidly increased in response to chemical stimulants such as those released during exercise. Nitric oxide secretion is also elevated in response to increases in shear stress that is, the force exerted on the endothelium by blood flow. This would result in flow-induced arterial vasodilation and is another important mechanism for increasing blood flow when required.

Endothelial dysfunction (inability to facilitate vasodilation and therefore increase blood flow) is thought to occur in the early stages of atherosclerosis and is a trigger of myocardial ischaemia (Gielen *et al.* 2001). Cross-sectional studies have demonstrated that the coronary arteries of endurance-trained athletes have a significantly greater dilating capacity than those of inactive men (Haskell *et al.* 1993). Moreover, exercise training improves endothelium-dependent vasodilation in the coronary vessels of patients with coronary artery disease (Hambrecht *et al.* 2000). The mechanisms responsible for exercise-induced improvements in endothelial function include an increase in the activity of nitric oxide synthase, the enzyme responsible for nitric oxide production and an increased production of extracellular superoxide dismutase, an enzyme which prevents the premature breakdown of nitric oxide. Such effects allow for an appropriate distribution of blood to cardiac muscle at all times and represent a direct means by which exercise may aid in the prevention of CVD.

COAGULATION AND FIBRINOLYSIS

Coagulation refers to the solidification of blood into a gel, termed a clot or thrombus. The process of clot formation is referred to as thrombosis and this may be considered the acute phase of CVD. If a thrombus occurs in arteries that are narrowed by atherosclerosis it may cause a blockage resulting in a heart attack or a stroke depending on

Figure 5.9 Electron micrograph of erythrocytes enmeshed in fibrin.

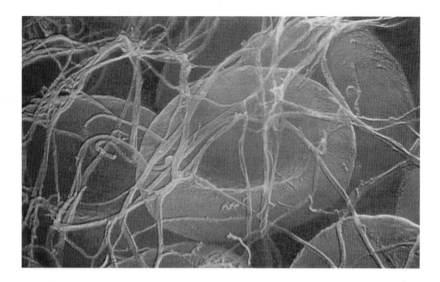

Source: Vander *et al.* (2001).

whether the site of the blockage is the arteries supplying the heart or those supplying the brain. The final event in the coagulation cascade is the conversion of the plasma protein fibrinogen into fibrin by the enzyme thrombin. Fibrin traps erythrocytes and other cells to form a blood clot (Figure 5.9). Elevated plasma fibrinogen concentration increases the likelihood of thrombus formation and is an independent CVD risk factor. Another factor that increases the risk of thrombosis is an increase in platelet aggregation, which may be defined as the tendency for platelets to stick together.

The opposite of coagulation is fibrinolysis, which refers to the break down of fibrin and removal of blood clots. This occurs when the plasma proenzyme plasminogen is activated to the enzyme plasmin, which digests fibrin thus dissolving the clot. One of the key plasminogen activators is tissue plasminogen activator (t-PA), which is secreted by endothelial cells. Thus, high concentrations of t-PA enhance fibrinolysis. Conversely, high concentrations of plasminogen activator inhibitor-1 (PAI-1) inhibit fibrinolysis because PAI-1 opposes the conversion of plasminogen to plasmin.

Acute exercise may lead to a pro-coagulant state due to increases in plasma fibrinogen concentration, the generation of thrombin, activation of platelets and haemoconcentration. This may partly explain the increased likelihood of sudden cardiac events during or shortly after heavy physical activity. In healthy individuals, however, activation of the coagulation system is balanced by a rapid increase in fibrinolytic activity.

Frequent physical activity has been shown to exert beneficial effects on both coagulation and fibrinolysis. These effects include a reduced platelet aggregation, reductions in plasma fibrinogen and PAI-1 concentrations and an increase in t-PA concentration (Imhof and Koenig 2001, Rauramaa *et al.* 2001). Collectively these changes would lower the risk of a heart attack or stroke.

INSULIN RESISTANCE

Insulin resistance may be defined as an inability of the cells within the body to respond normally to insulin. This is discussed in greater detail in Chapters 6 and 8. A surrogate marker for insulin resistance is hyperinsulinaemia, which refers to a high concentration of insulin in the blood. Insulin resistance/hyperinsulinaemia has been identified as a risk factor for heart disease in some studies. The effects of insulin resistance on heart disease risk may be mediated in part through other CVD risk factors since insulin resistance is associated with obesity, hypertension, hypertriglyceridaemia and low concentrations of HDL-cholesterol (see Chapter 8). However, at least one study has demonstrated that hyperinsulinaemia is an independent predictor of ischaemic heart disease after control for other CVD risk factors including those listed earlier (Després *et al.* 1996).

There is substantial evidence that physical activity is an effective method of enhancing insulin sensitivity and thus countering insulin resistance. Such an affect may be seen after a single exercise session although frequent exercise is required for continued benefit. This represents another mechanism by which physical activity may lower the risk of CVD. Much more is said regarding the role of physical activity in enhancing insulin sensitivity in Chapters 6 and 8 concerning type 2 diabetes and the insulin resistance syndrome respectively.

OVERWEIGHT AND OBESITY

Excess fat, particularly excess central/abdominal fat, increases the risk of CVD. As with insulin resistance the association may be mediated in part through other CVD risk factors. Overweight and obesity (see Chapter 7 for definitions) are associated with insulin resistance, type 2 diabetes, hypertension and dyslipidaemia all of which increase the risk of CVD. However, even after adjustment for these risk factors overweight has been shown to be an independent risk factor for the development of CVD in studies such as the Framingham Heart Study (Hubert *et al.* 1983). Physical activity is an effective means of preventing overweight and obesity as discussed in Chapter 7. This represents another mechanism by which regular physical activity may confer a low risk of CVD.

SUMMARY

- There are many mechanisms by which physical activity may modify CVD risk including an effect on lipoprotein metabolism, blood pressure, endothelial function, coagulation and fibrinolysis, insulin sensitivity and adiposity.
- Physical activity modifies several aspects of lipoprotein metabolism. In particular frequent exercise increases HDL-cholesterol concentration and it can also lower total cholesterol, LDL-cholesterol and triglyceride concentrations. The effects are often small but they are significant and there is some evidence of dose–response.
- A single-session of exercise has the potential to lower blood pressure for several hours thereafter. Frequent exercise may lead to a further lowering of blood pressure and

this may usefully contribute to the prevention and management of hypertension, one of the major risk factors for CVD.

- Frequent physical activity influences CVD risk in a more direct way by enhancing endothelial function. Improvements in endothelial function increase the ability of the coronary arteries to vasodilate, thus improving blood supply to the heart when necessary.
- The acute phase of CVD involves a thrombus or clot which can have fatal consequences. Frequent physical activity reduces the likelihood of thrombus formation and increases the capacity of the fibrinolytic system to dissolve blood clots.
- Hyperinsulinaemia, a marker for insulin resistance, has been identified as an independent risk factor for CVD. Physical activity has a positive influence on insulin sensitivity. As with blood pressure, effects may be seen following a single exercise session and frequent exercise is required for continued benefit.
- Overweight increases CVD risk and the risk increases more dramatically with obesity, particularly abdominal obesity. Physical activity plays an important role in the prevention and management of overweight and obesity.
- The evidence presented in this chapter provides plausible biological mechanisms supporting the epidemiological evidence linking physical inactivity and low levels of physical fitness with an increased risk of CVD.

STUDY TASKS

1 Draw a diagram to show the role of the major lipoproteins in the transport of cholesterol and triglyceride. Your diagram should include chylomicrons, VLDL, LDL and HDL as well as adipose tissue, muscle, the liver and the intestine.

2 Differences in lipids and lipoproteins between exercise and control groups at the end of intervention studies are often smaller than the differences observed between trained and untrained groups in cross-sectional studies. Give three possible explanations for this.

3 Describe the mechanism by which a single session of endurance exercise may lower blood pressure for several hours thereafter. What is the optimal exercise intensity for blood pressure reduction with exercise training?

4 Define the term endothelial function and briefly describe how physical activity can enhance this.

5 Describe the mechanisms by which physical activity may inhibit coagulation and promote fibrinolysis.

FURTHER READING

Durstine, J.L. and Haskell, W.L. (1994) 'Effects of exercise training on plasma lipids and lipoproteins', *Exercise and Sport Sciences Reviews* 22: 477–521.

Fagard, R.H. (2001) 'Exercise characteristics and the blood pressure response to dynamic physical training', *Medicine and Science in Sports and Exercise* 33: S484–92.

Frayn, K.N. (1996) *Metabolic Regulation – A Human Perspective*, London: Portland Press. Chapter 8: Lipoprotein Metabolism, pp. 197–217.

Hagberg, J.M., Park, J.J. and Brown, M.D. (2000) 'The role of exercise training in the treatment of hypertension: an update', *Sports Medicine* 30: 193–206.

Imhof, A. and Koenig, W. (2001) 'Exercise and thrombosis', *Cardiology Clinics* 19: 389–400.

Leon, A.S. and Sanchez, O.A. (2001) 'Response of blood lipids to exercise training alone or combined with dietary intervention', *Medicine and Science in Sports and Exercise* 33: S502–15.

6 Type 2 diabetes

Knowledge assumed
Basic human physiology and
biochemistry
Basic cell physiology

INTRODUCTION

Diabetes mellitus is a disease characterized by chronic hyperglycaemia (high blood glucose concentration). Over time hyperglycaemia is associated with significant damage to blood vessel walls throughout the body leading to a variety of complications which impair the quality of life and reduce life expectancy. The main cause of premature mortality with diabetes is cardiovascular disease. Moreover, diabetes treatment accounts for 9% and 14% respectively of the total healthcare budgets of the UK and US. The global prevalence of diabetes is approximately 3% but it is rising. The prevalence is higher in developed than developing countries and diabetes is the fourth or fifth leading cause of death in most Western countries.

Type 2 diabetes is by far the most common form of diabetes accounting for over 95% of diabetes cases worldwide. The incidence of type 2 diabetes is increasing in many countries and this trend is closely associated with the global increase in obesity prevalence (Chapter 7). Although type 2 diabetes is commonly thought of as a disease which afflicts only adults, cases are now occurring in children with increasing frequency. This is almost certainly linked to the rising prevalence of obesity in children (Chapter 7).

There is a genetic component to type 2 diabetes. However, recent evidence indicates that the majority of cases could be prevented by the adoption of a healthy lifestyle with physical activity as a major component.

TYPES OF DIABETES

Diabetes is not one disease but several diseases. Diabetes mellitus (sugar diabetes) is characterized by excessive thirst and frequent excretion of large amounts of urine containing an excess of sugar, hence the term 'diabetes' (meaning 'siphon') 'mellitus' (meaning 'sweet'). Diabetes insipidus is also characterized by excessive thirst and frequent urination but in this case the urine is watery and non-sweet, that is, insipid. Diabetes mellitus and diabetes insipidus have completely different causes. Diabetes insipidus is caused by a low secretion of vasopressin (antidiuretic hormone, ADH) from the pituitary gland and hence a low reabsorption of water in the kidneys. Diabetes insipidus is a rare disease and will not be discussed further here.

There are two main forms of diabetes mellitus (henceforth simply termed diabetes). Type 1 diabetes is commonly known as insulin-dependent diabetes mellitus (IDDM). It is caused by the total or near total destruction of the pancreatic beta cells (in the islets of Langerhans) by the body's own white blood cells (autoimmune disease). As a result, the pancreas is unable to produce insulin and this hormone must be injected regularly to control blood glucose concentrations (insulin cannot be given orally because gastrointestinal enzymes would digest it). Type 1 diabetes usually occurs before adulthood and therefore it is also termed juvenile-onset diabetes. On a global scale, type 1 diabetes accounts for less than 5% of all diabetes cases.

Type 2 diabetes is often referred to as non-insulin-dependent diabetes mellitus (NIDDM). In this case, the pancreatic beta cells are able to produce insulin but the body's cells are unresponsive to insulin. This is termed insulin resistance. In type 2 diabetes, insulin injections are not usually necessary although they are sometimes beneficial. Type 2 diabetes usually occurs in overweight and obese adults aged 40 and above and is sometimes termed maturity-onset diabetes. However, this term is imprecise since type 2 diabetes can and does occur in children. There is a genetic component to type 2 diabetes although estimates vary regarding the strength of this.

AETIOLOGY OF TYPE 2 DIABETES

Although there may be defects in insulin secretion in type 2 diabetes the prominent feature, as mentioned before, is insulin resistance. This means that for a given concentration of insulin less glucose is cleared from the blood into the cells. One indication of insulin resistance is fasting hyperinsulinaemia (high blood insulin concentration) in the presence of either normal or elevated blood glucose concentrations. The gold standard method for determining the blood glucose response to insulin, however, is the euglycaemic clamp technique. This involves intravenous infusion of insulin to produce the same plasma insulin concentration in all individuals. Simultaneously, glucose is infused intravenously to obtain euglycaemia (equal blood glucose concentration) in all individuals. The greater the quantity of glucose required to produce euglycaemia the more insulin sensitive the individual (Figure 6.1).

How does insulin resistance develop? One theory is that the cells become insensitive to the actions of insulin due to elevated body fat levels. This is plausible since most people with type 2 diabetes are overweight or obese (see Chapter 7 for definitions). One of the key functions of insulin is to stimulate the intracellular translocation of GLUT-4 glucose transporters to the cell membrane. GLUT-4 is strongly expressed in skeletal and heart muscle and in adipose tissue. GLUT-4 is stored in the Golgi apparatus of the cells but must be translocated to the cell membrane to facilitate diffusion of glucose into the cell. The greater the number of GLUT-4 transporters incorporated into the cell membrane the greater the rate of glucose transport. Obesity may desensitize muscle cells and adipocytes to the effects of insulin thereby reducing GLUT-4 translocation and thus glucose transport into the cells. Defects in muscle insulin sensitivity are thought to be the main reason for impaired glucose uptake in diabetics.

Figure 6.1 The euglycaemic clamp technique used to assess insulin resistance. Under equal plasma insulin concentrations non-diabetic subjects have a much greater rate of glucose disposal (via oxidation or storage as glycogen) than diabetic subjects, thus they have much greater insulin sensitivity.

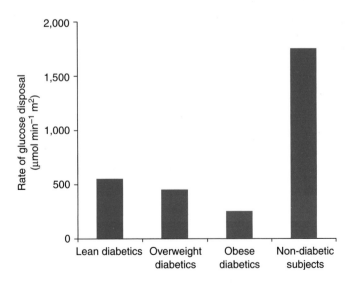

Source: Alberti *et al.* (1990).
Note: Not shown in this figure are data from obese non-diabetics. Such individuals have some degree of impaired glucose disposal in comparison to lean non-diabetics.

What are the consequences of insulin resistance? As the cells become insulin insensitive the response of liver, muscle and fat cells to insulin is compromised. In the liver, glucose production continues when it should be suppressed, that is, following meals. This is due to a process termed gluconeogenesis whereby non-carbohydrate precursors such as pyruvate, lactate, glycerol and amino acids are used to synthesize glucose. Although gluconeogenesis is a necessary response to fasting it is inappropriate following meals when exogenous glucose is available. In addition to this inappropriate hepatic glucose production, glucose uptake by muscle and fat cells is impaired with insulin resistance. The result is an elevation in blood glucose concentration due to both increased production and reduced removal of glucose.

Initially, an increase in blood glucose concentration due to insulin resistance is opposed by an increase in insulin secretion. This may be capable of maintaining blood glucose concentration at normal levels. Over time, however, insulin resistance increases further and eventually the pancreas cannot maintain a hyperinsulinaemic state. Insulin secretion now falls and although some insulin is still present, blood glucose concentrations rise further, perhaps to 20 mmol l^{-1} or more. Glycosuria (glucose in the urine) is now likely to occur. In the case of type 1 diabetes this may be severe enough to cause significant weight loss. Those with type 2 diabetes, however, do not normally excrete enough glucose in the urine to lose weight. Although glycosuria is indicative of diabetes it is not sufficient for a diagnosis since glucosuria may occur in the absence of diabetes and vice versa. Therefore, diabetes must be diagnosed from blood glucose concentrations (Box 6.1).

In addition to elevated blood glucose concentrations, type 2 diabetics exhibit raised non-esterified fatty acid (NEFA) concentrations. This is also a result of insulin resistance. Since the adipocytes have become insulin insensitive they are immune to the

BOX 6.1 DIAGNOSIS OF DIABETES MELLITUS

Diabetes mellitus is defined by hyperglycaemia. It may be diagnosed from either a fasting plasma glucose measurement or via an oral glucose tolerance test. The latter requires consumption of a 75 g glucose load after which blood glucose concentrations are monitored for 2 h. Intermediate stages between normal and diabetic have also been established by groups such as the American Diabetes Association and the World Health Organisation.

	VENOUS PLASMA GLUCOSE, mmol l^{-1} (mg dl^{-1})	
	FASTING	120 min AFTER GLUCOSE LOAD
Normal	<6.1 (110)	<7.8 (140)
Impaired fasting glucose	≥6.1 (110) to <7.0 (126)	—
Impaired glucose tolerance	—	≥7.8 (140) to <11.1 (200)
Diabetes mellitus	≥7.0 (126)	≥11.1 (200)

Source: Expert Committee on the Diagnosis and Classification of Diabetes Mellitus (1999).
Note: In the absence of symptoms, diagnosis must be confirmed by a repeat test on a separate day.

antilipolytic effects of insulin. Thus, triglycerides within the adipocytes are catabolized leading to the release of NEFAs and glycerol into the circulation. Elevated NEFA release, resulting in increased plasma NEFA concentrations, is desirable in some circumstances (e.g. during exercise or prolonged fasting). However, diabetic patients often have raised NEFA concentrations at inappropriate times (e.g. after a meal). These elevated NEFAs can interfere with the ability of muscle to take up glucose thereby exacerbating insulin resistance. Some of these NEFAs are oxidized in the liver resulting in the production of ketone bodies (ketogenesis). This can lead to a dangerous situation known as ketoacidosis whereby an excess of ketone bodies leads to an increase in the acidity (reduction in pH) of the blood. This condition is rare in those with type 2 diabetes, however, and is one of the distinguishing features between type 1 and type 2 diabetes clinically. Table 6.1 summarizes the mechanisms by which insulin resistance leads to elevated blood glucose and NEFA concentrations. Additional consequences of insulin resistance are discussed in Chapter 8.

Diabetes is associated with a variety of complications. These include atherosclerosis in small (microvascular) and large (macrovascular) blood vessels, kidney problems (nephropathy), nerve problems (neuropathy), eye problems (retinopathy and cataract) and hypertension. The risk of these occurring is related to the extent and duration of hyperglycaemia. High blood glucose concentrations are thought to facilitate a process termed glycation whereby glucose molecules combine with proteins thus negatively affecting their function. Therefore, the better the control of blood glucose the lower the risk of complications occurring. Two classes of drug are available to treat type 2 diabetes. The sulphonylureas act on the pancreatic beta cells to stimulate insulin release

Table 6.1 Major responses to insulin in normal situations and the influence of insulin resistance on these responses (NEFA = non-esterified fatty acid)

	NORMAL RESPONSE TO INSULIN	INSULIN RESISTANCE
Liver	• Glucose uptake • Glycogen synthesis • Suppressed gluconeogenesis	• Glucose release due to the lack of suppression of gluconeogenesis • Triglyceride and ketone synthesis and release due to high NEFA concentrations
Muscle	• Glucose uptake • Glucose oxidation • Glycogen synthesis	• Impaired glucose uptake, oxidation and storage
Adipocytes	• Glucose uptake and utilization • Triglyceride synthesis • Suppression of NEFA release	• Impaired glucose uptake and utilization • Inappropriate triglyceride catabolism due to lack of suppression via insulin • Release of glycerol and NEFAs
Outcome	• Normal blood glucose and NEFA concentrations	• Elevated blood glucose and NEFA concentrations

(these drugs are ineffective in type 1 diabetes) whereas the biguanide drug metformin has multiple metabolic effects. Its main effect is to improve insulin sensitivity thus suppressing gluconeogenesis in the liver and enhancing glucose uptake in skeletal muscle. Metformin is currently regarded as the drug of choice for overweight and obese individuals with type 2 diabetes.

PREVALENCE OF TYPE 2 DIABETES

Diabetes is one of the most common non-communicable diseases internationally. Estimates for the year 2000 suggest a global diabetes prevalence of 2.7% (151 million people) with type 2 diabetes accounting for 97% (147 million) of these cases. Moreover, projections indicate that these figures will increase over the next few years with 215 million people suffering from type 2 diabetes by 2010 (British Heart Foundation 2002). Diabetes prevalence tends to be higher in developed than developing countries and is particularly high in countries which have experienced rapid economic development. For example, in Singapore, a country that developed rapidly in the latter half of the twentieth century, the prevalence of diabetes was 7.0% in 2000. This was well above the average regional (South-East Asia) prevalence of 2.6% (Figure 6.2).

Diabetes rates in England are average for developed countries. In 1998, 3.3% of men and 2.5% of women were diagnosed as diabetic. Approximately 85% of these cases were due to type 2 diabetes. The true prevalence could be twice as high as this, however, because evidence suggests that up to 50% of diabetes cases go undiagnosed. Diabetes prevalence increases with age and tends to be higher in men than in women (Figure 6.3). Moreover, the prevalence of diabetes is rising in England. Between 1991 and 1998 diabetes prevalence increased by 65% in men and by 25% in women (British Heart Foundation 2002).

The prevalence of type 2 diabetes is 36% higher in men and almost twice as high in women living in deprived parts of England and Wales compared to those living in the most affluent regions. This may well be related to differences in lifestyle including dietary and exercise habits. The prevalence of diabetes also differs between ethnic groups living in England. Prevalence is at least five times higher among Pakistani and Bangladeshi men and women than it is among the general population. Prevalence is also higher amongst Black Caribbean and Indian men and women (British Heart Foundation 2002). It may be that these groups are genetically more susceptible to diabetes than other ethnic groups but it is possible also that differences in lifestyle between ethnic groups are partly responsible. Data on type 2 diabetes prevalence amongst children are sparse but evidence suggests that rates are increasing (Rosenbloom *et al.* 1999). This trend appears to be strongly related to the increasing rates of obesity amongst children (Rocchini 2002).

OBESITY AND TYPE 2 DIABETES

Although it is difficult to predict who will develop type 2 diabetes there are several factors which increase the likelihood of it occurring. These include genetic

Figure 6.2 Estimated prevalence of diabetes in major world regions in 2000.

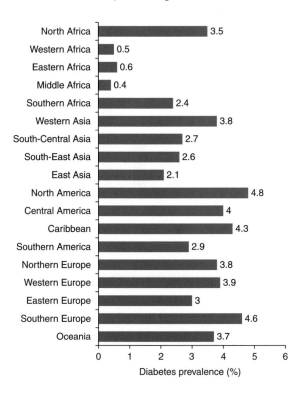

Source: Amos *et al.* (1997).
Note: Recent data indicate that diabetes prevalence has now risen to 7.3% in the US (Mokdad *et al.* 2001).

predisposition (having a parent, brother or sister who has type 2 diabetes), ethnic group, age, obesity, a sedentary lifestyle, cigarette smoking and high doses of certain diabetogenic drugs (e.g. corticosteroids). Some of these factors are modifiable whereas others are not. Obesity appears to be the most important modifiable factor. The magnitude by which obesity increases type 2 diabetes risk depends on several factors including the extent and duration of obesity. In the Nurses Health Study the increase in diabetes risk over an 8-year period ranged from 5.5 in overweight women to 60.9 in severely obese women (Figure 6.4).

Obesity also increases type 2 diabetes risk in children and adolescents. A recent study has documented the prevalence of impaired glucose tolerance in obese children for the first time. This study was conducted in the US. Impaired glucose tolerance was found in 25% of 55 obese children (4–10 years of age) and in 21% of 112 obese adolescents (11–18 years of age). Moreover, follow-up analysis was performed in two 6-year-old children found to have impaired glucose tolerance. Both children subsequently developed type 2 diabetes, one at age eight and the other at age 11. These findings are a great cause for concern bearing in mind the increasing prevalence of childhood obesity in many countries worldwide.

Figure 6.3 Prevalence of diagnosed diabetes in the UK in 1998 by sex and age.

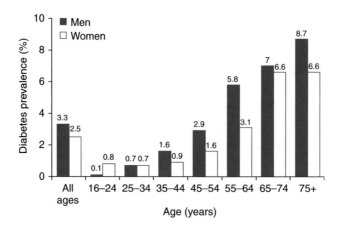

Source: British Heart Foundation (2002).
Note: Type 2 diabetes accounts for approximately 85% of all diabetes cases and over 90% of cases in adults aged 45 and above.

Figure 6.4 Data from the Nurses Health Study clearly demonstrate the influence of obesity on the risk of developing type 2 diabetes.

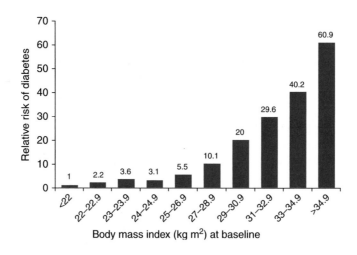

Source: Colditz *et al.* (1990).
Note: The figure shows the age-adjusted relative risk of developing type 2 diabetes over an 8-year period in American women aged 30–55.

Figure 6.5 The influence of abdominal obesity (as assessed by the waist–hip ratio) on the risk of developing type 2 diabetes over a 13.5-year period. Data are from the Göteborg cohort study involving middle-aged Swedish men.

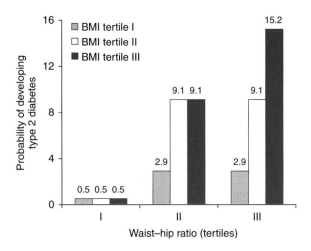

Source: Ohlson *et al.* (1985).

Individuals exhibiting abdominal obesity (Chapter 7) appear to be particularly susceptible to type 2 diabetes. Data from the Göteborg cohort study found that abdominal obesity was associated with an increase in type 2 diabetes risk independently from total body fatness (Figure 6.5). Moreover, this study may have underestimated the association between abdominal obesity and type 2 diabetes because the waist–hip ratio was employed as a proxy marker for abdominal obesity whereas the waist circumference is now considered to be a more accurate marker. The mechanism by which abdominal obesity increases type 2 diabetes risk is unclear. One theory is that visceral adipocytes are particularly resistant to the antilipolytic effects of insulin. This would result in increased catabolism of triglycerides and increased delivery of NEFAs to the liver via the portal vein. This could feasibly elevate glucose production in the liver via gluconeogenesis.

EVIDENCE THAT PHYSICAL ACTIVITY PREVENTS TYPE 2 DIABETES

Evidence has been accumulating over the last few decades which suggests that individuals leading a physically active lifestyle have a lower risk of developing type 2 diabetes than inactive individuals. Initially much of this evidence was anecdotal. In the latter part of the twentieth century, for example, it was found that approximately 50% of adult (aged 30 and above) Pima Indians living in Arizona were obese and had type 2 diabetes. This was in contrast to the situation earlier in the century when obesity and type 2 diabetes were rare in this group. It was hypothesized that these changes were due to a drastic change in lifestyle. In the early part of the twentieth century Pima Indians were reportedly very active and their diet was apparently low in calories and fat. By the latter half of the century the Pima Indian lifestyle had become 'Westernized' and it was now characterized by physical inactivity and excessive food consumption. This it appears, in combination with a strong genetic predisposition, is the explanation for their susceptibility to obesity and type 2 diabetes. A similar scenario exists for the Aborigines in Australia for whom the reported incidence of type 2 diabetes is 25%.

Observations such as those in Pima Indians led to more systematic study of the relationship between physical inactivity and type 2 diabetes. Initially this was in the form of cross-sectional studies. The majority of these studies indicated a lower prevalence of type 2 diabetes in active versus sedentary individuals (for a review see Kriska *et al.* 1994). However, it is impossible to establish from these studies whether inactivity is causing diabetes or *vice versa*. Thus, although these studies are informative the evidence is not categorical.

Some of the limitations of cross-sectional studies have been overcome using cohort studies. In these studies, large groups of individuals are recruited at baseline and then monitored over several years to determine if baseline physical activity levels are related to subsequent diabetes prevalence. A major advantage of this design is that experimenters can ensure that all subjects are free from disease at the beginning of the study. This removes the possibility that diabetes is influencing physical activity levels.

Several cohort studies have now been completed and most if not all support the conclusion that sedentary individuals are more likely than active individuals to develop type 2 diabetes. One example is the Physicians' Health Study (Manson *et al.* 1992). In this study, over 21,000 US male physicians aged 40–84 years at baseline were followed up for an average of five years. All subjects were free from disease at baseline. Physical activity levels were assessed at baseline using a single question: 'How often do you exercise vigorously enough to work up a sweat?' A lower risk of type 2 diabetes was observed in active men with some evidence of dose–response, that is, greater risk reduction with more frequent exercise (Figure 6.6). This relationship persisted following adjustment for age, body mass index, smoking, hypertension and other cardiovascular disease risk factors. Moreover, the relationship was particularly pronounced among overweight men suggesting that exercise may be particularly beneficial in this group.

An inverse association between physical activity and type 2 diabetes was also observed in a large cohort study of women. The Nurses Health Study (Hu *et al.* 2001) followed nearly 85,000 women in the US over a 16-year period (1980–96). These women were free from diagnosed cardiovascular disease, diabetes and cancer at baseline. Information regarding physical activity and other aspects of lifestyle was collected at baseline and at several other intervals during the study using questionnaires. From these the amount of time per week spent in moderate-to-vigorous activities (jogging, brisk walking, heavy gardening, heavy household work) requiring an expenditure of 3 METs or more was estimated. Consistent with the Physicians' Health Study a dose–response relationship was observed between activity status and diabetes risk (Figure 6.7). Moreover, the importance of taking a holistic approach to diabetes prevention was emphasized by the finding that the relative risk of developing type 2 diabetes was only 0.1 in nurses characterized by the following combination: good diet (dietary score in upper two quintiles), low body mass index (BMI) (< 25 kg m^2) and high physical activity levels (≥ 30 min day^{-1} of moderate to vigorous exercise). Based on this finding a population-attributable risk of 87% was calculated suggesting that 87% of diabetes cases could have been avoided if all women had been in these low-risk categories.

Figure 6.6 Findings from the Physicians' Health Study indicate that vigorous exercise ('enough to work up a sweat') is related to a lower risk of developing type 2 diabetes.

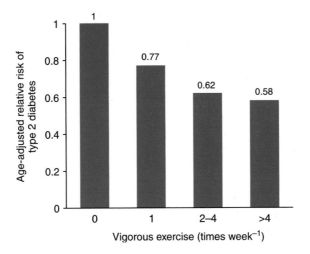

Source: Manson *et al.* (1992).
Note: This study involved over 21,000 US male physicians aged 40–84 years at baseline. The follow-up period averaged five years.

Figure 6.7 Relative risk of type 2 diabetes in relation to the weekly volume of exercise performed in the Nurses Health Study 1980–96.

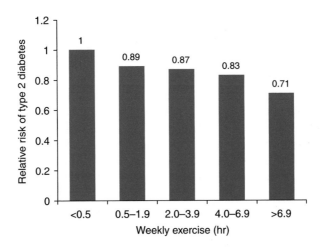

Source: Hu *et al.* (2001).
Note: Relative risks have been adjusted for possible confounding factors including age, BMI and the presence or absence of a family history of diabetes.

Although these cohort studies are convincing they still have limitations. As with cross-sectional studies physical activity is assessed via a questionnaire, sometimes using only a single question. Moreover, diabetes is determined by self-report and this may lead to inaccuracy due to undiagnosed cases (though this should be minimal in the case of physicians and nurses). These difficulties are overcome by intervention studies. Such studies are labour intensive and therefore involve smaller numbers than cohort studies. Moreover, the participants in intervention studies are at high risk for diabetes. Only a handful of well-controlled intervention studies have been performed to date but the results are promising.

The Malmö feasibility study (Eriksson and Lindgärde 1991) was a non-randomized intervention study conducted in southern Sweden. It involved two treatment groups and two 'comparison' groups. Treatment group one included 41 men with early stage type 2 diabetes, that is, a positive result on an oral glucose tolerance test but no overt symptoms of diabetes. Treatment group two included 181 men with impaired glucose tolerance. Comparison group one comprised 79 men with impaired glucose tolerance. Comparison group two comprised 114 men with normal glucose tolerance. Treatment groups followed a combined diet and exercise programme for five years whereas comparison groups served as controls. After five years, 54% of the group with early stage type 2 diabetes were in remission, that is, their blood glucose concentrations were no longer indicative of diabetes. Glucose tolerance was improved in 75.8% of cases in those receiving combined diet and exercise treatment for impaired glucose tolerance and only 10.6% of these men developed diabetes. In contrast, glucose tolerance had deteriorated in 67.1% of cases in those not receiving diet and exercise treatment for impaired glucose tolerance and 28.6% of these men developed diabetes. This equated to a 63% reduction in diabetes risk in men with impaired glucose tolerance who received diet and exercise treatment compared to those who did not. No cases of diabetes were diagnosed in the control group who had normal glucose tolerance initially.

More recently, the findings of the Malmö feasibility study have been confirmed by a study conducted in the city of Da Qing, China (Pan *et al.* 1997). In this study, 577 men and women with impaired glucose tolerance were randomized by clinic into either a control group or one of three intervention groups: diet only, exercise only or diet plus exercise. Follow-up tests were performed every 2 years for 6 years to identify individuals who developed type 2 diabetes. Results indicated a significant reduction in the risk of type 2 diabetes in all three intervention groups (Figure 6.8). In the exercise only group the reduction in risk amounted to 46% when data were adjusted for differences in baseline BMI and fasting glucose. The exercise prescription in this study was a minimum of one and preferably two 'units' of exercise per day. Units were defined in terms of exercise intensity and duration. Thus, one unit was equal to 30 min of mild exercise (e.g. slow walking, shopping, housecleaning), 20 min of moderate exercise (e.g. fast walking, cycling, heavy laundry), 10 min of strenuous exercise (e.g. slow running, climbing stairs, table tennis) or 5 min of very strenuous exercise (e.g. skipping, basketball, swimming).

Surprisingly, in the Da Qing study, the reduction in diabetes risk in the diet and exercise group was no greater than that experienced in the diet only and exercise only groups. This was despite the fact that the diet and exercise group received instructions and counselling for both diet and exercise that were similar to those for the diet only and exercise only interventions. Since the interventions were largely unsupervised a

Figure 6.8 Reduction in type 2 diabetes risk in men and women over a six-year period in the Da Qing Impaired Glucose Tolerance and Diabetes Study.

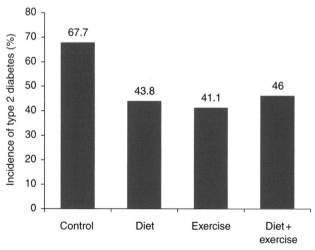

Source: Pan *et al.* (1997).

possible explanation is that the diet only group increased their activity levels and the exercise only group altered their diets. If this were the case then all three groups would have received the benefit of both diet and exercise. However, this is speculation.

Although the Malmö feasibility study and the Da Qing study have provided much stronger evidence supporting a crucial role for exercise in preventing type 2 diabetes the findings are not definitive. One aspect requiring clarification is the extent to which findings from Sweden and China can be generalized to other countries. A more fundamental limitation of these trials, however, it that neither was randomized (in the Da Qing study clinics rather than individual subjects were randomized). These issues have now been resolved by the findings from two randomized intervention trials published in *The New England Journal of Medicine* in 2001 and 2002.

The Finnish Diabetes Prevention Study (Tuomilehto *et al.* 2001) involved 522 middle-aged (40–65 years old), overweight (body mass index ≥ 25 kg m^2) men and women with impaired glucose tolerance. Subjects were randomly allocated into either an intervention group or a control group. Subjects in the intervention group received individual counselling to help them achieve five major goals: (1) a reduction in weight of 5% or more, (2) a reduction in total fat intake to less than 30% of energy consumed, (3) a reduction in saturated fat intake to less than 10% of energy consumed, (4) an increase in fibre intake to at least 15 g per 1,000 kcal and (5) moderate exercise for at least 30 min day^{-1} and totalling more than 4 h week^{-1}. Subjects in the control group were given oral and written information annually about diet and exercise but no specific individualized programmes or counselling. Oral glucose tolerance tests were performed annually. The mean duration of follow-up was 3.2 years.

Despite the modest weight loss (4.2 kg) the incidence of diabetes was more than halved in the intervention group as compared to the control group (11% versus 23% respectively). Moreover, no cases of diabetes developed in individuals who were successful in attaining four or more of the goals of the intervention programme regardless of whether these individuals were in the intervention group or the control group (Figure 6.9). Furthermore, among subjects in the intervention group who did not reach the goal of losing 5% of their initial weight but who did achieve the goal of exercising for more than 4 h week^{-1}, the odds ratio for diabetes was 0.2 compared to those in the intervention group who maintained a sedentary lifestyle. This suggests that even in the absence of major weight loss exercise is effective in preventing type 2 diabetes.

The results of the Finnish Diabetes Prevention Study were confirmed by a second randomized trial conducted in the US (Diabetes Prevention Program Research Group 2002). The Diabetes Prevention Program was a large multi-centre trial involving 3,234 men and women with impaired fasting glucose and impaired glucose tolerance. Participants were randomly assigned to either placebo, metformin or an intensive lifestyle-modification programme with the goals of at least a 7% weight loss and at least 150 min of physical activity per week. The incidence of type 2 diabetes during an average follow-up of 2.8 years was 11.0, 7.8 and 4.8 per 100 person-years in the placebo, metformin and lifestyle groups, respectively. The lifestyle intervention reduced the incidence of diabetes by 58% and metformin by 31% in comparison with placebo. The lifestyle intervention reduced the incidence of diabetes by 39% in comparison with the metformin trial. These results held across all age groups (Figure 6.10). Results were also similar in men and women regardless of ethnic group.

Figure 6.9 The incidence of type 2 diabetes in middle-aged men and women during follow-up according to success in achieving the five major goals of an intervention programme involving diet and exercise.

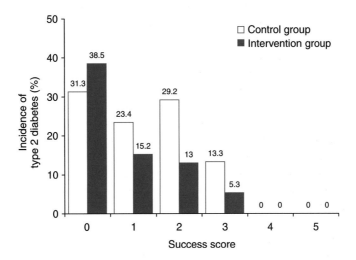

Source: Tuomilehto *et al.* (2001).
Note: Data are from the Finnish Diabetes Prevention Study.

Figure 6.10 The incidence of type 2 diabetes in placebo, metformin and lifestyle groups according to age category in the Diabetes Prevention Program.

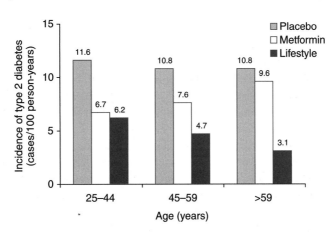

Source: Diabetes Prevention Program Research Group (2002).

A question not answered by the Finnish Diabetes Prevention Study and the US Diabetes Prevention Program is how long the effects of the lifestyle interventions can be sustained, that is, how long can the development of diabetes be delayed (Tataranni and Bogardus 2001). This is not known. Provided that the newly adopted lifestyle habits are maintained there is good reason to believe that the risk of diabetes will be minimized but evidence suggests that many people have difficulty in maintaining lifestyle changes following intervention programmes. One clear finding from the Finnish and US studies is that information alone is not effective in preventing diabetes in high-risk groups. In both studies, the control/placebo groups received information about diet and exercise. This was ineffective in reducing diabetes risk in comparison to the individualized guidance and supervision received by the intervention groups.

The Finnish Diabetes Prevention Study and the US Diabetes Prevention Program prove beyond doubt that inappropriate lifestyle plays a major role in the development of type 2 diabetes and that modifications to lifestyle can reduce the risk of developing type 2 diabetes. Neither trial reveals the relative contributions of improved diet and increased physical activity to reduced diabetes risk and this requires further study. However, the crucial role of physical activity is confirmed when considering the evidence collectively. First, exercise was a major component of the Finnish Diabetes Prevention Study and the US Diabetes Prevention Program. Second, increased physical activity alone was found to be effective in the Da Qing study. Third, many cohort studies demonstrate a relationship between inactivity and diabetes risk and fourth there are many plausible biological mechanisms to explain how physical activity reduces the risk of type 2 diabetes not least of which is the effectiveness of exercise as a means of weight control (Chapter 7).

How much exercise is required to reduce the risk of type 2 diabetes? Is there an optimal mode, duration and intensity of exercise for reducing diabetes risk? In the Finnish Diabetes Prevention Study the recommendation was a minimum of 30 min day^{-1} and 240 min week^{-1} of 'moderate' intensity exercise. In the US Diabetes Prevention Program the prescription was a minimum of 150 min week^{-1} (just over 20 min day^{-1}) of 'moderate' intensity exercise. In the Da Qing study the recommendation varied from 5–10 min day^{-1} of 'very strenuous' exercise to between 30 and 60 min day^{-1} of 'mild' exercise. A variety of activities were employed in these studies including walking, running, swimming, cycling, circuit training, volleyball, basketball, dancing, skipping and even household tasks. Probably the focus should be on increasing energy expenditure, as this will be the most effective means of controlling weight. In this respect there will be a trade off between the intensity and duration of exercise. Finally, there is some evidence from cohort studies of a dose–response relationship between physical activity and the reduction in risk of type 2 diabetes indicating that greater amounts of exercise are associated with greater reductions in risk. Further research is required to help refine the exercise prescription for diabetes prevention.

MECHANISMS OF INTERACTION BETWEEN EXERCISE AND TYPE 2 DIABETES

Many studies have shown that physical inactivity is related to impairments in insulin sensitivity and glucose tolerance. An example is the study of Rogers and colleagues (1990). They performed oral glucose tolerance tests on 14 masters athletes during a normal training period and following 10 days of detraining. Following detraining glucose tolerance was maintained at the expense of hyperinsulinaemia in 10 of these athletes (Figure 6.11). Moreover, in the other four athletes there were impairments in both insulin sensitivity and glucose tolerance (Figure 6.12). These findings suggest that physical inactivity leads to insulin resistance in all individuals and that in some individuals, perhaps those with a genetic predisposition, there will also be a reduction in glucose tolerance.

Figure 6.11 Loss of insulin sensitivity with inactivity in 10 masters athletes assessed 16–18 h after a usual training session (exercise) and following 10 days without exercise (detraining).

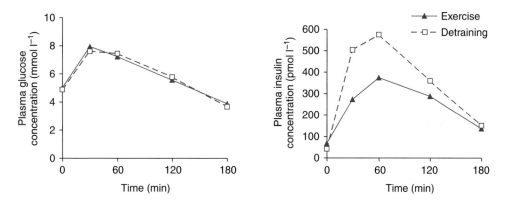

Source: Rogers *et al.* (1990).
Note: Values were recorded during an oral glucose tolerance test where 100 g of glucose was ingested at time zero.

Figure 6.12 Loss of insulin sensitivity and glucose tolerance with inactivity in four masters athletes assessed 16–18 h after a usual training session (exercise) and following 10 days without exercise (detraining).

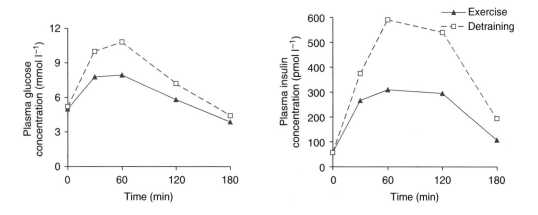

Source: Rogers *et al.* (1990).
Note: Values were recorded during an oral glucose tolerance test where 100 g of glucose was ingested at time zero.

Similar findings have resulted from studies examining extreme levels of physical inactivity. For example, Lipman and colleagues (1972) found impairments in glucose tolerance in eight healthy young men following five weeks of bed rest. The impairment was less severe, however, in those permitted one hour of vigorous supine exercise each day. Thus, it appears that regular exercise can prevent the development of type 2 diabetes by maintaining glucose tolerance. This is supported by the findings of the Diabetes Prevention Program. All participants in this study had impaired glucose tolerance initially but the lifestyle intervention was effective in normalizing glucose tolerance in 40–50% of participants (Figure 6.13).

The loss of insulin sensitivity upon cessation of exercise occurs very quickly. In some studies a decrease has been observed only three days after the last bout of exercise. This indicates that exercise must be performed regularly for the maintenance of insulin sensitivity. Moreover, the effects of exercise are also seen in untrained individuals following a single bout of exercise. Therefore, a prolonged period of exercise training is not required for the attainment of improved insulin sensitivity. Comparisons in young and old individuals indicate a loss of insulin sensitivity with ageing and this is a possible explanation for the higher prevalence of type 2 diabetes in elderly people. It is not clear to what extent the loss of insulin sensitivity is a natural consequence of ageing and to what extent it is due to the associated reduction in physical activity which often occurs in elderly individuals. Logic would suggest, however, that planned regular exercise is likely to be of particular benefit to elderly individuals in helping to improve insulin sensitivity and glucose tolerance.

Many mechanisms have been proposed to explain how physical activity leads to improvements in insulin sensitivity and glucose tolerance (for a review see Ivy *et al.* 1999). It appears likely that events within skeletal muscle account for the majority of

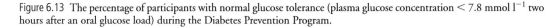

Figure 6.13 The percentage of participants with normal glucose tolerance (plasma glucose concentration < 7.8 mmol l^{-1} two hours after an oral glucose load) during the Diabetes Prevention Program.

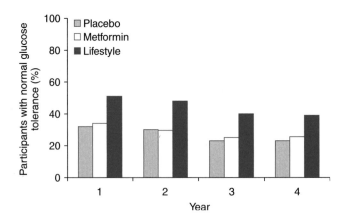

Source: Diabetes Prevention Program Research Group (2002).
Note: By design no participants had normal glucose tolerance at baseline.

the improvement in glucose tolerance because it has been estimated that 70–90% of the glucose ingested during an oral glucose tolerance test is cleared by skeletal muscle. Much attention has focussed on the role of GLUT-4 receptors in skeletal muscle (for a recent review see MacLean *et al.* 2000). Single and repeated bouts of exercise have been shown to increase the concentration of GLUT-4 protein in skeletal muscle and this should facilitate glucose transport into muscle cells. Moreover, an increase in glucose delivery to muscle would be aided by the increase in muscle blood flow that occurs during and following exercise. Glucose delivery would be further enhanced via adaptations to exercise training such as increased skeletal muscle capillarization. Other possibilities include an improved functioning of insulin receptors, an increased activity of enzymes involved in various aspects of glucose metabolism and an increase in muscle mass, which would increase the storage area for glucose.

Aside from the role of muscle it is also possible that exercise affects metabolism within the liver. Exercise may improve hepatic insulin sensitivity and this may result in a reduction in gluconeogenesis. This would be particularly important in the fasted state since hepatic glucose production is the main determinant of fasting blood glucose concentration. Gluconeogenesis may also be reduced due to a reduction in NEFAs in the circulation which is likely to occur with regular exercise.

Finally, exercise may improve insulin sensitivity via its affects on adipocytes. There is evidence that insulin receptor density and insulin-stimulated glucose transport are inversely related to adipocyte size. Exercise-induced weight reduction should lead to a reduction in adipocyte size and thus an improvement in the insulin sensitivity of adipocytes. This mechanism would be especially effective if it operated in visceral adipocytes since these are particularly resistant to the effects of insulin. Thus, weight loss may be an important mechanism by which exercise improves insulin sensitivity and glucose tolerance. However, some of the benefits of exercise appear to be independent of weight loss because intervention studies such as the Finnish Diabetes Prevention Study have shown a reduction in the risk of type 2 diabetes in the absence of major weight loss.

SUMMARY

- Type 2 diabetes is a disease characterized by insulin resistance and impaired glucose tolerance leading to hyperglycaemia.
- Type 2 diabetes accounts for the vast majority of diabetes cases in the UK and elsewhere.
- Type 2 diabetes is diagnosed using either fasting blood glucose concentrations or an oral glucose tolerance test.
- Type 2 diabetes is associated with a variety of complications including atherosclerosis, nephropathy, neuropathy, retinopathy and hypertension. These impact upon quality of life and life expectancy.
- The prevalence of type 2 diabetes is rising amongst adults in the UK and other developed countries. The prevalence of type 2 diabetes is also rising amongst children in some countries.

- Obesity, particularly abdominal obesity, is a major risk factor for type 2 diabetes. Other risk factors include age, genetic predisposition and ethnic background.
- Evidence from observational studies indicates that physical inactivity is associated with an elevated risk of developing type 2 diabetes.
- Evidence from non-randomized and randomized intervention trials shows that physical activity can help to reduce the risk of developing type 2 diabetes.
- Exercise can improve insulin sensitivity and glucose tolerance in those with impaired glucose tolerance. These effects are transient indicating that frequent exercise is required to maintain benefit.
- Many mechanisms have been proposed to explain how exercise improves insulin sensitivity and glucose tolerance. One likely mechanism is an increased concentration of GLUT-4 receptors in skeletal muscle.

STUDY TASKS

1 Distinguish between type 1 and type 2 diabetes. Discuss the similarities and differences between these diseases. Describe the complications which may arise from diabetes.
2 Describe how insulin resistance leads to elevated blood glucose and NEFA concentrations. How does triglyceride catabolism within adipose tissue contribute to hyperglycaemia? Describe one complication that may occur as a consequence of elevated NEFA concentrations.
3 Give examples of observational studies supporting a role for exercise in preventing type 2 diabetes. Discuss the strengths and limitations of these studies.
4 Briefly describe the findings of randomized intervention trials which have examined the effectiveness of physical activity in preventing type 2 diabetes. How have these studies advanced knowledge and what important questions do they leave unanswered?
5 Describe the proposed mechanisms by which exercise improves insulin sensitivity and glucose tolerance. Categorize these mechanisms into those operating following a single bout of exercise and those requiring chronic training. Discuss the implications of different modes of exercise with respect to these mechanisms.

FURTHER READING

American Diabetes Association (2002) 'The prevention or delay of type 2 diabetes', *Diabetes Care* 25(4): 742–9.

Frayn, K.N. (1996) *Metabolic regulation – a human perspective*, London, Portland Press, 219–232.

Ivy, J.L., Zderic, T.W. and Fogt, D.L. (1999) 'Prevention and treatment of non-insulin dependent diabetes mellitus', *Exercise and Sport Sciences Reviews* 27: 1–35.

Kelley, D.E. and Goodpaster, B.H. (2001) 'Effect of exercise on glucose homeostasis in Type 2 diabetes mellitus', *Medicine and Science in Sports and Exercise* 33: S495–S501.

Krentz, A.J. and Bailey, C.J. (2001) *Type 2 Diabetes*, London: The Royal Society of Medicine Press Limited.

Kriska, A.M., Blair, S.N. and Pereira, M.A. (1994) 'The potential role of physical activity in the prevention of non-insulin dependent diabetes mellitus: the epidemiological evidence', *Exercise and Sport Sciences Reviews* 22: 121–43.

Knowledge assumed
Principles of indirect calorimetry
and calculation of energy
expenditure
Basic statistics (including
percentiles, correlation
coefficients and statistical power)

7 Obesity and energy balance

INTRODUCTION

Obesity may be defined as excess of body fat such that health is endangered. Obesity increases the risk of many diseases including cardiovascular disease (CVD) and diabetes. It is also an important component of the insulin resistance syndrome as discussed in Chapter 8. There has been a dramatic increase in the prevalence of obesity in many developed countries in recent decades. This trend has been observed in men, women and children. The increased prevalence in children is a particular cause for concern because obese children are more likely than non-obese children to become obese adults. The estimated financial cost of obesity in the UK is £2.5 billion a year. Of this sum, £0.5 billion is spent on treatment costs within the National Health Service (NHS) and £2 billion or more a year is lost due to the impact on the economy (National Audit Office 2001).

Although some people are genetically more susceptible to obesity than others the underlying cause of obesity is an imbalance between energy intake and energy expenditure. In this chapter we will examine recent trends in obesity prevalence and highlight some of the literature regarding the role of inactivity as a cause of obesity.

DEFINITION OF OBESITY

The most commonly adopted criterion for obesity is the body mass index (BMI). This is calculated as weight in kilograms divided by height in metres squared ($kg\,m^{-2}$). Table 7.1 lists the classification of overweight and obesity by BMI. Overweight denotes an excess of weight/fat but not to the point where health is impaired. This is currently a matter of debate, however, because there is some evidence that the health risk may increase at BMI levels even lower than $25\,kg\,m^{-2}$. The term obesity indicates a condition in which there is firm evidence to suggest a significant increase in disease and all-cause mortality risk.

There are two main reasons for the widespread use of the BMI. First, weight and height are easy to measure. Second, in most individuals the BMI gives a more accurate indication of body fatness than merely using weight-for-height. One limitation of the BMI is that it can give an inaccurate indication of body fatness in some individuals. Most people are overweight because they are over fat but some individuals with high BMIs are muscular rather than fat. For these individuals a high BMI would not indicate an increased risk of disease. Another limitation of the BMI is that it has not been validated in all ethnic groups. Thus, it may be that the cut-off points displayed in Table 7.1 are not appropriate for some ethnic groups.

Table 7.1 Classification of overweight and obesity by BMI

	OBESITY CLASS	BMI ($kg\,m^{-2}$)
Underweight		<18.5
Normal		18.5–24.9
Overweight		25.0–29.9
Obesity	I	30.0–34.9
	II	35.0–39.9
Extreme obesity	III	≥40.0

Source: Expert Panel on the Identification, Evaluation and Treatment of Overweight in Adults (1998).

An alternative to the BMI is to measure body fatness using field techniques such as skinfold measurements. However, the reproducibility of skinfold measurements can be poor and there can be large differences between values obtained by different experimenters. Moreover, as with the BMI, equations to predict body fatness from skinfold thickness are not available for all ethnic groups. More accurate laboratory-based methods are available, such as hydrostatic weighing and dual-energy X-ray absorptiometry, but these are expensive and/or time-consuming and therefore not practical when dealing with large numbers. Another problem with using body fatness as an indication of obesity is that there are no universally established guidelines at present. Wilmore and Costill (1999) have proposed the following percentage body fat guidelines for men and women: men: 20–25% – borderline obese, >25% – obese; women: 30–35% – borderline obese, >35% – obese. However, they acknowledge that exact standards for body fat percentages have not been established.

In recent years scientists have begun to appreciate that it is not just total fatness which affects disease risk but also the location of body fat. In this respect individuals who carry a lot of fat around the abdomen are at increased risk of many diseases. Abdominal fat is stored both underneath the skin (subcutaneous abdominal fat) and within the abdominal cavity (visceral fat). Visceral fat is thought to be particularly harmful in terms of disease risk. This is discussed in more detail in Chapter 8.

Abdominal fat can be measured using sophisticated laboratory techniques such as computed tomography (CT) or magnetic resonance imaging (MRI). However, these techniques are expensive and most research relies on surrogate measures of abdominal adiposity. Initially the waist–hip ratio was used as a measure of abdominal adiposity but this has been superseded by the waist circumference, which gives a more accurate estimate of the disease risk associated with abdominal adiposity. Guidelines from the National Heart, Lung and Blood Institute in the US state that a waist circumference greater than 102 cm (40 inches) in men or greater than 88 cm (35 inches) in women indicates a high risk for diseases such as diabetes, hypertension and heart disease (Expert Panel on the Identification, Evaluation and Treatment of Overweight in Adults 1998).

One final area that needs addressing before turning to the issue of the prevalence of obesity is that of defining obesity in children. This area is problematic for several reasons. First, definitions of obesity are confounded by changes due to growth and maturation. Second, the relationship between fatness in children and disease endpoints such as diabetes and heart disease is less clear than it is for adults. This is partly due to the longer interval between the development of obesity and the occurrence of disease, which necessitates a longer period of study. However, the recent increase in both the prevalence and extent of obesity in children may be changing this (Figure 7.1).

There is no universally accepted definition for obesity in children. The usual approach is to use data from a reference group and employ the 85th and 95th percentiles (for either BMI or percentage fat) as cut-off points for overweight and obesity, respectively. However, such an approach can yield widely different estimates depending on whether the BMI or percentage fat percentiles are used. Moreover, if a standard (non-percentile-based) cut-off point for BMI or body fatness is used this will lead to different estimates again. There is no ideal solution to this problem at present. However, reference group percentiles established in a particular year are a useful method of tracking changes in obesity prevalence over time.

Figure 7.1 According to a report in *The Sunday Times* (Harlow 2002) headlined 'Obese young America has its coronaries early', obesity-related heart problems are occurring more often in American children and at a younger age. The boy in the photo died of obesity-related heart failure. He was only 7 years old.

Source: Photo courtesy of the Hickey family.

PREVALENCE OF OBESITY

In the UK, the average BMI of both men and women has increased steadily since the beginning of the 1980s and overweight (BMI $>25 \, \text{kg m}^{-2}$) is now the norm (Table 7.2). Nearly two-thirds of men and just over half of all women in the UK are currently overweight or obese and approximately 1 in 5 men and women is obese (British Heart Foundation 2002).

The prevalence of overweight and obesity increases with age. In England, about 28% of men and 27% of women aged 16–24 are overweight or obese whereas 76% of men and 70% of women aged 65–74 fall into this category (Figure 7.2). Obesity prevalence also varies between ethnic groups in the UK. Black Caribbean and Pakistani women are particularly susceptible to obesity. One in three women in each of these groups has a BMI $>30 \, \text{kg m}^{-2}$. Obesity is more common in adults employed in manual occupations, particularly women. This is surprising in view of the evidence, presented later in this chapter, that physical activity is associated with a lower prevalence of obesity. Possible explanations for the higher prevalence of obesity in those engaged in manual occupations include poor dietary habits and low levels of leisure-time physical activity.

Table 7.2 BMI for men and women (aged 16 and above) in the UK at various intervals between 1980 and 1998

YEAR	BMI (kg m⁻²) – MEN			BMI (kg m⁻²) – WOMEN		
	MEAN	$\geq$25 (%)	$\geq$30 (%)	MEAN	$\geq$25 (%)	$\geq$30 (%)
1980	24.8	43.0	8.0	24.0	34.0	9.0
1986	24.9	45.0	8.0	24.6	36.0	12.0
1988	23.8	—	—	23.2	—	—
1991	25.7	—	12.7	25.3	—	15.0
1993	25.9	57.6	13.2	25.7	48.6	16.4
1994	26.0	58.1	13.8	25.8	48.7	17.3
1995	26.1	59.3	15.3	25.9	50.4	17.5
1996	26.3	61.0	16.4	26.0	52.0	18.4
1997	26.5	62.2	17.0	26.2	52.5	19.7
1998	26.5	62.8	17.3	26.4	53.3	21.2

Source: British Heart Foundation (2002).

Figure 7.2 Percentage of overweight and obese men and women in England in 1998 by age range.

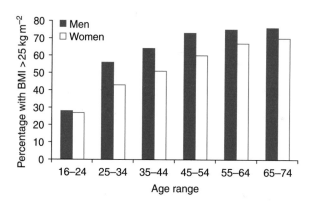

Source: National Audit Office (2001).

Consistent with the trends in adults, overweight and obesity prevalence has increased over time in children. Although prevalence figures were relatively stable between 1974 and 1984, Chinn and Rona (2001) noted increases in both English and Scottish boys and girls between 1984 and 1994. Their definition of overweight and obesity was the BMI percentile at a given age that was estimated to pass through BMI values of 25 and 30, respectively, at age 18. The most recent data for overweight and obesity prevalence

Figure 7.3 The prevalence of obesity in men and women in selected countries.

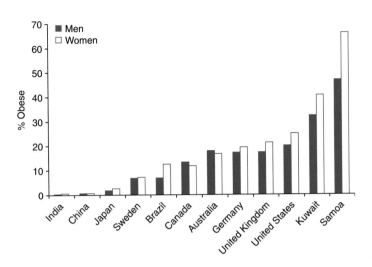

Source: Adapted from the British Heart Foundation (2002).
Note: Obesity is defined here as a BMI >30 kg m^{-2}.

in English children appears to be from a study conducted in 1996 (Reilly and Dorosty 1999). Prevalence of overweight ranged from 22% at age 6 years to 31% at age 15 years and that of obesity ranged from 10% at age 6 years to 17% at age 15 years. In this study the 85th and 95th BMI percentiles from reference data collected between 1978 and 1990 were used to indicate overweight and obesity, respectively. The data confirm the increasing prevalence of overweight and obesity amongst children in the UK. This is a cause for concern due to the positive relationship between childhood obesity and obesity in later life.

Thus far we have discussed obesity prevalence in the UK. What is the situation elsewhere in the world? Figure 7.3 displays obesity prevalence data for men and women in a selection of countries worldwide. Samoa has the highest obesity prevalence of any country in the world. Note also that obesity prevalence tends to be higher in women than in men. Moreover, the prevalence tends to be higher in developed countries (e.g. the UK and the US) than in developing countries (e.g. China and India). Figure 7.4 documents the annual increase in the prevalence of obesity for the countries included in Figure 7.3. This shows that obesity prevalence is increasing in all of these countries.

HEALTH RISKS OF OBESITY

Obesity increases the risk of all-cause mortality by approximately 50%. It has a greater impact, however, on the risk of developing associated diseases, in particular type 2 diabetes, as shown in Figure 7.5. In the UK, it is estimated that obesity is responsible

Figure 7.4 Annual increase in the prevalence of obesity between 1980 and 1998 in selected countries.

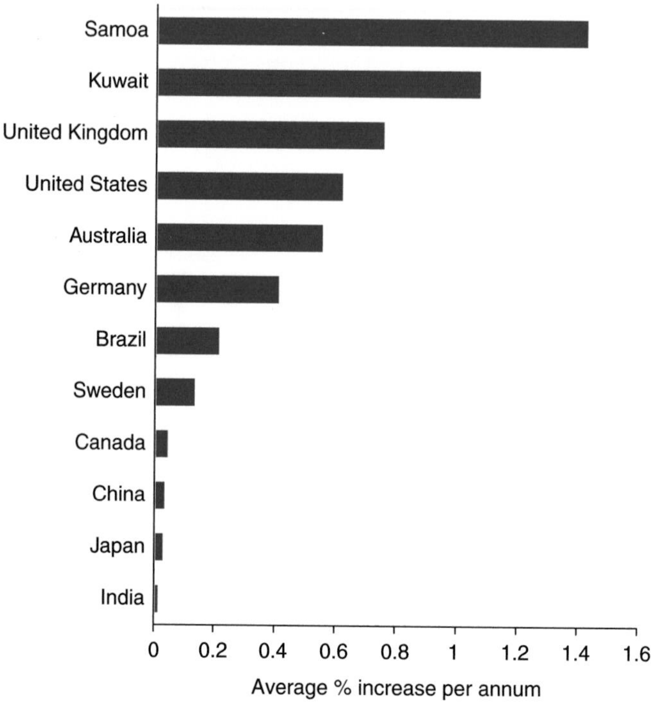

Source: Adapted from the British Heart Foundation (2002).
Note: Obesity is defined here as a BMI >30 kg m^{-2}.

for 18 million sick days and 30,000 deaths per year. These deaths shorten life by 9 years on average and result in 40,000 lost years of working life (National Audit Office 2001).

GENETIC INFLUENCE ON OBESITY

That genes have an influence on body fatness is indisputable. A clear example of this can be seen in a Danish adoption study. In this study Stunkard and colleagues (1986) compared the BMI of 540 adult adoptees with that of their biological as well as their adoptive parents. Ninety per cent of the adoptees had been placed in their adoptive homes within the first year of life. Stunkard and colleagues (1986) found a clear relationship between the weight class of the adoptees and that of their biological parents but no relationship between the weight class of the adoptees and that of their adoptive parents (Figure 7.6). This suggests that genes are a strong determinant of body fatness and that childhood family environment has little or no effect.

Although the findings of Stunkard and colleagues demonstrate the influence of genes on fatness this does not mean that obesity is inevitable from conception in some

Figure 7.5 The relative risk of obese (compared to non-obese) individuals developing associated diseases.

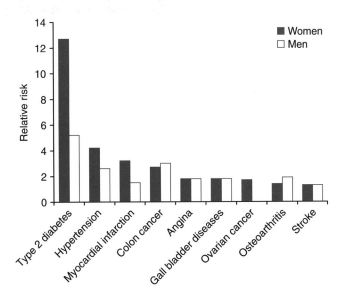

Source: National Audit Office (2001).

Figure 7.6 Genetic influence on overweight as indicated by the fact that the BMI of adopted children is positively associated with the BMI of their biological parents (left panel) but not that of their adoptive parents (right panel).

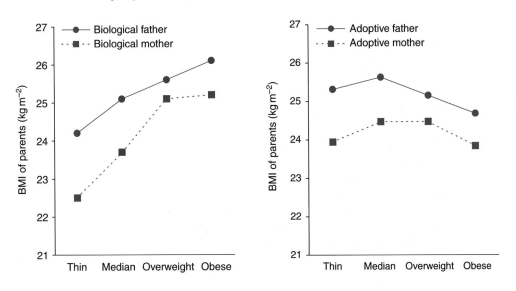

Source: Stunkard *et al.* (1986).

Figure 7.7 Genetic influence on diet-induced weight change as indicated by the similarity in weight gain (left panel) and visceral fat gain (right panel) in 12 pairs of monozygotic male twins after 100 days of overfeeding.

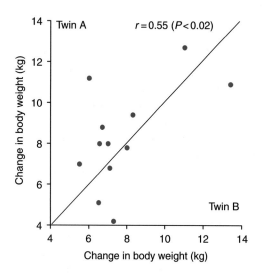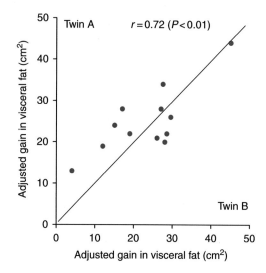

Source: Bouchard *et al.* (1990).
Note: Visceral fat gain was adjusted for the gain in total fat mass.

unfortunate individuals. Obesity is a result of an interaction between genes and the environment. Famine and/or high levels of physical activity may prevent the expression of any genetic tendency towards fatness. A good example of how genes interact with food intake is provided by a study of overfeeding in monozygotic (identical) twins (Bouchard *et al.* 1990). In this study, 12 pairs of male monozygotic twins were overfed by 353 MJ (84,000 kcal) over a 100-day period. Men gained an average of 8.1 kg in weight but the range of weight gain varied from 4.3 to 13.3 kg. Moreover, there was a significant relationship between weight gain within twin pairs indicating a genetic influence on weight gain. This influence was more pronounced when examining gain in visceral fat (Figure 7.7). These findings demonstrate that genes influence an individual's susceptibility to weight gain through overeating.

ENERGY BALANCE AND OBESITY

If we are to maintain a stable body weight we must be in energy balance, that is, energy intake must match energy expenditure. As we have just seen, overeating will lead to an increase in fat storage and therefore body weight. This is due to an imbalance between energy intake and energy expenditure, that is, energy intake exceeds energy expenditure. In the case of Bouchard's (1990) overfeeding study it was clearly overeating which led to the positive energy balance. In this study, the overfeeding was intentional. In 'real life', however, overeating is not usually intentional and often goes unnoticed until weight gain has occurred. What causes humans to subconsciously overeat? One factor thought to play a major role is a high fat diet. There is currently great debate regarding the role of high fat diets in causing obesity. Let us briefly examine the evidence suggesting that high fat diets lead to overweight and obesity.

There are several lines of evidence to support a link between high fat diets and obesity. First, converting dietary fat into body fat is a very efficient process. Second, fat is energy dense (containing $38 \, kJ \, g^{-1}$ compared to $17 \, kJ \, g^{-1}$ for carbohydrate and protein and $29 \, kJ \, g^{-1}$ for alcohol). Thus, diets high in fat may lead to passive (unintentional) overconsumption of energy because appetite is regulated by the bulk rather than the energy density of food (Prentice 1998). Third, under normal conditions, carbohydrate, protein and alcohol are not converted to fat. For each of these an increase in intake will stimulate an increase in oxidation. This is because there is limited potential to store carbohydrate and protein in the body and there is no storage site for alcohol. In contrast there is enormous potential for storing fat in the body. Thus, fat intake does not necessarily stimulate fat oxidation and a long-standing positive fat balance may cause obesity (Swinburn and Ravussin 1993).

Some scientists dispute the role of dietary fat as a major determinant of body fat. Walter Willett argues that in recent years there has been a decline in percentage fat intake in the US, yet at the same time there has been a 'massive' increase in obesity prevalence (Willett 1998). As we shall see later in this chapter there has also been a decline in fat intake in the UK in recent decades, at a time when obesity prevalence has been increasing. These trends suggest that inactivity rather than overeating is responsible for the increasing prevalence of obesity in many countries. Before examining this relationship further we will address two issues related to resting metabolic rate: (1) does a low resting metabolic rate cause obesity? (2) Does exercise increase the resting metabolic rate?

EXERCISE, RESTING METABOLIC RATE AND OBESITY

Twenty-four hour energy expenditure can be divided into three components namely resting metabolic rate, the thermic effect of feeding and the thermic effect of physical activity (Figure 7.8). Resting metabolic rate (RMR) may be defined as the energy required to sustain life while resting. Strictly speaking, RMR differs from basal or sleeping metabolic rate but for the purposes of this discussion we shall use the term RMR to denote the energy expenditure while asleep or awake but inactive and in the absence of food intake, digestion and absorption. In most individuals RMR accounts for 60–75% of the energy expended over a 24-hour period. The thermic effect of feeding represents the increase in energy expenditure associated with digesting, absorbing and storing food. In most individuals it accounts for approximately 10% of daily energy expenditure. The thermic effect of activity is the energy expended in all non-resting activities be they occupational, recreational or domestic. For most people the thermic effect of activity accounts for between 15% and 30% of daily energy expenditure.

Since RMR accounts for a large percentage of daily energy expenditure in most individuals it has long been hypothesised that some individuals may be susceptible to obesity because they have a low RMR. Many studies have been conducted in both children and adults to investigate this issue. The findings do not generally support a role

Figure 7.8 The three major components of daily energy expenditure: RMR, the thermic effect of feeding and the thermic effect of physical activity. Numbers in parentheses represent the approximate contribution of each component to total energy expenditure.

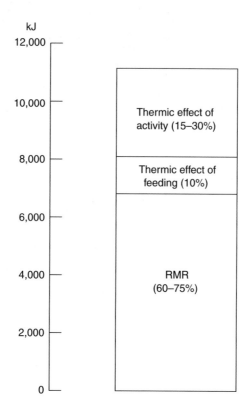

Source: Poehlman (1989).

for RMR in the aetiology of obesity. Comparisons of RMR in obese and non-obese individuals have usually found higher rather than lower values in the obese (Stensel *et al.* 2001). This finding is not surprising since obese individuals are heavier than non-obese individuals and body mass is a major determinant of RMR. It is possible that RMR is low in obese individuals prior to them becoming obese. However, measurements of RMR in non-obese individuals who are at risk of obesity by virtue of having obese parents usually yield values similar to those obtained for individuals not at risk of obesity (Goran *et al.* 1995).

A more robust approach for assessing the role of RMR in the development of obesity is longitudinal observation. Ravussin and colleagues (1988) found that individuals who gained more than 10 kg in weight over a 4-year period had lower RMRs initially than individuals who did not gain weight, thus providing some support for the hypothesis that a low RMR is a cause of obesity. However, other longitudinal studies have failed to reproduce this finding (Goran *et al.* 1998). Moreover, most studies of post-obese individuals who have lost large amounts of weight report RMR values similar to those of

subjects who have never been obese (Wyatt *et al.* 1999). Thus, most evidence does not support the contention that a low RMR is a cause of obesity. However, this possibility cannot be discounted because obesity may result from a daily energy imbalance of only 105 kJ (25 kcal) and even the most sophisticated of today's techniques would be unable to identify this energy imbalance as a defect in energy expenditure (Goran 2000).

One often-quoted benefit of exercise is that it raises the metabolic rate and in so doing helps to prevent weight gain. Let us examine this issue briefly. It is clear that the metabolic rate remains elevated above basal levels for a while following exercise. This has been determined from measurements of oxygen consumption and is termed excess post-exercise oxygen consumption or EPOC. EPOC is due to a variety of factors associated with the preceding exercise bout including the need to reduce body temperature and to restore muscle and liver glycogen stores. The duration of EPOC is positively related to the intensity and duration of the preceding exercise bout (Bahr *et al.* 1987, Bahr and Sejersted 1991). It usually lasts between 1 and 12 h. RMR differs from EPOC in that it is measured following an overnight fast and 8 h of sleep. Although some studies have found an increase in RMR following single (acute) and repeated (chronic) bouts of exercise, many have failed to detect an effect and therefore this issue needs clarifying. It is clear, however, that a single bout of exercise may increase the metabolic rate for several hours thereafter. Thus, individuals who exercise twice a day may have an almost permanent elevation in metabolic rate due to the repeated effects of acute bouts of exercise. Dieting, on the other hand, causes a reduction in RMR and exercise may be useful in helping to offset this reduction.

PHYSICAL INACTIVITY AS A CAUSE OF OBESITY

The fact that the prevalence of overweight and obesity has increased so markedly in recent years in the UK and in many other countries suggests that changes to eating patterns and/or physical activity levels are responsible. This is supported by the observation that the prevalence of obesity tends to be higher in developed countries, where the food supply is abundant and mechanisation has reduced the requirement for physical activity, than in developing countries (Figure 7.3). Are overeating and physical inactivity equally responsible for the current obesity trend or is one of these the major culprit? This is difficult to assess due to the difficulty in determining energy intake and expenditure accurately. Typically these are assessed via self-report questionnaires and there is a tendency for people to under-report their food intake and over-report their physical activity levels. Nevertheless, there is some evidence indicating that physical inactivity may be the major cause for the current rise in the prevalence of overweight and obesity.

Using data from the National Food Survey (adjusting for meals eaten outside the home, and for consumption of alcohol, soft drinks and confectionery), Prentice and Jebb (1995) estimate that average *per capita* energy intake has declined in Great Britain since 1970. Despite this decline, the prevalence of obesity doubled between 1980 and 1991 in Great Britain. The lack of association between these trends suggests that physical inactivity must play a role. Prentice and Jebb (1995) examined this issue with reference to data for television viewing and car ownership from the Central Statistical Office. These proxy measures of physical inactivity were more closely related to the changes in obesity prevalence than were energy intake and fat intake (Figure 7.9), leading Prentice and Jebb (1995) to conclude that inactivity is as important as diet in the aetiology of obesity and possibly represents the dominant factor.

A more recent study from the US also provides convincing evidence that inactivity is the single most important cause of weight gain over time. Weinsier and colleagues (2002) observed two groups of premenopausal women over a year. One group maintained their normal body weight while the other group gained 9.5 kg. Energy expenditure was determined during diet-controlled, energy-balance conditions in both groups of women at the beginning and end of the study using the doubly labelled water technique (Box 7.1). The women who gained weight had a significantly lower activity energy expenditure (total energy expenditure minus energy expenditure due to sleeping and the thermic effect of feeding) than those who did not gain weight both at baseline and at the end of the study (Figure 7.10). Weinsier and colleagues (2002) estimated that physical inactivity alone accounted for >75% of the weight gain observed in the gainers.

Besides the two notable examples we have just discussed there are many other studies demonstrating that physical inactivity is associated with overweight and obesity (Williamson *et al.* 1993, Haapanen *et al.* 1997, Kahn *et al.* 1997). This is not to say that diet is unimportant or that physical inactivity is the predominant cause of obesity in all cases. There is reason to believe, however, that physical inactivity is the dominant factor responsible for the current increase in obesity prevalence in the UK and in many other developed countries. Further evidence to support this belief is provided by James (1995) who estimates that energy intake has fallen by an average of 3150 kJ day^{-1} (750 kcal day^{-1}) in the UK since 1970. Despite this fall James has calculated that adults put on an average of 2.5 kg in weight between age 25 and age 75. This can be explained

Figure 7.9 Trends in diet (left panel) and activity (right panel) in relation to the prevalence of obesity in Great Britain.

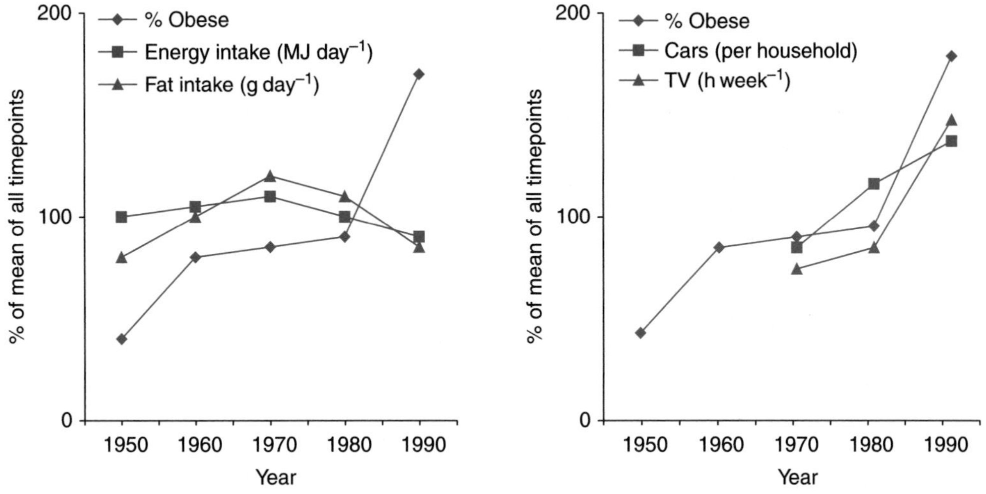

Source: Adapted from Prentice and Jebb (1995).

BOX 7.1 MEASUREMENT OF ENERGY EXPENDITURE USING DOUBLY LABELLED WATER

This is a non-intrusive method for measuring energy expenditure in free-living situations. It is objective and accurate and thus preferable to questionnaire-based methods but it has the disadvantage of being expensive. The principle is as follows:

- subjects drink water ($^2H_2{}^{18}O$) containing stable (non-radioactive) isotopes of hydrogen (^2H, or deuterium) and oxygen (^{18}O or oxygen-18);
- the isotopes distribute throughout all body fluids;
- ^2H leaves the body as water (^2H_2O) in urine, sweat and vapour from breathing;
- ^{18}O leaves the body as both water ($H_2{}^{18}O$) and carbon dioxide ($C^{18}O_2$);
- the difference between the rates of loss of ^{18}O and ^2H enables carbon dioxide production to be estimated;
- oxygen consumption (and thus energy expenditure) is calculated from carbon dioxide production.

by an imbalance of only 210 kJ day^{-1} (50 kcal day^{-1}). Therefore, the inference is that physical activity must have fallen by 3,360 kJ day^{-1} (800 kcal day^{-1}). The National Audit Office (2001) has documented possible reasons for the decline in physical activity in England and these are reproduced in Box 7.2. The role of exercise in managing obesity is addressed in Chapter 12 (Therapeutic exercise).

Figure 7.10 Activity energy expenditure (total energy expenditure minus energy expenditure due to sleeping and feeding) in women who gained or did not gain weight over a 1-year period.

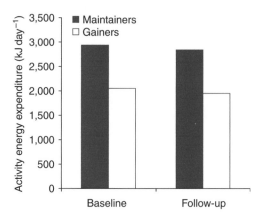

Source: Weinsier *et al.* (2002).
Note: Total energy expenditure was measured using the doubly labelled water technique.

BOX 7.2 POSSIBLE REASONS FOR A REDUCTION IN THE AMOUNT OF PHYSICAL ACTIVITY IN THE UK IN RECENT YEARS (NATIONAL AUDIT OFFICE 2001: PP. 13–14)

- a reduction in occupational exercise. The extra physical activity involved in daily living 50 years ago, compared with today, has been estimated to be the equivalent of running a marathon a week;
- a reduction in exercise due to greater use of the car and wider car ownership;
- the decline of walking as a mode of transport. One reason for this is heightened fears about personal safety, which affect some groups of the population more than others. For example, children, women and older people, especially those living in inner cities, are likely to feel particularly vulnerable;
- an increase in energy-saving devices in public places, such as escalators, lifts and automatic doors;
- less opportunities for young people to take physical exercise. Factors influencing this include increasing fears among parents about their children's safety when unsupervised, and a reduction in the amount of physical education and sport undertaken in some schools;
- the substitution of physically active leisure with sedentary pastimes such as television, computer games and the internet;
- fear of racial harassment and cultural beliefs which may prevent people from certain black and minority ethnic groups form taking exercise. Different avenues may therefore be required to promote physical exercise for these groups.

SUMMARY

- Obesity is a condition in which there is an excess of body fat such that health is impaired. The most commonly accepted criterion for obesity in adults is a BMI ≥ 30 kg m^{-2}.
- The prevalence of obesity has increased dramatically in the UK and many other developed and developing countries in recent years. Increases have been noted in both sexes and in children as well as adults.
- Obesity is associated with many health risks including an increased risk of type 2 diabetes, heart disease and hypertension. The risk of these diseases is particularly high in individuals with abdominal obesity.
- Genes determine who is most at risk of obesity but appropriate environmental conditions are required for these genes to express themselves.
- For body mass to remain stable energy intake must balance energy expenditure. If energy intake exceeds energy expenditure then weight gain is likely to occur.
- Most evidence does not support the theory that obesity is caused by a low resting metabolic rate.
- Metabolic rate may be increased for several hours after exercise but frequent exercise is required to maintain this increase.
- Both overeating and physical inactivity cause obesity but there is evidence to suggest that physical inactivity is the major cause of the current obesity epidemic.

STUDY TASKS

1 Identify the cut-off points for overweight and obesity and explain the rationale for these. List three advantages and two disadvantages of the use of the BMI as a measure of obesity. Which simple measurement could be used to add precision in estimating the health risk associated with obesity?
2 Explain why definitions of obesity in children are problematic. Describe two BMI-based approaches that have been used to identify obesity in children. What are the strengths and weaknesses of these two approaches?
3 Discuss the arguments for and against high fat diets as a cause of obesity.
4 Identify and explain the major components of daily energy expenditure. What role does RMR play in the development of obesity? Discuss the inter-relationships between exercise, EPOC and RMR.
5 Give examples of evidence suggesting that physical inactivity is a major cause of obesity. Evaluate the strengths and limitations of this evidence with reference to the study design and methods used.

FURTHER READING

Goran, M.I. (2000) 'Energy metabolism and obesity', *Medical Clinics of North America* 84: 347–62.
Hill, J.O. and Peters, J.C. (1998) 'Environmental contributions to the obesity epidemic', *Science* 280: 1371–74.

Jebb, S.A. and Moore, M.S. (1999) 'Contribution of a sedentary lifestyle and inactivity to the etiology of overweight and obesity: current evidence and research issues', *Medicine and Science in Sports and Exercise* 31 (Supplement): S534–41.

McArdle, W.D., Katch, V.I., and Katch, V.L. (2001) *Exercise Physiology: Energy, Nutrition and Human Performance*, 5th edn. Lippincott Williams and Wilkins, Philadelphia. Chapter 30: Overweight, obesity, and weight control, pp. 820–63.

National Audit Office (2001) 'Tackling obesity in England. Report by the Comptroller and Auditor General', HC 220 Session 2000–2001: 15 February 2001. Available at: http://www.nao.gov.uk/publications/nao_reports/00–01/0001220.pdf accessed 8 May 2002.

8 Insulin resistance syndrome

Knowledge assumed
Actions of insulin
Basic metabolism of fat and carbohydrate
Basic cardiovascular physiology

INTRODUCTION

So far risk factors for cardiovascular disease (CVD) have been discussed individually in relation to the effects of physical activity (see Chapter 5). However, some risk factors tend to cluster together. These include dyslipidaemia (specifically, high triglycerides and low high-density lipoprotein (HDL)-cholesterol), impaired glucose regulation or diabetes, obesity (particularly of the upper body type) and hypertension. The phrase 'cluster together' means that these risk factors coexist more commonly than would be expected by chance. For example, diabetes and obesity are twice as common among

Figure 8.1 Relative risk of CHD in people with increasing numbers of metabolic risk factors.

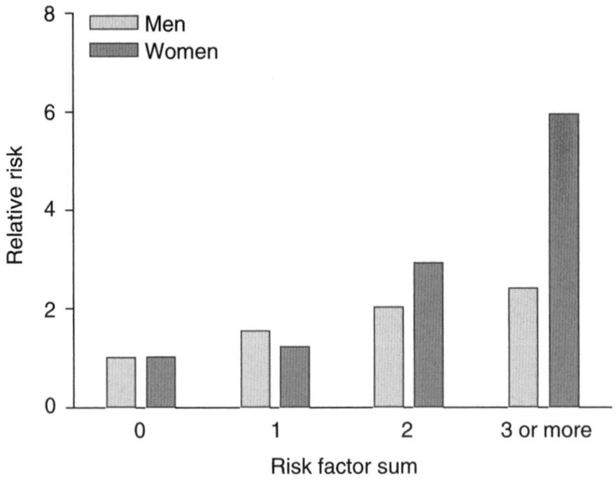

Source: Adapted from Wilson *et al.* (1999).
Note: Lighter bars, men; darker bars, women.

people with hypertension as among those with normal blood pressure. As a combination, risk factors become much more powerful predictors of disease. Data from the Framingham Offspring Study[1] shows that clusters of three or more factors increased the risk of coronary heart disease (CHD) more than two-fold in men and nearly 6-fold in women (Figure 8.1) (Wilson *et al.* 1999).

This clustering of risk factors is important for at least three reasons: first, it suggests the existence of a common aetiology; second, it makes it difficult to treat people because drugs are designed to target one pathology; and third, (as the reader will realize) physical activity may be an especially attractive preventive or therapeutic intervention if it is beneficial for more than one component of the cluster.

DEFINITION OF THE INSULIN RESISTANCE SYNDROME

Gerald Reaven was the first to argue that the defining feature of this cluster of abnormalities could be insulin resistance (Reaven 1988). He suggested that the abnormalities comprised a syndrome, common even among the apparently healthy population and which he called Syndrome X. The more descriptive terms 'insulin resistance syndrome' and 'metabolic syndrome' are now usually employed.

The principal components of this syndrome are listed in Box 8.1. Almost all have been related independently to the risk of CVD. As discussed in Chapter 6, insulin resistance is also a strong marker for the risk of developing type 2 diabetes and CVD accounts for the majority of deaths among diabetics. Thus there are sound reasons to suggest that the principal features of the insulin resistance syndrome are '... involved to a substantial degree in the cause and clinical course of the major diseases of Western civilisation' (Reaven 1994).

BOX 8.1 ABNORMALITIES THAT CHARACTERIZE THE INSULIN RESISTANCE SYNDROME

- Diabetes, impaired glucose tolerance or impaired fasting glycaemia
- Hyperinsulinaemia due to insulin resistance
- Raised arterial blood pressure*
- Raised plasma triglycerides and/or low HDL-cholesterol*
- Upper body or general obesity*
- Preponderance of small, dense low LDL particles
- High level of postprandial lipaemia
- Impaired endothelial function
- Procoagulant state
- Microalbuminuria*, †

* For diagnostic criteria, according to the World Health Organization, see Alberti et al. (1998).
† Abnormally high excretion of albumin in urine probably indicates vascular damage affecting the glomeruli of the kidney.

PREVALENCE

The prevalence of the insulin resistance syndrome is poorly described and estimates differ according to the definition and inclusion criteria adopted. As with any syndrome, not all features are present in the same individual. The prevalence in Europe (based on healthy Caucasians from 21 centres) has been reported to be about 15% (Ferrannini et al. 1996). This is probably an underestimate, however, as people already diagnosed as hypertensive or diabetic were excluded, as were some ethnic groups. In another study, only about one third of adult Americans studied were free of all the major syndrome abnormalities (Ferrannini et al. 1991). Within this population, 17% of the obese and 56% of hypertensives had three or more abnormalities. Overall, available data from industrialized societies suggest that up to one quarter or one third of adults without diagnosis of diabetes exhibit at least several features of the insulin resistance syndrome.

There appears to be a genetic predisposition to this syndrome among some ethic groups. For example, hyperinsulinaemia is more prevalent among Mexican-Americans than among non-Hispanic whites in the US. In the UK, the high prevalence of CHD and type 2 diabetes among immigrants from the Indian subcontinent may be attributable to the insulin resistance syndrome. Environmental factors must also be important, however, because genetic factors cannot account for the marked increase in prevalence over recent years.

ABNORMALITIES ASSOCIATED WITH INSULIN RESISTANCE

Insulin resistance is usually defined in terms of the lack of effect of insulin on glucose disposal. However, insulin affects many other metabolic processes. As resistance to its actions develops these are impaired, leading to abnormalities. The mechanisms that link insulin resistance to the major syndrome features (high triglycerides/low HDL-cholesterol, hypertension and obesity) are explained below, insofar as they are understood.

Lipid and lipoprotein metabolism

Insulin exerts multiple influences on lipid metabolism that affect plasma lipoprotein variables (Figure 8.2). Collectively, they promote the uptake and storage of fatty acids in adipose tissue, inhibit their mobilization from adipose tissue and decrease secretion of very low density lipoprotein (VLDL) from the liver. When insulin resistance develops these normal effects are impaired, leading to high triglycerides, low HDL-cholesterol and probably (in the longer term) to a preponderance of small dense LDL particles. This combination of lipid abnormalities confers a high level of cardiovascular risk and is sometimes called the 'atherogenic lipoprotein phenotype'. The principal mechanisms involved are set out in Table 8.1, which should be read with reference also to Figure 8.2.

Because insulin coordinates metabolism during the hours after a meal the consequences of resistance to its effects on lipid metabolism are seen most clearly during the postprandial period. After a typical meal containing 30–40 g of fat, plasma triglyceride concentration rises by about 50%, reaching a peak between 3 and 4 h later. In insulin-resistant people, not only are fasting triglycerides higher but the postprandial rise in triglycerides is also exaggerated and prolonged. Chylomicrons and VLDL circulate longer, facilitating exchange of triglycerides in their core with HDL and LDL. This depletes HDL of cholesterol and leads to triglyceride-poor VLDL that are degraded to

Table 8.1 Consequences of insulin resistance for lipid metabolism

NORMAL INSULIN-MEDIATED PROCESS	IMMEDIATE CONSEQUENCES OF INSULIN RESISTANCE	SECONDARY CONSEQUENCES OF INSULIN RESISTANCE
Suppression of NEFA release from adipose tissue	Excessive NEFA release and elevated plasma NEFA concentration	Increased secretion of VLDL-triglyceride from the liver; impaired glucose disposal
Suppression of hepatic synthesis and secretion of VLDL-triglyceride	Inappropriate postprandial secretion of VLDL, hence exaggerated postprandial lipaemia	Low HDL-cholesterol and preponderance of small, dense LDL
Activation of lipoprotein lipase in adipose tissue	Impaired postprandial clearance of triglycerides from plasma, hence exaggerated lipaemia	Low HDL-cholesterol

Source: Adapted from Frayn (1993).
Note: NEFA, non-esterified fatty acids; HDL, high density lipoprotein; VLDL, very low density lipoprotein; LDL, low density lipoprotein.

Figure 8.2 Influence of insulin on lipid metabolism to promote lipid synthesis and storage.

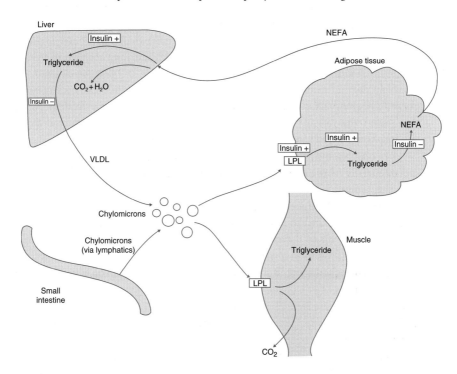

Source: Adapted from figures in Frayn (1996).
Note: LPL, lipoprotein lipase; Insulin +, insulin stimulates; Insulin −, insulin inhibits; NEFA, non-esterified fatty acids; VLDL, very low density lipoproteins.

small dense LDL, effects which are thought to hasten the progression of atherosclerosis. Since people are non-fasting for most of the day, atherosclerosis is regarded as a postprandial phenomenon (Karpe and Hamsten 1995).

Hypertension

Insulin-resistant states are consistently associated with hypertension. However, this is nowhere near as easy to explain as the association between insulin resistance and disordered lipid metabolism. Several potential mechanisms have been advanced but none is supported by a convincing body of evidence. Three are explained briefly here. First, hyperinsulinaemia enhances renal sodium retention by increasing reabsorption in the distal tubules of the kidney. Plasma volume expands, leading to an increase in blood pressure. Second, insulin resistance increases sympathetic nervous activity that may be expected to increase blood pressure via an increase in total peripheral resistance. Third, hyperinsulinaemia creates a growth-promoting milieu that may induce vascular smooth muscle hypertrophy, perhaps in resistance vessels. This would also increase blood pressure through an increase in peripheral resistance.

Obesity

Obesity is also an important feature of the insulin resistance syndrome. If insulin resistance is indeed the primary defect, this suggests that obesity and insulin resistance are linked. There is some evidence for this. Nearly half the variation in insulin sensitivity amongst individuals is accounted for by variations in body fat content, even within relatively normal ranges of body mass index (BMI). Thus, nearly all subjects who are obese have poor insulin sensitivity, even if they are apparently healthy. Weight reduction lowers the risk of type 2 diabetes and, in persons already affected by the disease, can improve insulin sensitivity and glucose tolerance.

The observation that visceral adiposity is a risk factor for type 2 diabetes, independently of the degree of overweight, suggests that insulin resistance is associated with this type of fat distribution in particular. The reasons for this are not fully understood but visceral adipose tissue appears to have a higher sensitivity to lipolytic agents than other depots and to be rather resistant to suppression of lipolysis by insulin. Both characteristics tend to increase day-long plasma non-esterified fatty acids (NEFA) concentrations, leading to increased fat oxidation, impaired glucose uptake and, eventually, insulin resistance. Figure 8.3 compares plasma responses of glucose and insulin to

Figure 8.3 Differences in postprandial responses of glucose, insulin and triglycerides between men with either high or low levels of visceral obesity, matched for total fat mass.

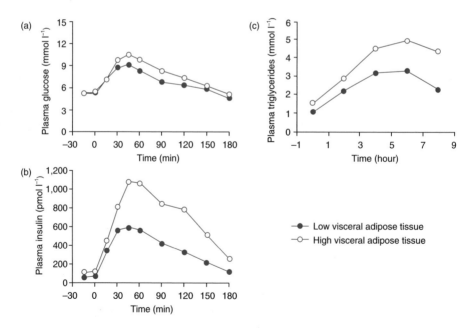

Sources: Adapted from Pouliot *et al.* (1992) and Couillard *et al.* (1998).
Note: Plasma concentrations of glucose (panel (a)) and insulin (panel (b)) after 75 g glucose tolerance test; plasma triglyceride concentration (panel (c)) after a mixed meal (64%, 18% and 18% of energy from fat, carbohydrate and protein, respectively).

an oral glucose challenge in men with low or high levels of visceral adipose tissue, with similar levels of overall obesity. Both responses were significantly higher in men with high visceral obesity, showing that this exaggerates hyperglycaemia and hyperinsulinaemia (and by inference insulin resistance).

INFLUENCE OF PHYSICAL ACTIVITY

Skeletal muscle is the body's largest insulin-sensitive tissue and the major influence on whole-body responsiveness to insulin. Conversely, insulin resistance resides largely in skeletal muscle. Insulin sensitivity is enhanced by physical activity and low levels of physical activity are related to most of its associated abnormalities. The preventive potential of physical activity may be particularly cogent for two reasons: first, these metabolic abnormalities may be present for up to 10 years before they are detected; and second, there is evidence that physical activity has favourable effects on blood pressure, lipoprotein metabolism and body fatness above and beyond those mediated through changes in insulin sensitivity (see Chapters 5 and 7). These have already been discussed individually and so consideration here is restricted to the limited evidence about physical activity and the cluster of abnormalities that comprise the insulin resistance syndrome.

Associations with level of physical activity

Several epidemiological studies have tested the hypothesis that the insulin resistance syndrome is more prevalent in people who are inactive or unfit than in their active or fit counterparts. For example, the cohort study of English civil servants known as Whitehall II found an inverse association between reported levels of physical activity and the presence of three or more features of the syndrome (Brunner *et al.* 1997). In that study men were deemed to have an abnormality if their value for any component, for example, hypertension, high fasting triglycerides, placed them in the highest risk quintile within the population of men under study. This approach is a practical solution to the problem of defining the syndrome but may limit the inference that can be made to populations in which these abnormalities may be present to a greater or lesser extent.

A different, and arguably more meaningful approach, was adopted in the US Aerobics Center Longitudinal Study. These researchers used 'clinically relevant thresholds' as the criteria for possessing four individual features of the syndrome (Whaley *et al.* 1999). For example, because a waist circumference > 100 cm has been associated with a significant increase in the risk of becoming insulin resistant or of developing CVD, this was adopted as the threshold for elevated central adiposity. Researchers then compared the risk of accumulating markers of the syndrome between people in different fitness categories. Low-fit men (lowest 20% for maximal time on a treadmill test, taking account of age) were three times as likely to accumulate these markers as those who were moderately fit and 10 times as likely to accumulate markers as those who had a high fitness level (highest 20% on the same test). Moreover, the association between fitness and the accumulation of metabolic abnormalities was graded across fitness categories suggesting that, as the number of abnormalities increased, the difference between the fitness groups widened. Similar, albeit somewhat weaker, relationships were found among women. A strength of this study was the large numbers studied (15,537 men and 3,899 women). A weakness may be that these people probably represent a fairly healthy cohort; only 5.6% of men and <0.6% of women showed three or more metabolic abnormalities and the prevalence of smoking was low.

A large study of Norwegian men and women found dose–response relationships between level of physical activity or serum lipid concentrations and BMI (Thune *et al.* 1998). Uniquely, these researchers made two sets of measurements, with an interval of seven years. Differences between sedentary and exercising groups were even more pronounced after seven years than at baseline. Moreover, *changes* in physical activity over this period were associated with *changes* in blood lipids and with *changes* in body weight in a dose-dependent manner (Table 8.2). Put another way, those with the greatest increase in their physical activity level during the 7-year interval showed the least unfavourable changes in metabolic markers. This constitutes evidence to counter the argument that an individual's propensity to be physically active may be inherited alongside a healthy metabolic profile (see discussion of confounding in Chapter 2).

Effects of increasing physical activity

Besides epidemiological studies, evidence from intervention studies shows the importance of physical activity for the metabolic abnormalities associated with the insulin resistance syndrome. These are probably influenced more by the volume of training (energy expenditure) than by its intensity.

Indirect evidence for this assertion comes from the US Runners' Study. This large cross-sectional study found strong positive relationships between distance run per week and HDL-cholesterol concentration among both male and female runners (Figure 8.4). Smaller, laboratory studies have reported findings pointing to the same conclusion. Those from Laval University in Québec are good examples. Training at 50–70% $\dot{V}O_2$max induced significant reductions in body weight, plasma insulin and LDL-cholesterol concentrations, as well as increases in HDL-cholesterol. As Figure 8.5 shows, improvements in risk factors were related to the degree of weight loss (an indicator of the increased energy expenditure) rather than to improvements in $\dot{V}O_2$max, which of course reflects training intensity (Després and Lamarche 1994). Insulin sensitivity has also been reported to improve after high-volume training at moderate intensity that does not result in increases to $\dot{V}O_2$max.

The importance of the weight loss associated with increased physical activity for improvements to metabolic markers has been demonstrated in randomized controlled trials. For example, in a landmark study, Wood *et al.* from Stanford University reported that diet-induced weight loss and exercise-induced weight loss led to similar increases in HDL-cholesterol (Wood *et al.* 1988).

Thus, when the objective is to prevent or treat the insulin resistance syndrome, the goal is a substantial increase in the energy expended through physical activity in order to induce negative energy balance. This prescription fits well with reports that blood

Table 8.2 Serum lipid concentrations and body mass index (BMI) at baseline and changes in these variables after 7 years of follow-up in 5,220 Norwegian men aged 20–49 years at entry

CHARACTERISTIC	BASELINE (MEAN ± SD)	7 YEARS LATER (MEAN ± SD)	CHANGE IN LEVEL OF LEISURE-TIME PHYSICAL ACTIVITY*					P FOR TREND
			≤−2 (n = 261)	−1 (n = 1337)	0 (n = 2681)	1 (n = 823)	≥2 (n = 118)	
Total cholesterol and *change* in total cholesterol (mmol l^{-1})	5.93 ± 1.26	6.05 ± 1.23	0.32	0.14	0.12	0.05	0.09	<0.001
Total cholesterol/HDL-cholesterol ratio and *change* in this ratio	4.36 ± 1.46	4.71 ± 1.63	0.59	0.40	0.35	0.22	0.02	<0.001
BMI and *change* in BMI (kg m^{-2})	24.2 ± 2.8	24.9 ± 2.9	1.0	0.8	0.7	0.6	0.2	<0.001

Source: Thune et al. (1998).
Note: * Leisure-time physical activity was self-reported. Changes in lipids and BMI were adjusted for potentially confounding changes, that is, age at baseline and changes in smoking, intake of 'table fat' and coffee drinking.

Figure 8.4 Concentrations of plasma HDL-cholesterol in relation to regular, self-reported running distance in runners.

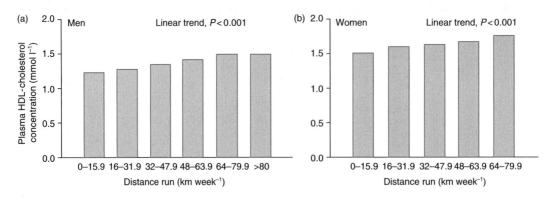

Source: Williams (1996, 1997).

Figure 8.5 Relationships between training-induced changes in the ratio of LDL-cholesterol to HDL-cholesterol and body mass (upper panel, a) and $\dot{V}O_2$max (lower panel, b).

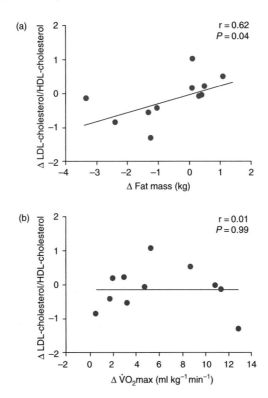

Source: Poirier *et al.* (1996).

pressure is reduced as effectively or more effectively by moderate-intensity exercise as by more vigorous exercise. Bearing in mind that vigorous exercise is in any case contraindicated in people with (or at risk of developing) the insulin resistance syndrome, low to moderate-intensity aerobic exercise of long duration may have to be undertaken on an almost daily basis to expend sufficient energy. The term 'metabolic fitness' has been coined to describe the improvements in metabolic variables derived through such training regimens (Després 1997).

EXERCISE AND POSTPRANDIAL LIPOPROTEIN METABOLISM

As explained above, many of the abnormalities of the insulin resistance syndrome can be linked to the impairment of events during the postprandial period. Plasma triglycerides are elevated, with repeated exaggerated episodes of postprandial lipaemia leading to low HDL-cholesterol and a preponderance of small, dense LDL. Obesity, particularly the abdominal type (Figure 8.3, panel (c)), is associated with high levels of postprandial lipaemia. Moreover, when triglycerides are high blood has an increased propensity to clot and there are detrimental effects on endothelial function. For all these reasons, the influence of exercise on postprandial events is a topic of considerable research interest. The most frequently used experimental model is a high-fat mixed meal. That is, the meal contains not only fat but also protein and carbohydrate so that effects mediated by changes to the associated insulin response are revealed.

Postprandial lipaemia has been reported to be lower in endurance-trained athletes than in sedentary controls. One early study found that the rise in plasma triglycerides after a high-fat meal (a Macdonald's breakfast!) was 43% lower in endurance-trained men than in untrained men (Figure 8.6). However, if training is interrupted for a few days, postprandial lipaemia increases rapidly. For example, just $2\frac{1}{2}$ days without training has been reported to lead to a 45% increase in the lipaemic response to dietary fat (Hardman *et al.* 1998). Therefore the characteristically low lipaemic response of trained people may be due, at least in part, to the fact that they have always exercised recently.

A single session of exercise decreases the plasma triglyceride response to a subsequent high-fat meal by up to a third. This is shown in Figure 8.7 that presents data from a repeated measures laboratory study in middle-aged men (Gill *et al.* 2001). On one occasion they walked briskly for 90 minutes at 60% $\dot{V}O_2$max one afternoon before eating the test meal at breakfast time the following morning; on the other they refrained from all exercise the day before the test meal (control). Prior exercise decreased postprandial triglycerides, mainly in the VLDL fraction. It also led to a lower insulin response (indirect evidence for improved sensitivity) and increased whole-body fat oxidation.

Exercise does not have to be vigorous in order to reduce postprandial lipaemia. This was clearly shown by a study in which exercise intensity was 'traded' for duration (Tsetsonis and Hardman 1996). Postprandial lipaemia was measured on three mornings, again in a repeated measures design. These were: after two days with minimal activity (control); after a 90-minute walk at 60% $\dot{V}O_2$max the previous afternoon; and after walking for twice as long at half the intensity (Figure 8.8). Prior exercise reduced postprandial lipaemia by nearly a third, irrespective of its intensity, providing further

Figure 8.6 Plasma triglyceride responses to a meal containing fat (approx. 70 g) and carbohydrate in endurance-trained and untrained men who were matched for age, height and weight.

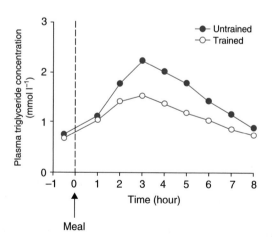

Source: Redrawn from Merrill *et al.* (1989).

Figure 8.7 Effects of a single 90-minute session of brisk walking at 60% $\dot{V}O_2$max on responses to a high-fat mixed meal in middle-aged men.

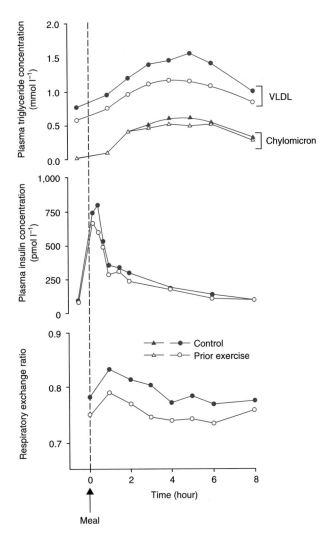

Source: Adapted from (Gill *et al.* 2001).

evidence that the total energy expended may be the most important determinant of the effects of exercise on markers of the insulin resistance syndrome.

The mechanisms by which prior exercise reduces postprandial lipaemia are incompletely understood but must involve either enhanced clearance of triglyceride or a reduced rate of entry into the circulation – or both of these. Hydrolysis by the enzyme lipoprotein lipase (LPL) is regarded as the rate-limiting step in triglyceride clearance. As indicated in Figure 8.2, this enzyme is situated on the luminal surface of the capillary endothelium and hydrolyzes lipoprotein triglycerides, liberating fatty acids that are taken up into tissues.

Figure 8.8 Influence of low and moderate intensity exercise of equivalent energy expenditure on plasma triglyceride responses to a high-fat mixed meal in young adults.

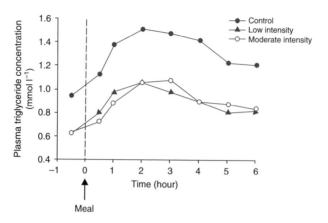

Source: Tsetsonis and Hardman (1996).

Exercise increases LPL activity in skeletal muscle but not in adipose tissue. This effect is delayed and transient, with maximal increases in LPL mRNA occurring around four hours post-exercise (Seip *et al.* 1995). This time frame is consistent with the maximal attenuation of triglyceride concentrations following exercise. Enhanced triglyceride clearance is thus one mechanism by which prior exercise reduces postprandial lipaemia.

A second mechanism may be reduced hepatic VLDL secretion. Although there is no direct evidence for this in humans, it could account for the increase in postprandial fat oxidation after exercise shown in Figure 8.7. Prior exercise might alter the hepatic partitioning of fatty acids, enhancing their oxidation so that fewer were available for synthesis and secretion as triglycerides in VLDL.

Besides their influence on lipoprotein metabolism, exercise-induced changes to LPL exert an important influence on energy balance and thus body fat levels. This enzyme is effectively a 'gate-keeper' governing the proportion of fatty acids from triglyceride-rich lipoproteins taken up into muscle or adipose tissue. The ratio of its activities in adipose tissue/muscle has been reported to increase 9-fold when endurance-trained athletes inter-rupted their training for two weeks (Simsolo *et al.* 1993). Thus, regular exercise favours oxidation of dietary fatty acids in skeletal muscle whereas inactivity favours adipose tissue storage. As fat balance largely determines energy balance (discussed in Chapter 7), this may oppose weight gain. Thus, the enhancement of LPL activity by exercise nicely illustrates its diverse but interrelated effects on features of the insulin resistance syndrome.

PREVENTION

Both a Western diet (high in fat and refined carbohydrate) and physical inactivity appear to increase the risk of developing insulin resistance and its associated abnormalities. Obesity further increases this risk and is linked to both of these through effects on energy balance. The main interventions available for prevention and/or treatment of the insulin resistance syndrome are therefore lifestyle change and drugs.

As mentioned at the beginning of this chapter, the multiple abnormalities of the insulin resistance syndrome greatly increase the risk of CVD. This makes pharmacological treatment difficult because drugs target individual pathologies and may have neutral or even negative effects on other syndrome features. For example, treatment with diuretics reduces blood pressure but also increases total cholesterol; treatment with beta-blockers reduces blood pressure but leads to a decrease in HDL-cholesterol. Thus the overall effect of drug therapy on CVD risk is not always clear. An alternative pharmacological strategy may be to treat the underlying cause of the insulin resistance syndrome, that is, to prescribe drugs that improve insulin sensitivity. There is no single drug, however, which will simultaneously treat all its abnormalities. Multiple drug regimens are available but are difficult to adhere to, particularly for older people. Finally, all drugs have side effects that have to be set against their benefits.

Physical activity, with its multiple beneficial effects on syndrome features, is an attractive preventive measure – particularly when accompanied by weight loss. Given the high prevalence of the syndrome, prevention may be the most important strategy. The most effective regimen will involve high expenditure of energy through regular exercise on most days of the week. The frequency of activity is important to maintain low plasma triglycerides and maximize blood-pressure lowering effects. Of course, increasing physical activity also involves risks (musculo-skeletal injuries, orthopaedic problems, increased risk of a cardiac event) that need to be considered alongside benefits. These risks will be discussed in Chapter 13. Physical activity may also be beneficial therapeutically but many of the individuals concerned carry excess weight and it is difficult for them to expend sufficient energy in physical activity without fatigue. Moreover, there is at least one important weakness in the rationale for physical activity in individuals who already exhibit multiple features of the insulin resistance syndrome. Experimental studies in this group are lacking – almost all the evidence referred to above is in apparently healthy people. Genetic factors predisposing to the syndrome may limit the efficacy of physical activity in modifying its abnormalities.

SUMMARY

- The insulin resistance syndrome is the name given to the clustering of risk factors for CHD. Physical inactivity, obesity and genetic make-up probably interact with dietary factors to explain its high prevalence in developed countries.
- Insulin resistance appears to be the defining feature of the syndrome.
- Associated abnormalities include: hyperinsulinaemia, high triglycerides, low HDL-cholesterol, hypertension and obesity (particularly of the abdominal type).
- Lipoprotein lipid abnormalities derive from effects of insulin resistance on postprandial lipoprotein metabolism.
- Insulin resistance resides largely in skeletal muscle. Physical (in)activity is therefore a major influence on whole-body measures of insulin resistance/sensitivity.

- Physical inactivity and low fitness are associated with increased prevalence of the insulin resistance syndrome.
- Prevention is important; by the time the insulin resistance syndrome is identified in an individual, its features have been established for a long time.
- Physical activity benefits multiple features of the syndrome. Drugs target one abnormality.

STUDY TASKS

1 Explain, with the use of a diagram, why insulin resistance leads to high triglycerides and low HDL-cholesterol. Give two reasons why is there an inverse relationship between serum or plasma concentrations of triglycerides and HDL-cholesterol, explaining these as fully as possible.

2 Turn to Table 8.2. Write a sentence summarizing the trend in change in total cholesterol by change in leisure-time physical activity between baseline and 7 years later. Suggest two reason why, even in men with the greatest increase in physical activity level, total cholesterol was higher 7 years later than at baseline. Which category would a man with the mean BMI for this group be placed in: desirable weight for height, overweight or obese?

3 What mechanism(s) might explain the effect of a single session of exercise in reducing postprandial lipaemia?

NOTES

1 This study followed the children of participants in the original Framingham Study – one of the first cohort studies conceived to gain insight into the causes of CHD.

FURTHER READING

Barnard, J.R. and Wen, S.J. (1994) 'Exercise and diet in the prevention and control of the metabolic syndrome', *Sports Medicine* 18: 218–28.

Buemann, B. and Tremblay, A. (1996) 'Effects of exercise training on abdominal obesity and related metabolic complications', *Sports Medicine* 21: 191–212.

Després, J.-P. (1997) 'Visceral obesity, insulin resistance, and dyslipidemia: contribution of endurance training to the treatment of the plurimetabolic syndrome', *Exercise and Sport Sciences Reviews* 25: 271–300.

Eriksson, J., Taimela, S. and Koivisto, V.A. (1997) 'Exercise and the metabolic syndrome', *Diabetologia* 40: 125–35.

Gill, J.M.R. and Hardman, A.E. (2003) 'Exercise and postprandial lipid metabolism: an update on potential mechanisms and interactions with high-carbohydrate diets', *Journal of Nutritional Biochemistry* 14: 122–32.

Knowledge assumed
Simple cell biology, including role
of nucleic acids
Basic anatomy and systems
physiology
Basic measures in epidemiology

9 Cancer

INTRODUCTION

Cancer has afflicted humans throughout recorded history. The origin of the word cancer has been credited to Hippocrates (460–370 BC) who used the terms 'carcinos' and 'carcinoma' to describe tumours. Cancer is not one disease but a set of diseases characterized by unregulated cell growth leading to invasion of surrounding tissues and spread to other parts of the body. It is a leading cause of morbidity and mortality, accounting for around a quarter of all deaths in countries like the US, the UK and Canada where the lifetime risk of developing cancer is more than 1 in 3. There are more than 200 different types of cancer but four – lung, breast, large bowel (colorectal) and prostate cancer – account for over half of cancer deaths in developed countries.

Cancer has multiple causes but the impact of lifestyle factors is illustrated by the enormous geographical differences in incidence worldwide. For example, Japan has an incidence of skin cancer that is 155 times lower than that in Australia (Table 9.1). These differences do not seem to be explained by genetic factors related to race, as studies of migrants have shown. When Chinese people migrate to the US or Hawaii, their incidence rates of prostate and breast cancer increase towards those in the indigenous population, while stomach cancer decreases. These changes are not seen, however, if the migrants maintain their traditional Eastern diet, pointing to a Western diet as one causative factor for these cancers. Contrary to public perception, therefore, some risk factors for cancer can be changed and some cancers prevented.

Although a role for energy balance in cancer causation was advanced almost three centuries ago, it is mainly in the last decade that population studies have linked physical activity to cancer risk. The extent, consistency, strengths and limitations of this evidence will be discussed later but first it is necessary to understand a little more about carcinogenesis (the process by which cancers are generated) and about how tumours develop.

CARCINOGENESIS

Normal body cells grow, divide and die in an orderly fashion. In humans, they are pre-programmed to reproduce up to a maximum of 50 or 60 times. If the genes of a normal cell are badly damaged, or if it becomes detached from its proper place, it will 'commit suicide' so that these faults are not passed on to daughter cells. Cancer cells do not exhibit this capability for self-destruction, called apoptosis, and so reproduce uncontrollably. Box 9.1 lists some important ways in which cancer cells differ from normal cells.

Cancer begins with one cell that loses vital control systems. Instead of dying in an orderly way, cancer cells outlive normal cells and continue to form new abnormal cells until a lump called a tumour is formed. As it grows, a tumour invades and destroys

Table 9.1 Examples of contrasting incidence rates of cancers in different countries

CANCER	HIGH	LOW	RELATIVE RISK (HIGH/LOW)
Skin	Australia	Japan	155
Prostate	US	China	70
Colon	US	India	19
Stomach	Japan	Kuwait	22
Cervix	Brazil	Israel	28
Liver	China	Canada	49

Source: Adapted from King (2000).

BOX 9.1 DIFFERENCES BETWEEN NORMAL CELLS AND CANCER CELLS

Normal cells can:	Cancer cells:
• Reproduce themselves exactly	• Carry on reproducing
• Stop reproducing at the right time	• Do not obey signals from neighbouring cells
• Stick together in the right place (cell adhesion)	• Can become detached from the primary tumour and travel to other parts of the body
• Self-destruct if they are damaged	• Do not become specialized but stay immature
• Become specialized or mature	• Do not die if they move to another part of the body

surrounding tissues. Its centre gets further and further from blood vessels in the area. By interacting with normal cells, the cancerous cells promote the development of new blood vessels thereby ensuring an adequate supply of oxygen and nutrients and promoting further growth.

One of the most troublesome characteristics of cancer cells is that they travel to other sites in the body, where they begin to grow and replace normal tissue. This process, called metastasis, occurs because cancer cells can lose the molecules on their surface that keep normal cells in the right place. Cancer cells travel in the bloodstream or lymph vessel and stop at the first place they get stuck. In the bloodstream, this is the next capillary bed they encounter – often in the lungs because venous blood from most organs goes next through these capillaries.

What initiates carcinogenesis?

Cells become cancerous because of damage to their DNA – the nucleic acid that is the basis of the genetic code. Genes tell the cell how to make many different proteins with important functions. Mutations (damage to a gene or loss of a gene) may mean that a signalling protein may be permanently switched on. Other proteins, whose job is to control and limit cell division, may be permanently switched off.

Three different types of genes are important in making a cell cancerous:

- Genes that encourage the cell to multiply. (Many cells only multiply to repair damage, for example after a wound.) If these genes, called oncogenes, become abnormal, they tell the cell to multiply all the time.
- Genes that stop the cell multiplying and act as a brake to the oncogene's accelerator. If one of these genes becomes damaged, the cell may carry on and on multiplying – it becomes immortal.
- Genes that repair other damaged genes. If these genes are damaged, other mutations are not repaired but replicated during the process of cell division and inherited by all subsequent daughter cells.

How do mutations arise?

Fortunately, it is not easy for a normal cell to turn into a cancer cell. Although DNA is continuously exposed to damaging agents from within as well as outside the body, damage to DNA is normally repaired efficiently so that mutations are not inherited by daughter cells. Mutations can happen by chance when a cell is reproducing but this often leads the cell to self-destruct. Or cells carrying a mutation may be recognized as abnormal by the immune system and killed. Thus, most pre-cancerous cells die before they can cause disease and only a few develop into a cancer. Moreover, carcinogenesis results from the accumulation of errors and it can take a long time before enough mutations happen for a cell to become cancerous. (This is why cancers are more common in older people – there has been more time to be exposed to carcinogens and more time for errors to happen when cells reproduce.)

Something that damages the genetic machinery of a cell and makes it more likely to be cancerous is called a carcinogen. People can inherit damaged DNA but fewer than 15% of all cancers are familial. Most often, a person's DNA becomes damaged by exposure to some environmental factor – chemicals, radiation or viruses. For some cancers, initiating agents have been clearly identified. These include lung cancer (tobacco smoke) and leukaemia (ionizing radiation) but it is difficult to define initiating events in cancers of the colon, prostate and breast. Natural events such as free radical generation may be the driving force for these common cancers. Once carcinogenesis has been initiated, proliferative signals could derive from exogenous factors such as diet, viral infection or hormones (contraceptive pill, hormone replacement therapy) or endogenous factors such as hormonal changes.

Cancer is therefore a multi-factorial disease. There is no single cause for any one cancer. For example, tobacco smoke contains potent carcinogens – smoking 20–30 cigarettes a day increases the risk of lung cancer 40-fold – but not everyone who smokes gets lung cancer, so other factors must be at work. Epidemiology has provided some clues about factors that influence risk (Box 9.2).

PHYSICAL ACTIVITY AND COLORECTAL CANCER

Colon cancer is the most commonly investigated cancer in relation to physical activity. The colon or large intestine forms a rectangle in the abdominal cavity that frames the tightly packed small intestine. Its main function is to store waste material until this is eliminated from the body. By contrast, the rectum, which links the colon to the anus, is empty except when the urge to defaecate is initiated. Some epidemiological studies present data describing cancers of the colon and rectum collectively (colorectal). Others report data for these two sites separately. Risk factors for colorectal cancer that are widely recognized include family history, high meat consumption, low intake of vegetables, high body mass index (BMI), smoking and alcohol consumption. The overall contribution of lifestyle factors to colorectal cancer is regarded as important. It has been estimated that 66–75% of colorectal cancer cases could be avoided by changes in lifestyle (World Cancer Research Fund 1997).

BOX 9.2 ESTABLISHED RISK FACTORS FOR SOME OF THE MAIN CANCERS

- Age – the single most important factor.
- Presence of genes that increase susceptibility. For example, genes (named BRCA1 and BRCA2) have been identified for breast cancer.
- Impaired immune function – those with problems of immune system, for example, AIDS are more likely to get some forms of cancer.
- Diet – diets high in fruit and vegetables are protective against several common cancers. Diets high in fat, meat, salt and alcohol increase the risk of some cancers.
- Agents in the day-to-day environment – for example, tobacco smoke, sun, natural and man-made radiation, work place hazards, asbestos.
- Viruses encountered – viruses can help to cause some cancers. This does not mean that cancer can be caught like an infection but that a virus can cause genetic changes in cells that make them more likely to become cancerous. Examples include hepatitis B virus (liver cancer) and human papilloma virus (cancer of cervix).

Around 50 observational studies of physical activity and colon cancer have been conducted.[1] Eighty per cent have demonstrated a large and statistically significant reduction in risk among the most physically active men and women (Friedenreich 2001). The consistency of these findings across occupational and leisure-time activity, different study designs (cohort, population-based case-control, hospital-based case-control) is all the more remarkable because methods of assessing physical activity have often been quite crude. The average risk reduction has been 40–50%, but up to 70% reductions were found in some studies. Overall, the evidence that physical activity has a preventive role in colon cancer has been assessed as 'convincing' according to criteria developed by the World Cancer Research Fund and the American Institute for Cancer Research (Friedenreich 2001).

In marked contrast to findings for colon cancer, there is general agreement across studies that there is no association between physical activity and the risk of cancer of the rectum. This probably accounts for the fact that studies combining colon and rectal cancers have tended to find weaker relationships with physical activity than those reporting findings for colon cancer alone.

The initial associations between physical activity and colon cancer were derived from observations that people involved in active occupations were less likely to develop colon cancer. These studies, published in the mid-1980s stimulated further investigations, not only of occupational activity but also of leisure time and total physical activity.

There are several indications that high levels of physical activity maintained over a long period confer the strongest protection. For example, a large case-control study assessed energy expenditure, based on reported intensity and duration of activities at home, leisure and work for (i) the referent year, (ii) 10 years ago and (iii) (for older participants) 20 years ago (Slattery *et al.* 1997). These researchers obtained data for 2,073 cases and a similar number of controls. Lack of a lifetime history of vigorous leisure-time activity (more than 4.2 MJ week^{-1} at an intensity of 23–27 kJ min^{-1}) was associated with an increased risk for colon cancer in men (odds ratio 1.63, 95% CI

1.14–2.67) and in women (odds ratio 1.59, 95% CI 1.21–2.10). Long-term activity was also evaluated prospectively in more than 17,000 Harvard alumni (Lee *et al.* 1991). (The reader will recall that this study obtained detailed information on leisure-time activity as well as on walking and stair climbing.) Those men who were highly or moderately active at several assessments had half the risk of developing colon cancer, compared with those who were not (RR 0.50, 95% CI 0.27–0.93). Physical activity assessed at any single time period did not show a protective effect.

There is some evidence for a dose–response relationship between physical activity and colon cancer risk. For example, in one cohort study from Norway, combining occupational and leisure-time activity revealed significant relationships with total physical activity among women and among men over 45 years (both *P* for trend = 0.04) (Thune and Lund 1996). Similarly, the US Nurses' Health Study (a cohort study of more than 120,000 female nurses which began in 1976) found a significant association between level of leisure-time physical activity and the risk of colon cancer (Martínez *et al.* 1997). Figure 9.1 shows that participating in 21 MET-h week^{-1} of activity was associated with a 50% reduction in colon cancer risk, compared with women in the least active group. This is equivalent to around 5 h of moderate or 3.5 h of high-intensity physical activity.

How do we know that it is actually the physical activity that is protecting people from colon cancer? The issue of confounding is an important one because physically active people tend to eat healthy diets (e.g. less red meat, more fibre) and are less prone

Figure 9.1 Relative risk of colon cancer according to level of leisure-time physical activity in the US Nurses' Health Study.

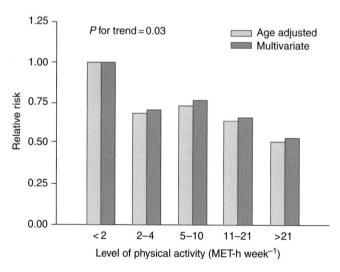

Source: Martínez *et al.* (1997).
Note: Multivariate analysis adjusted for age, cigarette smoking, family history, BMI, post-menopausal hormone use, aspirin use, intake of red meat and alcohol consumption.

to overweight than their sedentary peers. Studies that have attempted to adjust for confounding factors have found that the associations between colon cancer risk and level of physical activity were not altered materially. For example, in the Health Professionals Follow-up Study, a cohort of around 50,000 men was followed to study the role of diet in chronic diseases. Physically active men were more likely to use multivitamins than inactive men and had lower intake of saturated fat, higher intakes of fibre, lower prevalence of smoking and lower BMI (Giovannucci *et al.* 1995). After controlling for all these risk factors, as well as for aspirin use and family history, the protection associated with physical activity was reduced but not to an important degree, that is, from 56% to 47%. A later study examined the influence of 13 potentially confounding factors (age, sex, BMI, smoking, use of non-steroidal anti-inflammatory drugs, energy intake and seven dietary variables) on the association between long-term vigorous physical activity and colon cancer (Slattery and Potter 2002). There was no significant attenuation of the 40% reduction in risk for any of these factors. Thus, it can be concluded that activity is not merely a marker of a healthier lifestyle, but exerts an independent protective effect against colon cancer.

Energy balance as a whole seems to be associated with the risk of cancer. This may be illustrated from the findings of the large US case-control study referred to here (Slattery *et al.* 1997). In addition to estimating energy expenditure in physical activity, these researchers made measurements reflecting two other factors which determine energy balance, that is, BMI (a crude measure of energy storage) and energy intake. Either a high BMI or a high energy intake conferred a significant increase in the risk of colon cancer (by 94% and 74%, respectively). The most interesting finding, however, emerged when the interactions between physical activity, energy intake and BMI were examined (Table 9.2). At high levels of physical activity, the risk of colon cancer was not significantly influenced by BMI or energy intake. Among people with low levels of physical activity, two things changed: (a) BMI became a more important indicator of risk and (b) the risk associated with a high energy intake increased. (This is an example of 'effect modification', that is, the effect of one exposure differs according to the level of another.) This finding suggests that the influence of physical activity on the risk of colon cancer may be mediated through systemic metabolic effects related to energy balance. This possibility is discussed later in the section on potential mechanisms.

Table 9.2 Risk of colon cancer in people with high energy intake and high BMI

ACTIVITY STATUS	ODDS RATIO	95% CI
Low physical activity	3.35	2.09–5.35
High physical activity	1.28	0.81–2.03

Source: Slattery *et al.* (1997).
Note: Risk estimates were adjusted for confounding factors. Referent group: men who were active, consumed low levels of energy and had low BMI.

PHYSICAL ACTIVITY AND BREAST CANCER

The evidence for an association between physical activity and breast cancer, although neither as strong nor as consistent as that found for colon cancer, can also be classified as 'convincing' (Friedenreich 2001). Some two-thirds of around 40 published studies have observed a reduction in breast cancer risk among those women who were most active in their occupational and/or leisure-time activities. This risk reduction ranged from 50–70% to 20–30%, with an average of 20–40%. One or two reports exist, for example from follow-up of the Framingham Heart Study cohort, of an *increased* risk of breast cancer in women with high levels of physical activity. However, in these studies methods for assessments of physical activity had important limitations.

What type of activity and how much is associated with reduction of the risk of breast cancer? More than half the studies that measured only occupational activity and 70% of those that measured only leisure-time activity have found risk decreases in the most active women. However, all five of the studies that measured total activity (i.e. occupational, leisure time and, in one instance, household activity) found decreases in risk. This suggests that total activity – regardless of context – is what matters. (Measuring either occupational or leisure-time activity alone inevitably probably leads to misclassification and weakens associations.)

The 'dose' of physical activity required for breast cancer risk reduction can be estimated from studies that have provided sufficient detail on the activity level at which risk decreases were observed. The prospective Nurses' Health Study (Rockhill *et al.* 1999) is one of fewer than 20 such studies. Figure 9.2 shows the risk of breast cancer

Figure 9.2 Relative risk for breast cancer according to level of physical activity between 1980 and 1994 among women who were aged 30–55 in 1976.

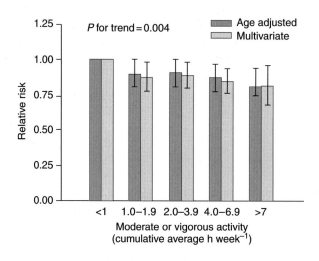

Source: Rockhill *et al.* (1999).
Note: Multivariate analyses adjusted for age and nine other potentially confounding factors.

in women who reported increasing levels of activity – measured as MET-h week^{-1}. The data are a cumulative average of reports obtained at 2-year intervals over a 14-year period and so represent long-term habits of activity/inactivity. There was a significant trend towards lower risk among more active women and women with an average of seven or more hours of moderate or vigorous activity per week had a nearly 20% lower risk of breast cancer than those in the least active group. There was no evidence that vigorous activity was more likely than moderate activity to reduce risk.

Overall assessment of the dose–response data suggests that a total of 30–60 min day^{-1} of moderate- to vigorous-intensity activity is probably needed for the reduction of breast cancer risk, that is, around 25 MET-h week^{-1} (IARC 2002). Frequency and duration of activity seem more important than intensity but this could be explained by the low prevalence of high intensity activity among the populations of women studied.

Could confounding factors explain the finding that physical activity reduces the risk of breast cancer? Besides age, important risk factors for breast cancer include: family history, variables which reflect exposure to oestrogens, high energy intake, high intake of fat and – for post-menopausal breast cancer, obesity or adult weight gain. Several of these could distort the estimated effect of physical activity – but not always in the direction of exaggerating its benefit. For example, if physically active women have a higher energy intake than inactive women this would attenuate estimates of risk reduction. On the other hand, if active women tend to consume diets particularly low in fat, which might artefactually *increase* estimates of risk reduction – a greater concern. The issue of whether or not to adjust for factors that influence exposure to oestrogens is an interesting one. For a variable to be considered a confounding factor, it must not be in the causal pathway from exposure to disease (Slattery and Potter 2002). So, if physical activity were associated with breast cancer through its ability to reduce exposure to oestrogens (see section on mechanisms in this chapter), adjustment for menstrual history or age of menarche would not be inappropriate. However, if physical activity acts through other mechanisms, these factors could be important confounding variables. Similarly, because physical activity may influence breast cancer risk through its ability to maintain appropriate body weight, it may not be appropriate to adjust for obesity. This decision is even harder because obesity is a risk factor for post-menopausal breast cancer but not for pre-menopausal breast cancer,[2] and numbers may be insufficient to justify analysing data for these two groups separately.

In practice, all the major studies of physical activity have controlled for potentially confounding factors, including obesity and those related to exposure to oestrogens. This does not materially alter the risk reduction associated with high levels of physical activity, as can be seen by comparing age-adjusted and multivariate analyses in the prospective Nurses' Health Study (Figure 9.2) or in the Canadian case-control study referred to earlier (Figure 9.3). Thus, if physical activity does act to reduce cancer risk through improved weight regulation, its benefits for post-menopausal women may be greater than the estimates of risk reduction suggest.

A few studies have attempted to measure physical activity comprehensively. One in particular deserves mention because the methodology shows the researchers' appreciation of the complexity of the relationship between physical activity and breast cancer. Friedenrich and colleagues obtained information about lifetime total physical activity (including variables of intensity, frequency and duration) from childhood until the referent year in 1233 cases and 1237 controls drawn from the general population

Figure 9.3 Odds ratios for lifetime total (occupational, leisure, household) activity of Canadian women with breast cancer, relative to controls.

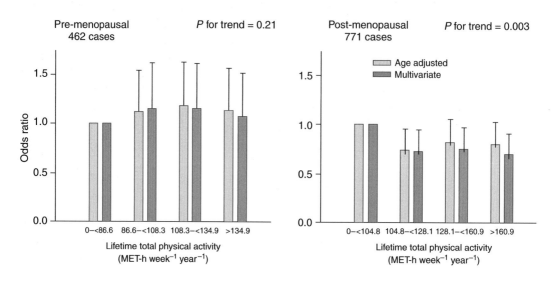

Source: Friedenerich *et al.* (2001).
Note: Left panel, pre-menopausal women; right panel, post-menopausal women. Multivariate analyses corrected for age and seven other potentially confounding factors.

(Friedenreich *et al.* 2001). The greatest risk reductions were observed for activity sustained throughout the lifetime (Figure 9.3) and for activity done between menopause and the referent year. The findings of a major cohort study, the Women's Health Study, also point to the importance of activity after the menopause; these researchers found a significant inverse trend between physical activity and breast cancer risk among post-menopausal but not pre-menopausal women (Lee *et al.* 2001a).[3] On the other hand, another large well-designed cohort study of Norwegian women found that physical activity was associated with greater risk reductions in pre-menopausal than in post-menopausal women (Thune *et al.* 1997). The inter-relationships between physical activity, breast cancer risk and menopausal status therefore remain unclear.

PHYSICAL ACTIVITY AND OTHER CANCERS

In addition to breast and colon cancer, the associations of physical activity with several other common cancers have been investigated. These include cancers of the prostate, endometrium, ovary, lung and pancreas. Of these, the most extensive body of evidence is available for prostate cancer.

The main risk factors for prostate cancer are age, race and family history – all non-modifiable. However, because rates for this cancer increase among migrants who move from areas of low incidence to areas of high incidence, lifestyle factors are also implicated. Around 20 epidemiological studies on physical activity and prostate cancer are available, all from developed countries. Again, a variety of different methods have been used to measure physical activity. Some 60% of studies suggested a reduction in risk in the most active men but only half of these reported that this reduction was statistically significant; a quarter of all studies found no association and nearly 17% found an increased risk in physically active men (Friedenreich and Thune 2001). Thus, studies are inconsistent in their findings and, if there is a reduction in risk, it is probably modest. These conclusions also hold if only the better studies are considered.[4] For example, the most recent report from the Harvard Alumni cohort found no significant associations with prostate cancer risk (Lee *et al.* 2001b). In contrast, a cohort study of >3 million Swedish men, identified from nationwide census data in 1960 and 1970, found that the relative risk for prostate cancer increased with decreasing level of occupational activity (four categories, based on job classification) (Norman *et al.* 2002). This effect was discerned despite the incomplete and crude methods for assessment of physical activity used. On the other hand, it could be exaggerated because the researchers lacked information on potentially confounding factors.

The results of around 10 epidemiological studies on endometrial cancer are consistent in suggesting a 20–40% decrease in risk for women with the highest level of activity. Most have taken into account other known risk factors, including body mass, so it is unlikely that these associations are due to confounding. Similarly, a majority of a small number of studies of lung cancer have found a significantly reduced risk of lung cancer in men with the highest activity levels and four studies found evidence for a dose–response relationship. It is therefore possible (Table 9.3) that physical activity is linked to a reduced risk of cancers of the lung and endometrium. Evidence for a role of physical activity in cancer of the ovary, testes, kidney and pancreas is insufficient to draw any conclusion.

POTENTIAL MECHANISMS

There is clearly an effect of physical activity on cancer, as shown by the summary of the extent and quality of the epidemiological evidence presented in Table 9.3. However, the studies included in this table are all observational and overwhelmingly in Caucasian populations from Europe and North America. (No reports are available from clinical trials.) Evidence for biologically plausible mechanisms which could explain these associations would strengthen the argument that physical inactivity is a causal factor in the development of cancer. Several such mechanisms have been proposed; these may be divided into systemic mechanisms that could pertain to several types of cancer and site-specific mechanisms.

Systemic mechanisms

These include modifications to circulating levels of metabolic hormones and growth factors, decreased body fat content and possibly enhanced immune function. One of the most important metabolic hormones, insulin, is clearly influenced by exercise – as discussed in Chapter 6. Insulin has a general anabolic role, stimulating net protein synthesis. For this reason, hyperinsulinaemia constitutes a growth-promoting milieu that may facilitate carcinogenesis. Elevated blood insulin concentrations have been

Table 9.3 Summary of epidemiological evidence to September 2000 on the associations between physical activity and cancer by criteria for causality

CANCER SITE	CONSISTENCY OF EVIDENCE FOR RISK REDUCTION WITH INCREASED PHYSICAL ACTIVITY	STRENGTH OF RISK ASSOCIATION		DOSE–RESPONSE	BIOLOGICAL PLAUSIBILITY	OVERALL LEVEL OF EVIDENCE
		RANGE OF RELATIVE RISK	AVERAGE RISK REDUCTION (%)			
Colon	39 of 46 studies	0.3–1.0	40–50	23 of 29 studies	Yes, several hypotheses	Convincing
Breast	24 of 36 studies	0.3–1.6	30–40	15 of 23 studies	Yes, several hypotheses	Convincing
Prostate	15 of 26 studies	0.5–2.2	10–30	9 of 19 studies	Yes, some hypotheses	Probable
Lung	6 of 8 studies	0.4–1.3	30–40	4 of 6 studies	Unclear	Possible
Endometrial	8 of 11 studies	0.1–1.0	30–40	4 of 7 studies	Yes, a few hypotheses	Possible
Testicular	3 of 8 studies	0.5–3.3	20	3 of 5 studies	Unclear	Insufficient
Ovarian	2 of 5 studies	0.3–2.1	0	2 of 3 studies	Yes, a few hypotheses	Insufficient

Source: Adapted from Friedenreich (2001).

associated with increased risk of breast cancer and individuals with colon cancer have been reported to have a higher than expected incidence of the metabolic syndrome – which is characterized by hyperinsulinaemia (Chapter 8). Exercise enhances insulin sensitivity, reduces plasma concentrations and may therefore contribute to its protective effect against cancers.

High levels of insulin-like growth factors (IGFs) and low levels of the proteins to which they are bound in the bloodstream have been associated with an increased risk of colorectal, breast, prostate and lung cancers. IGFs are peptide hormones that are synthesized in direct response to growth hormone. As their name implies, they have insulin-like actions in that they stimulate cell turnover in most body tissues. IGFs are down-regulated by increased production of their binding proteins, which can occur with physical activity. Thus, IGFs may link physical activity to decreased cancer risk.

Obesity increases the risk for post-menopausal breast cancer, endometrial cancer and colorectal cancer. Post-menopausal weight, weight gain and abdominal adiposity have all been associated with breast cancer risk. Thus, physical activity may decrease cancer risk through improved weight regulation (Chapter 7). Men and women who are physically active have only slightly higher energy intake than their sedentary peers but are leaner, suggesting that net available energy is lower in active people. This would fit with findings in animals that energy intake restriction inhibits carcinogenesis. Exercise may also prevent cancer development through a reduction in the highly metabolically active abdominal fat mass – particularly visceral fat. Rather small (<2 kg) decreases in visceral fat have important effects on insulin sensitivity, the relevance of which has already been mentioned.

The body's innate immune system has the potential to destroy tumour cells and prevent tumour growth. So, if immune surveillance is impaired, malignant cells are more likely to survive and the risk of some cancers increases. For example, patients with AIDS are at increased risk of developing lymphomas. Effects of endurance exercise on immune function have been described (Pedersen and Hoffman-Goetz 2000). The relationship with intensity and/or volume of activity appears to be 'J'-shaped, with the lowest risk among individuals who undertake regular moderate exercise (Woods et al. 1999). (Over-training and/or intense competition leads to immunosuppression.) The hypothesis is that there exists a level of physical activity that results in enhanced immune function, leading to a reduced risk for cancer. Moderate intensity exercise leads to increases in the number and/or activity of macrophages and natural killer cells. Both types of cell are involved in the first line of defence against viral infections, in early recognition of tumour cells and against tumour spread. There are, however, two weaknesses in the argument that effects on immune function contribute to a reduced risk of cancer in physically active people: first, the majority of human cancers are insensitive to control through the innate immune system; second, the evidence that immune function is enhanced above ordinary levels through moderate exercise is scant and beset with methodological problems.

Site-specific mechanisms

Cancers of the breast, prostate, testes and endometrium, are related to lifetime exposure to endogenous sex steroid hormones. For example, measures that reflect a high level of exposure to oestrogens, for example, early menarche, late menopause or an increased number of ovulatory cycles, increase a woman's risk for breast cancer. In contrast, women with irregular menses (thus reduced progesterone and oestradiol) have only half the risk of breast cancer as women with regular cycles. In men, a strong linear trend of increasing risk of prostate cancer with increasing plasma concentrations of testosterone has been observed.

Participation in exercise may therefore reduce the risk of hormone-related cancers by lowering concentrations of sex hormones. Young women who participate at a high level in vigorous sports such as gymnastics, ballet and endurance running have late menarche and exhibit a high incidence of primary and secondary amenorrhoea (Loucks 1996). Many have irregular, often anovulatory, menstrual cycles, the prevalence of which increases with the volume of training. However, the majority of the physical activity recorded in observational studies of cancer is not vigorous and less is known about the extent to which this might be associated with menstrual dysfunction. For this reason, data from two US cohorts (reported as one study) are important. In one, total physical activity and vigorous recreational activity were both positively related to cycle length. In the other, vigorous exercise during a given cycle was associated with an increase in the length of that cycle (Sternfeld *et al.* 2002). Researchers have also compared ovarian steroids in college-age women who engaged in moderate leisure-time exercise (running 20–30 km week^{-1}, plus gymnastics, tennis or dancing) and in BMI-matched sedentary controls (Broocks *et al.* 1990). The recreational athletes had substantially lower concentrations of oestrogens. These studies both support of the view that it is not only high intensity, high volume training that disrupts menstrual function.

Among post-menopausal women, exercise may decrease exposure to oestrogens by avoiding weight gain. Women in this age group continue to produce oestrogen through the peripheral conversion, mainly in fat cells, of adrenal androgens. Hence, lower levels of body fat in post-menopausal women who are physically active may lead to lower oestrogen exposure. Much less is known about the effects of exercise on sex hormones in men than in women. However, circulating levels of testosterone have been reported to be lower in endurance-trained men than in sedentary controls.

Effects of exercise on sex steroid hormones may be compounded because exercise decreases their bioavailability. These hormones are hydrophobic and so are carried in the blood bound to a plasma protein, sex hormone binding globulin. It is the free (unbound) hormone that binds to receptors within the cytoplasm of the target cell. In both sexes, physical activity is associated with an increase in sex hormone binding globulin, thereby decreasing unbound levels of oestrogens/androgens and reducing endogenous exposure to the active hormones. Moreover, triglycerides displace oestradiol from its tight binding to sex hormone binding globulin. Physically active women often have low plasma concentrations of triglycerides and this also would reduce their exposure to oestrogen.

One mechanism that might help to explain the lower incidence of colon cancer in physically active people involves bowel transit time. When individuals begin a running programme, bowel transit time may be reduced (Figure 9.4), decreasing the opportunity for carcinogens to have contact with bowel mucosa (Cordain *et al.* 1986). This would fit with findings that physical activity protects against cancer of the colon but not the rectum – which is only intermittently in contact with carcinogens in faecal matter. The evidence for an effect on colonic motility is limited, however, and mostly

Figure 9.4 Changes in bowel transit time in runners and controls.

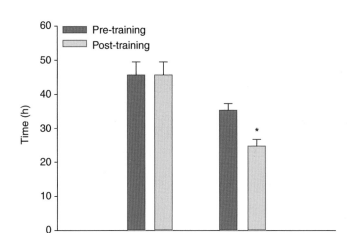

Source: Cordain *et al.* (1986).
Note: Runners trained for 6 weeks, three 30-min sessions per week. Controls remained sedentary.
* values for runners significantly different pre- versus post-training, $P < 0.05$. No between-group analysis reported.

relates to running – an activity that may have unique effects associated with repeated regular impacts. A further limitation is that, although stool bulk is a good (inverse) correlate of colorectal cancer risk, transit time is not a well-established risk factor. Another mechanism by which activity influences colon cancer risk might involve changes to prostaglandins (local signalling molecules). The level of leisure-time physical activity has been reported to be inversely related to the concentration of prostaglandin E_2 (Martínez *et al.* 1999) that increases the rate of colonic cell proliferation and decreases colonic motility.

POPULATION-ATTRIBUTABLE RISK

The proportions of breast and colon cancer that are attributable to inadequate physical activity are substantial. Population-attributable risks have been estimated for these cancers, making some assumptions about what constitutes 'inadequate'. Reported estimates are 13–14% for colon cancer and 11% for post-menopausal breast cancer (IARC 2002). These should be largely independent of body weight because most of the studies providing estimates of relative risk have adjusted for BMI. If part of the benefit of physical activity is through improved weight maintenance, these figures will underestimate the impact of inactivity.

A specific example provides an indication of the potential for cancer prevention through increasing the physical activity level in a population. Researchers took the distribution of activity in the Health Professionals Follow-up Study (Giovannucci *et al.* 1995) and modelled the effect of adding 3 h of walking to all participants. They found

that this would be expected to lead to a 17% decrease in the incidence of colon cancer (Colditz *et al.* 1997).

SUMMARY

- Cancer is a major cause of morbidity and mortality. Over half of cancer deaths are accounted for by cancers of the lung, breast, large bowel and prostate. Risk factors vary by tumour site.
- Carcinogenesis involves disruption of the orderly fashion in which normal body cells grow, divide and die.
- Increasing levels of physical activity are associated with reductions in the risk of several site-specific cancers. Evidence, predominantly in Caucasians, is strongest for cancers of the colon and breast.
- There is some evidence for dose–response relationships between level of activity and risk of colon and breast cancer but these are not well described. At least 30 min or more per day of moderate activity may be needed for optimal reduction in risk of colon cancer. For breast cancer risk reduction rather more, or more vigorous, activity may be needed.
- Potential systemic mechanisms which might influence the risk of cancer across sites include: changes to metabolic factors, in particular insulin, thus a less growth-promoting milieu; avoidance of weight gain; and improved immune surveillance.

- Hypothesized site-specific mechanisms include: for hormone-related cancers, a decrease through physical activity in lifetime exposure to sex steroid hormones; for colon cancer, a decrease in bowel transit time which would reduce exposure of the colonic mucosa to carcinogens.

STUDY TASKS

1　What are the possible explanations for the wide differences between countries in the incidence rates for specific cancers? Which seem most tenable and why?
2　How do cancer cells differ from normal cells? Explain how these characteristics lead to the development of a tumour.
3　Briefly describe the mechanisms by which high levels of physical activity may influence the risk of colon cancer.
4　Explain why a high proportion of epidemiological studies of breast cancer have used the case-control design. Give one example of such a study, describing the important features of methodology and the main findings.
5　Why does the relationship between body fatness and the risk of breast cancer differ in pre- and post-menopausal women? In addition, discuss the effect on population attributable risk for post-menopausal breast cancer of making the assumption that improved weight regulation is in the causal pathway linking physical activity to a reduction in risk.

NOTES

1　Case-control studies comprise a greater proportion of this literature (and that on other cancers), than of literature on coronary heart disease (CHD) and diabetes; the reason is that the incidence of site-specific cancers is much lower so it is difficult with a cohort study to obtain sufficient cases to give the power necessary to detect effects.
2　This is probably because adipose tissue is a much more important site of endogenous oestrogen after the menopause.
3　These two studies illustrate why so many studies in this area have used a case-control design. Lee and colleagues followed a cohort of 39,322 healthy women to obtain 411 breast cancer cases, one-third of the number studied by Friedenreich and colleagues in their case-control study, and even then had limited statistical power to detect small effects.
4　The relationship between CHD and physical activity has been shown to be strongest when only the better studies (based on quality of methodology, particularly in measuring activity) were considered.

FURTHER READING

Friedenreich, C.M. (2001) 'Physical activity and cancer prevention: from observational to intervention research', *Cancer Epidemiology, Biomarkers and Prevention* 10: 287–301.

Friedenreich, C.M., Bryant, H.E. and Coureya, K.S. (2001) 'Case-control study of lifetime physical activity and breast cancer risk', *American Journal of Epidemiology* 154: 336–47.

International Agency for Research on Cancer (2002) Handbooks of Cancer Prevention. Volume 6, *Weight control and physical activity*, Vainio, H. and Bianchini, F. (eds), Lyon: IARC Press.

Shephard, R.J. and Shek, P.N. (1998) 'Associations between physical activity and susceptibility to cancer: possible mechanisms', *Sports Medicine* 26: 293–315.

Slattery, M.L. and Potter, J.D. (2002) 'Physical activity and colon cancer: confounding or interaction?', *Medicine and Science in Sports and Exercise* 34: 913–9.

Thune, I. (2001) 'Physical activity and cancer risk: dose–response and cancer, all sites and site-specific', *Medicine and Science in Sports and Exercise* 33 (Supplement): S530–50.

WEB-BASED RESOURCES

American Cancer Society website at http://www.cancer.org/docroot/cri/content/cri_2_6x_the_history_of_cancer_72.asp?sitearea=cri

Cancer Research UK website at http://www.cancerhelp.org.uk/help/default.asp?page=85

10 Skeletal health

Knowledge assumed
Basic anatomy of the skeletal
system
Physiology of the endocrine
system
Simple biomechanics

INTRODUCTION

The skeleton enables movement for locomotion and provides physical support and
protection for internal organs. It also acts as a reservoir in the body for minerals,
particularly calcium. The structure of bone confers 'strength with lightness', so that
transporting the skeleton around is not a metabolic burden. As people age, bone

strength decreases and bones become more fragile with an increased propensity to fracture. Low muscle strength and poor balance in elderly people compound this problem by increasing the likelihood of a fall that may precipitate a fracture.

This chapter reviews the evidence concerning the role of physical activity in the maintenance of skeletal health and the prevention of osteoporosis. Knowledge of the anatomy of bone – as an organ and as a tissue – helps us to understand how different types of activity affect the load-bearing competence of the skeleton. The first section therefore describes the basic anatomy of bone and some aspects of its physiology.

BIOLOGY OF BONE

An adult has 10–12 kg of bone, a dynamic tissue with a high metabolic activity. It comprises organic material, an inorganic matrix and a small amount of water. The organic component is mainly collagen. The inorganic component is almost all hydroxyapatite, a mineral composed of calcium and phosphate. Bone is not a homogeneous tissue, however, and these components are organized in different ways in cortical and trabecular bone.

Cortical bone is dense and 'ivory-like', properties well suited to its functions of support and protection. It forms the external part of the long bones and is thickest in the shaft where it encloses a cavity filled with yellow, fatty marrow (Figure 10.1). Towards the ends of a long bone, this cavity is replaced by trabecular bone – also called cancellous or 'spongy' bone. Trabecular bone is much less dense than cortical bone and is made up of a lattice of thin calcified struts (trabeculae) that form along the lines of greatest stress. Different types of bone predominate at different skeletal sites, according to the functional requirements. For example, trabecular bone makes up 40% of vertebrae but only 1% of the mid-radius.

Lining the medullary cavity of compact bone and covering the trabeculae of spongy bone is the endosteum. In both types of bone, cells lining the endosteum are metabolically active and much involved in bone formation and resorption. Trabecular bone has a particularly high metabolic rate – its open structure allows bone marrow, blood vessels and connective tissue to be in contact with the endosteum.

Bone cells regulate bone metabolism and confer adaptive potential by responding to various environmental signals. There are three types of cells: osteoblasts, osteocytes and osteoclasts. Osteocytes are mature cells embedded within small cavities in bone. Their main role is to activate bone turnover and regulate extracellular calcium. Osteoblasts produce bone matrix and build new bone. Osteoclasts remove old bone. The activities of osteoblasts and osteoclasts are closely coupled during a process called bone remodelling. Even after growth has ended, the skeleton is in a continuous state of remodelling and between 1% and 10% of skeletal mass is remodelled each year. Remodelling takes place in cycles lasting between 3 and 5 months.

The process of remodelling is shown schematically in Figure 10.2. Osteoclasts are abundant at the surfaces of bone undergoing erosion. They secrete enzymes that create an acid environment to resorb (digest) old bone, creating a cavity. After a delay, osteoblasts fill this cavity with a volume of new bone that then undergoes remineralization. Bone resorption initiates bone formation and, under most circumstances,

Figure 10.1 Structure of a long bone.

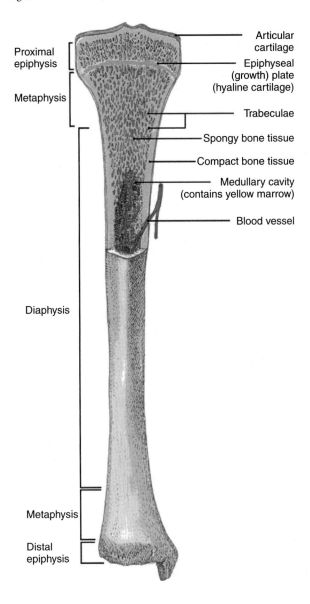

Source: Wheater *et al.* (1987).

restores lost bone. However, as age advances, less new bone is formed than is resorbed in each remodelling site, leading to bone loss and structural damage. It follows that, in older people, increased turnover enhances age-related bone loss.

The remodelling process is influenced by the hormones which regulate plasma calcium, that is, parathyroid hormone, vitamin D and, to a lesser extent, calcitonin. Parathyroid hormone acts to raise plasma calcium levels via effects on bone, gut and

Figure 10.2 Remodelling cycle in trabecular bone: (a) inactive surface, (b) resorption by osteoclasts, (c) final resorption cavity and (d) formation.

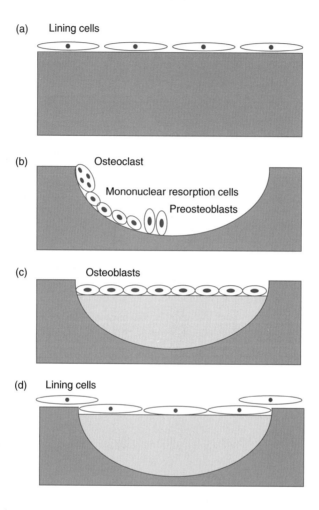

Source: Khan *et al.* (2001).

kidneys; it stimulates bone resorption, enhances calcium absorption and reduces calcium excretion. Vitamin D is converted in the skin from a precursor. The main action of its metabolites, which behave as hormones, is to stimulate the absorption of ingested calcium. It must also be concerned with calcification of the bone matrix as vitamin D deficiency gives rise to rickets in children and osteomalacia in adults. Secretion of calcitonin increases when plasma calcium is elevated. Its main effect is to inhibit the activity of osteoclasts, reducing resorption so that less calcium is released into the plasma.

Other hormones influence calcium metabolism although they are not involved in the regulation of plasma calcium. The most important of these is oestrogen. This hormone helps to conserve bone mass by limiting bone resorption and turnover. It also increases intestinal calcium absorption and reduces urinary calcium excretion, both bone-conserving effects. Oestrogen withdrawal therefore results in an increase in the intensity of remodelling, accelerating bone loss.

BONE MINERAL DENSITY

Most of the strength of bone derives from its density, the remainder from the quality of its architecture. There is no satisfactory measure of the competence of bone architecture, however, so bone density, which depends on its mineral content, is employed as a measure of bone strength. Bone density is measured by imaging techniques, most commonly dual-energy X-ray absorptiometry (DXA), quantitative ultrasound and quantitative computerized tomography (CT). The principles of these techniques, which measure different properties, are explained in Box 10.1. Bone mass measured by DXA, the technique most widely used, explains up to 90% of the variance in the breaking strength of bone. At a group level, DXA measurements are quite good at predicting fracture risk. Indeed the World Health Organization definitions of osteoporosis and osteopenia (low bone mineral density (BMD)) are based on DXA scan results. Ultrasound techniques are relatively new and so the evidence related to their potential to predict fracture risk is not extensive.

Bone mass increases during growth and reaches a peak towards the end of the second decade. Peak rates of bone accrual are about 20% greater in boys than in girls so that, from puberty onwards, bone mass is greater in men than in women. Bone mass remains fairly stable until about 50 years of age, when progressive loss begins (Figure 10.3). In women, the rate of bone loss accelerates sharply at the menopause to about 10% per decade, levelling off to about 3% per decade after age 75.

Twin and family studies show that differences in bone size, shape and BMD are largely attributable to genetic factors. However, modifiable lifestyle factors also play an important role. Inadequate intake of calcium impairs bone accrual during growth and leads to bone loss in adults. Minimal requirements for adults are probably about 400 mg day^{-1} but people in Western countries usually ingest more than this. Recommended daily intakes allow a safe margin, taking account of variation in bioavailability, that is, 800–1,300 mg for children, 700–1,000 mg for adults and 1,500 mg for post-menopausal women not taking hormone replacement therapy (lower values UK recommendations, higher values US). Physically active individuals probably consume more calcium than sedentary people because of their higher energy intake (intake of micronutrients is strongly related to energy intake). Vitamin D promotes calcium absorption but there are few dietary sources (fatty fish like herring and mackerel, eggs and fortified margarine and breakfast cereals). For most people the main source of vitamin D is from the action of sunlight but deficiency is unlikely unless people are confined indoors.

ADAPTATION TO LOAD-BEARING

Bone is deposited in relation to the load it must bear. It is this principle which makes it biologically plausible that exercise strengthens bone and attenuates bone loss; with greater loading, the load-bearing capacity of bone increases – and vice versa. The strains (deformations) produced during loading stimulate an adaptive response in bone that is

BOX 10.1 MEASURES OF THE PROPERTIES OF BONE

Dual energy X-ray absorptiometry (DXA)

DXA uses X-ray beams of two distinct energy levels to distinguish the relative composition of bone and non-bone compartments of the body. The measurements are based on the degree to which the X-ray beam is attenuated by the material of the tissues. Two measures are derived: Bone mineral content (BMC), the total grams of bone mineral within a measured region of bone; and bone mineral density* (BMD), the grams of bone mineral per unit of bone area scanned. BMC is highly dependent on bone size, thus a larger person will have a greater BMC than a smaller person. When bone strength is increased through changes in size as well as in mineral content (as might be the case for physical activity during growth) BMD alone would not detect this.

- The main limitation of DXA is that, although it measures all bone within a given area, it does not assess bone architecture nor does it differentiate between trabecular and cortical bone.
- Advantages of DXA include the low level of radiation exposure and its accuracy and precision. Scans take as little as 5 min and can measure bone at clinically relevant sites.

Quantitative ultrasound

Two ultrasound transducers (transmitter and a receiver) are positioned on each side of the tissue to be measured (usually the calcaneus). Measurements reflect the nature and extent of the distortion of a short burst of variable frequency ultrasound pulse as it passes through bone.

- Limitations include doubts about how well measurements made at the calcaneus reflect the characteristics of bone at the common sites of fracture.
- Advantages are that ultrasound measurements reflect bone architecture as well as bone mineral. They are also cheaper than DXA, can be used in the field and do not involve exposure to ionizing radiation.

Quantitative computed tomography

This technique uses X-rays to create an image of specific thin layers through the body that are built up to provide a measure of the density of bone. It measures BMC, BMD and axial cross-sectional area.

- The advantage of this technique is that it can measure type of bone present, as well as size, shape and bone mass.
- Limitations include difficulties in making measurements at the femoral neck and poorer precision, relative to DXA. This technique also involves higher exposure to radiation than DXA and is more expensive.

Biochemical markers of bone metabolism

These provide a 'snapshot' of the status of bone remodelling. Serum osteocalcin and skeletal alkaline phosphatase are markers of bone formation. Resorption is usually assessed by measuring collagen degradation products in urine. Problems associated with using these markers include high measurement error and the high normal range of biological variability within and between individuals.

* This use of the term density is not technically correct; in physics, density is defined as mass per unit volume. The quotient of BMC and area gives a two-dimensional picture and is therefore often described as an *areal density*.

Figure 10.3 Changes in bone mineral density over the life-span. Peak bone mass, attained in early adulthood, is 30–40 % higher in men than in women.

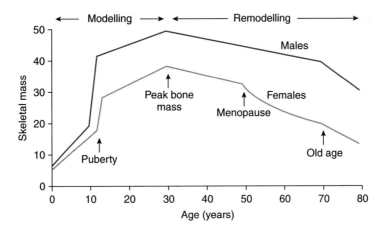

Source: Birdwood (1995).

determined by the magnitude, rate and distribution of strains as well as on the number of repetitions (strain cycles). It derives from bone cells in the region where the strains are experienced and is thus described as a 'local response to local loading'.

The general principles governing the response of bone to load bearing were established through *in vivo* experiments with the turkey ulna (Lanyon 1996) and subsequently supported by studies in other species, including humans. Disuse results in an increase in remodelling activity that is dominated by resorption and consequently loss of bone. However, exposure to even very short periods of dynamic strains within the physiological range prevents this and results in bone formation which is proportional to peak strain magnitude. Strain rate (the rate at which strain develops and releases) is another determinant of bone's adaptive response. A minimum number of strain cycles is necessary but bone's response to this aspect of loading appears to saturate quickly, suggesting that many repetitions of exposure to a given strain stimulus confer no additional advantage to that achieved by a few. An unusual strain distribution enhances the response at a given strain magnitude.

The 'mechanostat' theory holds that the structure of bone is adjusted so as to keep strain in bone within an optimal range. A minimal effective strain is necessary for bone maintenance, or else bone is lost. Thus, immobilization and space flight both lead to net bone loss. For example, during 17 weeks of strict bed rest, healthy men lost 4% of bone mineral density at the lumbar spine and femoral neck and 10% at the calcaneus (LeBlanc *et al.* 1990). No change was seen at the radius, showing that the effect is localized to those bones normally exposed to compressive loading during weight bearing. 'Normal' strains in the physiological range maintain bone remodelling and thus strength but, when loading-induced strain exceeds this range, new bone is added in response to the mechanical demand, increasing bone strength. Only when strains exceed those to which a particular skeletal site has previously been exposed, is an osteogenic response initiated – in other words, the principle of overload applies.

The mechanisms by which bone cells recognize changes in loading and initiate an osteogenic response are still being unravelled. Somehow, many cells behave in a coordinated fashion to achieve the modelling and remodelling necessary to adjust bone strength to the loads it must bear. It appears that a mechanical force generates shear stresses in bone extracellular fluid that stimulate a response from osteocytes and bone-lining cells. Biochemical compounds called second messengers then result in the differentiation of osteoblasts from progenitor cells, leading to increased bone-forming activity.

OSTEOPOROSIS: DEFINITION, CONSEQUENCES AND PREVALENCE

Osteoporosis (literally meaning 'porous bones') is a skeletal disorder that reduces bone strength, predisposing to an increased risk of fracture. Bones fracture easily, often during activities of daily living. Both the mineral density and the architecture of bone are compromised (Figure 10.4) but diagnosis relies on measurements of BMD at the hip as a proxy measure of bone strength. The public health issue is primary osteoporosis, that is, that which often follows menopause in women[1] and occurs later in life in men. A typical woman loses about 15% of her bone mass in the first decade after menopause and some women lose as much as 30% by age 70.

Osteoporotic fractures are one of the most common causes of disability and loss of independence and quality of life. They are also a major contributor to medical care costs in many regions of the world. For example, in the US such fractures probably cost around $20 billion per year. In Switzerland, they account for more hospital bed days than heart attack and stroke combined. Moreover, the social burden associated with osteoporotic fractures will increase, especially in industrialized countries, as the population ages (see Chapter 1).

Osteoporotic fractures

Almost all types of fracture are increased in patients with low BMD but the most vulnerable skeletal sites are those where trabecular bone predominates. Its greater

Figure 10.4 Osteoporosis changes in lumbar vertebrae. The strong vertebral bodies of early adult life (a) lose much of their structure and become prone to crush fractures (b).

(a)

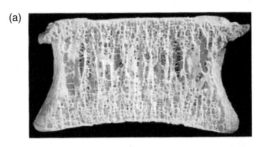

(b)

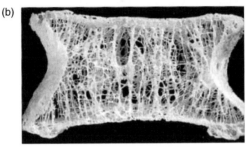

Source: Birdwood (1995).

metabolic rate means that it responds more quickly than cortical bone to changes in environmental influences, internal or external. Loss of circulating oestrogen, and its bone-conserving effects, around the menopause is the most important cause of bone loss in women. Box 10.2 shows risk factors for osteoporosis.

The most common osteoporotic fractures are of the proximal femur (hip), vertebrae (spine) and distal end of radius and ulna (wrist). Bone loss is not the only factor involved. Hip fractures result from an age-related increase in falls as well as from an age-related increase in bone fragility: 90% occur with a simple fall from a standing height or less. The incidence of hip fractures rises exponentially with age. Since women have lower BMD than men, live longer, experience more bone loss and have more falls, more than three-quarters of these disabling fractures occur in women. Half the patients who fracture their hip cannot walk independently afterwards and one third are discharged to a nursing home. Seventeen per cent of 50-year-old white women and 6% of white men of this age will have a hip fracture during their lifetime. (The risk for black people is much lower.)

Vertebral crush fractures result in loss of weight-bearing competence of the vertebral bodies. They also occur more often in women than in men. Most are precipitated by routine everyday activities. The associated loss of height can be considerable and gives rise to secondary problems because abdominal and thoracic organs are compressed, leading to chronic, disabling pain and deformity.

In perimenopausal women, the wrist is the most common site of fracture. Wrist fractures are usually associated with a fall, typically outdoors and often in icy weather.

BOX 10.2 RISK FACTORS FOR OSTEOPOROSIS

RISKS FOR LOW BMD	RISKS FOR FRACTURES
Female sex	History of falls
Increased age	Slow walking speed
Oestrogen deficiency	Low level of physical activity
White race	Low quadriceps strength
Low body weight	Impaired vision
History of fracture as adult	Environmental hazards in the home (e.g. rugs)
History of fracture in parent	Tall stature
Smoking	
Eating disorder	
Early menopause	
High caffeine intake	
Alcohol abuse	

Few patients are completely disabled by a wrist fracture, but fewer than half experience a satisfactory return to function.

Treatments for osteoporosis

Treatment focusses on agents that reduce bone loss. Calcium supplementation in the later post-menopausal years is associated with maintenance, but not gain, of skeletal mass and a decrease in the risk of hip fracture (24% reduction with 1,000 mg day^{-1}). Deficiency of vitamin D is not uncommon among the frail elderly living in institutions, probably because of poor exposure to sunlight. Physiological doses are used to correct subclinical deficiency, but not as a pharmacological treatment.

Drugs that are effective in decreasing fracture risk include bisphosphonates (potent inhibitors of bone turnover) and oestrogen in hormone replacement therapy. Selective oestrogen-receptor modulators block the effect of oestrogen on breast and uterine tissue and are designed to provide the benefits of oestrogen without the increased risk of breast and/or uterine cancer reported in some prospective studies. Finally, calcitonin may be effective because it reduces bone resorption by inhibiting osteoclastic activity.

PHYSICAL ACTIVITY AND RISK OF HIP FRACTURE

In one excellent prospective study, risk factors for hip fractures were assessed in nearly 10,000 white American women aged 65 or more over four years (Cummings *et al.* 1995). A woman whose mother had a hip fracture was at least twice as likely to have a fracture herself as a woman without such a history, indicating that there is a strong genetic component to fracture risk. Inactivity was one of a number of other risk factors. Specifically, women who were on their feet for less than 4 h day^{-1} had twice the risk of women who were on their feet for longer. Women who regularly walked for exercise had a 30% lower risk of fracture than women who did not walk regularly. Of course, exercise may be a marker for health and functional status, confounding these findings. However, these associations remained even when the data were adjusted for self-rated health and for tests of neuromuscular function. The benefit from walking might seem surprising, as this is a low impact activity. However, it was independent of bone density and so might derive from effects of walking on bone architecture and/or the risk of falling. In a smaller cross-sectional study of women in England, walking a mile frequently at a brisk or fast pace was associated with BMD at the proximal femur (Coupland *et al.* 1999).

Hip fracture is one health outcome where weight gain is advantageous. In the American prospective study referred to above (Cummings *et al.* 1995), the more weight a woman had gained since age 25, the lower her risk of hip fracture. This may be because soft tissue covering the hip may influence energy absorption during a fall. It might also be because individuals carrying more weight tend to have stronger bones.

BMD AND PHYSICAL ACTIVITY

Two main factors determine whether or not someone develops osteoporosis. These are the peak bone mass and the rate of subsequent bone loss. Physical activity has the potential to influence both factors because it subjects the skeleton to increased ground reaction forces and to forces produced by muscles. What is the evidence?

Physical activity and bone gain during growth

Studies in animals consistently show that growing bone has a substantially greater capacity to add new bone than does mature bone. Therefore, assuming that physical activity enhances bone gain during growth in humans as it does in animals, childhood and adolescence may represent a 'window of opportunity' for interventions aimed at reducing the risk of osteoporosis in later life. The extent of this opportunity is under-lined by the fact that children gain as much bone in the 2 years around the pubertal growth spurt as they will lose after their adult peak has been reached.

Cross-sectional studies have reported findings that suggest an effect on BMD of physical activity in childhood. In a study of Finnish girls and women, physical activity was the only non-growth-related factor associated with BMC and BMD (Uusi-Rasi *et al.* 1997). Females who exercised regularly in a club at a competitive level had 5% higher and 6.5% higher BMD at the femoral neck and lumbar spine, respectively, than females who did no exercise other than school physical education.

Studies of tennis and squash players are particularly instructive because these individuals have a history of unilateral bone loading. For example, researchers from the UKK Institute in Tampere, Finland studied 91 tennis players aged between 7 and 17 years and maturity-matched[2] controls who did not play tennis. BMD was measured at skeletal sites in the upper limb that are loaded during tennis and, for comparison, at the distal radius – a site *not* loaded in this activity (Haapasalo *et al.* 1998). Among players who were pre-pubertal, differences in BMD between the playing and non-playing arm were similar at all arm sites in players and controls. However, players who were at or beyond the adolescent growth spurt (average age 12.6 years) had much greater side-to-side differences in BMD than controls. Side-to-side differences in BMD at the radius were similar in players and controls. Two conclusions may be drawn from this study: first, the effect of loading through physical activity on the skeleton is site-specific (in line with principles described earlier); second, before puberty, bone's responsiveness to loading is poor.

Several cohort studies have examined determinants of BMC and BMD during growth and included measures of physical activity. The most comprehensive is probably the Amsterdam Growth and Health Study in which 84 males and 98 females were followed from age 13 until age 28. Anthropometric characteristics and lifestyle factors were measured six times during the follow-up period. When the subjects were 27 years old, researchers measured BMD at the lumbar spine using DXA and then used multiple regression techniques to find which variables best predicted this (Welten *et al.* 1994). An important methodological point is that care was taken to distinguish weight-bearing activity from other activity. In men, the best predictors of BMD at age 27 were weight-bearing activity during the 15-year follow-up period and body weight. In women, only body weight was a significant predictor.

These findings are broadly in line with those of the Cardiovascular Risk in Young Finns Study (Välimäki *et al.* 1994). Physical activity was measured more crudely than in the Amsterdam Growth Study but data were obtained for the femoral neck as well as for the lumbar spine. The Finnish study found that exercise, measured over the previous 10 years, was the most important determinant of BMD in 264 adults at age 20–29. It contributed significantly to BMD at the femoral neck in both sexes and at the lumbar spine in men. Thus, as in the Amsterdam Growth Study, the influence of exercise during youth stood out more strongly in men than in women.

Only a few controlled exercise intervention studies with change in bone mineral as the main outcome measure have been undertaken in children. Two 8-month studies of prepubertal children (one randomized by school, the other randomized within one school) found significantly (1.2–5.6%) more bone mineral gain in the intervention group than in controls. Both interventions were intense, however, demanding 75% and 150% more weight-bearing activity than controls, beyond that which is typically provided in physical education classes. Three studies have compared the response of bone to an exercise intervention in distinct maturational groups: taken together, their findings suggest that bone mass and structure are particularly responsive during the earliest onset of puberty in girls, that is, on average, around 10–12 years.

Thus, studies in children show that growing bones respond to changes in the mechanical loading environment. It is not possible to define an optimal period for this osteogenic response but there is some evidence that this could be pre-/early puberty. Long-term exercise-induced increases to growth hormone, a major influence on bone mineral change and growth during these years, could be one mechanism by which skeletal loading through exercise interacts with maturational status but this suggestion is speculative.

Physical activity and bone in pre-menopausal women and in men

Cross-sectional studies have consistently reported that pre-menopausal women athletes have higher bone mineral than controls (Snow-Harter and Marcus 1991, Drinkwater 1994). They have illustrated the specificity of the osteogenic effect by comparing BMD at different skeletal sites in groups of athletes whose training regimens produce different types of skeletal loading. In one such study, BMD was measured using DXA in competitive athletes all of whom had trained sport-specifically for at least 3 years and for ≥ 300 h year^{-1} (Heinonen *et al*. 1995). Values for the athletes were compared with two non-athletic reference groups, sedentary women and a physically active reference group (≥ 3 or more recreational exercise sessions per week). Figure 10.5 shows BMD (adjusted for differences in body weight) at six skeletal sites, presented as a percentage of the values for the sedentary reference group. Across all measured sites, athletes whose training caused high strain and/or high strain rates (squash players and weight lifters) had the highest BMD. The BMD values for cyclists (the only non-weight-bearing sport) and the physically active reference group did not differ from sedentary controls. A study of women Australian Masters athletes (average age 46) confirmed that it is weight-bearing exercise that is important by showing that swimmers, despite having a training history of more than 20 years, had values for BMD that did not differ significantly from those of non-sporting controls (Dook *et al*. 1997).

Studies comparing athletes with non-athletes have limited usefulness, however, because they cannot control for bias and confounding. Self-selection bias is inevitable (people with strong bones may tend to take up sport). Potential confounding factors include differences in lifestyle (healthy nutrition and avoidance of smoking in athletes) or physical activity history during childhood and adolescence. Better designs are (1) side-to-side comparisons in racket games players or (2) intervention studies where changes in exercisers can be compared with changes in controls.

An example of the former is the Finnish study by Kannus and colleagues. These researchers reported side-to-side differences in BMC in the humerus of 105 nationally ranked women tennis players and 50 healthy controls. Among players who started training for tennis as adults, side-to-side differences in BMD were about 5% higher than in controls (Figure 10.6). Thus, exercise can augment the mature skeleton (as well as the growing skeleton) in a site-specific manner. Kannus and colleagues also examined the influence of biological age at which playing was started on side-to-side differences, using recall of age at menarche as their marker. These were around twice (17–24%) as great among women who started playing before menarche than those who started after menarche (8–14%) (Figure 10.6). This finding appears to conflict with that of Haapasalo (mentioned earlier) who found indirect evidence that, before puberty, bone's responsiveness to loading is poor. Comparison is problematic, however, because of different methodologies (Haapasalo defined biological age using specific maturity stages). Both studies showed, albeit through cross-sectional data, that exercise exerts a potent effect on bone during the pubescent years.

Controlled intervention trials of bone-loading in pre-menopausal women in their twenties and thirties have found small (1–3%) benefits in BMD, compared with controls. In some, the benefit was a gain in BMD but in others it was a reduction of the loss seen in controls. Interventions reported have included jogging, strength

Figure 10.5 Differences in BMD in young adult women athletes and in a physically active referent group, compared with values in a sedentary control group.

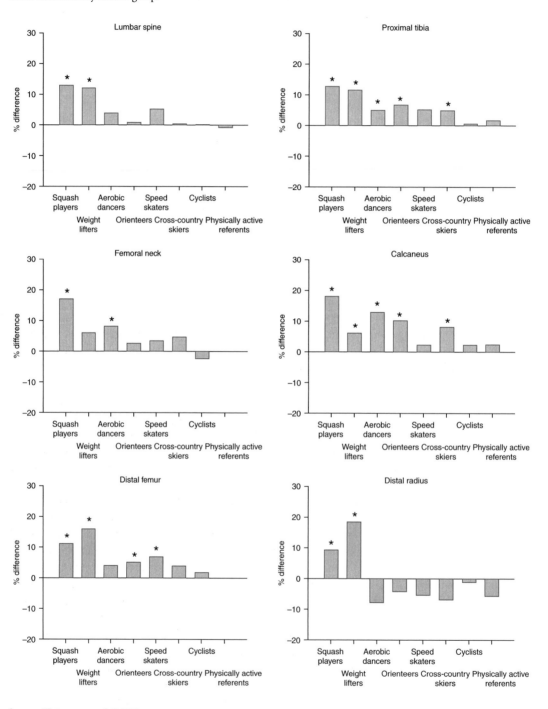

Source: Heinonen *et al.* (1995).
Note: Sports were selected because they load different skeletal sites. Data are mean percentage difference.
* Significantly different from sedentary control group.

Figure 10.6 Side-to-side differences in BMC of the humeral shaft in nationally ranked (a) female and (b) male players of racket games. Data are; females – mean and 95% CI, males – mean and standard deviation.

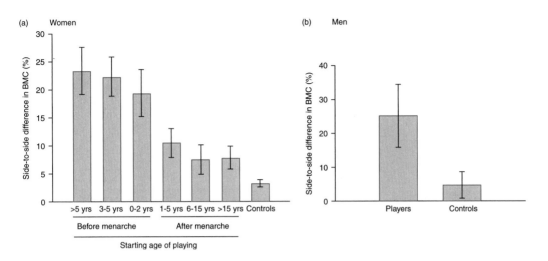

Source: Kannus *et al.* (1995) and Kontulainen *et al.* (1999).

training, weight lifting, aerobics and high-impact jumping activities. The main findings from one large, well-designed study are shown in Figure 10.7 (Heinonen *et al.* 1996). Sedentary women aged between 35 and 45 were randomly assigned to either a training group or a control group. Women in the training group did progressive high-impact exercises (jumping and step exercises) 3 times per week for 18 months. BMD was measured using DXA, with careful attention to precision and accuracy, both of which can be difficult to achieve over a long observation period. At the skeletal sites loaded by the exercise regimen, BMD increased more in exercisers than in the controls. For example, a mean increase of 1.6% (95% confidence interval 0.8–2.4) was seen at the femoral neck.

Studies that found a positive effect of exercise on bone have varied considerably in the duration of the intervention and subjects' ages. The common feature of these studies seems to be the nature of the intervention, that is, exercises were specifically selected for their bone-loading potential. Several used jumping exercises, which can create ground reaction forces up to 6 times body weight. By contrast, a low-impact intervention study that resulted in an increased muscle mass, even though it lasted for 3 years, did not alter BMD (Sinaki *et al.* 1996). Effective bone-loading exercise does not need to be strenuous in the sense that it is associated with a high oxygen uptake, but should involve exposure of skeletal sites to high and, ideally, unusual strains. For example, a study where pre-menopausal women gained 3% BMD at the hip required women to perform only very small jumps, about 50 per day (Bassey and Ramsdale 1994).

Far fewer studies have been conducted in men than in women (because their risk of osteoporosis is lower) but their findings are broadly similar (Khan *et al.* 2001). Cross-sectional comparisons of athletes and controls have found significantly higher BMD in athletes at skeletal sites loaded in their sports. Side-to-side differences in the BMC of

Figure 10.7 Percentage change over 18 months in BMD at different skeletal sites in sedentary women aged 35–45.

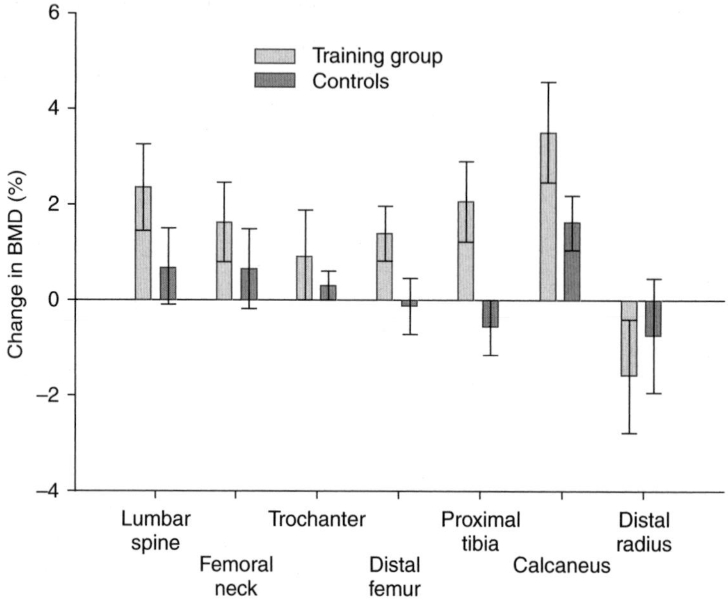

Source: Heinonen *et al.* (1996).
Note: Women in the training group (*n* = 39) did progressive, high-impact exercises 3 times per week. Controls (*n* = 45) were asked to maintain pre-trial levels of physical activity. Data are mean and 95% CI.

the arm bones have been reported to be 13–25%, depending on the site measured, compared with differences in controls of only 1–5% (Kontulainen *et al.* 1999). These data are presented in Figure 10.5 alongside the data already referred to for women. Several of the small number of controlled intervention studies in men have found small (2–3%) but significant gains in BMD.

Physical activity and BMD in post-menopausal women

Can healthy older women augment or maintain their bone mineral by increasing their physical activity and thus reduce their risk of fracture? Many prospective, controlled trials have addressed this question. The topic is complex, however, because of potential interactions with hormone replacement therapy (oestrogen may facilitate the osteogenic effect of physical activity) and because bone loading is a site-specific effect and a variety of exercise interventions have been used.

Many studies have examined the effect of exercise regimens based on strength training or high-impact loading. Two well-designed studies are cited here as examples. In a year-long randomized intervention trial, Nelson and colleagues studied post-menopausal white women aged between 50 and 70 (Nelson *et al.* 1994). None was taking hormone replacement therapy. Exercising women did high-intensity strength training for 45 min, 2 days per week. The major muscle groups attached to the bones of the lumbar spine and the hip were trained with exercises at 80% of one repetition maximum, using the principle of progressive overload. Compared with controls, the women who trained gained strength as well as total body BMC and BMD at the lumbar spine and femoral neck. The benefit of training, that is, relative to controls who lost bone, for BMD was 2.8% and 3.4%, respectively.

Using a randomized, controlled design, researchers compared the effects of high-impact activities (jogging, running, stair-climbing) or strength training on BMD in previously sedentary post-menopausal women (Kohrt *et al.* 1997). The women who trained did so for 45 min, 3 or 4 times a week for 11 months and calcium supplementation ensured that all women ingested 1,500 mg day^{-1}. Both exercise programmes achieved a 1–2% increase in BMD at the lumbar spine but only the impact-loading programme augmented BMD at the femoral neck (Figure 10.8).

Combining the findings of a number of studies, two meta-analyses have concluded that exercise regimens 'prevented or reversed' around 1–3% of bone loss per year at both the lumbar spine and femoral neck in post-menopausal women (Kelley 1998, Wolff *et al.* 1999). 'Prevented' in this context means that in a number of studies a *decrease* in BMD in controls contributed to the benefit of exercise, assessed as the difference in response over time between exercisers and controls. However, another meta-analysis concluded that, overall, physical activity had no statistically significant effect on BMD at any site (Bérard *et al.* 1997). They did, however, note a 'significant effect of physical

Figure 10.8 Comparison of the effects of impact loading and resistance training on BMD in post-menopausal women.

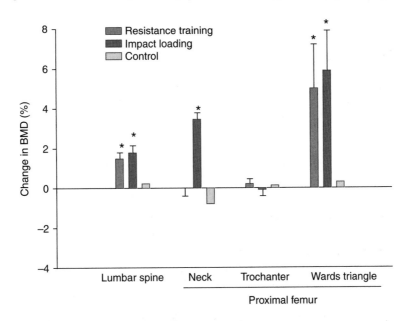

Source: Kohrt *et al.* (1997).
Note: Percentage change at the lumbar spine and at three different sites at the hip. Ward's triangle is a defined area of the proximal femur. Bars are SE. Different from change in control group, * $P > 0.05$, * $P > 0.01$.

activity on BMD at the lumbar spine in studies published after 1991'. One could argue that more importance should be attached to later studies because researchers have increasingly recognized that exercise intervention has to load the skeletal sites of interest. (Some early studies neglected this important principle and measured BMD at, for example, the radius when the exercise regimen employed loaded the lower limbs.)

Thus, exercise intervention in older women can maintain bone mineral or attenuate the rate of loss, but does not serve to add substantial amounts of new bone. An interesting methodological point is that the effects of exercise reported for non-randomized controlled trials have been almost twice as high as those for randomized controlled trials (Wolff *et al.* 1999), giving an indication of the importance of confounding introduced by non-random allocation of subjects to groups. Whether bone-loading exercise increases bone formation or decreases resorption (or both) is unclear. It is known, however, that oestrogen acts mainly by reducing resorption. Therefore, data showing that adding exercise to hormone replacement therapy enhances bone gain suggests that these two influences may act through different mechanisms.

PHYSICAL ACTIVITY AND RISK OF FALLS

Falls are an important cause of fractures, particularly fractures at the hip and radius. They result in disability, immobility, loss of independence and often death. Regular exercise can improve muscle strength and balance and so may decrease the risk of falling. The skeletal muscles that maintain body posture function almost continuously, making tiny adjustments, largely unconsciously, to maintain a stable upright posture. This motor activity is regulated by sensory feedback from several sources, that is, the eyes, the vestibular system and proprioceptors. As people age, all these systems deteriorate and the propensity to fall is increased. Age-related decreases in muscle mass (and therefore strength) (see Chapter 11) exacerbate the problem.

Regular exercise can modify several intrinsic risk factors for falls, that is, poor levels of muscle strength, range of motion, balance, gait and reaction time. Systematic review of randomized, controlled intervention studies, which aimed to improve some or all of these found that four demonstrated a significant reduction in falls, four showed a numerical but not statistically significant reduction and three (the oldest studies) found no benefit from the exercise intervention (Carter *et al.* 2001). One large study of 1,090 people over 70, living at home in Australia, used a factorial design to examine the potential of three different interventions to reduce falls (Day *et al.* 2002). Researchers looked at interventions designed to improve (1) strength and balance through exercises, (2) home hazard management and (3) vision, singly and or all combinations, allocating subjects randomly to 1 of 8 equal-sized groups (one was control, no intervention). Exercise, either alone or in combination with other interventions, conferred a significant decrease in the risk of a fall. The exercise regimen adopted by the subjects was modest, 1 h week^{-1} of supervised exercises for 15 weeks supplemented by twice weekly home exercises for the remainder of the 18-month trial. Based on this study and the pooled results of earlier studies, it is improved balance – rather than improved endurance, flexibility or strength) – which reduces the risk of falls. This is a relatively new research area, however, and the optimal exercise prescription to prevent falls has not yet been defined.

PREVENTIVE POSSIBILITIES

For osteoporosis, prevention is better than cure. Pharmacological therapy in patients with established disease cannot restore lost bone. To decrease her lifelong risk of fracture, a woman must maximize peak bone mass, maintain this through middle age and attenuate the rate of loss of bone after the menopause. In the later decades of life, she must try to decrease the risk of falls.

A life-long habit of weight-bearing exercise is clearly important. Its effects are particularly potent during growth, when gains in BMD of 5–10% are possible. For optimal effect, mechanical loading should expose multiple skeletal sites to high and varied strains through high impact and/or heavy resistance exercises. Whether bone gain during growth can be maintained during adulthood if the level of activity declines is not clear. One study has reported that BMC returns to pre-training levels when training stops (Dalsky *et al*. 1988), emphasizing the reversibility of the benefits. Rapid loss of all exercise benefits is not, however, inevitable. For example, one 5-year prospective study found that at least part of the increase in BMD associated with exercise during adolescence persisted despite decreased sporting activity (Kontulainen *et al*. 2001).

In adults, the potential for exercise to influence bone is smaller than during growth. Based on intervention studies, the benefit of exercise for BMD is around 1% in both pre- and post-menopausal women. How important, clinically, is this? Estimates suggest that an increase in BMD of this magnitude could, if maintained, result in a 10%

decrease in fracture risk (Eastell and Lambert 2002). This is clearly worthwhile but the overall benefit may be even greater if exercises to improve balance reduce the risk of falls. In practice, two issues limit the implementation of targeted bone-loading exercises as a strategy to reduce fracture risk, particularly in older women. These are (1) poor compliance with high-impact exercises and (2) the associated risk of injury. For these reasons researchers have examined the potential of aerobic exercise to limit age-related bone loss. For example, in one randomly controlled trial women aged 52–53 followed a programme of walking, stair climbing, cycling and jogging (55–75% $\dot{V}O_2$max), 3–4 times per week for 18 months (Heinonen *et al.* 1998). These aerobic exercisers avoided the loss of BMD at the femoral neck that was seen in the control group.

Even brisk or fast walking, an acceptable form of exercise for older women, may be a sufficient osteogenic stimulus for the lower limb skeleton: it alters the loading direction and rate because of the shorter heel strike; and it leads to higher ground and hip reaction forces. Although walking has consistently been associated with a lower risk of osteoporotic fracture in surveys, longitudinal studies of its influence on BMD in post-menopausal women have yielded conflicting findings.

SUMMARY

- Bone is a dynamic tissue that responds to changes in the internal or external environment. Functional loading is the most important influence on bone remodelling.
- Strain rate and an unusual strain distribution are important determinants of the site-specific effects of mechanical loading on osteogenesis.
- Bone mass increases during growth and reaches a peak towards the end of the second decade. It then remains fairly stable until about 50 years, when progressive loss begins. Age-related loss of bone can lead to osteoporosis, which compromises bone strength and leads to increased risk of fracture.
- Strong evidence suggests that weight-bearing physical activity plays a key role in the normal growth and development of a healthy skeleton.
- The potential of exercise to augment bone mineral in the mature skeleton is small. In pre menopausal women its effect is mainly conservation, although specific bone-loading exercise can lead to modest bone accrual. In older women its effect is to reduce the rate of bone loss.
- Women with a physically active lifestyle, including walking for exercise, have a lower risk of osteoporotic fracture.
- Many fractures are caused by falls and exercise can decrease the risk of falls through improving balance, strength and maybe neuromuscular coordination.

STUDY TASKS

1 Describe the general principles that govern the effect of exercise on BMD.
2 Identify the common sites of osteoporotic fracture and suggest specific exercises that might be expected to elicit an osteogenic response at each of these sites.

3 Explain why the age-related rise in hip fractures occurs 5–10 years later in men than in women. How might exercise alter the risk of this fracture even if it does not increase BMD?

4 Explain as fully as possible why studies of athletes who play racquet games are so informative in the context of the influence of exercise on BMD.

NOTES

1 Secondary osteoporosis is a result of medical conditions, diseases or medications.
2 This is a strong design feature; for growth-related outcomes, like BMD, it is preferable (but more difficult) to match groups of children by maturity rather than chronological age.

FURTHER READING

Bailey, D.A., Faulkner, R.A. and McKay, H.A. (1996) 'Growth, physical activity and bone mineral acquisition', *Exercise and Sport Science Reviews* 24: 233–66.

Drinkwater, B.L. (1994) '1994 C.H. McCloy Research Lecture: does physical activity play a role in preventing osteoporosis?', *Research Quarterly for Exercise and Sport* 65: 197–206.

Khan, K., McKay, H., Kannus, P., Bailey, D., Wark, J. and Bennell, K. (2001) *Physical Activity and Bone Health,* Champaign, IL: Human Kinetics.

MacKelvie, K.J., Khan, K.M. and McKay, H.A. (2002) 'Is there a critical period for bone respons to weight-bearing exercise in children and adolescents? A systematic review', *British Journal of Sports Medicine* 36: 250–7.

Snow-Harter, C. and Marcus, R. (1991) 'Exercise, bone mineral density, and osteoporosis', *Exercise and Sport Science Reviews* 19: 351–88.

Part III
Ageing, Therapeutic Exercise and Public Health

Knowledge assumed
Basic exercise physiology

11 Exercise and ageing

INTRODUCTION

Chapter 1 highlighted that an improvement in life expectancy is leading to an increase in the total number of older people worldwide. This trend is expected to continue into the foreseeable future and brings challenges for society. As described in several earlier chapters, the prevalence of many diseases (e.g. cancer, heart disease, diabetes, osteoporosis) and disease risk factors (e.g. hypercholesterolaemia, hypertension, obesity) increases with age. Thus, although people are living longer, many are burdened with disease or disability in the latter stages of their lives. Moreover, lifestyle and the ability to live independently may be impaired even in individuals free from disease due to a reduction in functional capacities (e.g. strength, endurance, flexibility) which limits their ability to perform everyday activities such as climbing a flight of stairs or crossing a street in the time allotted at pedestrian crossings. In this chapter we will examine how ageing leads to a decline in functional capacities in humans and the extent to which this can be offset by frequent exercise. We will also examine evidence that remaining active into old age enhances the capacity for independent living.

DECLINE IN FUNCTIONAL CAPACITIES WITH AGEING

Sports performance

The effect of ageing on our ability to exercise is clearly demonstrated by examining the UK age group records for the marathon (Figure 11.1). Beyond age 40, marathon run time increases gradually in men and women until age 70. This increase is equivalent to approximately 1% per year in men and 2% per year in women between the ages of 40 and 70. Beyond age 70 the decline in performance is more dramatic. A similar trend is evident when examining the UK age group records for 100 m (Figure 11.2). Once again the decline is greater in women than men with some evidence of an exponential deterioration in performance beyond age 70. These observations are consistent with findings from the US Masters Swimming Championships, which also document a dramatic decline in performance beyond age 70 in both men and women (Tanaka and Seals 1997). The above examples are based on the few individuals who maintain heavy training/competition, indicating an affect of age *per se* rather than physical inactivity. Age-related declines in sporting performance are due to declines in various aspects of physiological function and these will be examined in the following sections, beginning with maximum oxygen uptake.

Maximum oxygen uptake

Many studies have documented a decline in $\dot{V}O_2$max in ageing humans and this is the main physiological factor underlying the decrease in endurance performance with age. The approximate rate of decline in $\dot{V}O_2$max is 1% per year or 10% per decade from

Figure 11.1 The UK records for the marathon according to sex and age group as on 8 March 2003.

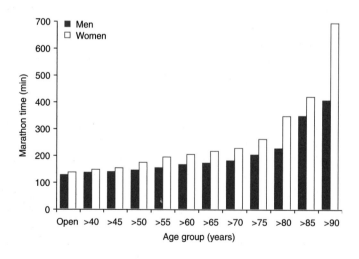

Source: United Kingdom Track and Field All-Time lists. Available at: http://www.gbrathletics.com/uk.

Figure 11.2 The UK records for the 100 m according to sex and age group as on 28 November 2002.

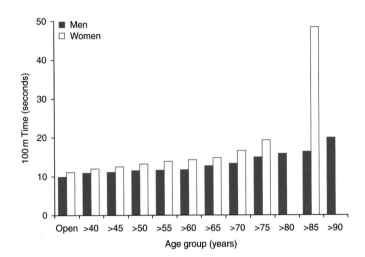

Source: British Masters Athletic Federation website. Available at: http://www.bvaf.org.uk.

the age of 25 onwards, although this varies depending on several factors including physical activity levels. Continual hard training may be able to prevent any decline in $\dot{V}O_2$max until the late thirties and individuals who continue exercising into old age retain higher $\dot{V}O_2$max values than those who stop training or remain untrained. Figure 11.3 illustrates the decline in $\dot{V}O_2$max from age 25 to 75 using cross-sectional data from athletes who continue training and from untrained healthy persons. Also included are data from three groups of older track athletes assessed on three occasions over a period of 20 years. The average age of these older athletes was 50, 60 and 70 years on the first, second and third assessments, respectively. The data show that $\dot{V}O_2$max values were better maintained in the high- and moderate-intensity training groups than in the low-intensity training group.

There is some evidence that the decline in $\dot{V}O_2$max with age is primarily due to an impaired efficiency of skeletal muscle to extract oxygen, at least within the age range of 20–50 years. This is indicated by the findings from a recent follow-up of the classic Dallas Bed Rest and Training Study (McGuire et al. 2001a,b). In the original study (in 1966), 5 healthy 20-year-old men were assessed: (1) at baseline, (2) after 3 weeks of bed rest and (3) after 8 weeks of intensive dynamic exercise training. Follow-up was performed 30 years later (in 1996) when the men were 50-years old. During this 30-year period the men had maintained varying levels of activity. Absolute $\dot{V}O_2$max values were 12% lower (2.9 versus 3.3 l min^{-1}) and relative $\dot{V}O_2$max values were 28% lower (31 versus 43 ml kg^{-1} min^{-1}) at age 50 compared to age 20. Although maximal heart rate had declined at follow-up, maximal cardiac output remained unchanged due to an increase in maximal stroke volume. Thus, the decline in $\dot{V}O_2$max was entirely due to a 15% reduction in the maximal difference between the oxygen content of arterial and mixed venous blood, $(a - \bar{v})O_2$diff. In other words, this study indicates oxygen

Figure 11.3 Cross-sectional data demonstrating the decline in $\dot{V}O_2max$ with age in untrained healthy persons and in athletes who continue to train. Also included are 20-year follow-up data from older track athletes who continued to train at either a high, moderate or low intensity.

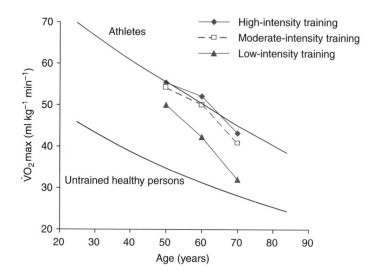

Source: Adapted from Pollock *et al.* (1997).
Note: The lines for 'athletes' and 'untrained healthy persons' represent average values obtained in many groups of athletes and untrained persons of different ages.

supply is not compromised with age, rather the ageing process impairs the ability of skeletal muscle to extract and/or utilize oxygen. Further research is required to confirm these findings.

What causes the reduction in oxygen extraction/usage with age? This is not known for certain but there are several likely causes. A large portion of the age-associated decline in $\dot{V}O_2max$ in non-trained individuals is due to the loss of muscle mass observed with advancing age (Fleg and Lakatta 1988). Moreover, a 20-year follow-up study of distance runners has documented a decrease in type I and type II muscle fibre areas as well as a decrease in skeletal muscle oxidative capacity as indicated by a lower activity of the enzyme succinate dehydrogenase (Trappe *et al.* 1995). It is also possible that capillary density and mitochondrial volume are decreased with age. A further possibility is that the distribution of blood is impaired during maximal exercise with age, perhaps due to impairments in the control of arterioles and capillaries such that channelling blood to the working muscles is less effective.

Muscle strength

There is an approximate 30% decline in muscle strength and a 40% reduction in muscle area between the second and seventh decades of life (Rogers and Evans 1993). This loss of muscle strength and mass, together with a possible decrease in the number of type II (fast twitch) muscle fibres, probably underlies the decline in sprint

Figure 11.4 Decline in isokinetic muscle strength ($60° \, s^{-1}$) of the knee extensors of the dominant side in men and women.

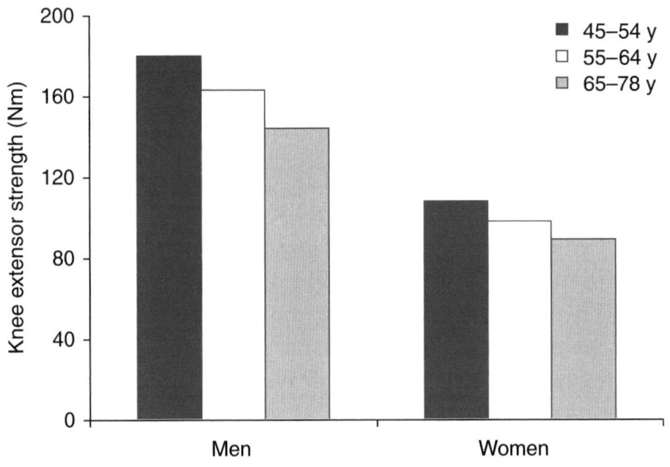

Source: Frontera *et al.* (1991).

performance with age shown in Figure 11.2. An example of the decline in muscle strength with age is illustrated in Figure 11.4. These data are from a cross-sectional study of 45–78 year old men and women. Muscle strength was determined using an isokinetic dynamometer. Note that ageing is associated with impaired muscle strength in both men and women (Frontera *et al.* 1991). When the data in Figure 11.4 were expressed per kilogram of muscle mass the differences between the age groups became smaller and there was no significant difference between the strength of males and females. This supports the hypothesis that the decline in muscle strength with age is largely due to a decline in muscle mass.

Other factors

The reductions in maximum oxygen uptake and muscle strength are the most notable and possibly the most debilitating effects of ageing but many other aspects of physiological function decline with age including lung function (vital capacity and forced expiratory volume), resting metabolic rate (largely due to the reduction in fat-free-mass) and flexibility (Fiatarone and Evans 1990). Moreover, as noted in Chapter 7, fat mass tends to increase with age (at least for the 'young' old) and this may further impair general mobility. However, as noted in Chapter 1, there is a rapid decline in physical activity with increasing age. Therefore, it is difficult to distinguish between the effects of age and those of decreased physical activity when assessing the age-associated decline in physiological function. Indeed some estimates suggest that 50% of the decline in functional capacities associated with ageing is actually due to disuse rather than ageing (Daley and Spinks 2000). In the following section we will examine the evidence that various aspects of physiological function can be improved in older individuals who engage in exercise training.

EXERCISE TRAINING AND FUNCTIONAL CAPACITY IN OLDER INDIVIDUALS

Exercise training can profoundly influence functional capacity in older individuals. As an example we may again refer to the UK age group records for running events. The UK record for the marathon for men aged over 70 is 3 h and 58 s while the men's record for 100 m in the over 70 age group is 13.34 s. Equivalent times for women for this age group are 3 h and 48.14 s for the marathon and 16.59 s for 100 m. These are remarkable performances and the average 25-year-old male or female would have difficulty in matching them. These performances are possible due to a combination of genetic make-up and continual hard training. In this section we will examine the extent to which untrained older individuals can improve aspects of their functional capacity through exercise training.

Maximum oxygen uptake

Several studies have demonstrated that the human body retains its ability to adapt to exercise training well into old age. A noteworthy example is a study involving 16 previously untrained men and women aged 70–79 years old (Hagberg *et al.* 1989). These individuals followed a 26-week endurance-training programme involving walking and slow jogging. Sessions were conducted 3 times per week. Exercise intensity ranged from 50% to 70% of VO_2max during the first half of the programme and increased to between 75% and 85% of VO_2max during the second half of the programme. This resulted in an 18% increase in VO_2max expressed in absolute units (1.88 versus 1.59 l min^{-1}) and a 20% increase in VO_2max expressed in relative units (27.1 versus 22.5 ml kg^{-1} min^{-1}). In practical terms, an increase of this nature would translate into a 1 mile h^{-1} increase in comfortable walking speed. Moreover, these data demonstrate that men and women retain the ability to respond to exercise training during their eighth decade of life.

Another study demonstrating that VO_2max remains trainable in older individuals is the follow-up to the Dallas Bed Rest and Training Study referred to in the previous section (McGuire *et al.* 2001a,b). The reader will recall that the original study (conducted in 1966) examined aspects of physiological function prior to and following 3 weeks of bed rest, and then again after 8 weeks of training. In the follow-up study, conducted 30 years later (in 1996), cardiovascular responses to sub-maximal and maximal exercise were examined prior to and following a 6-month endurance-training programme. This programme resulted in a significant improvement in VO_2max such that post-training values (l min^{-1}) in 1996 were similar to pre-bed rest values in 1966 (Figure 11.5). The investigators concluded that, 3 weeks of bed rest at age 20 had a more profound effect on VO_2max than did three decades of ageing. Furthermore, one hundred percent of the age-related decline in VO_2max was reversed by a 6-month

Figure 11.5 Maximum oxygen uptake in five male subjects prior to and following training in 1966 and again in 1996. Subjects were 20-years old in 1966. Note that the post-training $\dot{V}O_2$max attained in 1996 was the same as the pre-training $\dot{V}O_2$max attained in 1966 when expressed in $l\ min^{-1}$. This was not the case when values were expressed in $ml\ kg^{-1}\ min^{-1}$ because the subjects were 19 kg heavier post-training in 1996 compared to pre-training in 1966 (96 versus 77 kg).

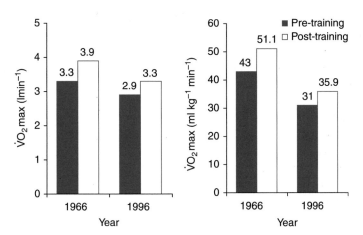

Source: Adapted from McGuire et al. (2001b).

endurance-training programme. However, no subject achieved the same $\dot{V}O_2$max attained after training 30 years earlier. This study clearly demonstrates the combined effects of ageing and physical inactivity on $\dot{V}O_2$max.

The increase in $\dot{V}O_2$max post-training in the follow-up to the Dallas Bed Rest and Training Study was primarily the result of peripheral adaptation with no improvement in maximal oxygen delivery. This is demonstrated by the data in Table 11.1. Maximal heart rate was decreased post-training compared to pre-training in 1996 but maximal cardiac output remained unchanged due to an increase in maximal stroke volume. The maximal $(a - \bar{v})O_2$diff. increased by 10%, however, and this was the key factor for the increase in $\dot{V}O_2$max in the 50-year-old men. Therefore, the mechanism for the training-induced increase in $\dot{V}O_2$max in older individuals may differ from that operating in younger subjects. In younger individuals oxygen delivery appears to be of primary importance as indicated by the 14–15% increase in stroke volume and cardiac output post-training, in 1966. The $(a - \bar{v})O_2$diff. increased by only 6% at this time (Table 11.1). Further research is required to determine the extent to which cardiac output and oxygen extraction can be improved following training in older individuals.

Several factors could be responsible for an improvement in maximal $(a - \bar{v})O_2$diff. following endurance-training in older individuals. These include an improvement in peripheral blood flow, an increase in capillary density and an increase in oxidative enzyme activity. Such changes have been observed in 60–70 year old men and women following a prolonged period (9–12 months) of endurance training involving walking/jogging at 80% of maximal heart rate for 45 min day^{-1}, 4 days week^{-1} (Coggan et al. 1992). Needle biopsy samples of the lateral gastrocnemius (calf) muscle obtained before and after training revealed significant increases in capillary density (Figure 11.6) and several enzymes associated with oxidative metabolism including

Table 11.1 Maximal values for heart rate, stroke volume, cardiac output and $(a-\bar{v})O_2$diff. before and after training in 1966 and again in 1996 in the same five subjects. Oxygen delivery (cardiac output) appears to be the major adaptation to training in 20-year-old men whereas oxygen extraction $(a-\bar{v})O_2$diff. appears to be the primary adaptation in 50-year-old men

	1966		1996	
	PRE-TRAINING	POST-TRAINING	PRE-TRAINING	POST-TRAINING
Heart rate (beat min^{-1})	193	190	181	171
Stroke volume (ml)	104	120	121	129
Cardiac output (l min^{-1})	20.0	22.8	21.4	21.7
$(a-\bar{v})O_2$diff. (ml O_2 in 100 ml blood)	16.2	17.1	13.8	15.2

Source: McGuire *et al.* (2001b).

Figure 11.6 Increased capillary density in the gastrocnemius muscles of 60–70-year-old men and women following a 9–12 month period of endurance training.

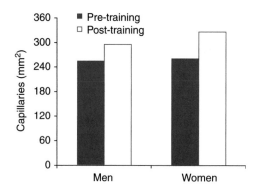

Source: Coggan *et al.* (1992).

succinate dehydrogenase, citrate synthase and β-hydroxyacyl-CoA dehydrogenase (Table 11.2). A significant increase in the percentage of type IIa muscle fibres together with a significant decrease in the percentage of type IIb muscle fibres was also noted post-training in this study. These are the same changes qualitatively as those seen in young adults. Such changes would enhance stamina/resistance to fatigue. Furthermore, these changes demonstrate that the skeletal muscle of men and women aged 60–70 years retains its ability to adapt to endurance training.

Muscle strength

As well as retaining its ability to adapt to endurance training, skeletal muscle also retains its ability to adapt to strength training. This is clearly demonstrated by a study

Table 11.2 Increased oxidative enzyme activities (mol kg^{-1} (protein) h^{-1}) in the gastrocnemius muscles of 60–70-year-old men and women following a 9–12 month period of endurance training

	MALES		FEMALES	
	PRE-TRAINING	POST-TRAINING	PRE-TRAINING	POST-TRAINING
Succinate dehydrogenase	1.11	1.83	0.76	1.05
Citrate synthase	2.97	3.83	2.21	2.58
β-hydroxyacyl-CoA dehydrogenase	5.95	8.45	5.29	7.19

Source: Coggan *et al.* (1992).
Notes: The standard unit for enzyme activity is μmol min^{-1} g^{-1}(wet weight). Values in the Table should be multiplied by a factor of three to give an approximate conversion to the standard unit. This assumes that muscle contains 20% protein (wet weight).

Figure 11.7 Improvements in strength (one-repetition maximum) of the knee extensors and knee flexors in men aged 60–72 years following a 12-week training programme.

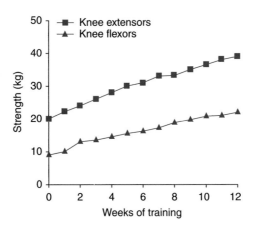

Source: Frontera *et al.* (1988).

involving 12 previously untrained men aged 60–72 years who completed a 12-week strength-training programme (Frontera *et al.* 1988). Training was conducted 3 days per week at an intensity of 80% of one-repetition maximum. Three sets of 8 repetitions were completed for the knee extensors and knee flexors on each training day. The findings demonstrated a progressive increase in muscle strength in both the knee flexors and knee extensors over the 12 weeks of the programme (Figure 11.7). Alongside the increase in strength, there was an increase in quadriceps muscle cross-sectional area as determined by computerized tomography scans (Figure 11.8). This muscle hypertrophy was in turn due to an increase in both type I and type II muscle fibre area. These findings have been confirmed in several other studies which collectively illustrate that older men and women experience similar strength gains as younger individuals after resistive

Figure 11.8 An increase in the cross-section area of the quadriceps muscles of the right and left legs following a 12-week strength-training programme in 12 men aged 60–72 years.

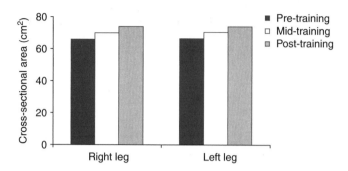

Source: Frontera *et al.* (1988).
Note: Muscle cross-sectional area was assessed using computerized tomography.

training (Rogers and Evans 1993). Such gains could have important implications for activities of daily living in elderly people. The ability to rise unaided from a low chair or toilet, for example, is dependent on quadriceps strength. Strength training may help preserve quadriceps strength allowing elderly individuals greater independence.

Other factors

Exercise training has been recommended for older individuals for a variety of reasons beyond any effects on VO_2max and muscle strength. It has been proposed that exercise training will increase energy expenditure in the elderly thus combating the increase in body fatness that often accompanies ageing. However, the evidence to support this suggestion is sparse (Westerterp 2000, Westerterp and Meijer 2001) and some studies have shown that any increase in energy expenditure due to exercise training in elderly people is nullified by a compensatory decrease in energy expenditure at other times of the day so that total daily energy expenditure remains unchanged (Morio *et al.* 1998, Westerterp and Meijer 2001).

Another proposed benefit of exercise for elderly people is that it may increase dietary intake. This would be beneficial because dietary intake declines in some individuals with age and there are indications that the diets of many elderly people are deficient in both macronutrients and micronutrients (Wakimoto and Block 2001). There is some evidence that exercise can increase food intake in older persons (Morley 2001) but this evidence is not irrefutable and further research is required to clarify this issue.

Other areas where exercise training may be beneficial for the elderly are postural stability and flexibility. Postural stability refers to the ability of an individual to retain balance and this is directly related to the risk of falling among older adults. Flexibility refers to the range of motion of single or multiple joints and this affects the ability to perform specific tasks. There is evidence supporting the use of exercise as a means of improving postural stability and flexibility in older individuals. Further study is required to determine the optimal exercise prescription for improving postural stability and flexibility in the elderly. In the meantime a broad-based exercise programme incorporating activities such as balance training, resistance exercise, walking, aerobic dance and stretching is recommended (American College of Sports Medicine Position Stand 1998).

EXERCISE, AGEING AND INDEPENDENT LIVING

The decreases in functional capacities noted here have important implications for the ability to perform many activities of daily living. Unfortunately, decreases in functional capacities (walking speed, quadriceps strength, joint flexibility) often go unnoticed until a threshold is reached when, suddenly, a person cannot do a particular task e.g. cross a road in time, get up from a low chair, climb a stair, open the cap on a jar, put socks on, etc. This results in a loss of independence and an inability to participate fully in life. As might be expected, the number of people reporting that they are unable to perform one or more activities of daily living increases with age (Daley and Spinks 2000).

Mobility

The level of proficiency in performing everyday tasks is related to the risk of disability. This was demonstrated in a 4-year follow-up study involving non-disabled older persons living in Iowa (Guralnik *et al.* 1995). Lower-extremity function was assessed by measuring standing balance, walking speed and the time taken to stand from a chair and sit back down. These measures were found to be highly predictive of subsequent disability.

Evidence from cohort studies indicates that a regularly active lifestyle may slow the decline in mobility performance. One example is The Longitudinal Aging Study Amsterdam (Visser *et al.* 2002). This was a 3-year follow-up study involving 2,109 men and women initially aged 55–85 years. Mobility performance was assessed using two tests: (1) the time taken to walk 6 m, (2) the time taken to stand up and sit down 5 times from a kitchen chair. Physical activity was assessed using an interviewer-administered questionnaire. After 3 years there was a decline in total physical activity (measured either as h day^{-1} or kcal day^{-1}) and mobility performance declined for 46% of the sample. Sports participation and a higher level of total physical activity, walking or household activity at baseline were associated with a smaller decline in mobility. Continuation of physical activity over time was also associated with a smaller decline in mobility.

Similar findings have emerged from cross-sectional studies. For example, a study of 619 healthy 70-year-old people in the city of Gothenburg, Sweden found that those who took a daily walk of at least 30 minutes had a significantly better climbing capacity (ability to climb a 40 cm high box without use of a handrail) than subjects who walked less (Frändin *et al.* 1991). Obviously these cross-sectional and cohort studies do not prove causality but intervention studies suggest a causal relationship as will be discussed in the next section.

Disease and disability

It is clear from the previous chapters that there is a wealth of evidence to support a role for physical activity in preventing diseases such as heart disease, diabetes, osteoporosis and cancer. There is also some evidence to suggest that physical activity can help preserve cognitive function in ageing humans (Chodzko-Zajko and Moore 1994) and findings from the Canadian Study of Health and Aging indicate that regular physical activity may help to prevent Alzheimer's disease (Lindsay *et al.* 2002).

In addition to preventing disease regular physical activity may also play a role in reducing the severity of some diseases and thus the need for hospitalization. A cohort study in Washington, Seattle, for example, examined the risk of cardiovascular disease hospitalizations in older adults (men and women aged 65 years and over) and found that walking more than 4 h week^{-1} was associated with a reduced risk of hospitalization over a 4.2-year follow-up period (Figure 11.9). These findings indicate that a sustained programme of walking may help to prevent cardiovascular disease events (LaCroix *et al.* 1996). In addition to this, exercise may also help to reduce hospitalizations due to hip fractures and falls as discussed in the previous chapter.

INTERVENTION TRIALS OF PHYSICAL ACTIVITY IN THE ELDERLY

Several intervention trials have been conducted to assess the extent to which exercise training can enhance the ability to perform activities of daily living in elderly men and

Figure 11.9 Relative risk of hospitalization due to cardiovascular disease (CVD) in men and women initially aged 65 years according to the amount of walking performed each week.

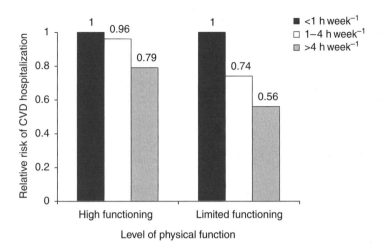

Source: LaCroix *et al.* (1996).
Note: Follow-up lasted for 4.2 years. Level of physical function was determined using a seven-point scale measuring limitations in physical tasks ranging from vigorous activities to self-care activities.

women. Some of these trials have been conducted in very elderly individuals living in nursing homes, others have assessed community dwelling elderly persons. Although the findings are not unanimous, several intervention studies show that exercise training, particularly resistance/weight training, can help to restore physical function thus improving quality of life and the ability for independent living.

The importance of leg strength for walking endurance was clearly demonstrated by a randomized intervention trial conducted in healthy elderly persons aged 65–79 years. Exercise intervention involved a 12-week resistance-training programme. This programme consisted of 3 sets of 8 repetitions of 7 exercises on 3 days week^{-1}. Resistance was initially set at 50% of one-repetition maximum but was increased to 80% of one-repetition maximum by week nine. This programme led to a significant improvement in leg-strength and walking endurance at 80% of baseline VO_2max (Figure 11.10). VO_2max was unaltered by the training programme (Ades *et al.* 1996). Improvements in walking endurance have also been demonstrated in nursing-home residents following a 12-week programme of supervised daily walking performed at a self-selected pace (MacRae *et al.* 1996).

The potential of resistance training to counteract physical frailty has also been demonstrated in a randomized controlled trial involving 100 very elderly people (mean age, 87 years; range, 72–98 years) resident in a nursing home (Fiatarone *et al.* 1994). Participants in the exercise intervention group followed a high-intensity (80% of one-repetition maximum) 10-week progressive resistance-training programme (3 sessions week^{-1}) targeting the hip and knee extensors. This programme increased muscle strength by 113%, walking speed by 12%, stair-climbing power by 28% and thigh muscle cross-sectional area (assessed using computed tomography) by 3%. There was

Figure 11.10 A 12-week weight training programme has been shown to improve leg strength (one-repetition maximum) and walking endurance (time to exhaustion at 80% of VO_2max) in healthy elderly persons aged 65–79 years.

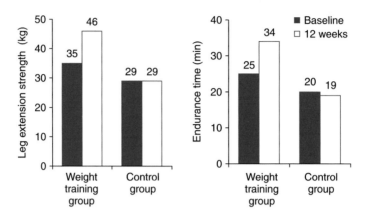

Source: Ades *et al.* (1996).

also an increase in spontaneous physical activity in the resistance-training group (assessed using activity monitors worn around both ankles). Over the same period there were small but significant reductions in walking speed and thigh muscle cross-sectional area in non-exercising participants.

The findings from intervention studies such as the ones described demonstrate that exercise training offers a valuable means of maintaining and improving functional capacities and mobility throughout the adult lifespan. This in turn should help to postpone disability, improve quality of life and enhance the capacity for independent living. Further research is required to determine if exercise operates in a dose–response manner to influence well-being and postpone dependency (Spirduso and Cronin 2001).

SUMMARY

- Functional capacities decline with age. Most noteworthy amongst these are maximum oxygen uptake and muscle strength. Flexibility and lung function also decrease with age and there are changes in body composition, most notably a decline in muscle mass.
- Loss of muscle mass is a major reason for the decline in muscle strength with age. It may also explain a large portion of the decline in maximum oxygen uptake.
- Some of the decline in functional capacity with age is due to inactivity rather than a genuine effect of ageing. Age group records for a variety of sports indicate that individuals who remain active are capable of very high levels of physical performance into their eighth decade of life.
- The body retains it ability to adapt to exercise training throughout life. Adaptations shown to occur in older individuals after a period of exercise training include increases in maximum oxygen uptake, skeletal muscle oxidative enzyme activity, skeletal muscle capillarization, muscle mass, muscle fibre area and muscle strength.

- The decline in functional capacities associated with ageing eventually impairs mobility and the ability to perform activities of daily living. This leads to a loss of independence and quality of life.
- An active lifestyle can help to counter the age-related decline in functional capacities and mobility. This reduces the risk of disability and hospitalization and allows individuals to retain their independence. Resistance training is particularly effective in this regard.

STUDY TASKS

1 Describe the major changes in functional capacities associated with ageing. What evidence is there to suggest that some of these changes are due to disuse rather than ageing?
2 Discuss the possible physiological mechanisms that might underlie a decline in $\dot{V}O_2$max with age. What evidence is there to support a role for these mechanisms in the age-related decline in $\dot{V}O_2$max?
3 Make a list of everyday tasks that older individuals may have difficulty in performing due to a decline in (a) $\dot{V}O_2$max, (b) leg strength and (c) flexibility.
4 Describe as fully as possible why resistance training may be particularly beneficial for older individuals.
5 Discuss the interaction between exercise training, nutrition status and body composition with respect to elderly individuals.

FURTHER READING

American College of Sports Medicine Position Stand (1998) 'Exercise and physical activity for older adults', *Medicine and Science in Sports and Exercise* 30: 992–1008.
Daley, M.J. and Spinks, W.L. (2000) 'Exercise, mobility and aging', *Sports Medicine* 29: 1–12.
Fiatarone, M.A. and Evans, W.J. (1990) 'Exercise in the oldest old', *Topics in Geriatric Rehabilitation* 5: 63–77.
Rogers, M.A. and Evans, W.J. (1993) 'Changes in skeletal muscle with aging: effects of exercise training', *Exercise and Sport Sciences Reviews* 21: 65–102.

12 Therapeutic exercise

Knowledge assumed
Cardiovascular and metabolic
adaptations to aerobic training
in healthy subjects

INTRODUCTION

This book is concerned mainly with the role of physical activity in preventing disease and maintaining positive health. It would not be complete, however, without some consideration of therapeutic exercise. This chapter sets out the rationale for including physical activity in the management of patients with various conditions and provides some assessment of the evidence as to its effectiveness. We do not set out to discuss the practicalities of exercise prescription for different patient groups. An excellent summary is available in the American College of Sports Medicine's 'Guidelines for exercise testing and prescription' Franklin *et al.* 2000).

The aims of therapeutic exercise may be broadly stated as:

• to help patients make the most of limited functional capacities, that is, reduce disability and handicap, for example, dyspnoea;
• to provide relief of symptoms;

- to reduce the need for medication;
- to reduce the risk of disease recurrence;
- to help patients overcome social problems and psychological distress associated with their illness.

A major barrier to the achievement of these aims is poor compliance by patients with exercise therapy. This is a lot lower than for pharmacological treatment and, as a result, exercise therapy can be difficult to implement on a wide scale. It requires good cooperation from the patient and is more complex to deliver.

CARDIAC DISEASE

Exercise rehabilitation is important in the management of patients with cardiac disease, hypertension and claudication. The most extensive experience is with cardiac rehabilitation.

Early in the twentieth century it was thought that, after a heart attack, patients needed prolonged bed rest to allow the injured area of the myocardium to heal. It was not until the 1950s that cardiologists, recognizing that this lead to deconditioning, boredom and depression, began to consider therapeutic exercise. This is now a core component of rehabilitation, not only for patients who have had a myocardial infarction but also for those who have had surgical procedures (coronary artery bypass grafts, percutaneous coronary angioplasty, even heart transplantation), or who have stable angina or chronic heart failure. Exercise intervention is complemented by education, relaxation therapy and individual counselling which aim to address the psychological and social needs of the patient (and often those of his/her spouse or carer) (Box 12.1).

Rehabilitation starts when patients are in hospital, where early mobilization counteracts the deleterious effects of bed rest (sometimes referred to as Phase I). Patients progress, within a few weeks of discharge, to a progressive programme of supervised activity initially based in the hospital where cardiac monitoring is available (Phase II). In Phase III, monitoring and supervision are reduced before patients move to a community-based and/or self-governed habit of exercise (Phase IV). The emphasis is on improving aerobic fitness but patients whose return to work involves lifting or other isometric exercise may also undertake strength training once a sufficient level of aerobic fitness has been achieved.

Secondary prevention (mortality and morbidity)

Meta-analyses are especially important in this area as, for practical reasons, many trials looking at the effect of rehabilitation have lacked the statistical power to identify effects on morbidity or mortality. Two widely-cited analyses of approximately 4,500 patients have demonstrated that patients randomized to cardiac rehabilitation after a myocardial infarction have a 20–25% reduction in all-cause and cardiac mortality, compared with those receiving conventional care (Oldridge *et al.* 1988, O'Connor *et al.* 1989). Many trials included in these analyses employed multiple interventions, however, so that the effect of exercise *per se* could not be stated. Subsequent analysis, limited to randomly

BOX 12.1 GOALS OF CARDIAC REHABILITATION

Medical goals, as set out by the World Health Organization

- Prevention of cardiac death
- Reduction of cardiac morbidity (e.g. another heart attack, closure of coronary artery bypass graft through re-stenosis)
- Relief of symptoms (e.g. breathlessness, angina)

Goals of the psychological component

- To improve quality of life through treating psychological distress and restoring confidence
- To help patients initiate and maintain lifestyle changes

Goals of the social component

- To help patients overcome problems related to handicap, for example, return to work, relationships with family and friends.

Interventions in pursuit of these goals

- Patient education, including information about their disease and behaviour change (diet, smoking, weight control, stress management)
- Exercise, first in a supportive, monitored environment, later in the community
- Individual counselling to help with social and psychological matters
- Relaxation therapy

controlled trials with rigorous inclusion and exclusion criteria, provided a summary of the findings of 51 studies with 8,440 patients (2,845 in exercise-only rehabilitation) (Jolliffe *et al.* 2003). This analysis demonstrated a 27% reduction in all-cause mortality and a 31% reduction in cardiac mortality for the exercise-only intervention, compared to 'usual care'. For a combined outcome of mortality, non-fatal heart attack and re-vascularizations, exercise rehabilitation was found to reduce adverse events by 20%. Thus the recommendation based on evidence for a rehabilitation programme with exercise as a prominent component can be categorized as Category A or 'convincing' (see Chapter 2), even when assessed solely on the basis of these 'hard endpoints'.

The mechanisms for these beneficial effects on mortality/morbidity are not known, although exercise training has been reported to increase myocardial perfusion. This could be due to better recruitment of coronary collaterals during maximal exercise but there is little evidence for this. An alternative mechanism could be slower progression of coronary artery occlusion of coronary vessels, although findings are inconsistent. One randomly controlled trial (113 male patients) that did support an effect on atherosclerosis was undertaken in Heidelberg, Germany. These researchers examined the effect of endurance exercise training on metabolic factors and on the severity and extent

of stenoses, visualized using coronary angiography (Niebauer *et al.* 1997). After 6 years, patients assigned to the exercise intervention[1] showed a significant retardation of lesion progression compared with controls (Figure 12.1). Individuals (exercisers and controls), who demonstrated regression of stenosis attended more group exercise sessions, reported more leisure-time activity and had the highest fitness levels. Regression was not associated with increased collaterals and changes in lipids did not differ from those in controls.

One promising avenue of research that might explain how training improves myocardial perfusion involves coronary endothelial function. As explained in Chapter 5, individuals with coronary artery disease demonstrate impaired endothelium-dependent

Figure 12.1 Long-term changes in the relative diameter of stenoses in a randomly controlled exercise intervention study after 6 years.

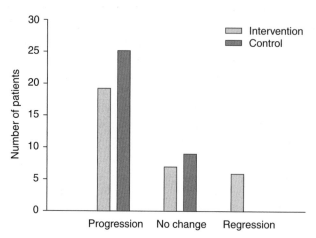

Source: Niebauer *et al.* (1997).
Note: Angiographic changes documented during the course of the study were analysed for each patient and classified as progression, no change or regression.

coronary vasodilatation. In an exploratory study, the Heidelberg group compared measures of coronary endothelial function in 10 patients who trained for 4 weeks with those in 9 randomly allocated controls. Training resulted in a 29% increase in blood flow reserve, a 105% increase in flow-mediated dilatation of coronary vessels and a 54% decrease in inappropriate vasoconstriction of these vessels (Hambrecht *et al.* 2000). These findings indicate enhanced vasodilatory capacity that would facilitate increases in myocardial blood flow at times of increased demand.

Effects on modifiable risk factors

Changes in multifarious risk factors probably contribute to the reduced mortality and morbidity associated with exercise rehabilitation. These include changes in lipids, blood pressure, insulin resistance and haemostatic factors, as discussed in Chapter 5. (Information on the latter two has seldom been reported.) It should be pointed out, however, that genetic factors, for example familial hyperlipidaemias, probably constrain the potential for risk factor reduction in some individuals. This may be one reason why changes in lipids with exercise in cardiac patients tend to be small and often indistinguishable from those in control groups.

Improvements in fitness

The improvements in functional capacity as a result of exercise rehabilitation are often undervalued. These matter because they help to maintain patients' quality of life and ensure that activities of daily living may be comfortably undertaken. As with healthy people, training improves $\dot{V}O_2$max. Improvements after 3–6 months of training range from 11% to 56% in patients recovering from myocardial infarction and from 14% to 56% in patients who have had coronary artery bypass grafting. These changes are much greater than those seen in healthy sedentary people, demonstrating the contribution from the natural process of recovery. Increases in VO_2max may be clinically important; in a 3-year multi-centre trial in the US, each 1-MET increase was associated with a 8–14% reduction in the risk of all-cause mortality at every follow-up period, that is, after 3, 5, 10, 15 and 19 years (Dorn *et al.* 1999).

In healthy, normally active individuals, it is central cardiovascular adaptations that mainly account for training-induced increases in VO_2max (for evidence, see standard text books of exercise physiology). In cardiac patients, peripheral adaptations in the trained skeletal muscles are more important determinants. Mitochondrial oxidative capacity is enhanced and, in the long term, muscle capillarization. These changes lead to increased extraction and utilization of oxygen. Responses to standard sub-maximal exercise (heart rate, blood lactate, catecholamines) are attenuated and the patient's perception of fatigue is reduced. In patients with angina the bradycardia induced by training reduces cardiac work and hence the frequency and duration of ischaemic episodes; their anginal threshold is raised and medication can be reduced.

Health status

The potential of exercise rehabilitation to improve patients' lives is perhaps best illustrated through studies of patients with chronic heart failure. For them, even small gains in exercise tolerance may have a profound effect on the quality of life. A study from the Toronto Rehabilitation Center demonstrates the potential functional and psychological gains in these individuals (Kavanagh *et al.* 1996). An experimental group (17 men, 4 women) followed a progressive, supervised programme of walking for 1 year and changes were compared with those in a convenience control group with the same condition (8 men, 1 woman). Walkers progressed over 16 weeks to 5.3 km per session and maintained this thereafter. Training improved $\dot{V}O_2$peak,[2] ventilatory threshold and resting heart rate as well as health status and habitual walking speed. Fatigue was significantly reduced in walkers, with trends towards decreased dyspnoea during day-to-day activities, improved emotional function and increased mastery (coping with the illness). Thus, even in patients with chronic heart failure, rehabilitation seems safe, feasible and effective.

Safety of cardiac rehabilitation

In the Toronto study just referred to, exercise precipitated few adverse events. Indeed the reduction of nearly one-third in cardiac mortality demonstrated by meta-analysis of exercise-only rehabilitation constitutes evidence for its safety. The incidence rate of cardiac events during exercise in outpatient rehabilitation programmes has been found to be 1 cardiac arrest per 111,996 patient-hours, 1 myocardial infarction per 293,990 patient-hours and 1 fatality per 783,972 patient-hours – all low absolute rates.

CLAUDICATION

Peripheral arterial disease is a manifestation of systemic atherosclerosis that leads to claudication, that is, walking-induced pain in the legs that is relieved only by rest. Treatment of claudication focuses on decreasing functional impairment, as well as on the underlying systemic atherosclerosis. Many patients are so deconditioned from lack of exercise that they become housebound or dependent on others. Rehabilitation offers a way to break into this cycle of disability.

That exercise improves walking ability in this patient group is well established. One meta-analysis showed that exercise improved pain-free walking time by an average of 180% and maximal walking time by an average of 120% (Gardner and Poehlman 1995). As might be expected, improvements were related to the duration, frequency and intensity of training and to the length of the programme. A subsequent analysis that excluded non-randomized trials found the average increase in maximal walking time was 150% (Leng et al. 2003). These improvements exceed those attained with medication, which range from 20 to 60%.

Improvements in walking ability help the patient in everyday life. For example, in one randomly controlled study, 6 months of exercise training led to a 38% increase in daily physical activity (measured using an accelerometer) which was related to the change in distance walked (Gardner et al. 2001). Exercise may also modify cardiovascular risk factors favourably and thus reduce the high risk of cardiovascular ischaemic events in this group, but there is little information.

How does exercise rehabilitation improve walking ability? Probably by attenuating the mismatch in leg muscles between oxygen supply and demand and thus reducing ischaemia. Oxidative metabolism of skeletal muscle is enhanced and these changes are related to increases in walking ability. There is also evidence for increases in capillary density and improved endothelium-dependent vasodilation, both of which would oppose ischaemia. Finally, rehabilitation probably improves walking economy (the rate of oxygen uptake at a given speed). Patients with claudication adopt a walking pattern that favours greater gait stability at the expense of speed. Reduction of pain improves biomechanical efficiency and thus walking economy. The relative intensity of the walking will be reduced, leading to less fatigue. In the study referred to earlier (Gardner et al. 2001), there was a 12% improvement in walking economy that was significantly related to change in walking distance.

HYPERTENSION

Non-pharmacological interventions are particularly important for the 90% of patients with essential hypertension[3] who have mild to moderate elevation of blood pressure, that is, systolic values of 140–180 mm Hg, diastolic values of 90–100 mm Hg. More than 70 trials of the blood pressure-lowering effects of exercise in hypertensive patients are available, with a total of more than 1,200 participants, men and women, mainly in middle age (Hagberg *et al.* 2000). Training periods studied range from 8 to 78 weeks. Overall, systolic blood pressure was reduced in 76% of groups and the weighted mean decrease was 10.6 mm Hg. Thus, these patients (with a weighted mean systolic pressure, before training, of 153 mm Hg) were still hypertensive after training, with systolic pressure >140 mm Hg. For diastolic pressure, 81% of patient groups exhibited a significant decrease with training (weighted mean 8.2 mm Hg). Thus, exercise reduced diastolic pressure from a weighted mean of 97 to 89 mm Hg, just below the conventional lower limit of diastolic hypertension of 90 mm Hg. These effects were independent of substantial weight loss.

Exercise may reduce blood pressure (particularly systolic pressure) somewhat more – and more consistently – in women than in men but it appears to be as effective in elderly patients as in those in middle age. (This is important as the prevalence of hypertension rises dramatically with age.) At least one ethnic group, hypertensive African Americans, appear to derive a substantial benefit from exercise. In hypertensives (as in healthy people, see Chapter 5), low-to-moderate intensity training is just as effective as higher intensity training, if not more effective. Groups that used training intensities <70% $\dot{V}O_2$max had about 50% greater systolic blood pressure reductions than groups training at higher intensities (Hagberg *et al.* 2000).

The blood pressure lowering effects of a single session of exercise in healthy people have already been described (Chapter 5). This phenomenon is evident also in patients with hypertension. For example, researchers used 24-hour ambulatory monitoring to compare blood pressure after 45 min of endurance exercise with values during a day without exercise (Taylor-Tolbert *et al.* 2000). Blood pressure was reduced for the first 16 h between 6/5 and 13/5 mm Hg and over the 24-hour period by an average of 7.4/3.6 mm Hg.

Thus physical activity, with decreasing dietary intake of salt, is the mainstay of the non-pharmacological management of patients with hypertension. Its modest effects will not normalize blood pressure except in those with values just over the designated thresholds. However, exercise frequently reduces the need for medication and will often benefit other CVD risk factors. (Hypertensive patients die primarily from CVD.) It is instructive to estimate the extent of the change in the overall risk of CVD for hypertensives that may be expected from therapeutic exercise (Box 12.2). This is clearly clinically important.

TYPE 2 DIABETES

As exercise renders the regulation of blood glucose concentration difficult in type 1 diabetics, it is not recommended as a therapeutic means to lower glucose levels for these patients.[4] By contrast, exercise is of great value for type 2 diabetics as it increases insulin sensitivity of the muscles (and probably the liver). The tissues need less insulin for the uptake and metabolism of a given amount of glucose and pancreatic secretion of insulin is spared. The treatment goal in these patients is to correct the metabolic abnormalities

BOX 12.2 ESTIMATING THE EFFECT OF EXERCISE TRAINING IN PATIENTS WITH HYPERTENSION UPON THE RISK OF DEVELOPING CARDIOVASCULAR DISEASE

The average risk of developing CVD can be estimated for individuals with particular combinations of risk factors, using data from the Framingham Study (Anderson *et al.* 1991). This provides a means of assessing the potential change in risk that may be expected from exercise-induced changes in risk factors.

- Almost 10% of 50-year-old men and women with blood pressure 153/97 mm Hg (average values from available trials of exercise), who are non-smokers with total cholesterol 5.33 mmol l^{-1}, HDL-cholesterol 1.09 mmol l^{-1} and without type 2 diabetes would develop CVD within 10 years (Case A in Figure 12.2). If training leads to typical changes in blood pressure, total and HDL-cholesterol, their risk is reduced by approximately 25%.
- If the same man or woman also has type 2 diabetes, their 10-year CVD risk rises to 16% (Case B in Figure 12.2). If training elicits typical changes in blood pressure, total and HDL-cholesterol and *eliminates* their type 2 diabetes (quite possible, for references see (Hagberg *et al.* 2000)), their risk would be reduced by approximately 50%.

Figure 12.2 Average 10-year risk of developing cardiovascular disease in hypertensive individuals with different combinations of risk factors, alongside the reductions in risk expected with training.

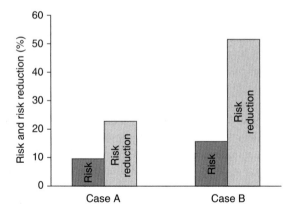

Source: Hagberg *et al.* (2000).
Note: Exercise training is assumed to lead to the average changes in risk factors reported for hypertensive patients, that is, Δ blood pressure −11/−8 mm Hg, Δ total cholesterol −0.18 mmol l^{-1} and Δ HDL-cholesterol +0.08 mmol l^{-1}.

associated with the insulin resistance syndrome (Chapter 8) and lower the risk for cardiovascular events and microvascular complications.

Evidence comes from both epidemiological and laboratory studies. Two large prospective studies show strong associations with better health outcomes in physically active than in sedentary diabetics. First, among diabetic men enrolled in the Aerobics Center Longitudinal study, 12-year mortality was 70% higher in men who reported being inactive than in those who were active (Wei *et al.* 2000). Second, in a subset of more than 5,000 diabetic women drawn from the US Nurses Health Study, time spent in moderate-to-vigorous activity per week was strongly and inversely related to the risk of CVD in a dose-dependent manner (Hu *et al.* 2001b). A similarly strong relationship was found for the volume of walking and walking pace was independently associated with a lower risk. Women who reported that their usual walking pace was 'brisk' experienced less than half the CVD as women who reported an 'easy' pace.

Laboratory studies show that these associations are biologically plausible. Exercise training improves insulin action in patients with type 2 diabetes. For example, Holloszy and colleagues trained a small group of patients vigorously for 1 year (70–85% VO_2max for 50–60 min day^{-1}, 5 days per week) (Holloszy *et al.* 1986). Insulin and glucose responses to an oral glucose tolerance test were determined before the training programme and again 18 h after the last session. Training reduced both responses significantly and fasting plasma glucose concentration was normalized (Figure 12.3), indicating improved insulin sensitivity.

The effect of training on insulin sensitivity has been measured directly using the glucose clamp technique in combination with measurements of glucose uptake (Dela *et al.* 1995). For 10 weeks, patients who volunteered for this study trained one leg – but not the other – by cycling. (This allows the untrained leg to act as a within-subject control.) Training improved insulin action and increased muscle glucose uptake across the trained leg, but not the untrained leg. These improvements were short-lived, dying away within a week.

Resistance exercise training has also been found to improve glycaemic control, decrease the dose of diabetes medication and reduced blood pressure in patients with type 2 diabetes (Castaneda *et al.* 2002). Patients in this randomized, controlled trial were all >55 years of age and had been diagnosed with diabetes at least 3 years earlier.

In addition to genuine training effects, exercise has acute effects on insulin sensitivity and glucose disposal. This was nicely illustrated by a Danish study (Larsen *et al.* 1997). Plasma concentrations of insulin, C-peptide (a marker for insulin secretion) and glucose, as well as rates of appearance and disappearance of glucose were determined in 9 sedentary diabetic men on 2 days, at an interval of 2 weeks. During 1 day, patients rested. On the other, they cycled for 45 min at approximately 50% VO_2max, beginning shortly after a standard breakfast. The exercise session reduced concentrations of insulin, glucose and C-peptide during a 4 h postprandial period, compared with the rest day. Interestingly, reducing the energy intake during breakfast (on a third study day) by an amount equivalent to the energy expended in the exercise session had exactly the same overall effect on postprandial responses of glucose and insulin. This suggests that the energy expenditure of exercise determines effects on glucose/insulin dynamics.

In addition to its effects on the underlying insulin resistance, regular exercise has beneficial effects on risk factors for CVD in patients with type 2 diabetes. For example in a

Figure 12.3 Plasma glucose and insulin responses to a 100 g oral glucose load in individuals with mild type 2 diabetes, before and after 12 months of regular, vigorous exercise training.

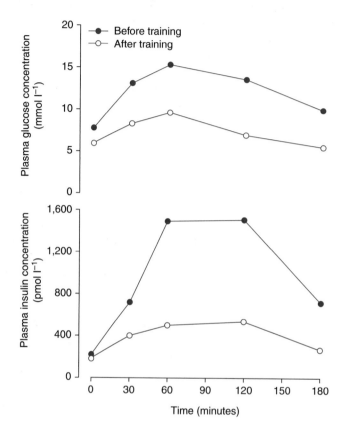

Source: Holloszy *et al.* (1986).
Note: After training glucose tolerance test was performed about 18 h after each individual's most recent bout of exercise.

Swiss study, 16 patients with well-controlled diabetes participated in a programme of aerobic exercise (walking, rowing, stationary bicycling, climbing stairs; average total duration 4 h week^{-1}) for 3-months (Lehmann *et al.* 1995). Training reduced triglycerides by 20%, increased HDL-cholesterol by 23% and reduced blood pressure by 8/8 mm Hg, as well as reducing body fat and the ratio of circumferences at the waist and hip.

Thus, the theoretical basis for exercise therapy in patients with type 2 diabetes is well established. Regular, frequent participation in exercise that involves large muscle groups and expends a lot of energy is indicated. In practice, this is not always straightforward because most patients are elderly, with cardiovascular and metabolic complications. Many are obese and 'diabetic foot' complications make weight-bearing activities difficult. Moreover, patients are usually advised to change their diet as well as to increase their physical activity. (Clinical guidelines recommend an intense, multifaceted lifestyle intervention to target all features of the disease. This has been found to reduce the risk of cardiovascular and microvascular events by about 50% (Gæde *et al.* 2003).)

OBESITY

For most people, physical activity accounts for only 15–30% of daily energy expenditure (Chapter 7). Nevertheless, it is the component with the greatest potential for alteration. For example in elite triathletes or cyclists in the Tour de France, physical activity may account for up to 75% of daily energy expenditure. Thus, there is great potential to increase energy expenditure through physical activity and, theoretically, exercise should be an effective method of reducing body fatness in obese individuals. In practice, however, this is not the case. Randomized trials consistently indicate that exercise has only a modest (1–2 kg) effect on weight loss, leading some to conclude that exercise makes only a 'marginal contribution' to the treatment of obesity (Garrow 1995). Why should this be?

One explanation is the short duration of most exercise training studies. The typical duration of a weight-loss study is 4 to 12 months, which is brief considering that obesity develops over many years. Another factor is exercise adherence, which is often poor. A third issue, linked with the previous two, is that energy expenditure is often insufficient to elicit major weight change. A further 'snag', as Garrow observes, is that the ability to exercise is lowest in the most obese individuals (Garrow 1995). Although these facts are discouraging, there is good evidence that exercise can be an effective method of weight loss in all individuals save those with extreme obesity (body mass index (BMI) $\geq$40 kg m^{-2}).

In one study demonstrating this, investigators examined weight and fat loss in nearly 200 obese Singaporean men undergoing a 5-month period of basic military training (Lee *et al.* 1994). Subjects performed 29 h of training per week, of which 14 h were described as 'physical'. No dietary restriction was imposed although the recruits did receive lectures on health and nutrition. Average body mass was reduced from 94.6 kg to 82.1 kg, an average loss of 12.5 kg of which 11.9 kg was fat mass and only 0.6 kg was fat-free mass. (This preservation of fat-free mass is a well-recognized advantage of exercise over dieting alone as a means of weight loss.) The weight loss reduced BMI from 31.5 to 27.4 kg m^{-2}. The greatest loss of weight/fat occurred in individuals with the highest initial levels of fat (Figure 12.4).

Exercise can be effective in the treatment of obesity in women as well as in men. Hadjiolova and colleagues studied 32 obese women over a 45-day period (Hadjiolova *et al.* 1982). Participants performed 10 h of exercise per day including walking and long distance races, gymnastics, games and dancing. Diet was maintained at pre-training levels. Body weight decreased from 95.1 to 82.7 kg (only 1.5 kg of this loss was fat-free mass) and body fat declined from 38.2% to 30.7%.

Although these two studies are extreme examples involving considerable amounts of exercise they do show that physical activity can be an effective weight-loss strategy, providing that energy expenditure is sufficient. This key point is confirmed by a review that examined the findings of studies comparing diet with exercise as a means of weight loss (Ross *et al.* 2000). Most studies found that dieting results in greater weight loss than exercise. In each case, however, the energy deficit created through dieting was greater than that created through exercise. Only two studies made fair comparisons, that is, the energy deficit created through dieting was the same as that created through exercise. In both these studies the amount of weight lost was independent of the method

Figure 12.4 Reductions in body mass, fat mass and fat-free mass in 197 obese Singaporean men following 5 months of military training.

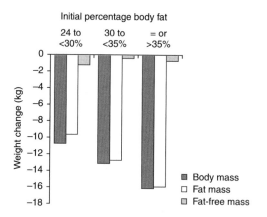

Source: Lee *et al.* (1994).

Note: Greater reductions in body mass and fat mass occurred in those with the highest level of body fat before training.

of eliciting the energy deficit, that is, 6.1 kg versus 6.2 kg with a 2,100 kJ day^{-1} (500 kcal day^{-1}) energy deficit in one study and 7.4 kg versus 7.5 kg with a 2,940 kJ day^{-1} (700 kcal day^{-1}) energy deficit in the other, for diet and exercise, respectively. Furthermore, exercise duration in these studies (43 min day^{-1} and 65 min day^{-1} respectively, both over a 12-week period) was attainable for many individuals. It was concluded that: '... exercise without diet restriction is an effective strategy for reducing obesity' (Ross *et al.* 2000).

Weight loss that occurs with exercise appears to be under a degree of genetic control, as shown convincingly by Bouchard and colleagues (Bouchard *et al.* 1994). These researchers conducted an exercise training study with seven pairs of male monozygotic twins. Daily energy and nutrient intake was kept constant throughout the study. Subjects exercised for nearly an hour at 50–55% of VO$_2$max, twice a day, 9 out of 10 days over a 93-day period. This caused an estimated energy deficit of 244 MJ (58,100 kcal) and a mean body mass loss of 5 kg, all of which was fat. Moreover, there was a large reduction in visceral adipose tissue, as assessed by computed tomography, from 81 to 52 cm^2. There was large inter-individual variation, however, in the response to the exercise-induced energy deficit that was much less within twin pairs than between twin pairs (Figure 12.5). This suggests that some individuals will experience a greater weight and fat loss with exercise training than others and that this is strongly influenced by genes.

An issue requiring further study is the extent to which exercise can reduce visceral fat. As mentioned earlier, visceral fat is particularly pernicious in terms of disease risk. Reductions in this, therefore, should be particularly beneficial to health. Diet-induced loss of visceral fat has been extensively studied. For every kilogram of weight loss achieved through dieting, total visceral fat is reduced by 2–3% (Ross 1997). Thus a 12-kg weight loss induced by diet would reduce visceral fat by up to one-third. The effects of exercise are less well studied. The study of Bouchard and colleagues (Bouchard *et al.*

Figure 12.5 Genetic influence on exercise-induced weight loss as indicated by changes in body weight (left panel) and visceral fat (right panel) in seven pairs of male monozygotic twins following a 244 MJ energy deficit induced by exercise over a 93-day period.

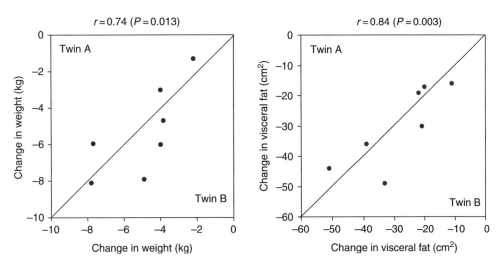

Source: Bouchard *et al.* (1994).

1994) confirms that exercise is an effective means of reducing visceral fat in overweight young men (Figure 12.5). However, based on limited data, it has been suggested that exercise might be more effective in reducing visceral fat in men than in women (Ross 1997). Further research is required to test this hypothesis and also to compare the effects of diet and exercise on visceral fat reduction. In combination, they are clearly effective; Figure 12.6 demonstrates changes in subcutaneous and visceral fat (assessed using magnetic resonance imaging) in two obese patients after a diet plus exercise intervention.

Most weight loss guidelines recommend a combination of diet and exercise and this appears to be the optimal strategy both for reducing weight and for maintaining weight loss. The latter point was nicely illustrated by a study of 629 women and 155 men enrolled on the National Weight Control Registry in the US (Klem *et al.* 1997). These men and women had been successful at long-term maintenance of weight loss – they had all lost an average of 30 kg and maintained a minimum weight loss of 13.6 kg for 5 years. Self-report data revealed that these individuals had low-energy intakes of energy and fat (averages of 5,778 kJ day^{-1} and 24% of energy) and high-energy expenditures (average 11,830 kJ week^{-1}), suggesting that a combination of diet and exercise was the key to the success of these previously obese individuals in maintaining weight loss. Such findings are not the norm, however, and most individuals who lose weight (whether through diet or exercise) subsequently regain it within 3–5 years. This has led some to propose that the most important benefit of exercise is in preventing weight gain, rather than treating it. There is evidence to support this view (Chapter 7). A summary of the recent American College of Sports Medicine guidelines on appropriate intervention strategies for weight loss is given in Box 12.3 (American College of Sports Medicine 2001).

Figure 12.6 Magnetic resonance images in the lumbar spine (level L4–L5 level and 5 cm above this) for a man and a woman before and after a 16-week programme of diet and exercise that resulted in a mean weight loss of 11 kg.

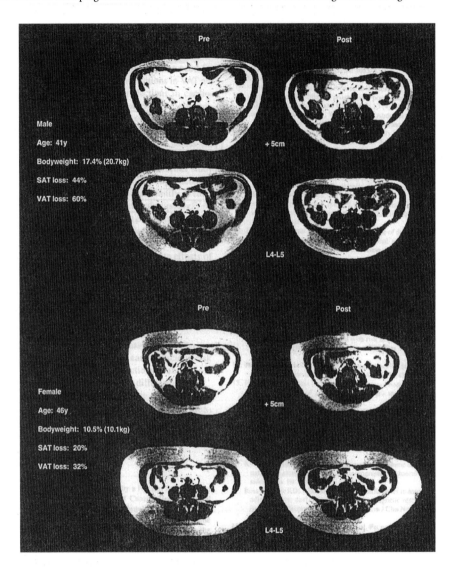

Source: Ross (1997).
Note: Adipose tissue is shown in white. SAT, subcutaneous adipose tissue; VAT, visceral adipose tissue. Note the reductions in SAT and VAT indicated by the reduced amount of whiteness.

RESPIRATORY DISEASES

The use of exercise training in children with asthma is controversial because there appear to be few effects on its defining feature, that is, bronchoconstriction. Training

BOX 12.3 SUMMARY OF THE AMERICAN COLLEGE OF SPORTS MEDICINE (2001) POSITION STAND ON APPROPRIATE INTERVENTION STRATEGIES FOR WEIGHT LOSS AND PREVENTION OF WEIGHT REGAIN IN ADULTS

It is recommended that

- individuals with a BMI >25 kg m^{-2} consider reducing their body weight and that those with a BMI ≥30 kg m^{-2} seek weight-loss treatment;
- overweight and obese individuals target reducing their body weight by a minimum of 5–10% and maintain at least this magnitude of weight-loss long term;
- individuals strive for long-term weight maintenance and the prevention of weight regain over the long term. Prevention of weight gain or weight regain is defined as maintaining a body weight within 2.3 kg of one's current weight;
- weight loss programmes target changing both eating and exercise behaviours;
- overweight and obese individuals reduce their current level of energy intake by 2,100–4,200 kJ day^{-1} (500–1,000 kcal day^{-1}) to elicit a weight loss of approximately 0.5–0.9 kg week^{-1} (1–2 pounds week^{-1}). In addition to reducing total energy intake, it is recommended that dietary fat intake be reduced to <30% of total energy intake;
- overweight and obese individuals progressively increase to a minimum of 150 min week^{-1} of moderate intensity physical activity. Eventually, this should be increased to between 200 and 300 min week^{-1} or ≥8,400 kJ week^{-1} (2,000 kcal week^{-1});
- resistance exercise supplements an endurance exercise programme in overweight and obese adults;
- pharmacotherapy for weight loss can only be used in individuals with a BMI ≥30 kg m^{-2}, or with a BMI ≥27 kg m^{-2} in the presence of additional comorbidities. Weight-loss medications should only be used under the supervision of a physician and in combination with modifications to eating and exercise behaviours.

does, however, lead to improved cardiorespiratory fitness and reduced breathlessness at a given exercise intensity in asthmatic children. There may also be psychosocial benefits. The need for medication may be reduced but this is a complex issue, because exercise is a potent stimulus to bronchoconstriction and children need prophylactic medication before each session. A session of exercise may bring on asthma symptoms in about 80% of people with the disease. However, in both adults and children with asthma there is evidence to suggest that in many cases exercise performance is more limited by lack of fitness than by underlying asthma. Therefore it is legitimate to encourage physical activity, assuming that underlying medication is adequate.

The evidence for the therapeutic value of exercise is, however, strong and extensive for chronic obstructive pulmonary disease (COPD). This term is applied to patients who have emphysema, chronic bronchitis or a mixture of both. The underlying pathology therefore differs but the symptoms are the same, that is, shortness of breath on minimal exertion because lung function is impaired. Most patients are elderly and ex- or current smokers. The development of COPD is silent and insidious because the healthy lung has good reserves of gas exchange capability. This reserve of function is eaten away by disease without any noticeable effects until, when approximately 60% of airway function is lost, symptoms develop. The disease is progressive and unlikely to undergo spontaneous natural remission. Once optimal medical treatment has been effected, rehabilitation focusses on the reduction of disability.

Rehabilitation is a relatively new feature of the management of patients with COPD, having been introduced in the US only in the 1980s (even later in Europe) when it was realized how much physical deconditioning and emotional responses to disability contributed to the resulting morbidity. Three features are common to most programmes, that is, exercise, disease education and psychosocial support. The exercise component is usually brisk walking or, less commonly, cycling. Training of the muscles of the upper extremities is sometimes included because this will diminish the ventilatory requirement of tasks using the arms.[5]

What does pulmonary rehabilitation achieve? There is ample evidence that this cannot alter parameters that reflect impairment, for example, FEV_1, blood gases or even maximal exercise capacity. Outcome measures are focussed on assessment of disability, such as walking performance, health status. These aim to reflect any changes in symptoms, improvements in function and independence in daily life (British Thoracic Society 2001).

In one large trial, 200 patients were randomized to a 6-week rehabilitation programme (education, including smoking cessation, recognizing and dealing with symptoms; aerobic exercise for arms and legs; and psychological issues relating to chronic disability) (Griffiths *et al.* 2000). Patients in the rehabilitation group were encouraged to exercise at home after the out-patient programme and all patients were followed for 1 year. Rehabilitation improved walking performance; after 6 weeks, patients in the rehabilitation group walked both faster and 50% further than controls in a symptom-limited 'shuttle'[6] walking test. Rehabilitation also reduced breathlessness and fatigue, improved patients' sense of control over their disease and improved their perception of their general health status. Some benefit was still evident 1 year later. During this year, patients in the rehabilitation group used fewer National Health Service resources (Table 12.1): they spent only half as many days in hospital as those in the control group, required fewer home visits from their general practitioner and less medication.

This study is not atypical. A review from the Cochrane Collaboration, based on 23 randomly controlled trials, concluded that rehabilitation for COPD results in moderately large and statistically significant improvements in health status (dyspnoea, fatigue, mastery) above the minimum clinically important difference and small improvements in walking distance (Lacasse *et al.* 2003).

What mechanisms are responsible for these improvements? The answer to this question is unclear. Training does not seem to lead to major adaptations of skeletal muscle metabolism in these patients, as it does in healthy people. One explanation is that patients cannot attain an intensity of exercise sufficient to stimulate these adaptations. The decrease in dyspnoea has been variously attributed to desensitization, (learning to overcome the anxiety associated with dyspnoea) or maybe to improved mechanical skill.

Table 12.1 Influence of rehabilitation on use of Health Service Resources (hospital and primary care) in patients with chronic obstructive pulmonary disease

	CONTROL $n = 101$	REHABILITATION $n = 99$
Days spent in hospital		
Respiratory illness	18.1 (9.3)	9.4 (10.2)[*]
All causes	21.0 (21.7)	10.4 (9.7)[*]
Consultations at primary-care premises		
Respiratory illness	4.5 (6.0)	4.7 (4.5)
All causes	7.3 (8.3)	8.6 (6.8)[*]
Primary-care home visits		
Respiratory illness	1.8 (3.2)	1.3 (2.4)
All causes	2.8 (4.6)	1.5 (2.8)[*]

Source: Adapted from Griffiths et al. (2000).
* Significantly different from control group, $P < 0.05$.

MENTAL ILLNESS

Very little is known about the role of exercise in treating mental illness other than depression, one of the most common mental illnesses. Clinically defined depression (for criteria see Biddle and Mutrie (2001)) affects 5–10% of the population of most developed countries. Its treatment, most frequently with drugs, is therefore a considerable burden on healthcare resources.

Meta-analytic reviews of exercise in the treatment of depression have found effect sizes in the range 0.5–0.7 standard deviation of change in depression scores (mainly based on the Beck Depression Inventory). This suggests that exercise does have an anti-depressant effect. However, the number of individual studies included in these analyses was rather small and only one was restricted to studies with subjects who had clinically-defined depression. Careful narrative review of 11 key studies conducted since 1970, all of which employed random assignment to groups and included only subjects defined as clinically depressed, concluded that exercise programmes consistently reduce depression (Biddle and Mutrie 2001). The reduction of depression was judged to be of the same order as that found for a variety of standard psychotherapeutic treatments. Effects are evident within 4–8 weeks and persist for up to 1 year. Little is known about the mechanisms by which exercise influences depression but no negative outcomes have been reported.

OTHER CONDITIONS

Physical activity and exercise are potentially valuable adjunct therapies in several other conditions, including osteoarthritis, osteopenia/osteoporosis, chronic low back pain and even chronic fatigue syndrome. Experience with all these patient groups is, however, limited and exercise interventions are in different stages of development, investigation and application.

Exercise is increasingly regarded as a key component of osteoarthritis management, although knowledge of long-term effects is inadequate. Comprehensive interventions including aerobic exercise (usually walking) and/or resistance exercise, pain management and education result in moderate improvements in measures of disability, physical performance (e.g. 6-minute walking distance, stair-climbing, getting in and out of a car) and perception of pain. Exercise does not worsen the disease and the limited information available suggests that it is relatively safe (e.g. only 2% of participants had serious musculoskeletal injuries related to exercise in the 18-month long US Fitness, Arthritis and Seniors Trial (Ettinger *et al.* 1997)). More experimental evidence about the influence (beneficial and detrimental) of exercise on joint structure and cartilaginous tissue is needed.

Physical activity is important in the prevention of osteoporosis (Chapter 10) but may have a therapeutic role also. However, only a handful of studies have specifically examined its effectiveness in women with a clinically defined condition. Most have found benefits, including reduced bone loss (compared with controls), improved balance and, in some instances, improvements in measures of psychological well-being and health status. There is no evidence, however, that therapeutic exercise reduces fracture risk and information on the risks involved is lacking. Nevertheless, it can be argued that exercise is the only single therapy that can simultaneously ameliorate low bone mineral density, augment muscle mass, promote strength gain, and improve dynamic balance – all of which are independent risk factors for fracture (Khan *et al.* 2001).

Chronic low back pain causes a great amount of suffering, loss of productivity and independence, as well as costs – to individuals and to societies. Its prevalence is increasing, partly because of the ageing of populations and partly because of changes in lifestyles and environment. Heavy physical work is one of the predisposing factors for low back pain but, paradoxically, exercise is now regarded as a first line therapy for sufferers. The most recent review of randomly controlled trials found strong evidence that exercise was as effective as conventional physiotherapy and more effective than usual care by a general practitioner (van Tulder *et al.* 2003). In contrast, exercise therapy is no better than other treatments for an acute episode of back pain.

SUMMARY

- Exercise contributes to the management of several patient groups. In some, for example cardiac patients, the course of disease may be favourably affected. In others, benefits are restricted to improved functional capacities, reduction of symptoms and improvements in health status (including sense of control over their disease).
- Exercise is a key component of rehabilitation for many cardiac patients, including those with chronic heart failure. Mortality and morbidity are reduced by at least 20% but the mechanisms involved are incompletely understood. Other benefits are apparent in improved functional capacities, reduced responses to sub-maximal exercise and improvements in measures of health status.

- Exercise improves walking ability in patients with claudication, probably to a greater degree than pharmacological interventions.
- Patients with cardiac disease, claudication, hypertension, diabetes and obesity often exhibit multiple risk factors. For them, exercise-induced changes in risk factors may be expected to decrease the risk of cardiovascular morbidity and mortality.
- Increased physical activity has the potential to elicit and maintain important fat loss in the obese. In practice, this is difficult to achieve. Most guidelines recommend a combination of diet and exercise for weight loss in obese patients.
- Exercise is increasingly employed in the rehabilitation of patients with COPD. In these, often elderly, patients even small improvements to functional capacities and quality of life are important.
- Patients with clinically defined depression probably benefit from exercise. Its anti-depressive effects are similar to those achieved through pharmacological therapy.

STUDY TASKS

1 Identify the principal goals of cardiac rehabilitation and discuss how exercise training contributes to the achievement of these goals.
2 Explain why patients with peripheral vascular disease experience pain on walking and why exercise training alleviates this.
3 Describe the main features of COPD and explain why patients with COPD find even walking distressing.
4 Explain the theoretical underpinning for the use of exercise in the management of obesity. Why is it difficult for obese patients to achieve substantial weight loss through exercise?
5 What, in your opinion, are the characteristics of an exercise regimen that aims to maximize the therapeutic value of exercise in patients with type 2 diabetes? Give your reasons in full, with reference to available evidence.

NOTES

1 The intervention also included dietary advice but the emphasis was on exercise.
2 This term is preferred to VO_2max if the classic criterion of a plateau in the oxygen uptake versus exercise intensity relationship is not met.
3 The reader will recall that almost 95% of patients with hypertension have blood pressures that are elevated for no apparent reason; they are said to suffer from 'essential' hypertension.
4 With careful control of insulin dose, type I diabetics can gain the usual benefits from a physically active lifestyle.
5 Many adaptations to training are specific to the muscle groups that are trained. To change respiratory responses to arm work, one must train the arms.
6 This test requires patients to walk up and down a 10 m course at a set speed which increases every minute until the patient can no longer, without troublesome symptoms, maintain the required speed.

FURTHER READING

American Association of Cardiovascular and Pulmonary Rehabilitation (1999) *Guidelines for Cardiac Rehabilitation and Secondary Prevention Programmes*, 3rd edn, Champaign, IL: Human Kinetics.

Coats, A.J.S., McGee, H.M., Stokes, H.C. and Thompson, D.R. (eds) (1995) *BACR Guidelines for Cardiac Rehabilitation*, Oxford: Blackwell Science.

Franklin, B.A., Whaley, M.H. and Howley, E.T. (eds) (2000) *ACSM's Guidelines for Exercise Testing and Prescription*. 6th edn, Philadelphia: Lippincott, Williams and Wilkins.

Morgan, M. and Singh, S. (1997) *Practical Pulmonary Rehabilitation*, London: Chapman and Hall Medical.

Knowledge assumed
Basic anatomy and physiology of the musculo-skeletal and endocrine systems
Principles of immune function and cells involved

13 Hazards of exercise

INTRODUCTION

Physical activity can be hazardous as well as beneficial to health. Jogging, walking and cycling inevitably increase exposure to the risk of injury through collisions with vehicles and falls due to uneven surfaces in pavements. Cycling is particularly hazardous. Around 500,000 injuries per year incurred during this activity are treated in US departments of emergency medicine and 800 people die; about one-third of injuries are to the head and these account for three quarters of deaths among cyclists. In the UK, 158 cyclists were killed on the roads in 1999 which was 5% of all fatalities.

Rather fewer injuries happen during swimming but deaths do occur from drowning in swimming pools, mainly among young children. Prolonged exercise in the heat can lead to hyperthermia, particularly if fluid intake is insufficient, and even to electrolyte imbalance. Hypothermia can be experienced by those engaging in water sports, hill-walking and even marathon running. (Deep body temperature can fall in individuals who cannot maintain a speed of walking or running sufficient to match heat production to heat loss.) Rhabdomyolisis (sporadic appearance in blood of abnormal levels of myoglobin) has been reported among endurance runners engaged in high volume training. There may be an increased likelihood of osteoarthritis in individuals who engage over many years in sports involving a lot of high impacts and torsional loading of joints.

Specific hazards are associated with physical activity for people with existing disease. Exercise can lead to hypoglycaemia in diabetics who take insulin or hypoglycaemic agents because it increases the rate of glucose uptake into muscle. Asthma may be precipitated by exercise – running in cold weather is a particularly potent trigger. In urban environments, air contains small amounts of gases and particulates other than its normal constituents. The increased ventilation of the lungs during exercise increases exposure to this pollution and may exacerbate respiratory problems in asthmatics. Even in healthy people, ozone and sulphur dioxide impair lung function.

The best-documented hazards of physical activity are: musculo-skeletal injuries; triggering of heart attack or sudden cardiac death; menstrual dysfunction and its associated osteopenia; and an increased risk of upper respiratory tract infections. Each is discussed below, with an emphasis on evidence relating to ordinary amounts of moderate exercise where this is available.

MUSCULO-SKELETAL INJURIES

Community studies in Europe suggest that every sixth unintentional injury is associated with leisure-time physical exercise, mainly sports. The majority are of low severity but a minority require hospitalization. At one university hospital in the Netherlands for example, sports injuries comprised about one fifth of all injuries treated over a 7-year period, making these the second highest cause of accidental injuries (Dekker *et al.* 2000).

Injuries associated with physical activity fall into two categories: overuse and acute traumatic. Incidence rates for acute exercise-related (including sport-related) injuries are rather low in the general population. For example, about 5% of European adults who participated in a telephone survey reported such an injury in the previous month. Rates are higher, of course, among populations that are vigorously active. Around 50% of people participating in team sports will sustain one or more injuries over a season and the annual rate of musculo-skeletal injuries among military trainees is between 25% and 50%.

The majority of sports injuries are to the lower limb (e.g. ligament sprains, meniscus tears) and two out of three occur during team sports. Soccer in particular gives rise to a high number of injuries, even when corrected for the number of people who play. Unfortunately, cervical spine injuries are occasionally incurred in sports such as rugby, diving, trampolining, gymnastics and horse-riding.

Running

Among recreational runners who are training steadily and participate in a long distance run every now and then, the yearly incidence rate for injuries is between 37% and 56%, that is, 2.5 and 12.1 injuries per 1,000 hours of running (van Mechelen 1992). Most injuries are to the lower limb, predominantly the knee, and the majority appear to be due to the constant repetition of the same movement and impact (overuse injuries). Many lead to a reduction of training or to the cessation of training. Weekly distance run is the most important determinant of running injuries, for both men and women. Other predisposing factors include previous injury (injury recurrence is common), lack of running experience, running to compete, a rapid increase in training distance or intensity. Running on hard surfaces and running in poor shoes are implicated in about 5% of injuries. Age and sex do not appear to be important aetiological factors.

Moderate levels of physical activity

Information about injury rates among people who engage in 'ordinary' amounts of moderate intensity activity is limited. Researchers have documented the prevalence and nature of injuries among participants in the Aerobics Center Study, a prospective study of a physical activity intervention (Hootman *et al.* 2002). Subjects (5,028 men, 1,285 women), who were aged between 20 and 85 and two-thirds of whom were physically active, provided information on physical activity habits and on injury experiences during one year. A quarter of participants reported at least one musculo-skeletal injury and 83% of these were activity-related, two thirds of them to the lower limb (Figure 13.1). Among both men and women, those participating in sports were the most likely to have an activity-related injury (27%), followed by runners (23–4%) and walkers (17–20%). However, 16% of subjects classified as sedentary also reported activity-related injuries, and so not all the injuries among the active groups can be attributed to physical activity purposefully taken for reasons of health benefit. In particular, those who walked for exercise experienced few 'excess' injuries, that is, above and beyond those reported in the sedentary group.

One of the few randomized intervention trials to report data on injuries is the physical activity versus Metformin trial conducted by the Diabetes Prevention Program Group. (Details of this study are discussed in Chapter 6.) Their findings are broadly in line with those from the Aerobics Center study. Among men and women at risk of type 2 diabetes who increased their physical activity level ('moderate exercise such as brisk walking', around 6 MET-h per week, for an average of 2.8 years) the incidence rate of musculo-skeletal injury was 24.1 per 100 person-years (Diabetes Prevention Program Group 2002). This was about the same as that experienced by the placebo group, which was 21.1 per 100 person-years.

Thus moderate amounts and intensities of physical activity are not associated with a high risk of musculoskeletal injuries. Walking for exercise carries a particularly low risk of injury, probably because the impact forces incurred are much lower than during running.

Figure 13.1 Distribution and percentage of activity-related musculo-skeletal injuries among participants in the US Aerobics Center Longitudinal Study.

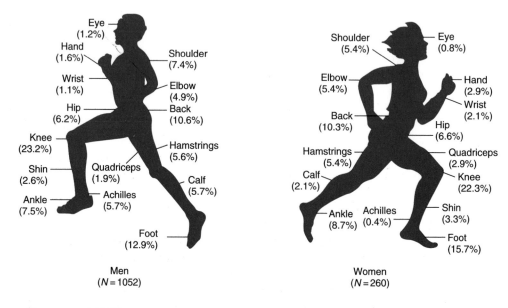

Source: Hootman *et al.* (2002).

Walking is very injury-free, even for the elderly. For example, among 21 men and women aged 70–79 years who trained by walking briskly for three sessions per week, increasing to 45 min per session, only one injury was sustained over 13 weeks (Pollock *et al.* 1991).

TRIGGERING OF HEART ATTACK, SUDDEN CARDIAC DEATH

Many people have atherosclerotic coronary arteries but relatively few experience a heart attack. Factors which 'trigger' an attack are therefore the subject of research interest. In approximately 5% of patients with myocardial infarction, vigorous exertion immediately precedes the onset of symptoms. Indeed, sudden death from cardiac causes occurs with an unusually high frequency during or shortly after vigorous exertion. Between 6% and 17% of all sudden deaths are exercise-related. Thus, vigorous exercise can trigger acute cardiac events. Just how risky is this for the heart and what factors alter the risk that it will trigger an event?

These questions have been addressed in epidemiological studies using the case-crossover method. This design allows transient risks, such as might occur during a period of vigorous exertion, to be quantified. In each of two major studies, one in Germany (Willich *et al.* 1993) and one in the US (Mittleman *et al.* 1993), researchers interviewed over a thousand patients soon after they were admitted to hospital with acute myocardial infarction. Patients' activities during the hour before the onset of symptoms were recorded, as well as their usual level and type of physical activity. In the German study, the risk of a heart attack during (or up to 1 h after) vigorous exertion was estimated to be twice as high as during less strenuous activity or no activity. In the American study, the risk associated with vigorous exertion was estimated to be six times greater than at all other times.

Of the 4.4% of American patients who had engaged in heavy exertion just before their heart attack, 70% were gardening, splitting wood, lifting or pushing (all mainly or partly isometric) and 30% were doing dynamic exercise such as jogging or racquet sports. Although the relative risk during vigorous exertion was increased 6-fold in these patients overall, it varied greatly according to their usual frequency of vigorous exertion, as shown in Figure 13.2. Thus it was 2.4 among those reporting regular vigorous exertion but 107 among individuals who were habitually sedentary, with clear evidence of a dose–response relationship. This effect modification by level of habitual exercise was even stronger in the German population studied (Willich *et al.* 1993).

Findings from the US Physicians' Health Study bolster these conclusions, using prospective data and taking sudden death from cardiac causes as the outcome measure (Albert *et al.* 2000). Among more than 12,000 men followed for 12 years, the risk of sudden cardiac death associated with an episode of vigorous exercise was 17 times higher than at all other times. Again, this increase in risk was strongly influenced by the habitual level of activity. The relative risk ranged from 74 in men exercising less often than once per week to 11 in men exercising five or more times per week.

Overall, these studies confirm that vigorous exertion is one trigger to myocardial infarction. However, they consistently show that the transient increase in risk is much smaller among people who are accustomed to vigorous exertion than in those who are sedentary.

Figure 13.2 Relative risk of myocardial infarction during a single session of heavy exertion, compared with all other times, according to the frequency of regular heavy exertion at an intensity ≥6 METs.

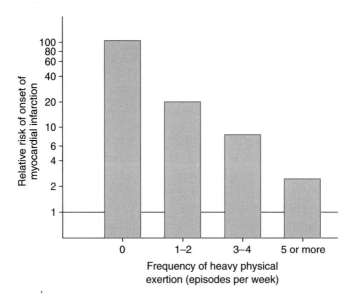

Source: Mittleman *et al.* (1993).
Note: The relative risk is shown on a logarithmic scale because the extremely high relative risk in habitually sedentary people (107) was so different from that in those who reported heavy exertion five or more times per week (2.4) ($P < 0.001$). The horizontal line represents the baseline risk, that is, the risk during no exertion or during light exertion.

It is important to realize that people who experience an exercise-related cardiac event invariably have underlying heart disease. In young adults, sudden exercise-related cardiac death is mainly attributable to cardiovascular abnormalities, usually congenital, the most common of which is hypertrophic cardiomyopathy. Among people over 35, autopsy studies show that the vast majority of sudden cardiac deaths are in individuals with severe atherosclerotic coronary artery disease. About 80% are due to cardiac arrest (through electrical instability) and the remainder to myocardial infarction. One mechanism may be that activation of the sympathetic nervous system during exercise leads to an acute increase in susceptibility to ventricular fibrillation. Alternatively, vigorous exercise may disrupt a vulnerable atherosclerotic plaque, leading to thrombosis and occlusion of a coronary vessel. Training decreases the sympathetic response and abolishes the platelet activation and hyper-reactivity that is observed in sedentary people during exercise. These adaptations would explain the blunting of the transient risk among very active individuals.

Paradoxically then, exercise is hazardous – as well as beneficial – to the heart. Does this diminish its role as part of a preventive strategy against CHD? Two points are important. First it is important to distinguish between the *relative* risk (discussed above) and the *absolute* risk. Whilst the risk during vigorous exercise may be high in relation to that at other times, the absolute excess risk during any particular episode of vigorous exercise is extremely low, about 1 death per 1.51 million episodes (Albert *et al.* 2000).

Even in the marathon, the prevalence of sudden death is low, about one in 50,000 to 74,000 competitors (Maron 2000). The frequency of sudden cardiac death in young athletes during competitive sports is even lower, about one in 200,000 student athletes per academic year (Maron 2000). Second, the evidence that habitual, moderate to vigorous exercise protects against CHD is compelling in its extent and consistency, as explained in Chapter 4. Thus, the transient increase in risk associated with a session of strenuous exercise is clearly outweighed by the strong cardioprotective effect of regular physical activity. The issue of benefit versus risk for CHD is discussed again in Chapter 14 in the context of public health.

MENSTRUAL DYSFUNCTION: CAUSES, CONSEQUENCES AND CORRELATES

Menarche has been reported to occur later in athletic girls, gymnasts and dancers for example, than in less active girls. However, this observation is probably accounted for by self-selection of late-maturing girls into these activities, rather than by a cause and effect relationship. By contrast, training is clearly a causal factor in the high prevalence of menstrual dysfunction among women athletes.

The first systematic study found that between 6% and 43% of women runners participating in the 1977 US National Collegiate Cross-Country Championships had secondary amenorrhoea and that its prevalence was linearly related to training distance (Feicht *et al.* 1978) (Figure 13.3). Training intensity was highest among the amenorrhoeic athletes who were also better runners than those who were menstruating regularly.

Research has subsequently shown that the prevalence of secondary amenorrhoea in adult athletes ranges from 3–66% (depending on the sport and the criteria used to

Figure 13.3 Incidence of secondary amenorrhoea in women runners in relation to distance run in training.

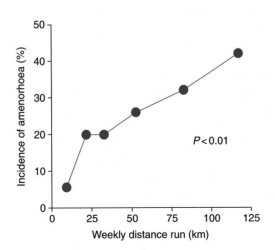

Source: Feicht *et al.* (1978).

define amenorrhoea), compared with only 2–4% of women in the general population. It is highest in sports where leanness influences performance or where weight categories restrict competition, for example endurance running, gymnastics and rowing. Intense training for non-sporting activity is also associated with amenorrhoea; for example, around 40% of ballet dancers are amenorrhoeic. Predisposing factors include youth (women who take up a sport as adults are less likely to become amenorrhoeic), a low level of body fatness and a sudden increase in training intensity or volume.

As well as secondary amenorrhoea, other menstrual dysfunctions are common among runners, that is, primary amenorrhoea, oligomenorrhoea, abbreviated luteal phases and low plasma concentrations of progesterone. The latter two are common even in regularly menstruating athletes. Menstruation is lacking or irregular because the normal endocrine control of the cyclic activities of the ovaries (set out in Box 13.1) is disrupted.

In oligo/amenorrhoea, the mid-cycle surge in luteinizing hormone (on which ovarian function critically depends) is blunted and the characteristic pulsatility of the secretory pattern of this hormone is decreased. The increase in follicle-stimulating hormone in the luteal-to-follicular transition is also attenuated. These abnormalities reflect disturbances of the neurosecretory functions of the hypothalamus.

BOX 13.1 PRINCIPAL PHASES OF THE OVARIAN CYCLE AND THEIR REGULATION

The menstrual cycle involves coordinated physical and hormonal changes illustrated in Figure 13.4.

- During the first (follicular) phase of each cycle one follicle grows and matures prior to releasing an egg. Oestrogens, mainly secreted by the developing follicle, are the dominant hormonal influence, preparing the uterus to receive a fertilized egg by stimulating proliferation of the endometrium.
- After ovulation, the remainder of the follicle collapses into a *corpus luteum* ('yellow body') that secretes large amounts of progesterone – the dominant hormone in the second (luteal) phase of the cycle. Progesterone optimizes conditions for implantation of the egg.

Cyclic variations in gonadotrophins from the anterior pituitary control these ovarian functions.

- High oestrogen levels at the end of the follicular phase stimulate pituitary output of follicle stimulating hormone and a surge of luteinizing hormone that precipitates ovulation.
- High concentrations of progesterone in the luteal phase have broadly the opposite effects, inhibiting gonadotrophin release.

Pituitary function is regulated by the hypothalamus. Hypothalamic neurones secrete 'releasing hormones' into blood vessels that link this part of the brain with the anterior pituitary. These hormones control gonadotrophin secretion. The links between the hypothalamus and the pituitary explain why a variety of emotional and physical factors can influence menstrual cyclicity.

Figure 13.4 Ovarian and endocrine changes during the normal menstrual cycle.

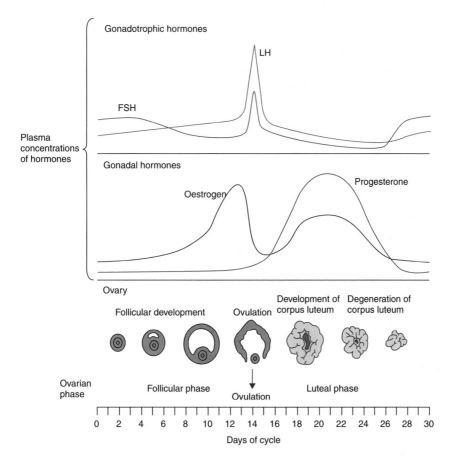

Source: Adapted from Sherwood (1991).

Reproductive function is often impaired, however, even in women who have a normal pattern of menstrual bleeding. Researchers have undertaken careful comparisons of the characteristics of menstrual cycles of recreational runners with those of sedentary age- and weight-matched controls (de Souza *et al.* 1998). The exercising women ran an average of 32 km (20 miles) per week, had a body fat level of 20% and a $\dot{V}O_2$max of 41.5 ml kg^{-1} min^{-1} – all characteristics consistent with a moderate habit of exercise rather than intense training and competition. Even though all the exercising women had repeatable menstrual cycle lengths in the normal range, their ovarian function was frequently abnormal: 55% of cycles monitored demonstrated either luteal phase deficiency (too short and/or inadequate because of low progesterone) (43%) or anovulation (12%). Cycles were more likely to be anovulatory as the severity of the disruption to endocrine function progressed.

Reproductive hormone responses are probably depressed by regular exercise in men as well as in women. Male endurance runners have been reported to exhibit plasma testosterone concentrations that are around 15% lower than those of sedentary men (Cumming *et al.* 1989). Evidence is scarce, however, and the implications of this sub-clinical effect are unclear.

Mechanisms of menstrual disorders in physically active women

Early hypotheses that reproductive function is disrupted when body fat levels fall below a critical threshold or because of the 'stress' of exercise have largely been disproved (Loucks 2001). An alternative 'energy availability' hypothesis holds that exercise has no suppressive effect on the reproductive system beyond the impact of its energy cost. This hypothesis is supported by reports that athletic women have lower energy intakes than would be expected for their activity level; by endocrine signs of chronic energy deficiency (decreased insulin, insulin-like growth factors (IGF-I) and thyroid hormones, elevated cortisol); by similarities between athletic amenorrhoea and anorexia nervosa; and by an extensive literature showing a dependence of reproductive function on energy availability in a range of mammalian species, including humans. According to this hypothesis, the links between the hypothalamus and the pituitary are disrupted when some unknown signal, possibly leptin, indicates that dietary energy intake is inadequate to cover the energy costs of both reproduction and locomotion.

Clinical consequences

'Athletic amenorrhoea' is reversed by modest weight gain and a reduced level of training (Drinkwater *et al.* 1986) and so is not necessarily, in itself, a long-term hazard to reproductive health. Its most obvious consequence is infertility; amenorrhoeic women are not developing egg cells that can be fertilized. Short luteal phases and low progesterone can also lead to infertility due to failures of implantation. Paradoxically, without contraception, irregularly menstruating athletes may be at increased risk for unwanted pregnancy because their day of ovulation is less predictable. One might also speculate that early cardiovascular disease may be a problem in amenorrhoeic athletes. There are reports of reduced HDL-cholesterol and of impaired endothelium-dependent dilatation in this group. Both these changes may be expected to increase the risk for cardiovascular disease.

The best-documented consequence of prolonged disruption to normal menstrual function is skeletal demineralization. Although there are no prospective data, this may be expected to increase the risk of stress fractures and, in the longer term, premature osteoporosis. Several reports in the early 1980s showed that women with exercise-associated amenorrhoea had lower spinal bone mineral density (BMD) than age-matched physically active or sedentary eumenorrhoeic women. Retrospective analysis of the menstrual histories of nearly one hundred runners found that spinal BMD correlated with the duration of their amenorrhoea (Drinkwater *et al.* 1990) (Figure 13.5). Thus the severity of bone loss increases with the degree of menstrual cycle disturbance. Moreover, as newer techniques became available, it has become clear that bone loss in amenorrhoeic athletes is not restricted to the spine but may be observed at

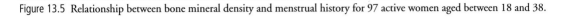

Figure 13.5 Relationship between bone mineral density and menstrual history for 97 active women aged between 18 and 38.

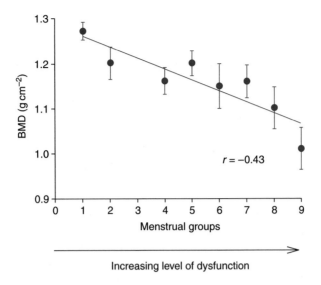

Source: Drinkwater *et al.* (1990).
Note: Values are mean and standard error. Numbers of women in each group are 21, 7, 2 (not plotted but included in regression), 5, 22, 9, 10, 10 and 11 for groups 1 to 9 respectively. Subjects were categorized according to both menstrual patterns of menstrual function at time of observation and previous menstrual history. Group 1 – regular menstrual cycles at time of study and previously. Group 9 – amenorrhoeic at the time of study and previously.

multiple skeletal sites, suggesting that this is a generalized effect and that even sites subjected to impact loading during exercise may be affected.

Skeletal demineralization is not restricted to women with exercise-associated oligo/amenorrhoea. Studies in physically active women with regular menstrual cycles but who are anovulatory and/or have short luteal phases have found that bone loss over one year is strongly associated with these disturbances. Thus, in some circumstances, exercise in physically active premenopausal women may exacerbate – rather than protect against – bone loss. No large prospective trials are available to evaluate the long-term consequences for skeletal health in women who have experienced long episodes of oligo/amenorrhoea. Eight-year follow-up data are available, however, for a group of 29 athletes; despite several years of normal menses or use of oral contraceptives, formerly oligo-amenorrhoeic athletes still had values for vertebral BMD that were 15% lower than those of the athletes who had regular menses throughout (Keen and Drinkwater 1997).

Mechanisms of bone loss in athletic amenorrhoea

The traditional explanation has been oestrogen deficiency. Oestrogens are consistently found to be low in active women with amenorrhoea and it is known that oestrogen deficiency is the principal cause of bone loss in women with ovarian failure. However, studies using biomarkers of bone cell activities and collagen turnover have challenged this view by showing that the pattern of bone remodelling in women with exercise-related amenorrhoea is not consistent with an oestrogen-deficient state. In oestrogen deficiencies, there is increased bone turnover with excessive bone *resorption* that is normalized by oestrogen replacement. By contrast women distance runners with long-term amenorrhoea show reduced bone *formation*, compared with eumenorrhoeic runners or age-matched sedentary eumenorrhoeic women (Zanker and Swaine 1998). Moreover, low BMD in amenorrhoeic athletes is much less responsive to exogenous oestrogen therapy than in women with ovarian failure.

An alternative to the oestrogen deficiency hypothesis is that low energy availability accounts for imbalanced bone remodelling in active amenorrhoeic women, as it does for the amenorrhoea itself. Energy deficit has been shown to elicit the metabolic aberrations (increased cortisol, low thyroid hormones, IGF-I deficiency) found in active amenorrhoeic women that can lead to inadequate bone formation.

Relation with eating disorders

The dependence of reproductive function and skeletal health on adequate energy availability is clear from the preceding discussion. Unfortunately, many very active women, far from maintaining an adequate diet, exhibit disordered eating.

Disordered eating may be intentional or unintentional but, either way, results in inadequate replenishment of the energy demands of exercise. This, in turn, may lead to deficiencies of essential micronutrients. Athletes may intentionally restrict food intake in a conscious attempt to lose weight or body fat in the interests of improved appearance or athletic performance. The spectrum of behaviours ranges from mild restriction of food intake to severe restriction (as in *anorexia nervosa*) to occasional, even regular, binge eating and purging (*bulimina nervosa*). Compulsive exercise, that is, exercise in addition to a normal training regimen, may also be practised. If maintained, these behaviours may result in psychological and other medical complications as well as in menstrual dysfunction and potentially irreversible bone loss.

The prevalence of disordered eating in athletes is high. For example, one study of young elite swimmers revealed that 60% of average weight girls and 18% of underweight girls were trying to lose weight; moreover, 12.7% were vomiting, 2.5% were using laxatives and 1.5% were using diuretics, all behaviours associated with morbidities (Dummer *et al.* 1987). Indeed, the prevalence of disordered eating in amenorrhoeic athletes is so high that the term 'Female athlete triad' has been coined to describe a syndrome comprising low bone mineral density, menstrual dysfunction and disordered eating (Otis *et al.* 1997).

UPPER RESPIRATORY TRACT INFECTION AND IMPAIRED IMMUNE FUNCTION

It was mentioned in connection with physical activity and the risk of cancer (Chapter 9) that the relationship between changes to the body's innate immune system and exercise intensity and/or volume appears to be J-shaped (Figure 13.6); so, although moderate exercise probably benefits immune function, prolonged intense exercise may impair it.

The immune system distinguishes host cells from those of invading organisms in two ways: through the adaptive immune system which detects a particular invading organism (specific recognition); and the innate system that detects such organisms in a non-specific manner. Evidence suggests that exercise appears to have effects on both the adaptive and the innate systems.

Epidemiological reports suggest that, during periods of heightened training or after marathon-type events, athletes are at increased risk of upper respiratory tract infections. For example, the incidence of such infections was studied in a group of 2300 marathon runners who had applied to enter the Los Angeles marathon (Nieman *et al.* 1990). After the race, runners reported information about their training habits and about upper respiratory tract infections and symptoms before and for one week after the race. Nearly 13% of participants reported having an infectious episode during the week following the race, compared with only 2.2% of similarly experienced runners who had applied but did not participate (for reasons other than sickness). Participants were six times as likely to have an infection during the week after the race than the non-participating runners. Runners training more than 96 km per week were twice as likely as those running less than 32 km per week to have experienced an infection during the two months leading up to the marathon. These findings are supported by several smaller studies from South Africa on runners participating in 56 km and 90 km ultra-marathons.

The innate and adaptive immune systems help to defend the body against upper respiratory tract infections. After prolonged, intensive exercise there are complex changes to the populations of cells that constitute a first line of defence against infection, that is,

Figure 13.6 Hypothesized relationships between exercise level, immune function and incidence of upper respiratory tract infection.

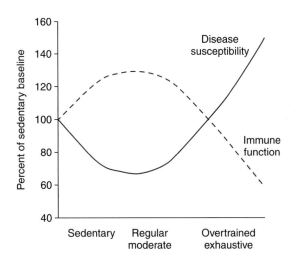

Source: Woods *et al.* (1999).

macrophages, neutrophils and natural killer cells. (Macrophages have phagocytic and cytotoxic capacities. Neutrophils, also phagocytic, are important in the non-specific killing of bacteria. Natural killer cells seek out and destroy virus-infected cells.) Macrophage anti-viral function, neutrophil function and NK cell activity are all impaired for several hours after a session of high intensity exercise, particularly if this is prolonged (Pedersen and Hoffman-Goetz 2000). One hypothesis is that the immune system's involvement in the inflammatory response following intensive exercise impairs its capability to protect against upper respiratory tract infection. The function of T lymphocytes (important cells of the adaptive immune system) is also altered following prolonged, intensive exercise. These cells are pivotal for anti-viral responses and are of particular relevance, given that athletes appear to suffer mainly from illnesses caused by respiratory viruses.

In the light of these findings, it has been suggested that a prolonged session of high intensity endurance exercise leads to transient but clinically important changes in immune function. During this 'open window' of altered immunity (which may last between 3 and 72 h, depending on the parameter measured), viruses and bacteria may gain a foothold. A weakness of this argument is that investigators have yet to link most markers of immunosuppression after exercise with an increased incidence of infections. However, a recent study reported a negative correlation between the concentration of an immune factor (immunoglobulin A) in the saliva and incidence of upper respiratory tract infection in elite swimmers during an intensive training period (Gleeson *et al.* 1999).

PREVENTION

Some of the hazards of exercise are preventable. In some sports protective equipment offers an obvious and effective strategy. Examples include helmets, mouth guards, shin pads and knee pads. The compulsory use of a face mask in ice hockey has virtually eliminated eye injuries. Safety is improved if cyclists display lights and wear reflective clothing. Helmets offer protection for the head for cyclists, although there are reports from Canada, Australia and the US that the increasing use of these has not been associated with a reduction in fatalities. Runners can decrease their risk of injury by wearing clothing that ensures that they can easily be seen and selecting their routes carefully.

At least one community-based attempt to prevent injuries has been reported. Swedish researchers compared injury rates in a year-long injury prevention intervention population with those in a comparable control population (Timpka and Lindqvist 2001). The intervention comprised: an injury prevention course for physical education teachers; a programme for coaches and referees on discouraging foul play; compulsory use of shin pads in soccer; increased supervision of novices in all sports; and courses for coaches on proper physical preparation. In the intervention population, the total morbidity rate for sports-related injuries decreased by 14% – the rate of moderately severe injuries halved and minor injuries increased but there was no change in the rate of severe injuries. There was no tendency towards a decreased injury rate among the over 40s, probably because they do not participate as much in the traditional, mainly team, sports targeted by the intervention.

Prevention of running injuries may best be tackled through education on rehabilitation after injury, early recognition of symptoms of overuse and training principles (van Mechelen 1992). Education on gradual entry into any sort of conditioning programme is particularly important for middle-aged and older people, especially if (often after long periods of a sedentary lifestyle) they intend to enter or re-enter the competitive arena.

Finally, most of the hazards of exercise may be avoided by pursuing a habit of moderate exercise, rather than high volume, intense training. As explained earlier, the transient risk of a cardiac event during exercise is much lower in people who are physically active on a regular basis than in those who rarely take exercise. Therefore sedentary individuals who begin low intensity activity and progress gradually to more and more intense activity will minimize this risk. Women who engage in moderate intensity physical activity and allow the physiological mechanisms of hunger and satiety to govern their eating behaviour are not at high risk of menstrual dysfunction or its consequences. Similarly, recreational exercisers are unlikely to experience problems with immune function.

SUMMARY

- Exercise-related injuries are common. Most are musculoskeletal, either overuse or acute traumatic. The majority are to the lower limb and two out of three occur during team sports.
- Vigorous exertion is one of a number of triggers to heart attack. On average, people are between two and six times more likely to have an attack during or shortly after exercise than at other times but this transient increase in risk is much greater among sedentary people than among those accustomed to vigorous exercise. It is outweighed by the decrease in risk long-term.
- Menstrual dysfunction is common among women who engage in large amounts of vigorous endurance exercise. Even when menstrual periods are regular there may be abnormalities that will reduce fertility.
- Bone mineral density is lower in amenorrhoeic athletes than in those with normal menstrual periods. There is concern that this bone loss may be largely irreversible.
- Immune function may be compromised for some hours after prolonged vigorous exercise and this may provide a 'window of opportunity' for infections to gain a foothold.
- Some hazards may be prevented through protective equipment. Those mainly associated with excessive exercise may be attenuated through maintenance of energy balance (particularly for women) and/or by moderation of the training regimen.

STUDY TASKS

1. What are the commonest musculo-skeletal injuries among runners? Discuss the factors that predispose to these and suggest preventive strategies.
2. Explain the statement 'exercise is both hazardous and beneficial for the heart'. On average, what is the relative risk associated with a single session of vigorous exercise and how does this differ between sedentary people and those who are highly active.

3 Distinguish between eumenorrhoea, oligomenorrhoea and amenorrhoea. Give examples of sports where women are at high risk of menstrual dysfunction and suggest reasons.

4 Describe one cross-sectional study that suggests that spinal bone mineral density in women athletes is related to their menstrual history. What are the limitations to this study?

5 Describe the likely relationship between immune function and the intensity/volume of exercise. Identify the weakness in this explanation of the increased prevalence of upper respiratory tract infections in runners after marathon-type events and suggest what studies might be undertaken to address this.

FURTHER READING

Bennell, K.L., Malcolm, S.A., Wark, J.D., Brukner, P.D. (1997) 'Skeletal effects of menstrual disturbances in athletes', *Scandinavian Journal of Medicine and Science in Sports* 7: 261–73.

Loucks, A.B. (2001) 'Physical health of the female athlete: observations, effects, and causes of reproductive disorders', *Canadian Journal of Applied Physiology* 26 (Supplement): S176–S185.

Nieman, D.C., Pedersen, B.K. (1999) 'Exercise and immune function: recent developments', *Sports Medicine* 27: 73–80.

Otis, C.L., Drinkwater, B., Johnson, M., Loucks, A., Wilmore, J. (1997) 'American College of Sports Medicine position stand. The female athlete triad', *Medicine and Science in Sports and Exercise* 29: 1–9.

van Mechelen, W. (1992) 'Running injuries: a review of the epidemiological literature', *Sports Medicine* 14: 320–35.

14 Physical activity, fitness and public health

Knowledge assumed
Common measures of disease prevalence
Role of dose–response relationships in causality in epidemiology

INTRODUCTION

The world is experiencing a transition from communicable to non-communicable diseases, in developing countries as well as those with established market economies. Non-communicable diseases contribute to about 60% of deaths worldwide and 43% of the global burden of disease (reflecting the sum of years of life lost because of premature mortality and years of life with disability). Moreover, it is estimated that, by 2020, these diseases will contribute to 73% of deaths and 60% of the global burden of disease (World Health Organization 1999). These shifts in the major causes of mortality, morbidity and disability necessitate changes to public health priorities. Non-communicable diseases, which include cardiovascular disease (CVD) and type 2 diabetes, share a relatively small number of preventable risk factors, especially lack of physical activity, tobacco use and an unhealthy diet. The public health approach seeks to change these features of the population's behaviour.

Population-attributable risk (PAR) (explained in Chapter 2) estimates the proportion of a public health burden that is caused by a particular risk factor. The PARs for the major risk factors for coronary heart disease (CHD) in the UK are shown in Figure 14.1; more than one-third of CHD can be attributed to physical inactivity. Equivalent figures for Australia and the US are 18% and 35%, respectively. Based on data from the US, the PARs for physical inactivity in type 2 diabetes and colon cancer appear to be of the same order. All these estimates make a number of assumptions in relation to the prevalence of inactivity. They also assume that ceasing to be sedentary reduces the risk of the disease in question. There is some epidemiological evidence for this for CHD (discussed in Chapter 4) but not for diabetes or colon cancer. Moreover, PARs inevitably overestimate the potential reduction in disease incidence because not all people will become physically active. Despite these limitations, they clearly show that increases in the physical activity levels of a population may be expected to reduce the incidence of several non-communicable diseases.

What implications does this information have for public health strategies? Two approaches to primary prevention may be identified; the 'high-risk' approach and the population approach. The first requires selective screening for risk factors, followed by therapeutic interventions with the group at greatest risk (in the present context, individual guidance on physical activity guidance and/or opportunities to participate in an exercise programme); the second aims to produce favourable shifts in the population distributions of risk factors (encourage everyone to do a little more). These approaches are not mutually exclusive. However, the priority for public health, as opposed to clinical medicine, is to reduce overall disease incidence and the most effective way to do this is probably to attempt to shift the whole distribution of risk. For physical inactivity, this requires a population-based strategy to increase activity across all sectors.

Figure 14.1 Proportion of all coronary heart disease in the UK attributable to the major risk factors.

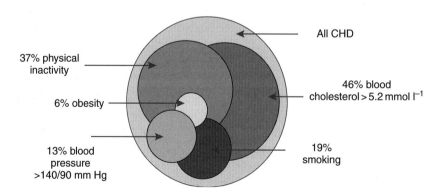

Source: Adapted from British Heart Foundation 2000.
Note: The overlapping reflects the fact that the total adds up to more than 100% because people have more than one risk factor.

Taking an example for blood pressure, data from the Asia Pacific Cohort Studies Collaboration indicate that an average 3 mm Hg reduction in diastolic blood pressure achieved by shifting the whole population blood pressure distribution down, has the potential to prevent 1.2 million deaths from stroke and 0.6 million from CHD every year by 2020 in the Asia Pacific region alone (Beaglehole 2001). This modest change is achievable through increasing physical activity levels.

RECOMMENDATIONS FOR PHYSICAL ACTIVITY

Early in the twentieth century there was concern in the UK at the poor fitness of recruits to the armed services. As this impaired the country's capability to wage war, the government took action to improve the fitness of young people, introducing 'physical training' (PT as it was called) into schools. Nowadays, governments around the world instigate strategies to increase fitness and/or physical activity in their populations for a different reason – the benefits to personal and public health.

The development of recommendations on physical activity began in the middle of the twentieth century when scientific interest in the biological effects of exercise and training gathered momentum. By the 1970s, this had generated a considerable literature about the type, intensity, frequency and duration of exercise needed to improve fitness – invariably assessed as $\dot{V}O_2$max. The first formal document was from the American College of Sports Medicine (ACSM) in their 'Position statement on the recommended quantity and quality of exercise for developing and maintaining fitness in healthy adults' (ACSM 1978). The recommendation was for 'continuous aerobic activity', 3–5 days per week at an intensity of 50 of 85% of $\dot{V}O_2$max for 15–60 min per session. This position stand, and the 1990 update (ACSM 1990), was soundly based in that if most healthy adults followed its recommendations they would improve their fitness. Many people assumed, probably correctly, that this regimen would also lead to health benefits but this was not the basis on which it was formulated.

The need to expand the 'exercise training-physical fitness' model to include a 'physical activity-health' model (Haskell 1994) was addressed during the 1990s, leading to recommendations from several authorities, namely: the ACSM/US Centers for Disease Control and Prevention (Pate *et al.* 1995); the US National Institutes of Health (National Institutes of Health Consensus Development Panel 1996); and the US Surgeon General's Report (US Department of Health and Human Services 1996). These recommendations (summarized in Box 14.1) have had a strong influence on public health strategies and statements on physical activity in developed countries worldwide (e.g. UK Department of Health's 1996 Strategy Statement on Physical Activity, the 1999 statement by the European Heart Network).

These recommendations differ in four important respects from earlier versions that were targeted at fitness improvements:

- By specifying 'moderate-intensity' activity.
- By asserting that multiple short spells of activity during a day are one way to fulfil the recommendations.

BOX 14.1 CORE RECOMMENDATIONS FOR PHYSICAL ACTIVITY TO IMPROVE HEALTH AND WELL-BEING (based on the US sources listed in the preceding text but adopted in many other countries)

- Children and adults should accumulate at least 30 min of moderate-intensity physical activity on most, preferably all, days of the week.
- Greater benefits will accrue from increasing either the duration or the intensity of the activity.
- The activity may be structured, as in recreational pursuits (e.g. swimming, cycling, aerobics classes, dancing), or based on 'lifestyle' activities (brisk walking, stair climbing, gardening etc.).
- Physical activity should be habitual and life long.

Notes:

1 The US Surgeon General's Report also recommended strength-developing activities once or twice a week.
2 There is concern that minimal compliance with these recommendations is insufficient to avoid weight gain. For this reason Health Canada stipulates 30–60 min per day of moderate activity.

- By specifying a 'lifestyle' approach as an alternative to structured exercise.
- By emphasizing the need for frequent, preferably daily, activity.

The rationale for these aspects of the recommendations is explained briefly in the next section – and more comprehensively by Haskell (Haskell 1994, 2001).

Moderate intensity[1]

In many epidemiological studies the type of physical activity associated with favourable health outcomes (lower risk of all-cause or CVD mortality, incidence of type 2 diabetes and some cancers) has been of light to moderate intensity. (Chapters 3, 4, 6 and 9 provide further discussion and main references.) Recent studies with careful classification of self-reported physical activity have confirmed these findings. The amount and/or speed of walking – moderate intensity exercise for most middle-aged people – has been specifically linked to the risk of each of these endpoints. Moreover, lower rates of CHD are consistently reported for people in the moderate category for physical activity or fitness than for those in the least active or fit categories (Figure 4.9, Chapter 4).

Exercise training studies have found that moderate intensity activity is sufficient to improve fitness in previously sedentary people (see section on walking) and benefit some health-related outcomes. For example, moderate exercise is at least as effective in reducing blood pressure as more vigorous exercise (Chapter 5); and low or moderate activity clearly improves 'metabolic fitness' (Chapter 8).

Two other considerations underpin the decision to recommend moderate, rather than vigorous, intensity physical activity for previously sedentary individuals. First, the hazards of physical activity appear to be associated more with its intensity than with its frequency or duration (discussed in Chapter 13). Unaccustomed vigorous activity is particularly hazardous for sedentary people – the group specifically targeted by public health recommendations. Second, experience worldwide with earlier recommendations and campaigns have shown how difficult it is to alter the proportion of people engaging in vigorous exercise.

Accumulating activity throughout the day

This principle assumes that multiple short periods of activity spread throughout the day will benefit health. According to this reasoning, it is the total amount of activity that is important, rather than the duration of any single bout. Evidence for this comes from several sources.

First, much of the activity reported in epidemiological studies and found to be associated with favourable health outcomes was probably undertaken on an intermittent basis rather than continuously for long periods. Examples include: walking, stair climbing, gardening, household chores. There are few data to confirm the (presumably fairly safe) assumption that most such activities are performed intermittently but one report from the Harvard Alumni study provides some evidence. Between 1988 and 1993 participants reported the frequency and average duration of each episode of activity; researchers found that longer sessions did not have a different effect on risk compared with shorter sessions, as long as the total energy expended was similar (Lee *et al.* 2000).

The second source of data on the validity of accumulating activity is research that has compared responses to contrasting patterns of activity of the same total duration. For example in a classic study, previously inactive middle-aged men did 30 min of jogging per day, 5 days per week for 8 weeks (DeBusk *et al.* 1990). One group did this in a single, 30-min session per day while a second group did three 10-min sessions per day (no control group). Both patterns of activity led to an increase in VO_2max and weight loss was similar in both groups. Another, randomly controlled study, allocated middle-aged women to train by brisk walking in either one 30-min session or three 10-min sessions per day (Murphy and Hardman 1998). Fitness improvements were similar in each walking group (relative to control) and three short sessions were at least as effective in decreasing body fatness as one long bout (Table 14.1). A subsequent study from the same group found that three 10-min sessions per day of brisk walking resulted in similar increases in high density lipoprotein (HDL)-cholesterol and similar decreases in total cholesterol and triglycerides as one 30-min session (Murphy *et al.* 2002).

If the principle that total energy expenditure mainly determines benefits to health-related outcomes, then it should be possible to 'trade' intensity for duration. We can be fairly confident that this is true for weight control because reviews and meta-analyses have consistently found that the total energy expended in physical activity or exercise determines its influence on body weight or fatness (Chapter 7). A few studies have specifically compared the effects on a health outcome of exercise sessions differing in intensity, while holding total energy expenditure constant. In one, described in more

Table 14.1 Changes with different patterns of brisk walking in previously sedentary, middle-aged women

	CONTROLS n = 10	THREE × 10-MIN SESSIONS, n = 12	ONE × 30-MIN SESSIONS, n = 12
Body mass, kg	+0.6 (0.7)	−1.7 (1.7)*	−0.9 (2.0)
Sum 4 skinfold thicknesses, mm	+2.6 (2.8)	−3.3 (3.5)*	−2.8 (3.8)*
Waist circumference, cm	+0.6 (1.0)	−3.0 (2.4)*	−1.8 (2.4)
Systolic blood pressure, mm Hg	−2.0 (6.9)	−7.4 (7.3)	−4.6 (5.9)
$\dot{V}O_2$max, ml kg^{-1} min^{-1}	−0.5 (0.1)	+2.3 (0.1)*	+2.4 (0.1)*

Source: Murphy and Hardman (1998).
* Values are mean (standard deviation). Change from baseline significantly different from change in controls, $P < 0.05$.
Training was either one 30-min session per day or three 10-min sessions per day, 5 days per week for 10 weeks.
Comparisons are with controls who remained sedentary.

detail in Chapter 8, researchers found that the postprandial triglyceride response was decreased by the same amount after either 90 min of exercise at 60% $\dot{V}O_2$max or after 180 min at 30% $\dot{V}O_2$max (Figure 8.8). Similarly, in a study of women with type 2 diabetes, insulin sensitivity was enhanced to the same degree after a longer session of exercise at 50% $\dot{V}O_2$max or a shorter session at 75% $\dot{V}O_2$max of equivalent energy expenditure (Braun *et al.* 1995). Thus, at least for these two outcomes, there is some evidence that intensity *can* be traded for duration.

However, given the prominence afforded in public health recommendations to the efficacy of accumulating physical activity throughout the day, research on this topic is inadequate: the total number of subjects in studies comparing short with longer bouts of activity is small; information on the effects of sessions of activity shorter than 8–10 min is lacking; few studies have compared the effects of longer bouts of moderate activity with those of shorter bouts of more vigorous activity; and only a small number of health-related outcomes have been studied.

Lifestyle activity

There is overlap here with topics discussed earlier as many so-called 'lifestyle' activities are of moderate intensity and undertaken intermittently. They are characteristically self-selected leisure, occupational or household activities of at least moderate intensity and engaged in as part of a daily routine. Observational and prospective epidemiological studies have linked these activities to health benefits but there are few intervention trials.

In one 2-year randomized (but not controlled) trial, called Project Active, researchers compared the effects of increasing activity through lifestyle activities with those of a traditional structured exercise programme (Dunn *et al.* 1999). Changes in fitness, body fatness and several risk factors for CVD were measured in 235 healthy, slightly overweight men and women aged 35–60. Estimated energy expenditure increased by a similar amount in both groups. Although the structured exercise group showed a greater improvement in fitness after 6 months, they failed to maintain this advantage and, by 24 months, there was no significant difference between groups in the increase in $\dot{V}O_2$max (mean values: lifestyle 0.77 ml kg^{-1} min^{-1}, structured 1.34 ml kg^{-1} min^{-1}). Both groups experienced similar (small) decreases in body fatness and blood pressure. This study and a few others (several of overweight or obese individuals) provide support for the proposition that increases in lifestyle activities lead to favourable changes in health-related outcomes. An important limitation to this literature, however, is the lack of randomized trials that include a control group.

Frequent, almost daily, activity

Physical activity does not need to result in a training effect to elicit a health benefit. Some health-related changes may be due largely to acute biological responses that persist for some time following each session. For example, blood pressure is decreased for up to 12 h after an exercise session (Chapter 5); and plasma triglyceride concentrations are reduced for even longer after a session of aerobic exercise (Chapters 5 and 6). However people need to be physically active on an almost daily basis if health benefits due to these acute responses are to be maintained. This is well illustrated by 'de-training' studies. Two beneficial metabolic characteristics (low postprandial triglycerides, good insulin sensitivity) have been shown to deteriorate rapidly when the habit of exercise is interrupted (Figure 14.2).

One small study is especially relevant because it looked at the acute effects of several short sessions of brisk walking (a lifestyle activity of moderate intensity), accumulated throughout the day (Murphy *et al.* 2000). Plasma triglycerides were measured in 10 middle-aged overweight people over three separate days during which they ate breakfast, lunch and an early evening meal. During one trial, subjects sat down all day (control); during another they walked for 30 min before breakfast; and during the other they walked for 10 min before each meal. Both patterns of brisk walking decreased triglycerides by a similar (statistically significant) amount (Figure 14.3). Thus, it is not only long, continuous episodes of activity which result in acute biological changes – accumulating activity throughout the day is effective too.

Overall evaluation of basis for newer aspects of physical activity recommendations

Despite the evidence described in the previous section, dose–response relationships with physical activity are poorly described for many health outcomes. The need for more research on the topic is clear and is being addressed. However, the evidence that physical activity benefits health is irrefutable and concerns about the inadequacy of information on dose–response should be viewed in the context of this certainty.

Public health recommendations for physical activity will be refined as dose–response relationships are better described. These will vary for different health outcomes, however and several biological changes probably contribute to a specific clinical benefit

Figure 14.2 (a) Changes in fasting and postprandial plasma triglyceride concentrations in 10 endurance-trained athletes during a 6.5-day interruption to training (mean and standard error) and (b) changes in insulin sensitivity in nine moderately trained men and women during a 7-day interruption to training (mean and standard deviation).

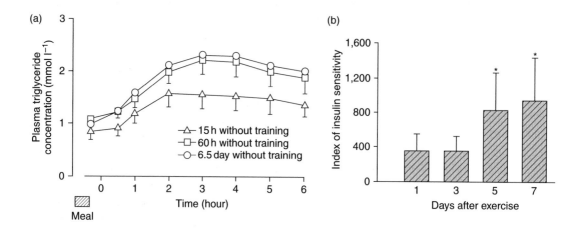

Sources: Hardman *et al.* (1998) and King *et al.* (1995).
Notes: (a) A high-fat mixed meal was completed at time 0 h. The area under the plasma triglyceride × time curve was 45% lower at 15 h than at 60 h ($P < 0.05$). (b) Insulin sensitivity measured as the product of insulin and glucose areas under concentration versus time curves; low values indicate good sensitivity. * Significantly different from 1 and 3 days after exercise.

Figure 14.3 Effect of 30 min of brisk walking on plasma triglyceride concentrations throughout the day.

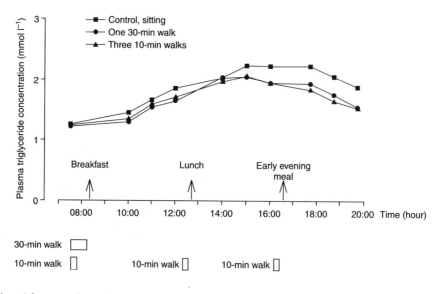

Source: Adapted from Murphy *et al.* (2000).
Notes: Ten subjects aged 34–66 undertook three trials; control (sitting down all day); one 30-min walk before breakfast; and three 10-min walks, one before each meal. Plasma triglycerides were significantly lower than control with each pattern of walking.

(e.g. physical activity may reduce the risk of a heart attack through effects on blood pressure, lipoprotein metabolism, insulin resistance and improved coronary endothelial function. Each mechanism may have a different dose–response relationship with physical activity). Furthermore, not all health outcomes will be related to the total energy expenditure of activity. For example, changes to bone mineral density would be expected to relate to the level of strain to which bone is exposed during activity. Public health recommendations can never reflect these complexities and so individuals (or those who counsel them) will always have to interpret recommendations in relation to their own particular needs and priorities.

Finally, as the Canadian HERITAGE Family Study has shown, individual responses to a given amount and/or type of activity are heterogeneous. (This study is investigating the heritable component of the heterogenicity in the responses to exercise.) People will get different 'rewards' for their investment in activity. Changes in fitness, HDL-cholesterol and blood pressure were all found to vary greatly among more than 700 participants despite a carefully standardized 20-week training programme (Bouchard and Rankinen 2001). This variation tended to cluster in families and so must reflect a degree of genetic predisposition and/or gene–environment interactions.

The relative importance of physical activity versus physical fitness for health benefits has been widely debated. As the level and intensity of activity is one determinant of fitness and the indices used to measure these parameters have different attributes, this is not always helpful. However, the recommendations summarized in Box 14.1 have been widely interpreted to mean that physical activity is the only goal and that fitness does not matter. This is wrong. It does matter. Fitness enables an individual to expend more energy or sustain a higher rate of energy expenditure without becoming fatigued. This helps weight regulation, enhances the acute biological responses to each session of activity and opens up a wide choice of leisure-time pursuits. A given task (e.g. shovelling snow, playing football with the children) demands a lower proportion of VO_2max for a fit person, so he/she can do it with something in reserve.

CHANGING PHYSICAL ACTIVITY BEHAVIOURS

This is the big challenge for public health and one that is the subject of much research interest. It is well documented that compliance with structured exercise programmes is poor – often at a level associated with smoking cessation or dieting. However, public health strategies now focus on regular moderate-intensity physical activity as part of an activity lifestyle rather than on structured programmes. This makes it important to understand the modifiable determinants of physical activity levels and sedentary behaviours. (Sedentary behaviour – measured for instance as computer use, television viewing, time spent in cars – is important for its contribution to the decrease in overall energy expenditure that may be a strong influence on average weight gains in populations.)

Environmental influences are important at the population level. For example, the associations of walking and cycling in relation to land use and transportation are now being studied. At the level of the individual, it is important to understanding the motivation of people who are active, the barriers perceived by those who are insufficiently active and the ways in which these change during the lifespan. In terms of motivation, increases in physical activity may be self-reinforcing; population-based surveys show significant associations between physical activity and general well-being and mood.

Behaviour change appears to involve movement through a series of stages, although change is cyclical and people may relapse. One widely used model defines these as: pre-contemplation (includes people who are not currently exercising and have no intention of doing so in the near future); contemplation (current non-exercisers who have an intention to start exercising in the near future); preparation (currently doing some exercise, but not regularly); action (those who are currently exercising but have only recently started); and maintenance (those currently exercising who have been doing so for some time). This model has been used to assess the distribution of physical activity behaviour in populations. In a meta-analysis of 68 such studies, involving 68,580 participants, it was estimated that 14% were in pre-contemplation, 16% in contemplation, 23% in preparation, 11% in action and 36% in maintenance (Marshall and Biddle 2001). This type of information is helpful in designing and targeting intervention strategies.

For a detailed discussion of the determinants of physical activity and the strengths and weaknesses of different physical activity interventions, readers are referred to specialist texts (e.g. Sallis and Owen 1999, Biddle and Mutrie 2001).

BENEFITS VERSUS RISKS

The relationship between the benefits and risks to health associated with physical activity is not well described. This relationship matters, both at the level of the individual – where it will be modified by pre-existing medical conditions (see Chapter 12), and at the level of the population. It will not be the same for all groups; risks may be greater for previously sedentary people and for the elderly.

Some risk/benefit analysis is available for cardiac events. In a retrospective case-control study of 133 men who died from primary cardiac arrest, information was obtained from the wives of the deceased (Siscovick et al. 1984). Among men with the highest habitual level of activity, an episode of vigorous exercise was associated with a 5-fold increase in risk, compared with a 56-fold increase in men whose habitual physical activity level was low. (This is entirely consistent with the evidence discussed in Chapter 13.) The unique finding of this study was that the overall risk of the physically active men, that is, during and not during vigorous exercise, was only 40% of that of the sedentary men. Thus, the transient increase in the risk of a cardiac event associated with a single session of exercise[2] is clearly outweighed by the long-term benefit.

Unfortunately, no comparable analysis is available for musculoskeletal injuries. This gives rise to concern because their prevalence will increase if the population becomes more active and more provision for treatment will be required. Injury avoidance may be particularly important for old people, for whom the consequences of a fall may be catastrophic.

Public health interventions need to provide guidance on how to maximize benefits and minimize risks. Of the variables that influence the 'dose' of physical activity, intensity is the most important in relation to risks. Vigorous activity may lead to a greater benefit for a specific health outcome than moderate activity but it is probably associated with greater risks. For example, the Aerobics Center Longitudinal Study found that brisk walking provides a greater net health benefit than running because of its lower risk profile (Hootman *et al.* 2002). Previously sedentary people should therefore begin with light/moderate activity and increase duration and frequency only gradually, refraining from activity during periods of ill health or when the environment is hazardous – through pollution, for example. Simple measures can reduce the risks associated with specific activities, for example, wearing protective clothing and equipment.

Finally, physical activity is not the only intervention aiming to benefit health that carries risks. Drugs have side effects, too, and they range from the discomforting to the life threatening. Their packaging therefore carries instructions on how to optimize effectiveness and minimize risks – rather like physical activity recommendations. In some circumstances, physical activity may be as (or more) effective than a drug in decreasing disease risk and it may incur fewer side effects. For example, the Diabetes Prevention Program Group trial compared physical activity and Metformin as means to prevent the development of type 2 diabetes in people with impaired glucose tolerance (Diabetes Prevention Program Research Group 2002). Subjects allocated to the drug therapy group were more likely not only to develop type 2 diabetes but also to experience a high incidence of gastrointestinal disturbances than those in the lifestyle intervention group.

WALKING AS THE BASIS OF PUBLIC HEALTH STRATEGY

Walking (amount and/or usual pace) has now been specifically studied in observational and prospective studies and shown to be independently associated with a lower risk of all-cause mortality, CHD/CVD and type 2 diabetes. Comprehensive analyses of walking behaviour and health outcomes have been published, particularly among cohorts of women. For example, the Women's Health Initiative Observational Study (Manson *et al.* 2002) found that both amount and pace of walking were strongly related to the risk of a cardiovascular event (Figure 14.4).

Walking at a 'normal/ordinary' pace, say (4.8 km h^{-1} or 3 mile h^{-1}) on level ground demands about 3.5 METs, increasing the metabolic rate more than 3-fold. This will constitute light activity for the average young man but vigorous activity for older or less fit individuals (Figure 14.5). For individuals with low $\dot{V}O_2$max values it is especially important to express relative intensity as %$\dot{V}O_2$max reserve (rather than as %$\dot{V}O_2$max, for explanation of the term $\dot{V}O_2$max reserve and its implications, see Chapter 2). For them a small increase in walking speed means a marked increase in the level of physiological stress.

Energy expenditure increases with walking speed, disproportionately so at higher speeds. When asked to walk 'briskly', most inactive middle-aged men and women select a pace eliciting nearly 60% $\dot{V}O_2$max, that is, sufficient to improve fitness. Slower walking will be similarly demanding for older people or for those with limitations to cardiorespiratory function. It is therefore not surprising that regular brisk or fast walking has been found to improve fitness in controlled trials in both men and women – the range of improvement in $\dot{V}O_2$max reported ranges from 9% to 28%. Regular walking has also been reported to improve plasma lipid profiles, decrease adiposity (or avoid increases in fatness seen in controls) and decrease blood pressure (Morris and Hardman 1997).

Figure 14.4 Effect of volume and pace of walking on the relative risk of CVD among post-menopausal women in the US Women's Health Initiative Observational Study (a) age-adjusted relative risk according to energy expenditure from walking and (b) multivariate relative risk (light bars) and relative risk adjusted for age and walking time (dark bars), according to walking pace.

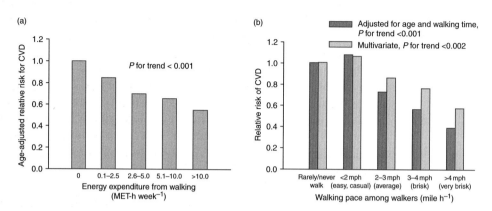

Source: Adapted from Manson *et al.* (2002).
Note: 10 MET-h is equivalent to walking for 3 h 20 min at an 'ordinary' pace of 4.8 km h^{-1} (3 mile h^{-1}).

Figure 14.5 Differences in the relative intensity of exercise (expressed as both %$\dot{V}O_2$max and as %$\dot{V}O_2$max reserve) for individuals with a range of $\dot{V}O_2$max values walking briskly at 5.6 km h^{-1} (3.5 mile h^{-1}), utilizing 3.8 METs.

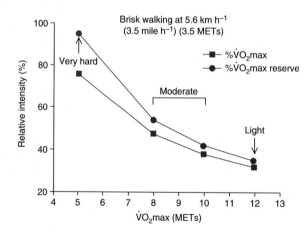

Source: Adapted from Howley (2001).

One reason walking for personal transportation is health-enhancing activity is that it is regular and performed on a near-daily basis. Commuting to work by walking has been studied by researchers from the UKK Institute in Tampere, Finland (Vuori *et al.* 1994). In a randomized, controlled study subjects walked an average of 36 min per trip, walking at a self-selected speed of about 6 km h^{-1} (3.75 mile h^{-1}), morning and evening, every working day for 10 weeks, at a relative intensity of just over 50% VO_2max. Walkers showed a small improvement in VO_2max, a decrease in heart rate during standard, sub-maximal exercise and a small increase in HDL-cholesterol.

Even as planned exercise, walking is very injury-free (Chapter 13). As mentioned in Chapter 13, among participants in the Aerobics Center Study, the prevalence of injuries in walkers was similar to that in sedentary people (Hootman *et al.* 2002). Moreover, increased duration of walking for exercise did not increase the risk of injury. These findings are important because fear of sustaining an injury and stopping activity because of an injury have both been associated with failure to start or maintain a physically active lifestyle.

Walking, which uses large skeletal muscles in a rhythmic, dynamic way, has been described as '...the nearest activity to perfect exercise' (Morris and Hardman 1997). While this may be true for health benefits derived from its increased cardiorespiratory and or metabolic demands, walking will not stimulate an optimal osteogenic response. Controlled trials have found either no effect of brisk or fast walking on BMD at the lumbar spine or a small benefit in post-menopausal women, compared with controls. However, even a small difference in BMD may reduce the propensity to fracture and regular walking may also diminish the risk of falling if strength and balance are improved (Chapter 10). Protection against hip fracture has been reported among walkers. The risk of hip fracture was reduced by 30% in white women who reported walking for exercise and there was a trend towards a greater reduction with increasing daily distance walked (Cummings *et al.* 1995). Moreover, older women enjoy walking and compliance is excellent. For example, one large trial ($n = 78$) reported 91% adherence among women aged between 60 and 70 during the first year of the intervention and 94% during the follow-up year (Brooke-Wavell *et al.* 2001).

Walking is cheap, safe, popular and sociable[3] and can take place in all sorts of environments, urban and rural. It is the obvious starting point for previously sedentary people. Promoting walking for health, and initiating environmental changes to facilitate walking, offers an opportunity to shift the population distribution of levels of activity. The potential benefits for public health may be illustrated through two examples. In the first, researchers took the distribution of physical activity measured in the Health Professionals Follow-up Study (Giovannucci *et al.* 1995) and modelled the effect of adding 3 h of walking to all participants. This would be expected to lead to a 17% decrease in the incidence of colon cancer (Colditz *et al.* 1997). The second example uses data from the Honolulu Heart Study in which 707 retired men of Japanese ancestry aged 61–81 years provided information on their regular walking distance. Of those who walked less than 1 mile per day, 43% died over the 12-year follow-up period, compared with 22% of those who walked more than 2 miles per day. Thus, for every five men who walked at least 2 miles a day, only fewer died over 12 years, compared with those who walked less than 1 mile a day. On the basis of these data, a walking group that includes 60 men aged 61–81 years may be expected to save one life each year.

A 'BEST BUY IN PUBLIC HEALTH'? (MORRIS 1994)

Current evidence indicates that the cost of medical care due to physical inactivity can range from about 2.4% (the Netherlands, without the cost of drugs), to about 6%

BOX 14.2 ECONOMIC BENEFITS FROM INCREASING LEVELS OF PHYSICAL ACTIVITY IN CANADA

Currency is US dollars (World Health Organization 1999).

- The increase from 21% in 1981 to 37% in 1995 in the proportion of people active enough to reduce the population risk of heart disease led to savings in health care costs of $190 million in 1995.
- The expected savings from achieving the 2003 target of increasing the physically active population by 10% are $5 billion (made up of cost of medical care, sick leave, lost revenues from taxes due to premature mortality).
- A 1% increase in the number of active Canadians may reduce the annual health care costs by $10.2 million for heart disease alone.
- The overall savings in the health care system is estimated at $364 per individual becoming active.
- A 25% increase in the proportion of the population that is physically active (to a total of about 50%) would stimulate productivity gains of between $2 and $5 for every dollar invested.
- Companies with employee 'active living' initiatives benefit by $513 per worker per year (from changes in productivity, absenteeism, staff turnover and injury).

(Canada) and 9.4% (USA – this includes the cost of obesity) of total health sector cost (World Health Organization 1999). As an example, estimates of the economic benefits in Canada, a country with comprehensive data on participation in physical activity over two decades, are given in Box 14.2.

These data on health economics are compelling but they are neither a sufficient nor a necessary argument for the promotion of physical activity. Low fitness and physical inactivity are a waste of human potential, at a personal level and at a population level. For this reason alone, physical activity should be widely and enthusiastically promoted.

SUMMARY

- Non-communicable diseases are a major and increasing public health burden, in developing countries as well as those with established market economies.
- Sedentary living is a major risk factor for several of these diseases, for example, CVD, type 2 diabetes, colon cancer. Estimates of PARs suggest that increasing physical activity levels would have an important impact on the incidence of these diseases.
- Public health recommendations stipulate that adults accumulate 30 min or more of physical activity of at least a moderate intensity on most days of the week.
- Like drugs, physical activity has some adverse side effects but these are mainly avoided if the intensity of activity is moderate.

- Brisk or fast walking will improve fitness in a majority of middle-aged and older men and in almost all adult women. Walking for exercise is very injury-free.
- The promotion of physical activity may lead to economic benefits for a country.

STUDY TASKS

1 Provide a reasoned argument for promoting moderate intensity activity, rather than vigorous activity, in the general population.
2 Explain why walking can be light or vigorous activity for different people.
3 It is asserted that one way to meet physical activity recommendations is to accumulate short bouts throughout the day. Do you think the available evidence is sufficient in quantity and quality to justify this assertion? Give full reasons for your point of view.
4 Explain why there is so much research interest in the dose–response relationships between physical activity and health outcomes.
5 Two strategies to improve public health through increasing physical activity are: to shift the whole population distribution of physical activity levels upward; and to increase activity in the least active groups. Discuss the relative strengths of these approaches.

NOTES

1 Absolute intensity 3–6 METs; relative intensity 40–60% $\dot{V}O_2$max reserve.
2 The media appreciate the relative risk (e.g. 5-fold, 56-fold) but, in reporting sudden exercise-related deaths, do not explain to their readership that the absolute risk of a cardiac event during exercise is very low (Chapter 13).
3 Dogs are good companions as well as people – in one Australian study 23% of all walking was dog walking!

FURTHER READING

Beaglehole, R. (2001) 'Global cardiovascular disease prevention: time to get serious', *The Lancet* 358: 661–3.

Canada's Physical Activity Guide (2000) Ottawa: Health Canada and Canadian Society for Exercise Physiology. Also available at http://www.hc-sc.gc.ca/hppb/paguide/index.html. Accessed 14.02.03.

Dunn, A.L., Andersen, R.E. and Jakicic, J.M. (1998) 'Lifestyle physical activity interventions: history, short- and long-term effects, and recommendations', *American Journal of Preventive Medicine* 15: 398–412.

Medicine and Science in Sports and Exercise 33, No. 6, Supplement (2001) Collection of papers from a symposium organised by Health Canada and the US Centers for Disease Control and Prevention '*Dose–response issues concerning physical activity and health: an evidence-based symposium*'.

Morris, J.N. and Hardman, A.E. (1997) 'Walking to health', *Sports Medicine* 23: 306–32.

US Department of Health and Human Services. (1996) *Physical activity and health: a report of the surgeon-general*. Atlanta, GA; U.S. Department of Health and Human Services, Centers for Disease Control and Prevention, National Center for Chronic Disease Prevention and Health Promotion.

Glossary

Abdominal fat   Fat on the trunk of the body between the waist and the diaphragm.

Accelerometer   A device that senses motion in one or more planes. It yields a count of movements in arbitrary units.

Accuracy   The extent to which measured values reflect the true values.

Acute biological response   Physiological or metabolic changes arising from a single session of exercise.

Adventitia   External coat of an artery or vein.

All-cause mortality   Death from any cause.

Amenorrhoea   Absence of menses. Primary amenorrhoea – normal menses never established; secondary amenorrhoea – cessation of menses after these were established.

Aneurysm   Rupture of an artery wall weakened by atherosclerosis, leading to internal bleeding.

Angina   Severe but temporary attack of cardiac pain.

Angiography   Radiography of arteries (e.g. coronary, carotid) after injecting a radio-opaque substance, such as iodine, into an artery.

Apoptosis   Active ('programmed') cell death.

Arteriovenous difference for oxygen   The difference between the oxygen content of arterial and mixed venous blood. This indicates how much oxygen has been extracted from arterial blood and utilized (predominantly) by muscle. Often written as $(a - \bar{v})O_2\text{diff}$.

Asthma Episodic obstruction resulting from airway inflammation characterized by cough, wheeze and breathlessness.

Atheroma Infiltration of lipid into the arterial wall, leading to tissue degeneration.

Atherosclerosis A progressive disease that leads to hardening and thickening of the walls of arteries and narrowing of these vessels.

β-hydroxyacyl-CoA dehydrogenase The rate-limiting enzyme in the mitochondrial β-oxidation pathway.

Bias Error that produces results that differ in a systematic manner from the true values.

Body mass index Body mass (in kg) divided by height (in m) squared, that is, body mass (kg)/height (m)^2. Used as a measure of obesity.

Bronchitis A lung disease characterized by excessive mucus production in the bronchial tree, causing coughing to get rid of sputum. Small airways become inflamed and narrowed and mucus may occlude small bronchi.

Cancer A set of diseases characterized by unregulated cell growth leading to invasion of surrounding tissues and spread to other parts of the body.

Carcinogen Agent capable of causing cancer.

Carcinogenesis Processes involved in the production of a cancer.

Cardiomyopathy Disorder of the heart muscle of unknown aetiology.

Case-control study A study comparing the occurrence of a possible cause/risk factor between cases (people with a disease or other outcome variable) and suitable controls (unaffected by the disease or outcome variable).

Case-report or case-series A study describing the characteristics of a patient or number of patients with a specific disease or attribute.

Cerebrovascular disease Stroke.

Cholesterol A steroid molecule necessary for the synthesis of steroid hormones and bile salts and an integral component of cell membranes.

Cholesterol esters Cholesterol in combination with long chain fatty acids, that is, esterified.

Chylomicron A lipoprotein, its main function is the transport of dietary fat (triglyceride) to adipose tissue and muscle.

Citrate synthase An enzyme involved in oxidative metabolism within the mitochondria. One of the enzymes in Kreb's cycle.

Chronic heart failure The inability of the heart to pump blood at a sufficient rate to meet the metabolic demands of the body.

Chronic obstructive pulmonary disease Progressive, sometimes partially reversible, airflow obstruction that does not vary over a long period. Predominantly caused by cigarette smoking that results in emphysema, chronic bronchitis and small airways disease.

Cohort study A study in which a group of people (a cohort), free of disease, are followed up to see how the development of new cases of the disease (or other outcome) differs between subgroups of the cohort classified according to their exposure to a potential cause/risk factor.

Confounding A factor associated both with an exposure (e.g. physical activity) and the outcome being studied which, if unequally distributed between the exposure subgroups, may confuse the findings. This distorts the estimated exposure effect.

Coronary collaterals Additional blood vessels that may grow in the heart, enhancing coronary blood flow.

Correlational study   A study describing relationships between potential risk factors and a disease (or other outcome). Populations or groups are the units of analysis, rather than individuals.

Cortical bone   Dense, strong ivory-like bone.

Cytotoxic   Toxic to cells.

Diabetes insipidus   A disease caused by a low secretion of vasopressin (antidiuretic hormone, ADH) from the pituitary gland and hence a low rate of reabsorption of water in the kidneys.

Diabetes mellitus   A disease characterized by either an inability of the pancreas to secrete insulin (type 1 diabetes) or an inability of the cells to respond to insulin (type 2 diabetes).

Diabetic foot   An informal term for the damages caused by microvascular disease of the extremities. Tissue damage leads to pain and, in severe cases, can lead to the need for amputation.

Disability   Restriction or lack of ability to perform an activity in a manner or within the range considered normal for a human being.

Dose–response   The relationship between level of exposure to a factor such as physical activity and the response to this in terms of health (or disease) outcome.

Dyslipidaemia   Abnormal concentrations in the blood of plasma lipoprotein lipids.

Dyspnoea   Uncomfortable sensation of breathlessness, difficulty in breathing or laboured breathing.

Effect modification   The magnitude or direction of the association under study differs according to the level of another factor.

Effect size   A statistic used to determine whether or not a difference between two means (different groups or same group in different conditions) is sufficiently large to be considered meaningful.

Emphysema   A lung disease characterized by enlargement of air spaces distal to the terminal bronchiole, with destruction of their walls. Parts of the capillary bed are destroyed.

Endosteum   The inner surface of bone that faces the bone marrow.

Endothelial function   Ability of the endothelium to invoke vasodilation or vasoconstriction by interacting with vascular smooth muscle.

Epidemiology   The study of the distribution and determinants of health-related states or events in specified populations, and the application of this study to control of health problems.

Euglycaemic clamp technique   Also known as the 'hyperinsulinaemic euglycaemic clamp' or the 'glucose clamp'. A technique used to determine insulin sensitivity by measuring how much glucose the body can dispose of (via oxidation and storage) in response to a fixed insulin concentration.

Eumenorrhoea   Normal menses, 10–13 cycles per year.

Excess post-exercise oxygen consumption   The elevation in oxygen consumption above resting levels which occurs following an acute bout of exercise.

Experimental study   A study in which researchers attempt to change a variable in one or more groups. Also called an intervention study.

Exposure   A measure of an individual's experience or 'dose' of a specified risk factor. (Exposure has two dimensions, level and duration; for physical activity it depends not only on the level of activity but also on number of years during which an individual has engaged in physical activity.)

Fat-free mass   Total body mass minus fat mass.

Fibrillation   Rapid uncoordinated contraction or twitching of cardiac muscle.

Fibrin   A protein polymer that traps erythrocytes and other cells in the blood to form a clot.

Fibrinogen   A plasma protein, the precursor of fibrin.

Fibrinolysis   The breakdown of fibrin in blood clots.

Flow-induced arterial vasodilation   Vasodilation in response to the increased shear stress on the endothelium when blood flow is increased.

Free radical   A highly chemically reactive molecule or molecular fragment that can damage cellular components such as DNA and lipid-rich membranes.

Generalizability   The extent to which results are applicable to different populations.

Gluconeogenesis   The synthesis of glucose from non-carbohydrate sources including pyruvate, lactate, glycerol and amino acids.

Glucose tolerance   The ability of the body to respond to the ingestion of glucose. Usually determined using the blood glucose concentration measured at the 2-h point in an oral glucose tolerance test.

GLUT4   A insulin-sensitive receptor located on membranes of cells in muscle and adipose tissue, which aids in the transport of glucose across the membrane into the cell.

Glycosuria   The presence of excessive amounts of glucose in the urine.

Gonadotrophins   Hormones that control the endocrine functions of the gonads (ovaries in women, testes in men).

Haemorrhagic   Due to a haemorrhage (bleed).

Health status   Disease-specific quality of life (a concept), usually measured with questionnaires.

High-density lipoproteins   Species of lipoproteins that, amongst other functions, promote the removal of excess cholesterol from cells in a process termed reverse cholesterol transport.

Homocysteine   A sulphur-containing amino acid, high plasma concentrations of which may be associated with an increased risk of cardiovascular disease.

Hypercholesterolaemia   Abnormally high concentration of cholesterol in the blood.

Hyperglycaemia   Abnormally high concentration of glucose in the blood.

Hyperinsulinaemia   Abnormally high concentration of insulin in the blood.

Hypertriglycerideaemia   Abnormally high concentration of triglycerides in the blood.

Hypertension   Abnormally high arterial blood pressure.

Hypertrophic cardiomyopathy   A familial cardiac disease characterized morphologically by an enlarged and non-dilated left ventricle.

Hypotension   Abnormally low arterial blood pressure.

Incidence   The number of new events/cases that develop in a defined population during a specified time interval.

Infarction   Death of a section of tissue because the blood supply has been cut off, as in myocardial infarction (heart attack).

Insulin resistance   A loss of sensitivity to the effects of insulin.

Insulin sensitivity   A measure of how effectively the cells remove glucose from the blood in response to insulin.

Insulin-dependent diabetes mellitus   Alternative name for type 1 diabetes.

Intima   Internal coat of a blood vessel.

Ischaemic   Impaired blood flow.

Isokinetic   Movement at a constant speed or angular velocity.

Ketoacidosis   A life-threatening situation in which an excess of ketone bodies leads to an increase in the acidity (reduction in pH) of the blood.

Ketogenesis   The formation of ketone bodies.

Lipaemia   Increased lipids, particularly triglycerides, in the blood.

Lipolytic   Chemical breakdown of fat by enzymes.

Lipoproteins   Macromolecular complexes composed of lipid and protein, responsible for transporting triglycerides and cholesterol in the blood.

Low-density lipoprotein   The main carrier of cholesterol in the blood, responsible for delivering cholesterol to the cells.

Lymphoma   Tumour of lymphatic tissue.

Macrophages   Cells that scavenge foreign bodies and cell debris.

Maximal oxygen uptake   The highest rate of oxygen uptake. This is reached when there is little or no further increase in oxygen uptake despite an increase in exercise intensity during a maximal exercise test. Expressed either in absolute terms (units: $l\ min^{-1}$) or relative to body mass ($ml\ kg^{-1}\ min^{-1}$). Sometimes predicted from heart rate and oxygen uptake during sub-maximal exercise. Used as a marker for aerobic/endurance fitness.

Media   Middle coat of a blood vessel.

MET   A multiple of the resting metabolic rate. One MET is defined as the energy requirement at rest, designated as an oxygen uptake of $3.5\ ml\ kg^{-1}\ min^{-1}$.

Meta-analysis   The statistical analysis of a collection of analytic results for the purpose of integrating the findings.

Metastasis   Process by which cancers escape to other parts of the body.

Metformin   A drug used in the treatment of type 2 diabetes.

Mutation   A heritable change in DNA.

Nitric oxide   A gas released by endothelial cells which acts as a vasodilator.

Non-esterified fatty acids   Fatty acids not combined with glycerol in triglyceride.

Non-insulin dependent diabetes mellitus   Alternative term for type 2 diabetes. An imprecise term since insulin is required by some individuals with type 2 diabetes.

Non-enzymatic glycation   A process whereby glucose molecules are bound to proteins to form glycoproteins.

Odds ratio   The ratio of the odds (likelihood) of exposure to the variable of interest in one group to the odds of exposure to this variable in another group.

Oligomenorrhoea   Infrequent menstruation, cycle prolonged beyond 35 days.

Oncogenes   A gene whose protein product contributes to carcinogenesis.

Osteoblasts   Cells that produce bone matrix to build new bone.

Osteoclasts   Cells responsible for bone resorption, removing old bone.

Osteocytes   Mature bone cells which may be involved in activation of bone turnover and regulation of extracellular calcium.

Osteomalacia   Demineralization of the mature skeleton, with softening of the bone and bone pain.

Osteopenia   Low bone mineral density without evidence of non-traumatic fractures.

Osteoporosis   A condition characterized by generalized skeletal fragility, leading to fractures with minimal trauma.

Phagocyte   A cell capable of engulfing bacteria or other particles.

Phospholipids Compounds of fatty acids, phosphoric acid and a nitrogenous base: important constituents of all cell membranes.

Plaques Complicated atheromatous lesions that are raised and obstruct blood flow.

Plasmin A proteolytic enzyme that causes fibrinolysis in blood clots.

Plasminogen A zymogen or proeznyme, the inactive precursor of plasmin.

Plasminogen activator inhibitor-1 Plasma constituent that inhibits fibrinolysis by opposing the conversion of plasminogen to plasmin.

Platelet aggregation The tendency for blood platelets to stick together.

Population-attributable risk The incidence of a disease or characteristic in a population that is associated with an exposure to a risk factor. Describes the relative importance of an exposure for that population.

Postprandial After a meal.

Precision The extent to which the same measurements, when repeated, yield the same values. Also called repeatability.

Prevalence The number of cases in a defined population at a specified point in time.

Primary care First level contact with the health care system (in UK, with general practitioners).

Primary prevention Prevention of the development of disease in healthy people.

Procoagulant Leading to formation of a blood clot.

Relative risk The ratio of occurrence of a disease (or other outcome) among exposed people to that among the unexposed.

Repeated measures An experimental design where measurements are repeated on the same individuals in different conditions.

Resorption The breaking down of bone into soluble constituents.

Resting metabolic rate The energy expenditure at rest following an overnight fast and 8 h of sleep.

Reverse-cholesterol transport The process whereby high-density lipoproteins collect cholesterol from cells and return it to the liver where it can be excreted as bile salts in the bile.

Rhabdomyolisis Sporadic appearance in blood of abnormal levels of myoglobin, indicative of muscle damage.

Rheumatic heart disease Damage to the myocardium due to rheumatic fever.

Rickets A disorder of calcium and phosphate metabolism, associated with deficiency of vitamin D, and beginning most often in infancy and early childhood. It leads to softening and bending of the long weight-bearing bones.

Risk difference The (absolute) difference in rates of occurrence between exposed and unexposed groups.

Sarcoma Cancer of connective tissues.

Secondary prevention Decrease in the risk of mortality and further morbidity in patients with existing disease.

Shear stress The force exerted on the endothelium by blood flow.

Statistical power The ability of a study to detect a specified (often 'clinically important') difference, that is, the probability of rejecting the null hypothesis when this is in fact false and should be rejected. It depends on sample size, and on the level of significance chosen.

Stenoses Narrowing, for example, of coronary vessels due to atherosclerosis.

Strain   Deformation of a material, measured as the change in dimension produced by force, divided by the original dimension. One 'strain' is thus equivalent to a 1% change.

Subcutaneous abdominal fat   Abdominal fat stored under the skin.

Succinate dehydrogenase   An enzyme involved in oxidative metabolism within the mitochondria. One of the enzymes in Kreb's cycle.

Syndrome   A group of symptoms which, occurring together, produce a pattern typical of a particular disease.

Thermic effect   Increase in energy expenditure. For example, the thermic effect of food is the increase in energy expenditure due to digestion, absorption, and storage of food; the thermic effect of activity is the increase in energy expenditure due to physical activity.

Thrombin   The enzyme responsible for converting fibrinogen into fibrin.

Thrombosis   Formation of a blood clot.

Thromboembolytic   Due to the formation of a thrombus (blood clot) that has blocked a blood vessel. Sometimes called an ischaemic stroke.

Thrombus   A blood clot.

Tissue plasminogen activator   A plasma protein secreted by endothelial cells that activates plasminogen, stimulating fibrinolysis.

Trabecular bone   An open type of bone (always enclosed in a hard outer crust of cortical bone) made up of a three-dimensional lattice-work of trabeculae. It has more remodelling sites and a more active metabolism than cortical bone.

Trabeculae   Curved plates and tubes organized to withstand the particular forces to which each part of a bone is normally subjected. They confer bone's essential property of 'strength with lightness'.

Training effect   An adaptive response to training, not merely a short-term biological response to a single session of exercise.

Triglyceride   A lipid molecule composed of glycerol and three fatty acids that is the storage form of fat in the body. From a biochemical perspective, it is correctly called triacyglycerol but the term triglyceride is still widely used, particularly in the clinical literature.

Tumour   A swelling or growth, that is, a mass of tissue which fulfils no useful purpose and which grows at the expense of the body. It can be benign or cancerous.

Type I (alpha) error   Rejecting the null hypothesis when this is true, that is, finding an effect when there is none (a 'false positive').

Type II (beta) error   Accepting the null hypothesis when this is false, that is, failing to find an effect when one is there (a 'false negative').

Validity   The extent to which a study measures what it purports to measure.

Visceral fat   Fat stored within the abdominal cavity.

Waist circumference   The preferred surrogate marker for abdominal obesity.

Waist–hip ratio   The ratio of waist circumference to hip circumference, used as a surrogate marker for abdominal obesity.

Bibliography

Ades, P.A., Ballor, D.L., Ashikaga, T., Utton, J.L. and Nair, K.S. (1996) 'Weight training improves walking endurance in healthy elderly persons', *Annals of Internal Medicine* 124: 568–72.

Ainsworth, B.E. and Macera, C.A. (1998) 'Physical inactivity', in R.C. Brownson, P.L. Remington and J.R. Davis (eds) *Chronic Disease Epidemiology and Control,* 2nd edn, Washington: American Public Health Association, pp. 191–213.

Ainsworth, B.E., Haskell, W.L., Leon, A.S., Jacobs, D.R., Montoye, H.J., Sallis, J.F. and Paffenbarger, R.S. (1993) 'Compendium of physical activities: classification of energy costs of human physical activities', *Medicine and Science in Sports and Exercise* 25: 71–80.

Ainsworth, B.E., Haskell, W.L., Whitt, M.C., Irwin, M.L., Swartz, A.M., Strath, S.J., O'Brien, W.L., Bassett, D.R., Schmitz, K.H., Emplaincourt, P.O., Jacobs, D.R. and Leon, A.S. (2000) 'Compendium of physical activities: an update of activity codes and MET intensities', *Medicine and Science in Sports and Exercise* 32 (9 Suppl): S498–504.

Albert, C.M., Mittleman, M.A., Chae, C.U., Lee, I.-M., Hennekens, C.H. and Manson, J.E. (2000) 'Triggering of sudden death from cardiac causes by vigorous exertion', *New England Journal of Medicine* 343: 1355–61.

Alberti, K.G. and Zimmet, P.Z. (1998) 'Definition, diagnosis, and classification of diabetes mellitus and its complications. Part 1: diagnosis and classification of diabetes mellitus: provisional report of a WHO consultation', *Diabetic Medicine* 15: 539–53.

Alberti, K.G.M.M., Boucher, B.J., Hitman, G.A. and Taylor, R. (1990) 'Diabetes mellitus', in R.D. Cohen, B. Lewis, K.G.M.M. Alberti, and A.M. Denman (eds) *The Metabolic and Molecular Basis of Acquired Disease*, Vol. 1, London: Baillière Tindall, pp. 765–840.

American Association of Cardiovascular and Pulmonary Rehabilitation (1999) *Guidelines for Cardiac Rehabilitation and Secondary Prevention Programmes*, 3rd edn, Champaign, IL: Human Kinetics.

American Cancer Society website at: http://www.cancer.org/docroot/cri/content/cri_2_6x_the_history_of_cancer_72.asp?sitearea=cri

American College of Sports Medicine (1978) 'Position stand: the recommended quantity and quality of exercise for developing and maintaining fitness in healthy adults', *Medicine and Science in Sports* 10: vii–ix.

American College of Sports Medicine (1990) 'Position stand: the recommended quantity and quality of exercise for developing and maintaining cardiorespiratory and muscular fitness in healthy adults', *Medicine and Science in Sports and Exercise* 22: 265–74.

American College of Sports Medicine (1998) 'Position stand: exercise and physical activity for older adults', *Medicine and Science in Sports and Exercise* 30: 992–1008.

American College of Sports Medicine (2001) 'Position stand: appropriate intervention strategies for weight loss and prevention of weight regain for adults', *Medicine and Science in Sports and Exercise* 33: 2145–56.

American Diabetes Association (2002) 'The prevention or delay of type 2 diabetes', *Diabetes Care* 25: 742–9.

Amos, A.F., McCarty, D.J. and Zimmet, P. (1997) 'The rising global burden of diabetes and its complications: estimates and projections to the year 2010', *Diabetic Medicine* 14: S7–85.

Anderson, K.M., Wilson, W., Odell, P.M. and Kannel, W.B. (1991) 'An updated coronary risk profile', *Circulation* 83: 356–62.

Australian Bureau of Statistics (2003) Australian Social Trends 1999. *Population Projections: Our Ageing Population*, Australian Bureau of Statistics: 18.11.02 Available at: http://www.abs.gov.au/ausstats/abs@.nsf/94713ad445ff1425ca25682000192af2/b7760619c3973594ca25699f0005d60f!OpenDocument accessed 10th March 2003.

Bahr, R. and Sejersted, O.M. (1991) 'Effect of intensity of exercise on excess postexercise O_2 consumption', *Metabolism* 40(8): 836–41.

Bahr, R., Ingnes, I., Vaage, O., Sejersted, O.M. and Newsholme, E. (1987) 'Effect of duration of exercise on postexercise O_2 consumption', *Journal of Applied Physiology* 62: 485–90.

Bailey, D.A., Faulkner, R.A. and McKay, H.A. (1996) 'Growth, physical activity and bone mineral acquisition', *Exercise and Sport Science Reviews* 24: 233–66.

Balady, G.J. (2002) 'Survival of the fittest – more evidence', *New England Journal of Medicine* 346: 852–4. Editorial.

Barengo, N.C., Nissinen, A., Tuomilehto, J. and Pekkarinen, H. (2002) 'Twenty-five-year trends in physical activity of 30- to 59-year-old populations in eastern Finland', *Medicine and Science in Sports and Exercise* 34: 1302–7.

Barker, D.J.P., Cooper, C. and Rose, G. (1998) *Epidemiology in Medical Practice*, 5th edn, New York: Churchill Livingstone.

Barnard, J.R. and Wen, S.J. (1994) 'Exercise and diet in the prevention and control of the metabolic syndrome', *Sports Medicine* 18: 218–28.

Bassey, E.J. and Ramsdale, S.J. (1994) 'Increase in femoral bone density in young women following high-impact exercise', *Osteoporosis International* 4: 72–5.

Baur, L.A. (2002) 'Child and adolescent obesity in the 21st century: an Australian perspective', *Asia Pacific Journal of Clinical Nutrition* 11: S524–8.

Beaglehole, R. (2001) 'Global cardiovascular disease prevention: time to get serious', *The Lancet* 358: 661–3.

Beaglehole, R., Bonita, R. and Kjellström, T. (1993) *Basic Epidemiology*, Geneva: World Health Organization.

Bennell, K.L., Malcolm, S.A., Wark, J.D. and Brukner, P.D. (1997) 'Skeletal effects of menstrual disturbances in athletes', *Scandinavian Journal of Medicine and Science in Sports* 7: 261–73.

Bérard, A., Bravo, G. and Gauthier, P. (1997) 'Meta-analysis of the effectiveness of physical activity for the prevention of bone loss in postmenopausal women', *Osteoporosis International* 7: 331–7.

Berlin, J.A. and Colditz, G.A. (1990) 'A meta-analysis of physical activity in the prevention of coronary heart disease', *American Journal of Epidemiology* 132: 612–28.

Biddle, S.J.H. and Mutrie, N. (2001) *Psychology of Physical Activity: Determinants, Well-being and Interventions*, London: Routledge.

Birdwood, G. (1995) *Understanding Osteoporosis and Its Treatment: A Guide for Physicians and Patients*, New York: Parthenon.

Blair, S.N. (1994) 'Physical activity, fitness and coronary heart disease', in C. Bouchard, R.J. Shephard and T. Stephens (eds) *Physical Activity, Fitness and Coronary Heart Disease*, Champaign, Illinois: Human Kinetics, pp. 579–90.

Blair, S.N., Cheng, Y. and Holder, J.S. (2001) 'Is physical activity or physical fitness more important in defining health benefits?', *Medicine and Science in Sports and Exercise* 33 (Supplement): S379–99.

Blair, S.N., Goodyear, N.N., Gibbons, L.W. and Cooper, K.H. (1984) 'Physical fitness and incidence of hypertension in healthy normotensive men and women', *Journal of the American Medical Association* 252: 487–90.

Blair, S.N., Kohl, H.W., Paffenbarger, R.S., Clark, D.G., Cooper, K.H. and Gibbons, L.W. (1989) 'Physical fitness and all-cause mortality: a prospective study of healthy men and women', *Journal of the American Medical Association* 262: 2395–401.

Blair, S.N., Kohl, H.W., Barlow, C.E., Paffenbarger, R.S., Gibbons, L.W. and Macera, C.A. (1995) 'Changes in physical fitness and all-cause mortality. A prospective study of healthy and unhealthy men', *Journal of the American Medical Association* 273: 1093–8.

Blair, S.N., Kampert, J.B., Kohl, H.W., Barlow, C.E., Macera, C.A., Paffenbarger, R.S. and Gibbons, L.W. (1996) 'Influences of cardiorespiratory fitness and other precursors on cardiovascular disease and all-cause mortality in men and women', *Journal of the American Medical Association* 276: 205–10.

Booth, F.W., Gordon, S.E., Carlson, C.J. and Hamilton, M.T. (2000) 'Waging war on modern chronic diseases: primary prevention through exercise biology', *Journal of Applied Physiology* 88: 774–87.

Bouchard, C. and Rankinen, T. (2001) 'Individual differences in response to regular physical activity', *Medicine and Science in Sports and Exercise* 33 (Supplement): S446–51.

Bouchard, C., Tremblay, A., Després, J.P., Nadeau, A., Lupien, P.J., Theriault, G., Dussault, J., Moorjania, S., Pineault, S. and Fournier, G. (1990) 'The response to long-term overfeeding in identical twins', *New England Journal of Medicine* 322: 1477–82.

Bouchard, C., Tremblay, A., Després, J.-P., Thériault, G., Nadeau, A., Lupien, P.-J., Moorjani, S., Prud'homme, D. and Fournier, G. (1994). 'The response to exercise with constant energy intake in identical twins', *Obesity Research* 2: 400–10.

Braun, B., Zimmermann, M.B. and Kretchmer, N. (1995) 'Effects of exercise intensity on insulin sensitivity in women with non-insulin-dependent diabetes mellitus', *Journal Applied Physiology* 78: 300–6.

British Heart Foundation (2000) *Coronary Heart Disease Statistics Database* 2000, London: British Heart Foundation.

British Heart Foundation (2002a) *Coronary Heart Disease Statistics*, British Heart Foundation Health Promotion Research Group, Department of Public Health, University of Oxford. Also available at: http://www.dphpc.ox.ac.uk/bhfhprg/stats/2000/index.html

British Heart Foundation (2002b) *Coronary Heart Disease Statistics*, British Heart Foundation Health Promotion Research Group, Department of Public Health, University of Oxford.

Also available at: http://www.dphpc.ox.ac.uk/bhfhprg/stats/2000/2002/mortality.html accessed 1st April 2002.

British Heart Foundation Statistics Database (2003) Coronary heart disease statistics 2003. Available at: http://www.heartstats.org/ accessed 14th February 2003.

British Masters Athletic Federation website (2003) Available at: http://www.bvaf.org.uk accessed 10th March 2003.

British Thoracic Society (2001) 'Pulmonary rehabilitation', *Thorax*, 56: 827–34.

Broocks, A., Pirke, K.M., Schweiger, U., Tuschl, R.J., Laessle, R.G., Strowitzki, E., Hörl, T., Haas, W. and Jeschke, D. (1990) 'Cyclic ovarian function in recreational athletes', *Journal of Applied Physiology* 68: 2083–6.

Brooke-Wavell, K., Jones, P.R.M., Hardman, A.E., Tsuritani, I. and Yamada, Y. (2001) 'Commencing, continuing and stopping brisk walking: effects on bone mineral density, quantitative ultrasound of bone and markers of bone metabolism in postmenopausal women', *Osteoporosis International* 12: 581–7.

Brunner, E.J., Marmot, M.G., Nanchalal, K., Shipley, M.J., Stansfeld, S.A., Juneja, M. and Alberti, K.G.M.M. (1997) 'Social inequality in coronary risk: central obesity and the metabolic syndrome. Evidence from the Whitehall II study', *Diabetologia* 40: 1341–9.

Buemann, B. and Tremblay, A. (1996) 'Effects of exercise training on abdominal obesity and related metabolic complications', *Sports Medicine* 21: 191–212.

Canada's Physical Activity Guide (2000) Ottawa: Health Canada and Canadian Society for Exercise Physiology. Also available at http://www.hc-sc.gc.ca/hppb/paguide/index.html accessed 14th February 2003.

Canadian Fitness and Lifestyle Research Institute (2002) Physical activity monitors for 1981, 1988, 1992, 1995, 1997, 1998, 1999, 2000, 2001: dates updated not given. Available at: http://www.cflri.ca/cflri/pa/index.html accessed 11th February 2003.

Cancer Research UK website at http://www.cancerhelp.org.uk/help/default.asp?page=85

Carter, N., Kannus, P. and Khan, K.M. (2001) 'Exercise and the prevention of falls in older people: a systematic literature review examining the rationale and the evidence', *Sports Medicine* 31: 427–38.

Castaneda, C., Layne, J.E., Munoz-Orians, L., Gordon, P.L., Walsmith, J., Foldvari, M., Foubenoff, R., Tucker, K.L. and Nelson, M.E. (2002) 'A randomized controlled trial of resistance exercise training to improve glycemic control in older adults with type 2 diabetes', *Diabetes Care* 25: 2335–41.

Chinn, S. and Rona, R.J. (2001) 'Prevalence and trends in overweight and obesity in three cross sectional studies of British children, 1974–94', *British Medical Journal* 322: 24–6.

Chodzko-Zajko, W.J. and Moore, K.A. (1994) 'Physical fitness and cognitive functioning in ageing', *Exercise and Sport Sciences Reviews* 22: 195–220.

Coats, A.J.S., McGee, H.M., Stokes, H.C. and Thompson, D.R. (eds) (1995) *British Association for Cardiac Rehabilitation Guidelines for Cardiac Rehabilitation*, Oxford: Blackwell Science.

Coggan, A.R., Spina, R.J., King, D.S., Rogers, M.A., Brown, M., Nemeth, P.M. and Holloszy, J.O. (1992) 'Skeletal muscle adaptations to endurance training in 60- to 70-yr-old men and women', *Journal of Applied Physiology* 72: 1780–86.

Colditz, G.A., Cannuscio, C.C. and Frazier, A.L. (1997) 'Physical activity and reduced risk of colon cancer: implications for prevention', *Cancer Causes and Control* 8: 649–67.

Colditz, G.A., Willett, W.C., Stampfer, M.J., Manson, J.E., Hennekens, C.H., Arky, R.A. and Speizer, F.E. (1990) 'Weight as a risk factor for clinical diabetes in women', *American Journal of Epidemiology* 132: 501–513.

Cordain, L., Latin, R.W. and Behnke, J.J. (1986) 'The effects of an aerobic running program on bowel transit time', *Journal of Sports Medicine* 26: 101–4.

Couillard, C., Bergeron, N., Prud'homme, D., Bergeron, J., Tremblay, A., Bouchard, C., Mauriège, P. and Després, J.-P. (1998) 'Postprandial triglyceride response in visceral obesity in men', *Diabetes* 47: 953–60.

Coupland, C.A.C., Cliffe, S.J., Bassey, E.J., Grainge, M.J., Hosking, D.J. and Chilvers, C.E.D. (1999) 'Habitual physical activity and bone mineral density in postmenopausal women in England', *International Journal of Epidemiology* 28: 241–6.

Cumming, D.C., Wheeler, G.D. and McColl, E.M. (1989) 'The effects of exercise on reproductive function in men', *Sports Medicine* 7: 1–17.

Cummings, S.R., Nevitt, M.C., Browner, W.S., Stone, K., Fox, K.M., Ensrud, K.E., Cauley, J., Black, D. and Vogt, T.M. (1995) 'Risk factors for hip fracture in white women', *New England Journal Medicine* 332: 767–73.

Currens, J.H. and White, P.D. (1961) 'Half a century of running: clinical, physiologic and autopsy findings in the case of Clarence DeMar ('Mr. Marathon')', *New England Journal of Medicine* 16: 988–93.

Daley, M.J. and Spinks, W.L. (2000) 'Exercise, mobility and aging', *Sports Medicine* 29: 1–12.

Dalsky, G., Stocke, K.S., Eshani, A.A., Slatopolsky, E., Wee, W.C. and Birge, S.J. (1988) 'Weight-bearing exercise training and lumbar bone mineral content in postmemopausal women', *Annals of Internal Medicine* 108: 824–8.

Day, L., Fildes, B., Gordon, I., Fitzharris, M., Flamer, H. and Lord, S. (2002) 'Randomised factorial trial of falls prevention among older people living in their own homes', *British Medical Journal* 325: 128–31.

DeBusk, R.F., Stenestrand, U., Sheehan, M. and Haskell, W.L. (1990) 'Training effects of long versus short bouts of exercise in healthy subjects', *American Journal of Cardiology* 65: 1010–13.

Dekker, R., Kingma, J., Groothoff, J.W., Eisma, W.H. and Ten Duis, H.J. (2000) 'Measurement of severity of sports injuries: an epidemiological study', *Clinical Rehabilitation* 14: 651–6.

Dela, F., Larsen, J.J., Mikines, K.J., Ploug, T., Petersen, L.N. and Galbo, H. (1995) 'Insulin-stimulated muscle glucose clearance in patients with NIDDM. Effects of one-legged physical training', *Diabetes* 44: 1010–20.

de Souza, M.J., Miller, B.E., Loucks, A.B., Luciano, A.A., Pescatello, L.S., Campbell, C.G. and Lasley, B.L. (1998) 'High frequency of luteal phase deficiency and anovulation in recreational women runners: blunted elevation in follicle-stimulating hormone observed during luteal-follicular transition', *Journal of Clinical Endocrinology Metabolism* 83: 4220–32.

Després, J.-P. (1997) 'Visceral obesity, insulin resistance, and dyslipidemia: contribution of endurance training to the treatment of the plurimetabolic syndrome', *Exercise and Sport Sciences Reviews* 25: 271–300.

Després, J.-P. and Lamarche, B. (1994) 'Low-intensity endurance exercise training, plasma lipoproteins and the risk of coronary heart disease', *Journal Internal Medicine* 236: 7–22.

Després, J.P., Lamarche, B, Mauriege, P., Cantin, B., Dagenais, G.R., Moorjani, S. and Lupien, P.J. (1996) 'Hyperinsulinaemia as an independent risk factor for ischaemic heart disease', *New England Journal of Medicine* 334: 952–7.

Diabetes Prevention Program Research Group (2002) 'Reduction in the incidence of type 2 diabetes with lifestyle intervention or Metformin', *New England Journal of Medicine* 346: 393–403.

Dook, J.E., James, C., Henderson, N.K. and Price, R.I. (1997) 'Exercise and bone mineral density in mature female athletes', *Medicine and Science in Sports and Exercise* 29: 291–6.

Dorn, J., Naughton, J., Imamura, D. and Trevisan, M. (1999) 'Results of a multicenter randomized clinical trial of exercise and long-term survival in myocardial infarction patients. The National Exercise and Heart Disease Project (NEHDP)', *Circulation* 100: 1764–9.

Drinkwater, B.L. (1994) '1994 C.H. McCloy Research Lecture: Does physical activity play a role in preventing osteoporosis?', *Research Quarterly for Exercise and Sport* 65: 197–206.

Drinkwater, B.L., Nilson, K., Ott, S. and Chesnut, C.H. (1986) 'Bone mineral density after resumption of menses in amenorrheic athletes', *Journal American Medical Association* 256: 380–2.

Drinkwater, B.L., Bruemner, B. and Chesnut, C.H. (1990) 'Menstrual history as a determinant of current bone density in young athletes', *Journal American Medical Association* 263: 545–8.

Dummer, G.M., Rosen, L.W., McKeag, D.B., Hough, D.O. and Curley, V. (1987) 'Pathogenic weight-control behaviors of young competitive swimmers', *Physician and Sportsmedicine* 5: 22–7.

Dunn, A.L., Andersen, R.E. and Jakicic, J.M. (1998) 'Lifestyle physical activity interventions: history, short- and long-term effects, and recommendations', *American Journal of Preventive Medicine* 15: 398–412.

Dunn, A.L., Marcus, B.H., Kampert, J.B., Garcia, M.E., Kohl, H.W. and Blair, S.N. (1999) 'Comparison of lifestyle and structured interventions to increase physical activity and cardiorespiratory fitness', *Journal of the American Medical Association* 281: 327–34.

Durstine, J.L. and Haskell, W.L. (1994) 'Effects of exercise training on plasma lipids and lipoproteins', *Exercise and Sport Sciences Reviews* 22: 477–521.

Eastell, R. and Lambert, H. (2002) 'Strategies for skeletal health in the elderly', *Proceedings of the Nutrition Society* 61: 173–80.

Egger, G.J., Vogels, N. and Westerterp, K.R. (2001) 'Estimating historical changes in physical activity levels', *Medical Journal of Australia* 175: 635–6.

Ekelund, L.-G., Haskell, W.L., Johnson, M.S., Whaley, F.S., Criqui, M.H. and Sheps, D.S. (1988) 'Physical fitnes as a predictor of cardiovascular mortality in asymptomatic North American men', *New England Journal of Medicine* 319: 1379–84.

Enos, W.F., Holmes, R.H. and Beyer, J. (1953) 'Coronary heart disease among United States soldiers killed in action in Korea: preliminary report', *Journal of the American Medical Association* 256: 2859–62.

Erikssen, G. (2001) 'Physical fitness and changes in mortality: the survival of the fittest', *Sports Medicine* 31: 571–6.

Eriksson, K.F. and Lindgärde, F. (1991) 'Prevalence of type 2 (non-insulin dependent) diabetes mellitus by diet and physical exercise: the 6-year Malmö feasibility study', *Diabetologia* 34: 891–8.

Eriksson, J., Taimela, S. and Koivisto, V.A. (1997) 'Exercise and the metabolic syndrome', *Diabetologia* 40: 125–35.

Erikssen, G., Liestøl, K., Bjørnhold, J., Thaulow, E., Sandvik, L. and Eriksson, J. (1998) 'Changes in physical fitness and changes in mortality', *Lancet* 352: 759–762.

Ettinger, W.H., Burns, R., Messier, S.P., Applegate, W., Rejeski, W.J., Morgan, T., Sumaker, S., Berry, M.J., O'Toole, M., Monu, J. and Craven, T. (1997) 'A randomized trial comparing aerobic exercise and resistance exercise with a health education programme in older adults with knee osteoarthritis. The Fitness Arthritis and Seniors Trial (FAST)', *Journal of the American Medical Association* 277: 25–31.

Expert Committee on the Diagnosis and Classification of Diabetes Mellitus (1999) 'Report of the expert committee on the diagnosis and classification of diabetes mellitus', *Diabetes Care* 22 (Supplement 1): S5–19.

Expert Panel on the Identification, Evaluation and Treatment of Overweight in Adults (1998) 'Clinical guidelines on the identification, evaluation and treatment of overweight and obesity in adults: executive summary', *American Journal of Clinical Nutrition* 68: 899–917. Also available at: http://rover.nhlbi.nih.gov/guidelines/obesity/ob_home.htm accessed 8th May 2002.

Fagard, R.H. (2001) 'Exercise characteristics and the blood pressure response to dynamic physical training', *Medicine and Science in Sports and Exercise* 33 (Supplement): S484–92.

Feicht, C.B., Johnson, T.S., Martin, B.J., Sparkes, K.E. and Wagner, W.W. (1978) 'Secondary amenorrhoea in athletes', *Lancet* ii: 1145–6.

Ferrannini, E., Haffner, S.M., Mitchell, B.D. and Stern, M.P. (1991) 'Hyperinsulinaemia: the key feature of a cardiovascular and metabolic syndrome', *Diabetologia* 34: 416–22.

Ferrannini, E., Vichi, S., Beck-Nielsen, H., Laakso, M., Paolisso, G. and Smith, U. (1996) 'Insulin action and age. European Group for the Study of Insulin Resistance (EGIR)', *Diabetes* 45: 947–53.

Fiatarone, M.A. and Evans, W.J. (1990) 'Exercise in the oldest old', *Topics in Geriatric Rehabilitation* 5: 63–77.

Fiatarone, M.A., O'Neill, E.F., Ryan, N.D., Clements, K.M., Solares, G.R., Nelson, M.E., Roberts, S.B., Kehayias, J.J., Lipsitz, L.A. and Evans, W.J. (1994) 'Exercise training and nutritional supplementation for physical frailty in very elderly people', *New England Journal of Medicine* 330: 1769–75.

Fleg, J.L. and Lakatta, E.G. (1988) 'Role of muscle loss in the age-associated reduction in VO_2max', *Journal of Applied Physiology* 65: 1147–51.

Forrest, K.Y.-Z., Bunker, C.H., Kriska, A.M., Ukoli, F.A.M., Huston, S.L. and Markovic, N. (2001) 'Physical activity and cardiovascular risk factors in a developing population', *Medicine and Science in Sports and Exercise* 33: 1598–1604.

Frändin, K., Grimby, G., Mellström, D. and Svanborg, A. (1991) 'Walking habits and health-related factors in a 70-year old population', *Gerontology* 37: 281–8.

Franklin, B.A., Whaley, M.H. and Howley, E.T. (eds) (2000) *ACSM's Guidelines for Exercise Testing and Prescription*, 6th edn, Philadelphia: Lippincott, Williams and Wilkins.

Frayn, K.N. (1993) 'Insulin resistance and lipid metabolism', *Current Opinion in Lipidology* 4: 197–204.

Frayn, K.N. (1996) *Metabolic Regulation – A Human Perspective*, London: Portland Press.

Friedenreich, C.M. (2001) 'Physical activity and cancer prevention: from observational to intervention research', *Cancer Epidemiology, Biomarkers and Prevention* 10: 287–301.

Friedenreich, C.M. and Thune, I. (2001) 'A review of physical activity and prostate cancer risk', *Cancer Causes and Control* 12: 461–75.

Friedenreich, C.M., Bryant, H.E. and Coureya, K.S. (2001) 'Case-control study of lifetime physical activity and breast cancer risk', *American Journal of Epidemiology* 154: 336–47.

Frontera, W.R., Meredith, C.N., O'Reilly, K.P., Knuttgen, H.G. and Evans, W.J. (1988) 'Strength conditioning in older men: skeletal muscle hypertrophy and improved function', *Journal of Applied Physiology* 64: 1038–44.

Frontera, W.R., Hughes, V.A., Lutz, K.J. and Evans, W.J. (1991) 'A cross-sectional study of muscle strength and mass in 45- to 78-year old men and women', *Journal of Applied Physiology* 71: 644–50.

Gæde, P., Vedel, P., Larsen, N., Jensen, G.V.H., Parving, H.H. and Pedersen, O. (2003) 'Multifactorial intervention and cardiovascular disease in patients with type 2 diabetes', *New England Journal of Medicine* 348: 383–93.

Gardner, A.W. and Poehlman, E.T. (1995) 'Exercise rehabilitation programs for the treatment of claudication pain: a meta analysis', *Journal of the American Medical Association* 274: 975–80.

Gardner, A.W., Katzel, L.I., Sorkin, J.D., Bradham, O.D., Hochberg, M.C., Flinn, W.R. and Goldberg, A.P. (2001) 'Exercise rehabilitation improves functional outcomes and peripheral circulation in patients with intermittent claudication: a randomized controlled trial', *Journal of the American Geriatric Society* 49: 755–62.

Garrow, J.S. (1995) 'Exercise in the treatment of obesity: a marginal contribution,' *International Journal of Obesity and Related Metabolic Disorders* 19 (Supplement 4): S126–9.

Gielen, S., Schuler, G. and Hambrecht, R. (2001) 'Exercise training in coronary artery disease and coronary vasomotion', *Circulation* 101: E1–6.

Gill, J.M.R. and Hardman, A.E. (2003) 'Exercise and postprandial lipid metabolism: an update on potential mechanisms and interactions with high-carbohydrate diets', *Journal of Nutritional Biochemistry* 14: 122–32.

Gill, J.M.R., Frayn, K.N., Wootton, S.A., Miller, G.J. and Hardman, A.E. (2001) 'Effect of prior moderate exercise on exogenous and endogenous lipid metabolism and plasma factor VII activity', *Clinical Science* 100: 517–27.

Giovannucci, E., Ascherio, A., Rimm, E.B., Colditz, G.A., Stampfer, M.J. and Willett, W.C. (1995) 'Physical activity, obesity, and risk for colon cancer and adenoma in men', *Annals of Internal Medicine* 122: 327–34.

Gleeson, M., McDonald, W.W., Pyne, D.B., Cripps, A.W., Francis, J.L., Fricker, P.A. and Clancy, R.L. (1999) 'Salivary gland IgA levels and infection risk in swimmers', *Medicine and Science in Sports and Exercise* 31: 67–73.

Glew, R.H., Williams, M., Conn, C.A., Cadena, S.M., Crossey, M., Okolo, S.N. and VanderJagt, D.J. (2001) 'Cardiovascular disease risk factors and diet of Fulani pastoralists of northern Nigeria', *American Journal of Clinical Nutrition* 74: 730–6.

Goran, M.I. (2000) 'Energy metabolism and obesity', *Medical Clinics of North America* 84: 347–62.

Goran, M.I., Carpenter, W.H., McGloin, A., Johnson, R., Hardin, J.M. and Weinsier, R.L. (1995) 'Energy expenditure in children of lean and obese parents', *American Journal of Physiology* 268: E917–24.

Goran, M.I., Shewchuk, R., Gower, B.A., Nagy, T.R., Carpenter, W.H. and Johnson, R.K. (1998) 'Longitudinal changes in fatness in white children: no effect of childhood energy expenditure', *American Journal of Clinical Nutrition* 67: 309–16.

Griffiths, T.L., Burr, M.L., Campbell, I.A., Lewis-Jenkins, V., Mullins, J., Shiels, K., Turner-Lawlor, P.J., Payne, N., Newcombe, R.G., Lonescu, A.A., Thomas, J. and Tunbridge, J. (2000) 'Results at 1 year of outpatient multidisciplinary pulmonary rehabilitation: a randomised controlled trial', *The Lancet* 355: 362–8.

Guralnik, J.M., Ferrucci, L., Simonsick, E.M., Salive, M.E. and Wallace, R.B. (1995) 'Lower-extremity function in persons over the age of 70 years as a predictor of subsequent disability', *New England Journal of Medicine* 332: 556–61.

Haapanen, N., Miilunpalo, S., Pasanen, M., Oja, P. and Vuori, I. (1997) 'Assocation between leisure time physical activity and 10-year body mass change among working-aged men and women', *International Journal of Obesity* 21: 288–96.

Haapasalo, H., Kannus, P., Sievänen, H., Pasanen, M., Uusi-Rasi, K., Heinonen, A., Oja, P. and Vuori, I. (1998) 'Effect of long-term unilateral activity on bone mineral density of female junior tennis players', *Journal of Bone and Mineral Research* 13: 310–9.

Hadjiolova, I., Mintcheva, L., Dunev, S., Daleva, M., Handjiev, S. and Balabanski, L. (1982) 'Physical working capacity in obese women after an exercise programme for body weight reduction', *International Journal of Obesity and Related Metabolic Disorders* 6: 405–10.

Hagberg, J.M., Graves, J.E., Limacher, M., Woods, D.R., Leggett, S.H., Cononie, C., Gruber, J.J. and Pollock, M.L. (1989) 'Cardiovascular responses of 70- to 79-yr-old men and women to exercise training', *Journal of Applied Physiology* 66: 2589–94.

Hagberg, J.M., Park, J.-J. and Brown, M.D. (2000) 'The role of exercise training in the treatment of hypertension: an update', *Sports Medicine* 30: 193–206.

Hakim, A.A., Curb, J.D., Petrovitch, H., Rodriguez, B.L., Yano, K., Ross, G.W., White, L.R. and Abbott, R.D. (1999) 'Effects of walking on coronary heart disease in elderly men. The Honolulu Heart Program', *Circulation* 100: 9–13.

Hajjar, D.P. and Nicholson, A.C. (1995) 'Atherosclerosis. An understanding of the cellular and molecularr basis of the disease promises new approaches for its treatment in the near future', *American Scientist* 3: 460–7.

Hambrecht, R., Wolf, A., Gielen, S., Linke, A., Hofer, J., Erbs, S., Schoene, N. and Schuler, G. (2000) 'Effect of exercise on coronary endothelial function in patients with coronary artery disease', *New England Journal of Medicine* 342: 454–60.

Hardman, A.E., Lawrence, J.E.M. and Herd, S.L. (1998) 'Postprandial lipemia in endurance-trained people during a short interruption to training', *Journal of Applied Physiology* 84: 1895–901.

Harlow, J. (2002) 'Obese young American has its coronaries early. The Sunday Times', 24th March, World News, p. 29.

Haskell, W.L. (1994) 'Health consequences of physical activity: understanding and challenges regarding dose–response', *Medicine and Science in Sports and Exercise* 26: 649–60.

Haskell, W.L. (2001) 'What to look for in assessing responsiveness to exercise in a health context', *Medicine and Science in Sports and Exercise* 33 (Supplement): S454–8.

Haskell, W.L., Sims, C., Myll, J., Bortz, W.M., Goar, F.G. and Alderman, E.L. (1993) 'Coronary artery size and dilating capacity in ultradistance runners', *Circulation* 87: 1076–82.

Hennekens, C.H. and Buring, J.E. (1987) *Epidemiology in Medicine*, Philadelphia: Lippincott, Williams and Wilkins.

Heinonen, A., Oja, P., Kannus, P., Sievänen, H., Haapasalo, H., Mänttäri, A. and Vuori, I. (1995) 'Bone mineral density in female athletes representing sports with different loading characteristics of the skeleton', *Bone* 17: 197–203.

Heinonen, A., Kannus, P., Sievänen, H., Oja, P., Pasanen, M., Rinne, M., Uusi-Rasi, K. and Vuori, I. (1996) 'Randomised controlled trial of the effect of high-impact exercise on selected risk factors for osteoporotic fractures', *The Lancet* 348: 1343–7.

Heinonen, A., Oja, P., Sievänen, H., Pasanen, M. and Vuori, I. (1998) 'Effect of two training regimens on bone mineral density in healthy perimenopausal women: a randomized controlled trial', *Journal of Bone and Mineral Research*, 13: 483–90.

Hill, J.O. and Peters, J.C. (1998) 'Environmental contributions to the obesity epidemic', *Science* 280: 1371–4.

Holloszy, J.O., Schultz, J., Kusnierkiewicz, J., Hagberg, J.M. and Ehsani, A.A. (1986) 'Effects of exercise on glucose tolerance and insulin resistance. Brief review and some preliminary results', *Acta Medica Scandinavica* 711: 55–65.

Hootman, J.M., Macera, C.A., Ainsworth, B.E., Addy, C.L., Martin, M. and Blair, S.N. (2002) 'Epidemiology of musculoskeletal injuries among sedentary and physically active adults', *Medicine and Science in Sports and Exercise* 34: 838–44.

Howley, E.T. (2001) 'Type of activity: resistance, aerobic, anaerobic and leisure-time versus occupational physical activity', *Medicine and Science in Sports and Exercise* 33 (Supplement): S364–9.

Hu, F.B., Stampfer, M.J., Colditz, G.A., Ascherio, A., Rexrode, K.M., Willett, W.C. and Manson, J.E. (2000) 'Physical activity and risk of stroke in women', *Journal of the American Medical Association* 283: 2961–7.

Hu, F.B., Manson, J.E., Stampfer, M.J., Colditz, G., Liu, S., Solomon, C.G. and Willett, W.C. (2001a) 'Diet, lifestyle, and the risk of type 2 diabetes mellitus in women', *New England Journal of Medicine* 345: 790–7.

Hu, F.B., Stampfer, M.J., Solomon, C.G., Liu, S., Colditz, G.A., Speizer, F.E., Willett, W.C. and Manson, J.-A. (2001b) 'Physical activity and risk for cardiovascular events in diabetic women', *Annals of Internal Medicine* 134: 96–105.

Hubert, H.B., Feinleib, M., McNamara, P.M. and Castelli, W.P. (1983) 'Obesity as an independent risk factor for cardiovascular disease: a 26-year follow-up of participants in the Framingham Heart Study', *Circulation* 67: 968–77.

Imhof, A. and Koenig, W. (2001) 'Exercise and thrombosis', *Cardiology Clinics* 19: 389–400.

Institute of European Food Studies, Trinity College, Dublin (1999) *A Pan-EU Survey on Consumer Attitudes to Physical Activity, Body Weight and Health*, Dublin: IEFS.

International Agency for Research on Cancer (2002) *Weight Control and Physical Activity*, H. Vainio and F. Bianchini, (eds) Handbooks of Cancer Prevention, Vol. 6, Lyon: International Agency for Research on Cancer Press.

Ivy, J.L, Zderic, T.W. and Fogt, D.L. (1999) 'Prevention and treatment of non-insulin dependent diabetes mellitus', *Exercise and Sport Sciences Reviews* 27: 1–35.

Jacobs, D.R., Ainsworth, B.E., Hartman, T.J. and Leon, A.S. (1993) 'A simultaneous evaluation of 10 commonly used physical activity questionnaires', *Medicine and Science in Sports and Exercise* 25: 81–91.

James, W.P.T. (1995) 'A public health approach to the problem of obesity', *International Journal of Obesity and Related Metabolic Disorders* 19: S37–45.

Joint Health Surveys Unit (1998) *Health Survey for England: the Health of Young People 1995–97*, London: The Stationery Office.

Joint Health Surveys Unit (1999) '*Health Survey for England: Cardiovascular Disease 1998*', London: The Stationery Office.

Jolliffe, J.A., Rees, K., Taylor, R.S., Thompson, D., Oldridge, N. and Ebrahim, S. (2003) 'Exercise-based rehabilitation for coronary heart disease (Cochrane Review)', in *The Cochrane Library*, Issue 1, Oxford: Update Software.

Jones, W.H.S. (1967). *Hippocrates* (translated by W.H.S. Jones). Cambridge, MA: Harvard University Press.

Kahn, H.S., Tatham, L.M., Rodriguez, C., Calle, E.E., Thun, M.J. and Heath, C.W. (1997) 'Stable behaviors associated with adults' 10-year change in body mass index and likelihood of gain at the waist', *American Journal of Public Health* 87: 747–54.

Kannel, W.B. (1983) 'High-density lipoproteins: epidemiological profile and risks of coronary artery disease', *American Journal of Cardiology* 52: 9B–12B.

Kannus, P., Haapasalo, H., Sankelo, M., Sievänen, H., Pasanen, M., Heinonen, A., Oja, P. and Vuori, I. (1995) 'Effect of starting age of physical activity on bone mass in the dominant arm of tennis and squash players', *Annals of Internal Medicine* 123: 27–31.

Karpe, F. and Hamsten, A. (1995) 'Postprandial lipoprotein metabolism and atherosclerosis', *Current Opinion in Lipidology* 6: 123–9.

Katch, F.I. and McArdle, W.D. (1993) *Introduction to Nutrition, Exercise and Health*, 4th edn, Philadelphia/London: Lea and Febiger.

Katzmarzyk, P.T. and Craig, C.L. (2002) 'Musculoskeletal fitness and risk of mortality', *Medicine and Science in Sports and Exercise* 34: 740–44.

Kavanagh, T., Myers, M.G., Baigrie, R.S., Mertens, D.J., Sawyer, P. and Shephard, R.J. (1996) 'Quality of life and cardiorespiratory function in chronic heart failure: effects of 12 months' aerobic training', *Heart* 76: 42–9.

Keen, A.D. and Drinkwater, B.L. (1997) 'Irreversible bone loss in former amenorrheic athletes', *Osteoporosis International* 7: 311–15.

Kelley, D.A. (1998) 'Exercise and regional bone mineral density in postmenopausal women', *American Journal of Physical Medicine and Rehabilitation* 77: 76–87.

Kelley, D.E. and Goodpaster, B.H. (2001) 'Effect of exercise on glucose homeostasis in Type 2 diabetes mellitus', *Medicine and Science in Sports and Exercise* 33: S495–501.

Keys, A. (1980) *Seven Countries. A Multivariate Analysis of Death and Coronary Heart Disease*, Boston: Harvard University Press.

Khan, K., McKay, H., Kannus, P., Bailey, D., Wark, J., Bennell, K. (2001) *Physical activity and bone health*, Champaign, IL: Human Kinetics.

Kimm, S.Y.S., Glynn, N.W., Kriska, A.M., Barton, B.A., Kronsberg, S.S., Daniels, S.R., Crawford, P.B., Sabry, Z.I. and Liu, K. (2002) 'Decline in physical activity in black girls and white girls during adolescence', *New England Journal of Medicine* 347: 709–15.

King, D.S., Baldus, R.J., Sharp, R.L., Kesl, L.D., Feltmeyer, T.L. and Riddle, M.S. (1995) 'Time course for exercise-induced alterations in insulin action and glucose tolerance in middle-aged people', *Journal Applied Physiology* 78: 17–22.

King, R.J.B. (2000) *Cancer Biology*, Harlow, England: Prentice Hall.

Klem, M.L., Wing, R.R., McGuire, M.T., Seagle, H.M. and Hill, J.O. (1997) 'A descriptive study of individuals successful at long-term maintenance of substantial weight loss', *American Journal of Clinical Nutrition* 66: 239–46.

Kohl, H.W. (2001) 'Physical activity and cardiovascular disease: evidence for a dose response', *Medicine and Science in Sports and Exercise* 33 (Supplement): S472–83.

Kohrt, W.M., Ehsani, A.A. and Birge, S.J. (1997) 'Effects of exercise involving predominantly either joint-reaction or ground-reaction forces on bone mineral density in older women', *Journal of Bone and Mineral Research* 12: 1253–61.

Kontulainen, S., Kannus, P., Haapasalo, H., Heinonen, A., Sievänen, H., Oja, P. and Vuori, I. (1999) 'Changes in bone mineral content with decreased training in competitive young adult tennis players and controls: a prospective 4-yr follow-up', *Medicine and Science in Sports and Exercise* 31: 646–52.

Kontulainen, S., Kannus, P., Haapasalo, H., Sievänen, H., Pasanen, M., Heinonen, A., Oja, P. and Vuori, I. (2001) 'Good maintenance of exercise-induced bone gain with decreased training in female tennis and squash players: a prospective 5-year follow-up study of young and old starters and controls', *Journal of Bone and Mineral Research* 16: 195–201.

Kramsch, D.M., Aspen, A.J., Abramowitz, B.M., Kreimendahl, T. and Hood, W.B. (1981) 'Reduction of coronary atherosclerosis by moderate conditioning exercise in monkeys on an atherogenic diet', *New England Journal of Medicine* 305: 1483–9.

Kraus, W.E., Houmard, J.A., Duscha, B.D., Knetzger, K.J., Wharton, M.B., McCartney, J.S., Bales, C.W., Henes, S., Samsa, G.P., Otvos, J.D., Kulkarni, K.R. and Slentz, C.A. (2002) 'Effects of the amount and intensity of exercise on plasma lipoproteins', *New England Journal of Medicine* 347: 1483–92.

Krentz, A.J. and Bailey, C.J. (2001) *Type 2 Diabetes*. London: The Royal Society of Medicine Press Limited.

Kriska, A.M., Blair, S.N. and Pereira, M.A. (1994) 'The potential role of physical activity in the prevention of non-insulin dependent diabetes mellitus: the epidemiological evidence', *Exercise and Sport Sciences Reviews* 22: 121–43.

Lacasse, Y., Brosseau, L., Milne, S., Martin, S., Wong, E., Guyatt, G.H., Goldstein, R.S. and White, J. (2003) 'Pulmonary rehabilitation for chronic obstructive pulmonary disease (Cochrane Review)', in *The Cochrane Library*, Issue 1, Oxford: Update Software.

LaCroix, A.Z., Leveille, S.G., Hecht, J.A., Grothaus, L.C. and Wagner, E.H. (1996) 'Does walking decrease the risk of cardiovascular disease hospitalizations and death in older adults?', *Journal of the American Geriatric Society* 44: 113–20.

Lanyon, L.E. (1996) 'Using functional loading to influence bone mass and architecture: objectives, mechanisms, and relationship with estrogen of the mechanically adaptive process in bone', *Bone* 18: 37S–43S.

LaPorte, R.E., Brenes, G., Dearwater, S., Murphy, M.A., Cauley, J.A., Dietrick, R. and Robertson, R. (1983) 'HDL Cholesterol across a spectrum of physical activity from quadriplegia to marathon running'. *The Lancet* 1: 1212–3.

Larsen, J.J., Dela, F., Kjær, M. and Galbo, H. (1997) 'The effect of moderate exercise on post-prandial glucose homeostasis in NIDDM patients', *Diabetologia* 40: 447–53.

Last, J.M. (1995) *A Dictionary of Epidemiology*, Oxford: Oxford University Press.

LeBlanc, A.D., Schneider, V.S., Evans, H.J., Engelbretson, D.A. and Krebs, J.M. (1990) 'Bone mineral loss and recovery following 17 weeks of bed rest', *Journal of Bone and Mineral Research* 5: 843–50.

Lee, C.C. and Blair, S.N. (2002) 'Cardiorespiratory fitness and stroke mortality in men', *Medicine and Science in Sports and Exercise* 34: 592–5.

Lee, C.D., Blair, S.N. and Jackson, A.S. (1999) 'Cardiorespiratory fitness, body composition, and all-cause and cardiovascular disease mortality in men', *American Journal of Clinical Nutrition* 69: 373–80.

Lee, I.-M. and Paffenbarger, R.S. (1996) 'Do physical activity and physical fitness avert premature mortality?', *Exercise and Sport Sciences Reviews* 24: 135–71.

Lee, I.-M. and Skerrett, P.J. (2001) 'Physical activity and all-cause mortality: what is the dose–response relation?', *Medicine and Science in Sports and Exercise* 33: S459–71.

Lee, I.-M., Paffenbarger, R.S. and Hsieh, C.-C. (1991) 'Physical activity and the risk of developing colorectal cancer among college alumni', *Journal of the National Cancer Institute* 83: 1324–9.

Lee, I.-M., Hsieh, C.C. and Paffenbarger, R.S. (1995) 'Exercise intensity and longevity in men: The Harvard alumni health study', *Journal of the American Medical Association* 273: 1179–84.

Lee, I.-M., Sesso, H.D. and Paffenbarger, R.S. (2000) 'Physical activity and coronary heart disease risk in men. Does the duration of exercise episodes predict risk?', *Circulation* 102: 981–6.

Lee, I.-M., Rexrode, K.M., Cook, N.R., Hennekens, C.H. and Buring, J.E. (2001a) 'Physical activity and breast cancer risk: the women's health study (United States)', *Cancer Causes and Control* 12: 137–45.

Lee, I.-M., Sesso, H.D. and Paffenbarger, R.S. (2001b) 'A prospective cohort study of physical activity and body size in relation to prostate cancer risk (United States)', *Cancer Causes and Control*, 12: 187–93.

Lee, I.-M., Sesso, H.D., Oguma, Y. and Paffenbarger, R.S. (2003) 'Relative intensity of physical activity and risk of coronary heart disease', *Circulation* 107: 1110–16.

Lee, L., Kumar, S. and Chin Leong, L. (1994) 'The impact of five-month basic military training on the body weight and body fat of 197 moderately to severely obese Singaporean males aged 17 to 19 years', *International Journal of Obesity and Related Metabolic Disorders* 18: 105–9.

Lehmann, R., Vokac, A., Niedermann, K., Agosti, K. and Spinas, G.A. (1995) 'Loss of abdominal fat and improvement of the cardiovascular risk profile by regular moderate exercise training in patients with NIDDM', *Diabetologia* 38: 1313–19.

Leng, G.C., Fowler, B. and Ernst, E. (2003) 'Exercise for intermittent claudication (Cochrane Review)', in *The Cochrane Library*, Issue 1, Oxford: Update Software.

Leon, A.S. and Sanchez, O.A. (2001) 'Response of blood lipids to exercise training alone or combined with dietary intervention', *Medicine and Science in Sports and Exercise* 33: S502–15.

Leon, A.S., Connett, J., Jacobs, D.R. and Rauramaa, R. (1987) 'Leisure-time physical activity levels and risk of coronary heart disease and death: the multiple risk factor intervention trial', *Journal of the American Medical Association* 258: 2388–95.

Lindsay, J., Laurin, D., Verreault, R., Hébert, R., Helliwell, B., Hill, G.B. and McDowell, I. (2002) 'Risk factors for Alzheimer's disease: a prospective analysis from the Canadian study of health and aging', *American Journal of Epidemiology* 156: 445–53.

Lipman, R.L., Raskin, P., Love, T., Triebwasser, J., Lecocq, F.R. and Schnure, J.J. (1972) 'Glucose intolerance during decreased physical activity in man', *Diabetes* 21: 101–7.

Loucks, A.B. (1996) The reproductive system, in O. Bar-Or *et al.* (eds) *Exercise and the Female – A Life Span Approach*, Vol. 9, Carmel, IN: Cooper Publishing.

Loucks, A.B. (2001) 'Physical health of the female athlete: observations, effects, and causes of reproductive disorders', *Canadian Journal of Applied Physiology* 26 (Supplement): S176–85.

McArdle, W.D., Katch, F.I. and Katch, V.L. (2001) *Exercise Physiology: Energy, Nutrition, and Human Performance*, Philadelphia: Lippincott, Williams and Wilkins.

McGill, H.C., Geer, J.C. and Strong, J.P. (1963) 'Natural history of human atherosclerotic lesions', in M. Sandler, and G.H. Bourne (eds) *Atherosclerosis and its Origin*, New York: Academic Press, pp. 39–65.

McGuire, D.K., Levine, B.D., Williamson, J.W., Snell, P.G., Blomqvist, G., Saltin, B. and Mitchell, J.H. (2001a) 'A 30-year follow-up of the Dallas bed rest and training study. I. Effect of age on the cardiovascular response to exercise', *Circulation* 104: 1350–7.

McGuire, D.K., Levine, B.D., Williamson, J.W., Snell, P.G., Blomqvist, G., Saltin, B. and Mitchell, J.H. (2001b) 'A 30-year follow-up of the Dallas bed rest and training study. II. Effect of age on cardiovascular adaptation to exercise training', *Circulation* 104: 1358–66.

MacKelvie, K.J., Khan, K.M, McKay, H.A. (2002) 'Is there a critical period for bone response to weight-bearing exercise in children and adolescents? A systematic review', *British Journal of Sports Medicine* 36: 250–7.

MacLean, P.S., Zheng, D. and Dohm, G.L. (2000) 'Muscle glucose transporter (GLUT4) gene expression during exercise', *Exercise and Sport Sciences Reviews* 28: 148–52.

MacRae, P.G., Asplund, L.A., Schnelle, J.F., Ouslander, J.G., Abrahamse, A. and Morris, C. (1996) 'A walking program for nursing home residents: effects on walk endurance, physical activity, mobility, and quality of life', *Journal of the American Geriatric Society* 44: 175–80.

Manson, J.E., Nathan, D.M., Krolewski, A.S., Stampfer, M.J., Willett, W.C. and Hennekens, C.H. (1992) 'A prospective study of exercise and incidence of diabetes among US male physicians', *Journal of the American Medical Association* 268: 63–7.

Manson, J.E., Hu, F.B., Rich-Edwards, J.W., Colditz, G.A., Stampfer, M.J., Willett, W.C., Speizer, F.E. and Hennekens, C.H. (1999) 'A prospective study of walking as compared with vigorous exercise in the prevention of coronary heart disease in women', *New England Journal of Medicine* 341: 650–8.

Manson, J.E., Greenland, P., LaCroix, A.Z., Stefanik, M.L., Mouton, C.P., Oberman, A., Perri, M.G., Sheps, D.S., Pettinger, M.B. and Sisovick, D.S. (2002) 'Walking compared with vigorous exercise for the prevention of cardiovascular events in women', *New England Journal of Medicine* 347: 716–25.

Maron, B.J. (2000) 'Sudden death in sports and the marathon', in D. Tunstall-Pedoe (ed.) *Marathon Medicine*, London: Royal Society of Medicine Press, pp. 208–25.

Marshall, S.J. and Biddle, S.J.H. (2001) 'The transtheoretical model of behavior change: a meta-analysis of applications to physical activity and exercise', *Annals of Behavioral Medicine* 23: 229–46.

Martínez, M.E., Giovannucci, E., Spiegelman, D., Hunter, D.J., Willett, W.C. and Colditz, G.A. (1997) 'Leisure-time physical activity, body size, and colon cancer in women', *Journal of the National Cancer Institute* 89: 948–55.

Martínez, M.E., Heddens, D., Earnest, D.L., Bogert, C.L., Roe, D., Einspahr, J., Marshall, J.R. and Alberts, D.S. (1999) 'Physical activity, body mass index, and prostaglandin E_2 levels in rectal mucosa', *Journal of the National Cancer Institute* 91: 950–3.

Medicine and Science in Sports and Exercise (2001) collection of papers from a symposium organised by Health Canada and the US Centers for Disease Control and Prevention 'Dose–response issues concerning physical activity and health: an evidence-based symposium', *Medicine and Science in Sports and Exercise* 33 (Supplement 6).

Merrill, J.R., Holly, R.G., Anderson, R.L., Rifai, N., King, M.E. and DeMeersman, R. (1989) 'Hyperlipemic response of young trained and untrained men after a high fat meal', *Arteriosclerosis* 9: 217–23.

Mittleman, M.A., Maclure, M., Tofler, G.H., Sherwood, J.B., Goldberg, R.J. and Muller, J.E. (1993) 'Triggering of acute myocardial infarction by heavy physical exertion. Protection against triggering by regular exertion', *New England Journal Medicine* 329: 1677–83.

Mokdad, A.H., Bowman, B.A., Ford, E.S., Vinicor, F., Marks, J.S. and Koplan, J.P. (2001) 'The continuing epidemics of obesity and diabetes in the United States', *Journal of the American Medical Association* 286: 1195–200.

Morgan, M. and Singh, S. (1997) *Practical Pulmonary Rehabilitation*, London: Chapman and Hall Medical.

Morio, B., Montaurier, C., Pickering, G., Ritz, P., Fellmann, N., Coudert, J., Beaufrère, B. and Vermorel, M. (1998) 'Effects of 14 weeks of progressive endurance training on energy expenditure in elderly people', *British Journal of Nutrition* 80: 511–19.

Morley, J.E. (2001) 'Decreased food intake with aging', *Journals of Gerontology, Series A Biological Sciences and Medical Sciences* 56A (Special Issue II): 81–8.

Morris, J.N. (1994) 'Exercise in the prevention of coronary heart disease: today's best buy in public health', *Medicine Science Sports Exercise* 26: 807–14.

Morris, J.N. (1996) 'Exercise versus heart attack: questioning the consensus', *Research Quarterly for Exercise and Sport* 67: 216–20.

Morris, J.N. and Hardman, A.E. (1997) 'Walking to health', *Sports Medicine* 23: 306–32.

Murphy, M.H. and Hardman, A.E. (1998) 'Training effects of short and long bouts of brisk walking in sedentary women', *Medicine and Science in Sports and Exercise* 30: 152–7.

Morris, J.N., Heady, J.A., Raffle, P.A.B., Parks, J.W. and Roberts, C.G. (1953) 'Coronary heart disease and physical activity of work', *The Lancet* ii: 1053–7, 1111–20.

Morris, J.N., Everitt, M.G., Pollard, R., Chave, S.P.W. and Semmence, A.M. (1980) 'Vigorous exercise in leisure-time: protection against coronary heart disease', *The Lancet* ii: 1207–10.

Morris, J.N., Clayton, D.G., Everitt, M.G., Semmence, A.M. and Burgess, E.H. (1990) 'Exercise in leisure time: coronary attack and death rates', *British Heart Journal* 63: 325–34.

Murphy, M.H., Nevill, A.M. and Hardman, A.E. (2000) 'Different patterns of brisk walking are equally effective in decreasing postprandial lipaemia', *International Journal of Obesity and Related Metabolic Disorders* 24: 1303–9.

Murphy, M.H., Nevill, A.M., Neville, C., Biddle, S.J.H. and Hardman, A.E. (2002) 'Accumulating brisk walking for fitness, cardiovascular risk, and psychological health', *Medicine and Science in Sports and Exercise* 34: 1468–74.

Myers, J., Prakash, M., Froelicher, V., Do, D., Partington, S. and Atwood, J.E. (2002) 'Exercise capacity and mortality among men referred for exercise testing', *New England Journal of Medicine* 346: 793–801.

National Audit Office (2001) Tackling Obesity in England. Report by the Comptroller and Auditor General. HC 220 Session 2000–01: 15 February 2001. Available at: http://www.nao.gov.uk/publications/nao_reports/00-01/0001220.pdf accessed 8th May 2002.

National Fitness Survey (1992) *National Fitness Survey: Main Findings*, London: Sports Council and Health Education Authority.

National Institutes of Health (1998) 'Clinical guidelines on the identification, evaluation, and treatment of overweight and obesity in adults: the Evidence Report', *Obesity Research* 6: 51S–209S.

National Institutes of Health Consensus Development Panel (1996) 'Physical activity and cardiovascular health', *Journal of American Medical Association* 276: 241–6. Also available at http://consensus.nih.gov/cons/101/101_statement.htm accessed 14th February 2002.

Nelson, M.E., Fiatorone, M.A., Morganti, C.M., Trice, I., Greenberg, R.A. and Evans, W.J. (1994) 'Effects of high-intensity strength training on multiple risk factors for osteoporotic fractures. A randomized controlled trial', *Journal of the American Medical Association* 272: 1909–14.

Niebauer, J., Hambrecht, R., Velich, T., Hauer, K., Marburger, C., Kälberer, B., Weiss, C., von Hodenberg, E., Schlierf, G., Schuler, G., Zimmermann, R. and Kübler, W. (1997) 'Attenuated progression of coronary artery disease after 6 years of multifactorial risk intervention: role of physical exercise', *Circulation* 96: 2534–41.

Nieman, D.C., Pedersen, B.K. (1999) 'Exercise and immune function: recent developments', *Sports Medicine* 27: 73–80.

Nieman, D.C., Johanssen, L.M., Lee, J.W. and Arabatzis, K. (1990) 'Infectious episodes in runners before and after the Los Angeles Marathon', *Journal of Sports Medicine and Physical Fitness* 30: 316–28.

Norman, A., Moradi, T., Gridley, G., Dosemeci, M., Rydh, B., Nyrén, O. and Wolk, A. (2002) 'Occupational physical activity and risk for prostate cancer in a nationwide cohort study in Sweden', *British Journal of Cancer* 86: 70–5.

O'Connor, G.T., Buring, J.E., Yusuf, S., Goldhaber, S.Z., Olmstead, E.M., Paffenbarger, R.S. and Hennekens, C.H. (1989) 'An overview of randomized trials of rehabilitation with exercise after myocardial infarction', *Circulation* 80: 234–44.

Oguma, Y., Sesso, H.D., Paffenbarger, R.S. and Lee, I.-M. (2002) 'Physical activity and all-cause mortality in women', *British Journal of Sports Medicine* 36: 162–72.

Ohlson, L.-O., Larsson, B., Svärdsudd, K., Welin, L., Eriksson, H., Wilhelmsen, L., Björntrop, P. and Tibblin, G. (1985) 'The influence of body fat distribution on the incidence of diabetes mellitus – 13.5 years of follow-up of the participants in the study of men born in 1913', *Diabetes* 34: 1055–8.

Oldridge, N.B., Guyatt, G.H., Fischer, M.E. and Rimm, A.A. (1988) 'Cardiac rehabilitation after myocardial infarction. Combined experience of randomised clinical trials,' *Journal of the American Medical Association* 260: 945–50.

Otis, C.L., Drinkwater, B., Johnson, M., Loucks, A., Wilmore, J. (1997) 'American College of Sports Medicine position stand. The female athlete triad', *Medicine and Science in Sports and Exercise* 29: 1–9.

Paffenbarger, R.S. and Hale, W.E. (1975) 'Work activity and coronary heart disease', *New England Journal of Medicine* 292: 545–50.

Paffenbarger, R.S., Wing, A.L. and Hyde, R.T. (1978) 'Physical activity as an index of heart attack risk in college alumni', *American Journal of Epidemiology* 108: 161–75.

Paffenbarger, R.S., Wing, A.L., Hyde, R.T. and Jung, D.L. (1983) 'Physical activity and incidence of hypertension in college alumni', *American Journal of Epidemiology* 117: 247–57.

Paffenbarger, R.S., Hyde, R.T., Wing, A.L. and Hsieh, C.-C. (1986) 'Physical activity, all-cause mortality, and longevity of college alumni', *New England Journal of Medicine* 314: 605–13.

Paffenbarger, R.S., Blair, S.N., Lee, I.-M. and Hyde, R.T. (1993a) 'Measurement of physical activity to assess health effects in free-living populations', *Medicine and Science in Sports and Exercise* 25: 60–70.

Paffenbarger, R.S., Hyde, R.T., Wing, A.L., Lee, I.-M., Jung, D.L. and Kampert, J.B. (1993b) 'The association of changes in physical activity level and other lifestyle characteristics with mortality among men', *New England Journal of Medicine* 328: 538–45.

Paffenbarger, R.S., Blair, S.N. and Lee, I.-M. (2001) 'A history of physical activity, cardiovascular health and longevity: the scientific contributions of Jeremy N. Morris, DSc, DPH, FRCP', *International Journal of Epidemiology* 30: 1184–92.

Pan, X.R., Li, G.W., Hu, Y.H., Wang, J.X., Yang, W.Y., An, Z.X., Hu, Z.X., Lin, J., Xiao, J.Z., Cao, H.B., Liu, P.A., Jiang, X.G., Jiang, Y.Y., Wang, J.P., Zheng, H., Zhang, H., Bennett, P.H. and Howard, B.V. (1997) 'Effects of diet and exercise in preventing NIDDM in people with impaired glucose tolerance', *Diabetes Care* 20: 537–44.

Pate, R.R., Pratt, M., Blair, S.N., Haskell, W.L., Macera, C.A., Bouchard, C., Buchner, D., Ettinger, W., Heath, G.W., King, A.C., Kriska, A., Leon, A.S., Marcus, B.H., Morris, J., Paffenbarger, R.S., Patrick, K., Pollock, M.L., Rippe, J.M., Sallis, J. and Wilmore, J.H. (1995) 'Physical activity and public health. A recommendation from the Centers for Disease Control and Prevention and the American College of Sports Medicine', *Journal of the American Medical Association* 273: 402–7.

Pedersen, B.K. and Hoffman-Goetz, L. (2000) 'Exercise and the immune system: regulation, integration, and adaptation', *Physiological Reviews* 80: 1055–81.

Pescatello, L.S., Fargo, A.E., Leach, C.N. and Scherzer, H.H. (1991) 'Short-term effect of dynamic exercise on arterial blood pressure', *Circulation* 83: 1557–61.

Petrie, J., Barnwell, B., Grimshaw, J. on behalf of the Scottish Intercollegiate Guidelines Network (1995) *Clinical Guidelines: Criteria for Appraisal for National Use*, Edinburgh: Royal College of Physicians.

Poehlman, E.T. (1989) 'A review: exercise and its influence on resting energy metabolism in man', *Medicine and Science in Sports and Exercise* 21: 515–25.

Poirier, P., Catellier, C., Tremblay, A. and Nadeau, A. (1996) 'Role of body fat loss in the exercise-induced improvement of the plasma lipid profile in non-insulin-dependent diabetes mellitus', *Metabolism* 45: 1383–7.

Pollock, M.L., Carroll, J.F., Graves, J.E., Leggett, S.H., Braith, R.W., Linacher, M. and Hagberg, J. (1991) 'Injuries and adherence to walk/jog and resistance training programs in the elderly', *Medicine and Science in Sports and Exercise* 23: 1194–200.

Pollock, M.L., Mengelkoch, L.J., Graves, J.E., Lowenthal, D.T., Limacher, M.C., Foster, C. and Wilmore, J.H. (1997) 'Twenty-year follow-up of aerobic power and body composition of older track athletes', *Journal of Applied Physiology* 82: 1508–16.

Pooling Project Research Group (1978) 'Relationship of blood pressure, serum cholesterol, smoking habit, relative weight and ECG abnormalities to incidence of major coronary events. Final report of the pooling project', *Journal of Chronic Disability* 31: 202–306.

Popkin, B.M. (1994) 'The nutrition transition in low-income countries: an emerging crisis', *Nutrition Reviews* 52: 285–98.

Pouliot, M.-C., Després, J.-P., Nadeau, A., Moorjani, S., Prud'homme, D., Lupien, P.J., Tremblay, A. and Bouchard, C. (1992) 'Visceral obesity in men: associations with glucose tolerance, plasma insulin, and lipoprotein levels', *Diabetes* 41: 826–34.

Powell, K.E., Thompson, P.D., Casperson, C.J. and Kendrick, J.S. (1987) 'Physical activity and the incidence of coronary heart disease', *Annual Review of Public Health* 8: 253–87.

Prentice, A.M. (1998) 'Manipulation of dietary fat and energy density and subsequent effects on substrate flux and food intake', *American Journal of Clinical Nutrition* 67 (Supplement): 535S–41S.

Prentice, A.M. and Jebb, S.A. (1995) 'Obesity in Britain: gluttony or sloth?', *British Medical Journal* 311: 437–9.

Rauramaa, R., Li, G. and Väisänen, S.B. (2001) 'Dose–response and coagulation and hemostatic factors', *Medicine and Science in Sports and Exercise* 33 (Supplement): S516–20.

Ravussin, E., Lillioja, S., Knowler, W.C., Christin, L., Freymond, D., Abbott, W.G.H., Boyce, V., Howard, B.V. and Bogardus, C. (1988) 'Reduced rate of energy expenditure as a risk factor for body weight gain', *New England Journal of Medicine* 318: 467–72.

Reaven, G.M. (1988) 'Role of insulin resistance in human disease', *Diabetes* 37: 1595–1607.

Reaven, G.M. (1994) 'Syndrome X: 6 years later', *Journal of Internal Medicine* 236: 13–22.

Reilly, J. and Dorosty, A. (1999) 'Epidemic of obesity in UK children', *The Lancet* 354: 1874–5.

Rocchini, A.P. (2002) 'Childhood obesity and a diabetes epidemic', *New England Journal of Medicine* 346: 854–5. Editorial.

Rockhill, B., Willett, W.C., Hunter, D.J., Manson, J.E., Hankinson, S.E. and Colditz, G.A. (1999) 'A prospective study of recreational physical activity and breast cancer risk', *Archives of Internal Medicine* 159: 2290–6.

Rogers, M.A. and Evans, W.J. (1993) 'Changes in skeletal muscle with aging: effects of exercise training', *Exercise and Sport Sciences Reviews* 21: 65–102.

Rogers, M.A., King, D.S., Hagberg, J.M., Ehsani, A.A. and Holloszy, J.O. (1990) 'Effect of 10 days of physical inactivity on glucose tolerance in master athletes', *Journal of Applied Physiology* 68: 1833–7.

Rosenbloom, A.L., Joe, J.R., Young, R.S. and Winter, N.E. (1999) 'Emerging epidemic of type 2 diabetes in youth', *Diabetes Care* 22: 345–54.

Ross, R. (1997) 'Effects of diet and exercise induced weight loss on visceral adipose tissue in men and women', *Sports Medicine* 24: 55–64.

Ross, R., Freeman, J.A. and Janssen, I. (2000) 'Exercise alone is an effective strategy for reducing obesity and related comorbidities', *Exercise and Sport Science Reviews* 28: 165–70.

Sallis, J.F. and Owen, N. (1999) *Physical Activity and Behavioural Medicine*, Thousand Oaks CA: Sage.

Sandvik, L., Erikssen, J., Thaulow, E., Erikssen, G., Mundl, R. and Rodahl, K. (1993) 'Physical fitness as a predictor of mortality among healthy, middle-aged Norwegian men', *New England Journal of Medicine* 328: 533–7.

Schriger, D.L. (2001) 'Analyzing the relationship of exercise and health: methods, assumptions, and limitations', *Medicine and Science in Sports and Exercise* 33 (Supplement):S359–63.

Scottish Executive Department of Health (2000) *The Scottish Health Survey 1998*, Edinburgh: The Stationery Office.

Seip, R.L., Angelopoulos, T.J. and Semenkovich, C.F. (1995) 'Exercise induces human lipoprotein lipase gene expression in skeletal muscle but not adipose tissue', *American Journal of Physiology* 268: E229–36.

Shaper, A.G. and Wannamethee, G. (1991) 'Physical activity and ischaemic heart disease in middle-aged British men', *British Heart Journal* 66: 384–94.

Shephard, R.J. (1986) *Fitness of a Nation: Lessons from the Canada Fitness Survey*, Basel: Karger, p. 95.

Shephard, R.J. and Shek, P.N. (1998) 'Associations between physical activity and susceptibility to cancer: possible mechanisms', *Sports Medicine* 26: 293–315.

Sherwood, L. (1991) *Fundamentals of Physiology: a Human Perspective*, Minnesota, West: St Paul.

Simsolo, R.B., Ong, J.M. and Kern, P.A. (1993) 'The regulation of adipose tissue and muscle lipoprotein lipase in runners by detraining', *Journal of Clinical Investigation* 92: 2124–30.

Sinaki, M., Wahner, H.W., Bergstralh, E.J., Hodgson, S.F., Offord, K.P., Squires, R.W., Swee, R.G. and Kao, P.C. (1996) 'Three-year controlled, randomized trial of the effect of dose-specified loading and strengthening exercises on bone mineral density of spine and femur in non-athletic, physically active women', *Bone* 19: 233–44.

Sinha, R., Fisch, G., Teague, B., Tamborlane, W.V., Banyas, B., Allen, K., Savoye, M., Rieger, V., Taksali, S., Barbetta, G., Sherwin, R.S. and Caprio, S. (2002) 'Prevalence of impaired glucose tolerance among children and adolescents with marked obesity', *New England Journal of Medicine* 346: 802–10.

Siscovick, D.S., Weiss, N.S., Fletcher, R.H. and Lasky, T. (1984). 'The incidence of primary cardiac arrest during vigorous exercise', *New England Journal of Medicine* 311: 874–7.

Slattery, M.L. and Potter, J.D. (2002) 'Physical activity and colon cancer: confounding or interaction?', *Medicine and Science in Sports and Exercise* 34: 913–19.

Slattery, M.L., Potter, J., Caan, B., Edwards, S., Coates, A., Ma, K.-N. and Berry, T.D. (1997) 'Energy balance and colon cancer – beyond physical activity', *Cancer Research* 57: 75–80.

Snow-Harter, C. and Marcus, R. (1991) 'Exercise, bone mineral density, and osteoporosis', *Exercise and Sport Sciences Reviews* 19: 351–88.

Spirduso, W.W. and Cronin, D.L. (2001) 'Exercise dose–response effects on quality of life and independent living in older adults', *Medicine and Science in Sports and Exercise* 33 (Supplement): S598–608.

Statistics New Zealand (2002) Population monitor: our ageing population 28.10.02. Available at: http://www.stats.govt.nz/domino/external/web/schools.nsf/htmldocs/Our+Ageing+Population accessed 10th March 2003.

Stensel, D.J., Lin, F.-P. and Nevill, A.M. (2001) 'Resting metabolic rate in obese and non-obese Singaporean boys aged 13 to 15 years', *American Journal Clinical Nutrition* 74: 369–73.

Sternfeld, B., Jacobs, M.K., Quesenberry, C.P., Gold, E.B. and Sowers, M. (2002) 'Physical activity and menstrual cycle characteristics in two prospective cohorts', *American Journal of Epidemiology* 156: 402–9.

Stunkard, A.J., Sorensen, T.I.A., Hanis, C., Teasdale, T.W., Chakraborty, R., Schull, W.J. and Schulsinger, F. (1986) 'An adoption study of human obesity', *New England Journal of Medicine* 314: 193–8.

Swinburn, B. and Ravussin, E. (1993) 'Energy balance or fat balance', *American Journal of Clinical Nutrition* 57 (Supplement): 766S–71S.

Tanaka, H. and Seals, D.R. (1997) 'Age and gender interactions in physiological functional capacity: insight from swimming performance', *Journal of Applied Physiology* 82: 846–51.

Tataranni, P.A. and Bogardus, C. (2001) 'Changing habits to delay diabetes', *New England Journal of Medicine* 344: 1390–2. Editorial.

Taubes, G. (1995) 'Epidemiology faces its limits', *Science* 269(14 July): 164–9. Editorial.

Taylor, H.L., Klepetar, E., Keys, A., Parlin, W., Blackburn, H. and Puchner, T. (1962) 'Death rates among physically active and sedentary employees of the railroad industry', *American Journal of Public Health* 52: 1697–707.

Taylor-Tolbert, N., Dengel, D., Brown, M.D. and Other, A.N. (2000) 'Ambulatory blood pressure after acute exercise in older men with essential hypertension', *American Journal of Hypertension* 13: 44–51.

Thomas, J.R. and Nelson, J.K. (2001) *Research Methods in Physical Activity*, 4th edn, Champaign, IL: Human Kinetics.

Thune, I. (2001) 'Physical activity and cancer risk: dose–response and cancer, all sites and site-specific', *Medicine and Science in Sports and Exercise* 33 (Supplement): S530–50.

Thune, I. and Lund, E. (1996) 'Physical activity and risk of colorectal cancer in men and women', *British Journal of Cancer* 73: 1134–40.

Thune, I., Brenn, T., Lund, E. and Gaard, M. (1997) 'Physical activity and the risk of breast cancer', *New England Journal of Medicine* 336: 1269–75.

Thune, I., Njølstad, I., M.-L., Lochen and Førde, O.H. (1998) 'Physical activity improves the metabolic risk profiles in men and women', *Archives of Internal Medicine* 158: 1633–40.

Timpka, T. and Lindqvist, K. (2001) 'Evidence based prevention of acute injuries during physical exercise in a WHO safe community', *British Journal of Sports Medicine* 35: 20–7.

Trappe, S.W., Costill, D.L., Fink, W.J. and Pearson, D.R. (1995) 'Skeletal muscle characteristics among distance runners: a 20-yr follow-up study', *Journal of Applied Physiology* 78: 823–9.

Truswell, A.S., Kennelly, B.M., Hansen, J.D.L. and Lee, R.B. (1972) 'Blood pressure of Kung Bushmen in northern Botswana', *American Heart Journal* 84: 5–12.

Tsetsonis, N.V. and Hardman, A.E. (1996) 'Reduction in postprandial lipaemia after walking: influence of exercise intensity', *Medicine and Science in Sports and Exercise* 28: 1235–42.

Tuomilehto, J., Lindström, J., Eriksson, J.G., Valle, T.T., Hämäläinen, H., Ilanne-Parikka, P., Keinänen-Kiukaanniemi, S., Laakso, M., Louheranta, A., Rastas, M., Salminen, V. and Uusitupa, M. (2001) 'Prevention of type 2 diabetes mellitus by changes in lifestyle among subjects with impaired glucose tolerance', *New England Journal of Medicine* 344: 1343–50.

United Kingdom Track and Field All-Time lists. Available at: http://www.gbrathletics.com/uk accessed 10th March 2003.

United States Department of Health and Human Services (1996) *Physical Activity and Health: A Report of the Surgeon-General*. Atlanta, GA: US Department of Health and Human Services, Centers for Disease Control and Prevention, National Center for Chronic Disease Prevention and Health Promotion.

Uusi-Rasi, K., Haapasalo, H., Kannus, P., Pasanen, M., Sievänen, H., Oja, P. and Vuori, I. (1997) 'Determinants of bone mineralization in 8 to 20 year old Finnish females', *European Journal of Clinical Nutrition* 51: 54–9.

Välimäki, M.J., Kärkkäinen, M., Lamberg-Allardt, C., Laitinen, K., Alhava, E., Heikkinen, J., Impivaara, O., Mäkelä, P., Palmgren, J., Seppänen, R., Vuori, I. and The Cardiovascular Risk in Young Finns Study Group (1994) 'Exercise, smoking, and calcium intake during adolescence and early adulthood as determinants of peak bone mass', *British Medical Journal* 309: 230–5.

Vander, A., Sherman, J. and Luciano, D. (2001) *Human Physiology. The Mechanisms of Body Function*, 8th edn, Boston: McGraw-Hill.

van Mechelen, W. (1992) 'Running injuries: a review of the epidemiological literature', *Sports Medicine* 14: 320–35.

van Tulder, M.W., Malmivaara, A., Esmail, R. and Koes, B.W. (2003) 'Exercise therapy for low back pain (Cochrane Review)', in *The Cochrane Library*, Issue 1, Oxford: Update Software.

Visser, M., Pluijm, S.M.F., Stel, V.S., Bosscher, R.J. and Deeg, D.J.H. (2002) 'Physical activity as a determinant of change in mobility performance: The Longitudinal Aging Study Amsterdam', *Journal of the American Geriatric Society* 50: 1774–81.

Vuori, I.M., Oja, P. and Paronen, O. (1994) 'Physically active commuting to work-testing its potential for exercise promotion', *Medicine and Science in Sports and Exercise* 26: 844–50.

Wakimoto, P. and Block, G. (2001) 'Dietary intake, dietary patterns, and changes with age: an epidemiological perspective', *Journals of Gerontology, Series A Biological Sciences and Medical Sciences* 56A (Special Issue II): 65–80.

Wannamethee, G.S. and Shaper, A.G. (2001) 'Physical activity in the prevention of cardiovascular disease: an epidemiological perspective', *Sports Medicine* 31: 101–14.

Wannamethee, S.G., Shaper, A.G. and Walker, M. (1998) 'Changes in physical activity, mortality, and incidence of coronary heart disease in older men', *The Lancet* 351: 1603–8.

Wei, M., Kampert, J.B., Barlow, C.E., Nichaman, M.Z., Gibbons, L.W., Paffenbarger, R.S. and Blair, S.N. (1999) 'Relationship between low cardiorespiratory fitness and mortality in normal weight, overweight and obese men', *Journal of the American Medical Association* 282: 1547–53.

Wei, M., Gibbons, L.W., Kampert, J.B., Nichaman, M.Z. and Blair, S.N. (2000) 'Low cardiorespiratory fitness and physical inactivity as predictors of mortality in men with type 2 diabetes', *Annals of Internal Medicine* 132: 605–11.

Weinsier, R.L., Hunter, G.R., Desmond, R.A., Byrne, N.M., Zuckerman, P.A. and Darnell, B.E. (2002) 'Free-living activity energy expenditure in women successful and unsuccessful at maintaining normal body weight', *American Journal of Clinical Nutrition* 75: 499–504.

Welten, D.C., Kemper, H.C.G., Post, G.B., Van Mechelen, W., Twisk, J., Lips, P. and Teule, G.J. (1994) 'Weight-bearing activity during youth is a more important factor for peak bone mass than calcium intake', *Journal of Bone and Mineral Research* 9: 1089–96.

Westerterp, K.R. (2000) 'Daily physical activity, aging and body composition', *Journal of Nutrition, Health and Aging* 4: 239–42.

Westerterp, K.R. and Meijer, E.P. (2001) 'Physical activity and parameters of aging: a physiological perspective', *Journals of Gerontology. Series A Biological Sciences and Medical Sciences* 56A (Special Issue II): 7–12.

Whaley, M.H., Kampert, J.B., Kohl, H.W. and Blair, S.N. (1999) 'Physical fitness and clustering of risk factors associated with the metabolic syndrome', *Medicine and Science in Sports and Exercise* 31: 287–93.

Wheater, P.R., Burkitt, H.G., Stevens, A. and Lowe, J.S. (1985) *Basic Histopathology, A Colour Atlas and Text*, Edinburgh: Churchill Livingstone.

Wheater, P.R., Burkitt, H.G. and Daniels, V.G. (1987) *Functional Histology: A Text and Colour atlas,* 2nd edn, Edinburgh: Churchill Livingstone.

Williams, P.T. (1996) 'High density lipoprotein cholesterol and other risk factors for coronary heart disease in female runners', *New England Journal of Medicine* 334: 1298–303.

Williams, P.T. (1997) 'Relationship of distance run per week to coronary heart disease risk factors in 8283 male runners', *Archives of Internal Medicine* 157: 191–8.

Williamson, D.F., Madans, J., Anda, R.F., Kleinman, J.C., Kahn, H.S. and Byers, T. (1993) 'Recreational physical activity and ten-year weight change in a US national cohort', *International Journal Obesity* 17: 279–86.

Willett, W.C. (1998) 'Is dietary fat a major determinant of body fat?', *American Journal of Clinical Nutrition* 67 (Supplement): 556S–62S.

Willich, S.N., Lewis, M., Löwel, H., Arntz, H.-R., Schubert, F. and Schröder, R. (1993) 'Physical exertion as a trigger of acute myocardial infarction', *New England Journal Medicine* 329: 1684–90.

Wilmore, J.H. and Costill, D.L. (1999) *Physiology of Sport and Exercise*, 2nd edn, Champaign, IL: Human Kinetics.

Wilson, P.W., Kannel, W.B., Silbershatz, H. and D'Agostino, R.B. (1999) 'Clustering of metabolic risk factors and coronary heart disease', *Archives of Internal Medicine* 159: 1104–9.

Wolff, I., van Croonenborg, J.J., Kemper, H.C.G., Kostense, P.J. and Twisk, J.W.R. (1999) 'The effect of exercise training programs on bone mass: a meta-analysis of published controlled trials in pre- and postmenopausal women', *Osteoporosis International* 9: 1–12.

Wood, P.D., Stefanick, M.L., Dreon, D.M., Frey-Hewitt, B., Garay, S.C., Williams, P.T., Superko, H.R., Fortmann, S.P., Albers, J.J., Vranizan, K.M., Ellsworth, N.M., Terry, R.B. and Haskell, W.L. (1988) 'Changes in plasma lipids and lipoproteins in overweight men during weight loss through dieting as compared with exercise', *New England Journal of Medicine* 319: 1173–9.

Wood, P.D., Terry, R.B. and Haskell, W.L. (1985) 'Metabolism of substrates: diet, lipoprotein metabolism and exercise', *Federation Proceedings* 44: 358–63.

Woods, J.A., Davis, J.M., Smith, J.A. and Nieman, D.C. (1999) 'Exercise and cellular innate immune function', *Medicine and Science in Sports and Exercise* 31: 57–66.

World Cancer Research Fund/American Institute for Cancer Research (1997) *Food, Nutrition and the Prevention of Cancer: A Global Perspective*, Washington, DC: WCRF/AICR.

World Health Organization (1946) Preamble to the Constitution of the World Health Organization as adopted by the International Health Conference, New York, 19–22 June 1946: signed on 22 July 1946 by the representatives of 61 States (Official Records of the World Health Organization, no. 2, p. 100) and entered into force on 7 April 1948.

World Health Organization (1999a) Active living, http://www.who.int/hpr/archive/active/evidence.html accessed 29th January 2003.

World Health Organization (1999b) Health Promotion. Active living: the challenge ahead: No last update given. http://www.who.int/hpr/archive/active/challenge.html accessed 11th March 2003.

Wyatt, H.R., Grunwald, G.K., Seagle, H.M., Klem, M.L., McGuire, M.T., Wing, R.R. and Hill, J.O. (1999) 'Resting energy expenditure in reduced-obese subjects in the National Weight Control Registry', *American Journal of Clinical Nutrition* 69: 1189–93.

Zanker, C.L. and Swaine, I.L. (1998) 'Bone turnover in amenorrhœic and eumenorrhœic distance runners', *Scandinavian Journal Medicine Science Sports* 8: 20–6.

Zmuda, J.M., Yurgaevitch, S.M., Flynn, M.M., Bausserman, L.L., Saratelli, A., Spannaus-Martin, D.J., Herbert, P.N. and Thompson, P.D. (1998) 'Exercise training has little effect on HDL levels and metabolism in men with initially low HDL cholesterol', *Athersclerosis* 137: 215–21.

Index